INTRODUCTION TO ORGANISATIONAL BEHAVIOUR

First edition December 1987
Revised and reprinted December 1988

ISBN 0 86277 206 0

A CIP catalogue record for this book is available
from the British Library

Published by BPP Publishing Ltd
BPP House
Aldine Place
142-144 Uxbridge Road
London W12 8AA

Printed and Bound in England
by Watkiss Studios Limited
Biggleswade, Beds. SG18 9ST

We are grateful to the Institute of Chartered Secretaries and Administrators, the
Chartered Institute of Management Accountants, the Chartered Association of
Certified Accountants and the Association of Accounting Technicians for
permission to include past examination questions in this text. The suggested
solutions have been prepared by BPP Publishing Limited.

©
BPP Publishing Ltd
1988

CONTENTS

CONTENTS

FOREWORD

Introduction

This study text is designed to prepare candidates for Paper 4 'Introduction to Organisational Behaviour' in Part One of the ICSA's professional qualification. The subject was entirely new when first set in June 1986 under the revised examination scheme, although 'behavioural' questions had previously been set in the old 'Communication' and 'Personnel: Principles and Policy' paper. In May 1987, a revised syllabus for the '87 – '88 academic year was published as part of the Joint Syllabus Scheme with the Institute of Personnel Management. This Study Text is structured to reflect this most recent syllabus, though the changes in *substance* to the 1986 syllabus were not significant.

A footnote to the syllabus addresses students as follows.

"This subject is intended not only to stand on its own as an essential component of the professional training programme, but also to provide necessary background which will inform the student's approach to other subjects, particularly Personnel Administration and Management: Principles and Policy.

Furthermore, it should be clearly understood that students will be expected to display only an introductory level of familiarity with the syllabus...although this will not absolve them from pursuing their studies in a careful, methodical and rigorous manner."

In fact, the papers so far set for this subject have required in-depth preparation and creative thinking in applying acquired knowledge to particular questions.

FOREWORD

The syllabus

Objective:

At the end of a programme of study of at least 60 hours, the student should be able to:

(a) comprehend some of the distinctive perspectives and methods of psychologists, social psychologists and sociologists and how these can be used in the study of people at work.

(b) comprehend the particular and complementary contribution of these disciplines to the study of the individual as a worker and the organisation and social context of work.

(c) comprehend, at an introductory level, a psychological and sociological analysis of employee and managerial actions and decisions in work organisations.

Content:

1: <u>The individual as a worker</u>

(a) Maturation, development and ageing. Implications for performance, learning and career development.

(b) The nature of skilled performance. Learning processes and the acquisition of skill.

(c) Motivation, job satisfaction and worker goals.
   i   Motivation, its nature and assessment. Major work-related theories of motivation, eg. process theories, expectancy theory, equity theory, content theories, need hierarchy theory, two factor theory, ERG theory.
   ii Job satisfaction, its nature and assessment. The quality of working life.
   iii Worker goals. The nature of intrinsic and extrinsic factors. The role of pay as an incentive.
   iv The relationship between motivation, performance and job satisfaction.

(d) Abilities, aptitudes and intelligence. The nature and assessment of intelligence and aptitude. Issues in the use of intelligence tests.

(e) Personality: the nature and assessment of personality. Individual differences in personality and their implications for work behaviour: authoritarianism, need for achievement, self-esteem.

(f) Social perception and sources of social influence. Communication processes. The role of reference groups. Attribution theory and the interpretation of information and events.

(g) The use of information and judgements about people at work.

(h) Attitudes at work. The nature of attitudes and their implications for behaviour. The influence of non-work factors on attitudes to work. Attitude surveys and attitude measurement.

(i) Frustration, aggression and individual forms of conflict. Stress at work and methods of coping.

(j) The individual and change. Resistance to change at work. Overcoming resistance to change.

2: The organisational and social context of work

(a) The nature of work organisations.
    i   Organisations as bureaucracies, rules and norms, the problems of bureaucracy.
    ii   The nature of organisational roles; the roles of manager, supervisor and worker.
    iii Sources of authority, power and control at work.

(b) Structuring the work environment.
    i   Choices of design of structure and jobs: contingency theory; socio-technical systems theory; matrix organisations.
    ii   Choices of design of the work-place and allocation of tasks; ergonomic and man-machine systems.
    iii The influence of size, market environment and technology on organisational structure and functioning.
    iv The influence of automation and computer technology and micro processing on organisations and jobs.

(c) The nature of the work group.
    i   The development, operation and influence of work groups.
    ii   Informal and formal work groups.
    iii Group pressures and conformity; influences on behaviour.
    iv Individual versus group performance.
    v   Group cohesion and influences on group effectiveness.

(d) Leadership at work.
    i   The nature of leadership. Theories of leadership. Leadership style.
    ii   Studies of leadership effectiveness.
    iii The supervisor, manager and shop steward as leaders.

(e) Work and non-work.
    i   Work as a central life interest.
    ii   Orientation to work.
    iii Theories of work and leisure.
    iv Sex differences and the occupational and family roles of men and women.

(f) Conflict and co-operation at work.
    i   Theories and sources of conflict and co-operation.
    ii   Interest groups: occupations, professions, unions, the influence of ideology.
    iii Managerial models of the worker, eg. scientific management, human relations, theory Y, complex man.
    iv Class, class-consciousness and alienation.
    v   Counter-organisations and organisational sub-cultures.

3: An overview of the behavioural sciences in organisations

Why managers and administrators need to make use of the behavioural sciences. The peculiar difficulties of the behavioural sciences (when compared with the natural sciences). Experimentation in the behavioural sciences. Description, explanation and prediction. Problems of application for behavioural science research. The 'rational' model of decision-making and its limitations. Organisational politics.

FOREWORD

Review of past papers

It might be helpful for you to have some idea of the topics examined so far in this paper.

Pilot Paper
1. Potential benefits of study of the behavioural sciences
2. Selection of a management style
3. Experimentation in the study of organisational behaviour
4. Communication breakdowns between managers and subordinates
5. Attitudes to work of manual and non-manual workers
6. Physiological and psychological effects of shift work
7. Value of systems view of organisation
8. Problems arising from existence of low-skilled, repetitive tasks
9. Is small beautiful?
10. Research on work group 'management' of incentive payment schemes

June 1986
1. Quality of working life
2. Selection of leadership style to fit situation
3. Bureacracies as non-responsive organisations
4. Differences between formal and informal groups
5. Benefits to managers of systems view of organisation
6. Alienation: is it inevitable?
7. Conflict: neither good nor bad
8. Behavioural implications of computers and IT in large organisations
9. Theory X assumptions
10. Resistance to different types of change

December 1986
1. Reasons for political behaviour
2. Value of Maslow hierarchy of needs in motivation
3. Culture and excellence
4. Human problems of shift work
5. Nature and desirability of 'leadership'
6. Significance of Hawthorne research, and reason for popularity
7. Barriers to communication
8. Personality
9. Social class system as a variable in behavioural analysis
10. Formal case for employment of full-time behavioural scientist

June 1987
1. Formation of cohesive groups
2. Job enlargement and job enrichment
3. Experimentation and other research methods
4. Organisational 'climate'?
5. Leadership 'qualities' and 'traits'
6. Communication methods and barriers in various situations
7. Resistance to change, and management action to overcome it
8. Behavioural problems associated with financial incentive systems?
9. Symptoms and causes of stress: remedial action
10. Benefits of study of Organisational Behaviour

FOREWORD

(NB. The most recent syllabus given above places more emphasis on 'the individual as worker' than the previous syllabus, under which all the above questions were set. This will be reflected in the structure and content of the study text.)

Examination format

Of the ten questions on the paper, FIVE only must be attempted.

All questions carry equal marks.

Time allowed – 3 hours.

Guidance for students

The syllabus for Introduction to Organisational Behaviour is large, but helpfully arranged to give you some idea of the areas to be covered: there are no relative weightings attached to the various sections, and some requirements are obviously set out more specifically than others.

Some topics and ideas inevitably overlap within the logical design of the syllabus, so you should beware the temptation to think within topic 'boxes' when answering questions in the exam. The syllabus can tell you in which areas you should concentrate your study: what it does not directly convey is the bias of the examination towards evaluation, the critical awareness required of you as you study and write about Organisational Behaviour. The questions set so far have invited candidates to *think objectively* about what they have read and observed, rather than to churn out facts or describe theories. You should think hard about how various ideas and theories might help managers 'in the real world' to improve the performance of the organisation they run. Use your common sense and judgement to evaluate ideas, but be receptive to those that you have never met before in your own practical experience. *Watch people* – particularly at work. The Examiner in his Report on the paper has stressed the need for an active, tough-minded response to the topics raised in the syllabus.

FOREWORD

The Examiner mentions four points in particular:

1. Many students demonstrate a 'naive optimism' about the beneficial effects of applying behavioural theories in organisations, stemming, perhaps, from 'a lack of awareness about the untidiness of the real world. The Examiner ... seeks some attempt at objectivity and some ability to stand back from the efforts of the behavioural scientists so that they can be viewed dispassionately, in a critical, though constructive, manner.' In some cases, this may simply involve the insertion of 'may' or 'might' into an otherwise simplistic assertion.

2. 'Candidates should note... that even if the syllabus appears academic, they will be expected to demonstrate some familiarity with applications, where appropriate... It should not be necessary for the Examiner to ensure that phrases like 'give examples' are included in each question: it should be widely understood by candidates (and by tutors) that the inclusion of practical instances is an essential aspect of demonstrating competence in this subject. Not only does familiarity with actual case-histories ... enable organisational behaviour to retain its links with reality, but such familiarity also helps to undermine the unhealthy attitude of utopian idealism with which some candidates approach the syllabus.'

3. Candidates should be aware of research conducted in the recent past (ie. not just the early landmarks), if they are to avoid a 'dangerously restrictive attitude to the content of the syllabus.'

4. Candidates must *answer the question posed*, especially where it calls for some analytical discussion, as opposed to descriptive narrative.

Other advice offered by the Examiner in his reports includes the following.

1. Answer all five questions. Roughly thirty minutes should be allocated to each question.

2. Attempt first the questions which you think will enable you to obtain your best marks.

3. Plan your answers with rough notes (to be crossed out when the answer is written).

4. Divide your material, at least into separate paragraphs, but preferably with the added use of side-headings and itemised points. (Coherent sentences should still be written, however.)

5. Start your answer with an introductory paragraph (perhaps defining key terms) and end with a summary or conclusion.

6. *Don't* write out the question before you start your answer (a signal to the Examiner that you are a little too desperate to get something on paper).

Editor's note

We have used the male pronoun 'he' and its variations throughout this study text, except where the discussion is specifically about women, or sex differences. This is purely to avoid cumbersome 'he or she' constructions; we are aware that this text is relevant to women as well as to men, and intend no prejudice in the use of this convenient form.

A BRIEF INTRODUCTION TO ORGANISATIONAL BEHAVIOUR

Understanding and control

1. It is important in any kind of organisation for a manager or administrator to:

    - *understand* what is going on at a given time, and why; and
    - use that understanding to *control* events.

    A *business* organisation in particular has to account to owners (ie. shareholders), investors and various regulatory bodies for its activities and its use of resources. It has certain responsibilities, as well as goals, and in order to fulfil both, it must exercise a measure of control on the diverse individuals and operations that make up 'the organisation' as a whole: it must channel all its energies and activities in controlled, desirable directions.

2. For example:

    (a) if something 'valuable' is happening in an organisation - productivity rising, costs falling etc. - its managers will wish to know what is going on, and how to recreate the conditions in order to reap the benefits again in future, perhaps as a permanent state of affairs;

    (b) if things are going wrong - absenteeism increasing, quality declining etc. - the manager will want to know why, as well as how to put things right, and hopefully how to spot similar trouble coming next time round so as to prevent it happening;

    (c) in the normal functioning of the organisation, the administrator will need to understand and anticipate the various events which occur - seasonal fluctuations of work load, staff/stock turnover etc. - in order to control the flow of information and resources which 'fuel' the organisation's activity.

3. Man has always sought ways of

    - describing,
    - analysing,
    - predicting and
    - controlling

    events and phenomena, from his first need to adapt to and control his environment in order to survive, through the more complex demands and power-plays of social interaction and politics.

Language, mathematics, logic – these were ways in which Man sought to make sense of himself and his environment, to impose order and meaning on events.

'Hard' and 'soft' information

4. Your studies for Part 1 of the ICSA examinations introduce you to two complementary approaches to a similar 'self-awareness' and control on the part of the *organisation*, ie:

    *   Quantitative Studies; and
    *   Organisational Behaviour.

    These are sometimes said to be 'hard' and 'soft' areas of study, respectively. 'Hard' refers to quantifiable information or phenomena (such as organisational size and structure, product diversity, revenue and cost, time-horizon, market share etc.) and 'soft' to more qualitative 'non-dollar' variables, such as style, culture, worker morale or customer satisfaction.

5. It is relatively simple to introduce and alter variables in 'hard' calculations, and to ask 'what if...?' questions to help planning and decision-making: eg. 'What would our profit margin be if we cut production costs by x% ? y% ? z% ?'

    It is not so easy to quantify (or even to predict accurately) the effects on business of, for example, the family circumstances of the Managing Director, a change of colour scheme in the office, or workers' dislike of a new machine. These are nevertheless areas of which a fully-equipped manager/administrator should be aware, in order to:

    (a) establish and facilitate essential *communication* within the organisation. Only through communication can the organisation deal with the problems created by the sheer *difference* of the individuals who make it up;

    (b) *motivate* or encourage the individuals to direct their efforts in ways which are desirable or at least acceptable to the organisation, by offering them fulfilment of their own various needs and goals.

    Such considerations are not just the province of those 'soft' (or 'enlightened') managers who are said to inhabit Personnel departments.

But what is 'organisational behaviour'?

6. Of course, in using words like 'behaviour' and 'self-awareness' of the organisation, we are lending it human characteristics that in itself it does not really possess. Organisation cannot be said to 'behave' in the sense that a man or animal does. However, they consist of *systems* which function in observable ways, and adapt to the internal and external environment, and of *individuals*, who do 'behave' - acting, reacting and interacting in the pursuit of individual and/or common goals.

7. 'Organisational behaviour', then, is a shorthand expression for all those actions, reactions and interactions, embracing:

    *   the behaviour of individuals and groups of individuals, within
    *   the structure, systems and functions of the organisation; and
    *   the 'outside' environment which shapes or influences all of the above.

8. The study of organisational behaviour is one to which various 'social sciences' can contribute: psychology, sociology, social psychology, economics, political science, anthropology etc.

    The multi-disciplinary nature of the study reflects the wide impact which organisations of different types have on societies and individual lives, and also the many levels on which individuals engage themselves in relationships with organisations.

The management of diversity

9. Each individual may be involved in the organisation which employs him or her in many different roles:

    (a) as an employee, but also as a manager of others - ie. in a subordinate and a superior role;

    (b) as a friend of other individuals, and as part of a specifically work-centred team;

    (c) as a provider of man hours, skill and experience - and as a seeker of money, satisfaction and/or other needs and desires;

    (d) as a committed member of the organisation, who shares its aims, and as a person with other allegiances - to family, leisure interests etc. - who may work simply to support his non-working life; some allegiances eg. to class or trade union may lead to outright conflict with the interests of the organisation as a whole;

    (e) as a unique individual with particular attitudes, beliefs, perceptions, aspirations and lifestyle - as well as a component, 'conforming' part of the organisation as a whole.

10. Charles de Gaulle once said of France: 'How can anyone govern a country that has 246 different kinds of cheese?'

    Much the same problem faces the manager and administrator in an organisation: the organisation itself may seem 'as one' - but it is made up of individuals, each of whom has his own perceptions of reality and other people, and each of whom desires and expects different things from his working life. How then is the organisation - and more specifically its managers and administrators - to 'govern' its human resources, to get the best possible performance from them? How can it know what they need and want from the organisation in return?

> The general considerations involved in organisational behaviour as an area of study, and as a necessary part of managerial 'equipment', will be discussed in more depth in the final section of this study text.
>
> First, we will start to discover something of the individual as worker - and the worker as an individual.

THE INDIVIDUAL AS A WORKER

Topics covered in this section

- Maturation, development and ageing
- Skills and learning
- Abilities, aptitudes and intelligence
- Motivation
- Job satisfaction and worker goals
- Personality
- Perception, social influence and attitudes
- Communication
- Use of information about people: personnel selection
- Conflict, stress and change

MATURATION, DEVELOPMENT AND AGEING

Points to be covered

- Aspects of development: personality
- Aspects of development: childhood and family
- Social interaction and child development
- Aspects of development: education
- The organisation and the developing individual
- The organisation's interest in personal development
- Attitude to development and ageing

Introduction

1. With time, individuals progress physically from the state of childhood to adulthood. The most basic products of this progression are:

    (a) growth; and
    (b) experience.

    These in turn are generally assumed to create 'maturity', although some individuals mature faster and further than others.

    'Maturation' is the process of growing up (ie. in children). 'Ageing' is the continuation of the process in adults. Both involve the 'development' of the individual, physiologically and psychologically.

2. The maturity of an individual - and the particular ways in which he has developed - may be of interest to the organisation which employs him in many different ways. Is he an 'adult' personality, needing and being able to handle responsibility over others, for example? Is he mature enough to feel secure with a degree of autonomy and independence? Is he, on the other hand, still willing and able to learn and adapt? Are his energies directed towards work goals, or is he not yet, or no longer, seeking fulfilment through his job?

    These things will be of interest to the organisation when it comes to:

    (a) recruiting suitable employees for a given task or position;
    (b) training them to required degrees of expertise in relevant areas;
    (c) offering the required motivation and incentives to elicit desired performance;
    (d) directing, controlling and assessing that performance; and
    (e) developing their careers in appropriate directions, and to suitable levels.

3. What, then, is a Personnel or other manager to 'go on' when making the judgements required by such concerns? What, in necessarily generalised terms, can he or she *expect* from the 'normal' process of maturation, development and ageing in the individual?

Aspects of development: personality

4. The complexities of the nature and assessment of 'personality' itself are discussed in a later chapter, but we will describe briefly here the kind of changes that it undergoes as 'development' takes place in an individual. We will simply take personality to be the sum of all the qualities that can be observed in a person's general pattern of behaviour. (Strictly speaking, we should divorce from this the purely intellectual and physical qualities, but since these also influence motivations, emotions etc., we will not make such distinctions for the moment.)

5. According to most accepted theories, the personality of any one individual is made up of various 'parts' - the psychological forces which dictate perception and response - which combine and interact to shape the behaviour of the 'whole person'. Add to this 'internal environment' the *external* environment - stimuli of all kinds to which the individual responds - and you start to appreciate the complex and interdependent forces which shape personality.

6. The relative strengths and weaknesses of the various 'parts' of an individual's personality, and the limitations or encouragement afforded by his external environment (eg. up-bringing, relationships, experience etc.) are obviously so variable that no two people are likely to mature and develop in exactly the same way, or at the same rate. However, in general terms, maturation involves:

   (a) the 'parts' of the individual becoming greater in number and complexity, shaped by a greater range of experience and stimuli - emotional, intellectual, sexual, social etc.;

   (b) the inter-relationship between those parts therefore becoming more complex, with greater potential for tension and conflict, but also for 'depth' of personality and self-awareness;

   (c) the relationship between the 'whole' individual and his external environment also becoming more complex. In particular, he will take on an increasing number of *roles* (psychologically and emotionally, as well as socially), as he becomes involved in life on more varied levels - family, work, political, social etc.

7. How do these things work themselves out in the behaviour of individuals, then? The general trend is towards increasing diversity and complexity, and usually therefore an increasing sense of 'self-hood', and the need to develop that personal potential.

8. According to Chris Argyris, psychologist and management writer, the sort of developments one might expect and observe in people as they mature are:

   (a) *an increasing tendency to activity, rather than passivity* - or 'doing' rather than 'being done to'. This is partly because of the widening scope for action, with learning and experience, and partly to do with a growing sense of self as a (more or less self-determining) 'agent';

(b) *diversification of behaviour patterns.* As the personality of the individual grows more complex, and as experience provides him with new stimuli, he progresses from a few relatively limited forms of behaviour to a wider and more subtle range of responses;

(c) *a tendency from dependence towards independence.* 'Independence' is obviously relative - truly autonomous individuals are rare indeed - but generally, childish dependence on others gives way to a degree of self-sufficiency. This may range from a recognition that one's basic needs will no longer all be met by someone else, to an active *need* for autonomy, self-expression, or perhaps a position of authority over others;

(d) *acceptance of equal or superior relationship to others.* Some people are happy to be in subordinate positions (eg at work) all their lives - but rarely in all areas of their lives. Generally, as we mature, we feel that a certain position is 'due' to our self image, our age and experience. In the family, we move naturally from the subordinate (child) to superior (parent) role, while in our other relationships, there is at least a tendency towards equality: a large age difference between two friends, for example, may create a subordinate-superior relationship while the younger of the two is still a child - but once both are adults, socially and psychologically, the relationship will tend towards a more equal footing. Progression 'upwards' is seen as socially desirable in most contexts - particularly at work, where promotion is often the prime 'carrot' in a company's reward/incentive scheme;

(e) *lengthening perspectives.* A person's sense of 'time' is highly subjective - digital watches and desk calendars notwithstanding. To a child, 20- or 30-year-olds seem immensely aged; a year seems like a long time (eg. to wait for Christmas to come around again); looking ahead, short horizons are generally all that seem necessary or possible (try asking a twenty-year-old to think about a pension scheme!). Increasingly, however, the pressures of responsibility, as well as experience/perception of the passage of time, lengthen the time-scales with which we are prepared to work: long-term planning, eg. of career moves, becomes more natural, and delayed gratification becomes more acceptable - eg. if you have to wait some years before your efforts are rewarded with promotion;

(f) *'deepening' and more stable interests.* This is not to say that all adults are 'deep' or 'serious-minded' nor all youngsters erratic and 'shallow'. However, experience generally provides a wider range of potential interests; priorities are altered as personality develops; the search for new experience/knowledge has gone beyond the 'basics', which may have seemed challenging enough when the individual was younger;

(g) *increasing self-awareness.* Humans are 'self-conscious' individuals: we behave partly in accordance with the image or concept that we have of ourselves, or 'the Self'. That self image is something we learn from interaction with other people, through their behaviour and attitudes towards us. Our self-image - and therefore our personality - is formed by experience over time, and is constantly adjusted. *Self control* may also be developed through increasing self-awareness in the mature individual - though that will also depend on social pressure and conscious decision.

"A young child's interests and enjoyments shift from minute to minute, and he is concerned only with here and now - he cannot wait till later for his ice-cream. He is self-centred and unaware of how his demands affect others: but he accepts a dependent position in which others largely control what he does. Mature adulthood is achieved when the individual has some ability to see himself from the point of view of others, to foresee consequences even years ahead, to pursue interests consistently, and to accept responsibilities equal to or superior to those of others."

(Writers on Organisations, survey of Chris Argyris' ideas on development)

---

9. It is important to remember that development is not only an 'internal' process involving psychological and emotional forces within the individual, but also a process of interaction with the 'external' environment. The individual learns about himself and about the 'rules' governing behaviour through taking on social roles, and through relationships with other people.

Aspects of development: childhood and family

10. The family is the earliest and one of the most important 'external' influences on personal maturation and development: it is both a *social unit* and an extremely complex *relationship*, so it embraces a wide variety of behaviour, and affects development on many levels. The sociologist might stress the development of social behaviour and roles within the family, while the psychologist would concentrate on childhood patterning and the development of personality.

One should also bear in mind that the behaviour, organisation and importance of 'The Family' itself will vary greatly from society to society: eg. *who* looks after the children, *how*, and *for how long*?

In Britain, childhood needs are generally given priority in the family, though not all societies are 'child-centred' in the same way. The childhood years, and the relationships and learning experiences associated with them, are considered crucial in determining what sort of adult will later emerge.

11. Functionalist sociologists (who, as their name implies, are concerned to analyse the function of the various parts of the social system in relation to each other and to the whole) include, in their analysis of the functions of the family:

   (a) the *socialisation* of children, ie. informal training encouraging the kind of values, attitudes and behaviour that their society will later expect of them;

   (b) *role definition*. The family is the first context in which individuals take on a role - as son, daughter, brother, sister etc - and learn what to expect, and what is expected of them, in relation to others (in appropriate roles as mother, father, adult, etc). The family also provides role patterns for sexual, social and 'economic' behaviour, eg. - to take a stereotypical example:

   > woman = wife and mother = household maintenance and child-rearing;
   > man = father = breadwinner etc.

   (c) the provision of emotional security, shelter, love etc. for all members of the unit, as an enduring 'home base' in the face of an impersonal society.

12. The above analysis assumes, of course, that the individual develops in a 'normal' family life that is secure, happy, socially constructive and mutually supportive. In fact his maturation and development may arise from an experience of struggle, unhappiness, disappointment, guilt and repression: it would be unrealistic to view marriage and family life as inviolable institutions in the modern world.

The analysis also asks us to assume that a certain type of socially acceptable family behaviour is universally 'normal' and correct - thereby ignoring the needs of the individuals involved and the localised social origins of the ideals, as well as the 'interests' that they might reflect.

In particular, it has been suggested that 'normal' family life is defined to suit the prevailing economic system (ie. developing properly submissive labour forces - wage-earning and domestic - for the future) and the preservation of the social status quo.

13. Moving into the psychological field, Buchanan and Huczynski, in their book 'Organisational Behaviour', suggest that 'Human beings do not behave in, and in response to, the world "as it really is"'... Human beings behave in, and in response to, the world as they *perceive* it.'

    The way an individual *perceives* people, events and the world around him be highly subjective and selective, and will partly be influenced by his *expectations*. These in turn arise out of *past experience*. The experience of the earliest 'formative' years of childhood and adolescence is therefore likely to colour the whole perceptual world of the emerging adult.

14. We have also noted the importance of *self awareness* in determining behaviour, and this too will be influenced in the early years. If a child is taught - by experiencing constant criticism or inadequate relationships, for example - to have a low self-image, or low expectations, his behaviour will tend to reflect this in later life, unless other influences intervene: his aspirations will be as low as his expectations, and his performance will conform to his lack of confidence.

Social interaction and child development

15. Child psychology and development is an enormous area of study in its own right. One major school of thought which you might find relevant, however, is *symbolic interactionism*.

    This is a theory of behaviour which originated with Charles Cooley (1865-1929) and George Herbert Mead (1863-1931), centring on the individual and how he is shaped by interaction with others. According to Mead the infant begins to learn about himself through the symbols by which he communicates with 'significant others' in his life. He learns the accepted meanings of symbols such as language, gestures, expressions, dress etc. and how to use them appropriately in response to the actions and reactions of others. The symbolic 'vocabulary' of the individual's roles (family, social, sexual etc.) becomes part of his consciousness - ie. is 'internalised' - as his sense of identity develops. He forms, modifies and adapts his behaviour in response to the reactions and expectations of others - not only in infancy, but throughout his life.

16. One corollary of all this, which a manager might find relevant, is the significance of *labelling* people. A 'label' given at home or at school (eg. X is a 'trouble-maker', or a 'loser' or 'a high achiever' etc.) comes to define what is expected of the individual (whether or not it is justified), and, because expectation influences behaviour, the label will tend to be 'self-fulfilling': the individual will be encouraged to live up (or down) to the label and its implications.

    This challenges the critical manager to look carefully at his prejudices and attitudes towards the people who work for him. It is something of a chicken and egg situation: does he have a poor opinion of their abilities because they really are lacking - or is he encouraging poor performance by his own lack of confidence and low expectations?

Conversely, positive expectations will tend to encourage aspiration, self-confidence and self-fulfilling performance.

17. We will be talking about *goals* in depth in the later chapters on Motivation, Job Satisfaction and Worker Goals, but we should mention briefly here the way in which the denial or satisfaction of childhood needs influences development.

The effect of childhood experience is complex. As we have suggested, learned roles and expectations may be carried over into adulthood: a child whose parents always withold total acceptance ('Well done, *but* you should have...') may accept a low self-image, or an extreme idea of the importance of 'achievement', and may therefore develop a tendancy towards conservatism; insecurity and rejection may similarly create a lack of confidence, and risk-aversion in the adult; children of poor or ill-educated parents may not expect or strive for anything better for themselves. What is known as the 'work ethic' may well arise from a childhood of 'delayed gratification', learning not to expect immediate reward or recognition for achievement.

18. Of course, *positive* patterns are also created, such as successful career models, stable relationships etc., which will be *emulated* and perpetuated by the next generation. There may even be an element of *competition* with parents or older contemporaries in certain areas.

19. On the other hand, the adult may adopt life-goals to *compensate* for childhood deprivation, or to *deny* or react against childhood experience.

If a child is deprived of eg. affection, security, material comfort, reward or recognition for achievement, that area of privation may become an object of aspiration in later life. A child from a very poor background may place monetary reward high on his list of priorities; another, having experienced rejection, may have stable relationships as a prime goal; an insecure or unstructured home life may create a deep need to be part of a 'safe' authority structure, while rigid discipline and repression may result in later rebellion, a need for autonomy, or self-determination; a child who is never praised or rewarded may seek a work environment which provides immediate recognition for achievement.

Aspects of development: education

20. As we have seen, 'learning' takes place throughout an individual's life, and certainly not just in the formal education system. Personal relationships within the family, and later with friends, neighbours, work mates etc. are instrumental in providing fresh information, teaching new skills and thereby altering or adjusting behaviour.

Moreover, various social groupings and systems - indeed society as a whole - provide the context within which this learning experience takes place, and each has an interest in communicating and gaining acceptance for the behaviour, values and attitudes they have accumulated. The individual's experience of family, work groups, the media, prevailing legal / economic / religious systems etc. are all part of his 'informal education'.

21. *Formal* education - in schools, colleges and other identifiable institutions - is nevertheless the only compulsory and relatively universal part of the education process, and as such has been the main focus of sociological observation.

Here again, study has concentrated on the way in which the 'socialisation' of individuals is carried out in educational institutions ie. the way that schools recognise and reinforce mainstream social values and attitudes, through:

(a) *reward and punishment:* eg. prizes for achievement, sanctions against failure or disruptive behaviour;

(b) *role definition:* eg. the separation of boys and girls, and the areas of study and behaviour expected of them;

(c) *'ethos':* definitions of success and failure, achievement, status (eg. values attached to academic subjects as opposed to vocational studies), acceptable behaviour etc.

The organisation and the developing individual

22. What emerges from all this is a picture of how an individual develops into the kind of adult that his managers and colleagues later come into contact with.

    We will discuss the implications of *how* an individual develops in a later chapter. The main implications of this development of (a) personality type and (b) goals will be for *motivation*: what kind of task, environment, relationship with management and rewards will satisfy the individual, or encourage the best possible performance from him (not necessarily the same thing)?

    But what are the implications of the fact of development itself?

23. Earlier in this chapter, we discussed some of the psychological forces and needs of the developing individual: activity, deep interests, long perspectives, independence, equality or superiority, self-awareness etc.

    Individuals spend so much of their time in organisations - and particularly in work organisations - that those needs will have to be at least partly fulfilled within the organisation. Indeed, for some individuals, their sense of identity is bound up with their working life to a large extent - 'what they do' symbolises 'what they are'.

    So how far does an organisation *co-operate* in, or actively *encourage* the personal growth and development of its employees?

24. Argyris suggests that there are 'basic incongruities' between what the formal business organisation requires of individuals, and the psychological needs of the individual striving to reach maturity. Moreover, individuals themselves *recognise* the conflict which arises between the demands of 'rational', efficiency-seeking organisations, and their own needs - creating the human and management problems of stress, dissatisfaction etc.

25. The rational model of the organisation assumes that it has specified objectives, and is designed logically so as to further the achievement of those objectives. There are various theories of how, and how far, an organisation can be structured and managed on 'universal principals'; to exclude any consideration of individual differences and personalities (although it is recognised that those differences do exist). Henri Fayol (1841 - 1925), for example, is one of the early, major exponents of 'classical' management thought.

The traditional formal organisation is broadly built on principles of:

- division of work ie. task specialisation. No one individual will be able to do everything, or have an overall view of the organisation's activity. Time and effort will be more efficiently utilised if individuals concentrate on and become expert in a narrow range of tasks;

- unity of direction, for the organisation as a whole; and therefore

- a structure of authority and responsibility, so that superiors can define, direct and control the work of subordinates, to make sure that each part contributes as required to the whole.

26. In such a structure (and in order for it to run smoothly), individuals tend to become content - or at least submissive - within the framework of organisation and control. They become consenting subordinates, with minimal control over their working environment. They feel their dependence on the organisation (for whatever financial rewards they are offered, a defined status in society etc.). They become largely passive, limited in their perspective (eg. of the overall purpose and value of their work), and willing to utilise only a few of their abilities (usually not the most important ones).

Argyris blames this failure to progress beyond infantile behaviours on the typical approach to management of organisations, and the lack of interpersonal competence in them (ie. the lack of constructive relationships). The immature outlook thus created merely perpetuates the assumption that the workers (and even lower managers) are short-sighted, petty, incapable of initiative and responsibility: the structure of authority and control from the higher levels of the hierarchy is further reinforced: a vicious circle.

27. Basically, however, the above kind of organisation would seem to provide the opposite of the conditions required for psychological maturation: the aims of the organisation would tend to frustrate the course of development needed by the individual for psychological health.

This is of course taking an extreme theoretical example of the formal organisation, without considering the alleviating effects of 'human relations' factors - such as the strength of worker relationships - or good management at a personal level. Increasingly management theory and practice do at least pay lip service to the realisation that *people* are the stuff of which organisations are made, or, as Peters and Waterman put it in 'In Search of Excellence', that "the individual human being still counts."

28. In any case, the frustration of personal development will be truer of the lower levels of the hierarchy, where one might expect to find the lowest degree of autonomy and responsibility. (These in particular are considered an important element of personal growth and 'self-actualisation', or the realisation of personal potential.)

Nor is low rank *per se* the only factor in the frustration of development. The progression towards responsibility, independence, serious interests and equal or superior social positions, for example, may be frustrated by social expectations or pressures: women, racial minorities etc. may have to struggle against a deeply-ingrained resistance to such aspirations on their part.

The impact of technology, eg. automation, on the working environment, although encouraging the acquisition of new skills, may also rob individuals of responsibility, choice, variety and a sense of value in the exercise of their duties.

The organisation's interest in personal development

29. Frustration, conflict, feelings of failure and low prospects etc. tend to show themselves in such effects as high labour turnover, absenteeism or pre-occupation with financial rewards (in compensation for lack of other satisfactions) – which can be as self-defeating for the organisation as they are unhealthy for the individual.

    The management task/problem, then, is to appreciate the normal, healthy process of human maturation and development, and make room for it – if not actively exploit its potential – within the organisation.

30. One of the prime attributes of 'excellent' companies identified by Peters and Waterman is what they call 'Productivity through People'.

> "We are not talking about mollycoddling. We are talking about tough-minded respect for the individual and the willingness to train him, to set reasonable and clear expectations for him, and to grant him practical autonomy to step out and contribute directly to his job." *In Search of Excellence.*

The emphasis is on *enabling contribution*. They quote IBM: "Our early emphasis on human relations was not motivated by altruism but by the simple belief that if we respected our people and helped them to respect themselves, the company would make the most profit."

'Happy workers' are unlikely to be an end in themselves. A business organisation tries to get the best *out* of its people, not necessarily *for* them – unless the one cannot be achieved without the other.

31. We should also note that there are a great many other work and non-work variables in the equation. A 'happy' workforce will not *necessarily* make the organisation profitable (eg. if the market is unfavourable): they will not necessarily be more productive (eg. if the task itself is badly designed, or resources scarce) nor even more highly motivated. Nor is there a magic formula for making them happy by offering them opportunities suitable to their personality development (increased responsibility etc.): their priorities may lie elsewhere, or they may be suffering frustration and failure in other areas of their lives that work cannot influence.

Implications of development for performance, learning and career development

32. The process of growth and change in the individual over time will be of interest to the organisation – and the other people who have to manage or simply get on with him – in many ways. It has implications for performance, learning and career development in so far as it reflects, or develops, the individual's:

(a) *personal maturity*. This is not necessarily a function of ageing, though it may be regarded as such eg. in the staff recruitment policies of the organisation. A responsible individual capable of considered decision-making and exercise of authority without it 'going to his head', or an individual wise in the ways of dealing with other people, may be considered as a 'mature' or adult personality - whatever his physical age;

(b) *experience*. Again, recruitment and training policies may express this in terms of 'job experience' or learned skills, but familiarity with occupational duties, procedures and techniques is only part of the picture. An individual may have gained experience in other areas of his life: experience of exercising authority, or submitting to it; of applying logic, or intuition, to problem-solving; of compromise, co-operation and conflict with other individuals; of learning and applying communication skills etc.;

(c) *adaptability*. This is another area in which age may be given undue consideration. Young people are thought to be more 'pliable' or adaptable, more able and more willing to learn and change: older people might be less flexible ('set in their ways' etc.) or simply, by education or practice, a generation behind the latest methods and technologies. This is oversimplified, of course, because an individual's education, training and career history may have made him highly adaptable and open to new ideas, whatever his age;

(d) *physical qualities*. Jobs which are physically demanding may require youthful strength and stamina - though again age itself need not be the deciding factor: physical condition and energy levels may depend on lifestyle, general health etc. Other qualities such as exceptional eyesight, co-ordination or dexterity may be required, and may be affected by the age and physical development of the individual - though again, not solely;

(e) *goals and priorities*. This is a major area in which individual growth and ageing may be of prime importance. One would expect the individual's goals, and the relative priorities which he gives to them, to change as each 'life stage' is reached. From the organisation's point of view, this will be interesting as a clue to the motivation of the individual (ie. what he is 'after', at a given time - relationships, career advancement, security etc.): the organisation can then offer him appropriate incentives and satisfactions, which will theoretically secure his good will and optimum performance. In particular, the organisation may be able to harness the individual's energies while they are most directly orientated towards work-related goals, ie. before disillusionment sets in, or other concerns eg. family or retirement plans, take over.

33. In the above comments, we have stressed the sort of positive qualities that an organisation might look for or wish to foster in its employees. Of course, we must also be aware that the progress of time, life experience and personal growth do not guarantee development in desirable directions. The 'development' of a particular individual may not result in emotional maturity, useful experience, physical prowess or clear motivation at all - as our own observation of people will show us.

34. Moreover, one must accept that organisations are generally highly selective in the qualities that they regard as truly desirable in the individuals that they employ, and not all of these qualities will be consistent with psychological maturity.

Independence, flamboyant individualism and creative thinking may be much prized qualities of maturity in some contexts - but if a person with those qualities were to be a low-ranking employee in a bureaucratic, 'do-it-by-the-book' organisation, the result would be misery both for himself and for the managers responsible for getting a 'sound', strictly controlled performance out of him. Such an organisation might rather look for conformity, low aspiration or high tolerance of monotony etc.

On the other hand the traditionally 'childlike' virtues of humility, simplicity or lack of worldly ambition are just as unlikely to be an asset to the individual in certain business contexts, ie. in jobs which require high-profile, highly-motivated, crafty, possibly ruthless individuals.

Attitude to development and ageing

35. You may have noticed that the individual's own perspective on development and ageing is somewhat different from the organisation's.

Self-awareness varies from individual to individual, but most people will either:

(a) consciously realise the direction and extent of their own maturation and development, and the psychological needs associated with it (eg. 'I require satisfaction from my job', or 'I won't grow unless I'm given more responsibility'); or

(b) have some 'picture' of it, as reflected by interaction with other individuals and the roles given to them by society (eg. 'I deserve a promotion - with my age and experience', or 'You can't teach an old dog new tricks').

The individual's performance, and his attitudes to learning and career development, will grow out of his perceived stage of development, and the needs or desires aroused in him.

36. As we have seen, however, the organisation itself may be judging the maturity and development of the individual by other criteria, and may be attaching a different importance to its judgements. For one thing, the larger it is, the more assumptions and generalisations about 'people' or 'the workforce' the organisation will have to make in its employee appraisal and formulation of management strategy. Even if the 'true and essential facts' about an individual's unique personality were ascertainable, it would be a time-consuming and expensive business.

37. The *perceived* or assumed implications of development and ageing will be all the organisation has to 'go on' - and it must make *some* assessment, unless it is prepared to take potentially expensive risks in recruiting, training and promoting people. For a manager looking at a 'curriculum vitae', job appraisal sheet or personnel file, it is often the common conceptions associated with age, experience etc. that will influence judgement.

SKILL AND LEARNING

Points to be covered

- The nature of skilled performance
- Learning processes: the learning curve
- The psychology of learning: the behaviourist approach
  - Pavlovian ('classical' or 'respondent') conditioning
  - Skinnerian ('instrumental' or 'operant') conditioning
- Learning psychology: the cognitive approach
- Learning about the organisation

The nature of skilled performance

1. 'Skill' to a psychologist covers a wide range of human abilities and behaviours, both:

   (a) routine, eg the ability to walk across a room, which when analysed is seen to be a very complex achievement, involving skill at controlling muscles, avoiding obstacles, judging distances and directions etc; and

   (b) specially acquired, eg the ability to play a musical instrument, or to operate a piece of machinery.

2. Common usage tends to define skill more narrowly, to cover the acquired abilities related, in particular, to performance in a work context. So it is possible to ignore the range of supposedly basic or 'natural' human abilities and talk about 'unskilled' or 'semi-skilled' labour.

   Even reading and writing, which are skills in the commonly accepted sense, are taken for granted in the assessment of 'skilled' performance: a cleaner in a factory might be designated an 'unskilled' worker, even though he will be exercising 'skill' as he reads warning notices, signs in and out of the building etc, (let alone the effective wielding of a broom in a complex environment).

   Some skills are commonly defined by organisations purely in terms of specialised functions - eg when a job advertisement specifies 'secretarial skills', it implies the ability to type, take shorthand or use office machinery. However, we do also speak of people being skilled in communication, diplomacy, teaching etc.

3. Non-manual (as opposed to manual) work is *assumed* to involve skill: manual work itself is often divided into categories according to varying *degrees* of skill required. So, for example, in a common sociological framework, 'working class' embraces three levels of society in Britain - ie. people in:

    (a) skilled manual jobs, eg. electricians and vehicle mechanics;
    (b) semi-skilled manual jobs, eg. machine operators and trawler men; and
    (c) unskilled manual jobs, eg. road sweepers and canteen assistants.

4. The degree of skill attributed to these jobs is clearly associated with:

    (a) the amount of *learning* required to master the necessary techniques and methods;

    (b) the amount of *understanding* that is involved in them (as opposed to rote-learning or simple 'habit-forming' by repetition); and also

    (c) the extent to which *initiative* is required in the application of those techniques and methods ie. the command of knowledge required to make any necessary analyses, judgements, plans, decisions etc. (so that diagnosing a fault and repairing a machine is more skilled work than simply operating it in accordance with learned methods).

5. These 'higher' aspects of skill distinguish it from mere learned ability such as is observable in animals. No-one doubts that animals are able to *learn*, and indeed the study of human learning processes is often approached through animal behaviour (eg. Skinner's rat and Pavlov's dogs). Animals are able to learn about and adapt to changes in their environment, to modify their behaviour according to changes in their circumstances. This is learning in one sense. Humans, however, go beyond this: we are not only able to learn about and adapt to our environment, but also:

    • to find ways of *manipulating* our environment; and
    • to exercise choice in the *goals* or purposes of our behaviour.

6. So human skills are extremely complex (especially if one recognises the psychologists' wider definition of them). The technological revolution is still struggling to design and build machines to reproduce human physical and mental processes, to perform tasks that humans do naturally and without effort.

    Learning, and the acquisition of skills, will therefore be of great importance to individuals and the organisations that employ them. The organisation will be interested in:

    (a) most commonly, the job-orientated 'manual' or 'technical' skills relevant to its particular field. This will have an impact on the recruitment, placement and career development of appropriately 'qualified' individuals;

    (b) the less easily defined skills in management, communication, inter-personal relations etc. that an individual might possess, or have the potential to develop;

    (c) learning potential. This will be relevant to recruitment and career development, and also to the induction and training methods used by the organisation; and

(d) learning progress. The speed with which an individual can be expected to learn and adapt should influence superiors' evaluations of the performance of their subordinates, especially in the case of new recruits, or the introduction of new technology or work methods.

Learning processes

7. 'Learning' is how we come to know things ie. a process of acquiring knowledge.

That knowledge, however, must go beyond simply having new ideas and thoughts in our minds: it must *change our behaviour*. The test of whether you have learned how to do something (or to do it better), is whether you can perform that action, where you couldn't have, previously. Likewise, if you have learned *about* something, you will take it into account in your decisions about behaviour, you will be able to think about it, talk about it (write exam essays about it?) etc.

This is also important for study of the learning process. Obviously, we cannot observe learning itself taking place inside the brain: it can only be *inferred* from changes in behaviour – assuming that human behaviour does not simply change for no reason.

8. Behaviour may be altered by a number of other processes or influences, which would not be defined as learning. We have already mentioned maturation and ageing, which are psychological and physiological processes, although the acquisition of knowledge does accompany them. There are many other shorter-lived and less constructive influences on behaviour, including stress, fatigue, alcohol, drugs and hypnosis.

The knowledge which leads to a change in behaviour comes through *experience*.

> **Learning** is the process of acquiring, through experience, knowledge which leads to changed behaviour.

Learning curve

9. It is possible to quantify and measure learning – ie. the degree of observable behaviour change. This makes it possible for organisations to:

(a) assess individual performance and progress;

(b) compare the performance and progress of different individuals; and

(c) establish 'norms' or standard levels of performance or progress, for a variety of planning and control applications.

10. A *'learning curve'* may be drawn up for an individual or group to represent progressive levels of performance (eg. output) in a particular task, over time. This makes it possible to trace the actual learning process in an individual worker or trainee.

In the graph below:

- the trainee's output levels off at 140 units per day: this may set the standard for output of a 'normally' proficient worker.
- it takes the trainee 4 months to reach this level: this may set the standard for allowed learning time.
- the trainee's progress is uneven. He learns slowly at first (having a lot to take in - not all, perhaps, related directly to the task): he then gains momentum, reaches a brief 'plateau' (while he consolidates what he has learned so far), and then develops more swiftly again, until he gains proficiency. Unless there is an injection of new equipment or methods, or fresh motivation, this will be his optimum performance level.

This is a common pattern for the acquisition of manual skills - though the speed of the learning process, the stage at which the plateau is reached etc. will vary from job to job and individual to individual.

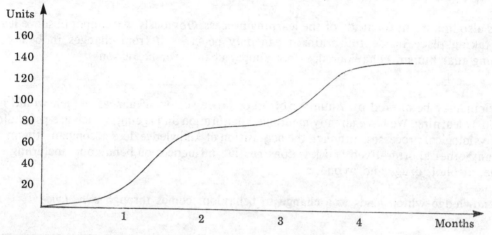

11. There is a more technical 'learning curve' theory, based on the idea that labour learns from experience, and as this experience is gained, the time required to complete a job lessens. This speeding up of a job with repeated performance is known as the learning effect or learning curve, and where it occurs, its effects on direct labour time and output may be calculated.

12. The theory was first developed in the US aircraft industry in the 1920s and 1930s. Since then, the learning curve concept has been extended to other industries and it has been found that the time required to do most tasks of a repetitive nature gets shorter as the tasks are done more and experience in doing them is built up. The concept of a learning curve or 'experience curve' has been extended to non-production activities, such as marketing efforts.

Some points to note about the use of this concept in production management are:

(a) that the learning effect will not be present for all types of work;

(b) that the learning effect does not continue indefinitely, so it is only a useful measurement in the production of items which are relatively short-lived or made in small quantities;

(c) that items which are made largely by labour effort naturally offer more opportunity for learning and improvement than those which are highly automated;

(d) that improvements in efficiency due to the ironing out of bugs at the very start of production, or better machinery and materials, are not directly attributable to the learning effect, and will distort the picture. The effect can be applied only to 'standard' methods;

(e) that the learning effect assumes stable conditions at work which will enable learning to take place: it may be impracticable eg. because of labour turnover; and

(f) that it also assumes a degree of motivation among employees. Problems may arise if:

   (i) trade unions object to the gradual reduction in standard production times per unit. Management may have to set a low standard from the outset, and put up with the shortfall until the learning curve 'catches up';

   (ii) the work force is paid a productivity bonus. The reduction in standard times might appear to be a threat to the size of bonuses, and cause dissatisfaction.

Experience

13. The experiences which cause observed changes in an individual's behaviour might be:

   (a) internal, ie. derived from inside the body; or

   (b) sensory, arising outside the body.

   However, it is not easy to draw a clear dividing line between the two: the mind is constantly processing the information of the senses, bringing to it all sorts of other recollections, associations and judgements. Our internal reactions - even to clearly sensory stimuli such as pain and pleasure - can be highly ambiguous. Our perceptions, feelings and recollections *about* an 'event' are as much part of the experience of it as the event itself.

14. It is important to realise that the mind does not simply record sensory impressions: it 'filters out', re-interprets and revalues experience.

   ● *We do not have total recall of everything we have read, seen, heard etc.* The mind is - necessarily - highly selective, unless a conscious decision is made to commit something to memory. Try to recall in detail an experience you are 'accustomed' to - walking down your street, the journey to work or college: identify the gaps in your mental picture.

   ● *Reflection on experience, after the event, can greatly alter its interpretation.* When we recall events in which we participated, we are able to disconnect or distance ourselves from the immediate sense impressions we received at the time, and reconstruct the 'scene' with ourselves as actors. We become objects in our own experience, rather than subjects through whom the scene is viewed.

   ● *The mind lends sensory experience its significance.* Not all new experiences *per se* have the effect of altering our behaviour: they must undergo a process of revaluation before they 'sink in', or become significant in modifying or determining future behaviour.

The psychology of learning: the behaviourist approach

15. The *behaviourist* (or '*stimulus-response*') approach to learning is based on:

    (a) the study of observable behaviour. Thought processes are not amenable to scientific study: only the relationship between visible stimuli and visible responses is important;

    (b) a theory of how people know things ('epistemology') called *empiricism* (or 'associationism', because of the association between stimulus and response). What we actually learn is sequences of muscle movements. The human mind is dependent on sensory input for thought. By 'abstraction', the mind concentrates on the main features of that input, arranges it and makes comparisons and associations. Patterns and concepts emerge from sensory data through this information-processing activity. The abstracted information is stored in the memory, and is also a source of new knowledge, through reflection and logical deduction;

    (c) the recognition that experience influences behaviour: past results teach us to modify our behaviour in future. This implies knowledge of the results ie. *appropriate feedback*, which may be rewarding ('*positive reinforcement*') or punishing ('*negative reinforcement*') - an incentive or a deterrent to similar behaviour in the future.

16. Behaviourist psychology concentrates on the connections between stimuli and responses. 'Learning' is the formation of *new* connections between stimuli and responses, through experience, or '*conditioning*'.

Pavlovian ('classical' or 'respondent') conditioning

17. According to stimulus-response psychology, there can be no response (behaviour) without a specific stimulus to invoke it. Pavlov (1849 - 1931) worked with dogs to demonstrate how an established behaviour can become 'attached' to a new stimulus: behaviour is not actually altered, but redirected. Responses which are amenable to conditioning (ie. to being attached to a given stimulus) are called 'respondents'.

18. There are 'unconditioned' stimuli and responses (also called *reflexes*). In the case of Pavlov's dogs, the sight and smell of meat made them salivate: the meat was an unconditioned stimulus - nothing else having to be 'done' to the dog to provoke a response - and the saliva is a natural or unconditioned response. Human reflexes, such as knee jerk, are of the same type.

19. Pavlov demonstrated what he called '*conditioned*' stimuli and responses. If a bell, for example, is rung while the dogs are shown the meat, the dogs will eventually associate the bell with the meat. The dogs learn, through the conditioning process, to 'attach' their normal response (salivation) to a new stimulus (bell), and will salivate at the sound of a bell. The dogs can be conditioned to *discriminate* between similar stimuli (so that they will respond to, say, a high-pitched bell only) or to *generalise* the stimulus (so that they will respond to any similar sound). If the meat is withheld for long, the association between bell and meat will break down, (the process of '*extinction*') and the dogs will gradually cease to give the conditioned response.

    Pavlov studied various subjects, stimuli and responses, at varying times and in varying conditions, and found conditioned response to be a consistently observable phenomenon. The argument is that human behaviour - and changes to it - are the result of conditioning: we learn by 'conditioned response'.

Skinnerian ('instrumental' or 'operant') conditioning

20. B F Skinner (1904 -) argued that behaviour *does* in fact occur in the absence of a specific stimulus: random or spontaneous behaviours of this kind are called *'operants'*, and are also susceptible to conditioning. Skinner demonstrated how new behaviours and behaviour patterns become established, through being associated with a stimulus - a reward or reinforcement of some kind: ie. unlike respondent conditioning, operant conditioning can be used to *shape* behaviour.

21. Any behaviour which is positively reinforced - even if it is completely random - will tend to be repeated in that same situation or context. The phenomenon is called 'instrumental' conditioning because behaviours conditioned in this way must be instrumental in gaining a reward which is:

    (a) of value to the subject. The subject has to be under the influence of some drive before it can be conditioned in this way; and

    (b) associated with the behaviour concerned. Skinner demonstrated that this does not necessarily involve total consistency in the correct behaviour = reward equation. *Intermittent reinforcement* - ie. where correct behaviour is rewarded only some of the time - can still condition behaviour: people still play on fruit machines and put money on the football pools, despite the infrequency of reward.

22. Skinner experimented with rats. He put a rat in a box with a lever which, when pressed, gave the animal access to food. The rat was hungry. As it wandered at random around the box, the rat in some way worked the lever (ie. by accident): that random act was reinforced with an appropriate reward, and gradually became established.

    By selectively reinforcing elements of otherwise random behaviour, Skinner found it possible to get birds to do 'tricks', like playing table tennis! He argued that complex human behaviour patterns develop in the same way: our environment and experience - with the various rewards and punishments that it brings - conditions and shapes selective aspects of our behaviour (see the *expectancy theory* of motivation, later).

23. Skinner directed his research to predicting human behaviour, and controlling it by manipulating appropriate variables: non-observable variables in behaviour - thought processes, 'psychic forces' etc. - were not considered useful to this end.

    Some of the practical applications of Skinner's work may be useful in organisational contexts.

    (a) The acquisition of skills may be considered a simple conditioning process of trial and error (punished) or success (rewarded). This is the basis of 'programmed learning' techniques, where individuals learn at their own pace through reinforcement of correct responses.

    (b) 'Behaviour modification' is the basis of therapy for mental and criminal disorders - but can be applied to the socialisation of individuals in other contexts. A range of acceptable behaviours is positively reinforced with praise or material reward, while undesirable behaviours are punished or simply not rewarded. 'Carrot and stick' motivation theories conform to this type.

Positive and negative reinforcement

24. According to Skinner, *negative* reinforcement (ie punishment) will produce behavioural change, but often in strange, unpredictable and undesirable ways, because of fear and hostility in the punished individual. 'The person who has been punished is not thereby simply less inclined to behave in a given way; at best he learns how to avoid punishment.'

    Positive reinforcement (ie. reward), on the other hand, is more effective in creating behavioural change in the desired direction. It also has the effect of enhancing the self-image of the person concerned, which, according to Peters and Waterman, is a prime factor in motivation. "Mere association with past personal success apparently leads to more persistence, higher motivation, or something that makes us do better."

    We will talk about reinforcement in a motivational context in the following chapter.

Research

Charles O'Reilly and Barton Weitz did a study of how 141 supervisors in an American retail chain used punishment as a means of controlling and correcting subordinates' behaviour.

'Incorrect' behaviour by subordinates included:

- lack of courtesy to customers
- sloppy appearance
- poor sales record
- slack timekeeping

Ways of dealing with these behaviours included:

- informal verbal warnings
- suspension
- loss of pay
- dismissal

Some supervisors made free and prompt use of these sanctions, while others were more 'sensitive' and lenient with their subordinates, and hated having to punish them. The departments run by these 'soft' supervisors showed poorer performance ratings.

It appeared that punishment *can* - contrary to the behaviourist position - be effective in modifying behaviour in a desired direction, if:

(a) it is perceived to maintain socially accepted standards (ie. where the desire for social acceptance, eg. by work colleagues, will also be brought to bear); and
(b) it is perceived by the punished person himself to have been legitimate or warranted.

Learning psychology: the cognitive approach

25. The cognitive or 'information processing' approach to learning is based on:

    (a) the belief that it is possible to make inferences about the internal, non-observable working of the mind;

    (b) a *rationalist* epistemology (theory of knowledge), which argues that the human mind is *not* dependent on information from the senses, but relies on *reasoning* as the basis for understanding. Sensory information is merely raw material on which the mind imposes organisation and meaning, not merely by sorting and abstracting, but by active and discriminating interpretation. Our image of the world is more elaborate than a mere sensory mosaic;

    (c) the realisation that experience influences behaviour through reinforcement – but in more complex ways than 'conditioning' implies. Feedback information on the results of past behaviour must be processed – received, interpreted and used in decision-making ie. whether to maintain successful behaviours or modify unsuccessful behaviours in future. We do not learn habits (as conditioning theories suggest) but ways of dealing with information, and choosing alternative methods of reaching our goals.

26. Cognitive psychology is concerned with the *plans* individuals elect to pursue, the methods they adopt and the effect of experience on those plans and methods.

    Our behaviour is 'purposive' (ie has a purpose). We choose or formulate plans which will fit our needs, motives, image of ourselves and our environment, in order to achieve those purposes. A 'plan' is a set of mental instructions or directions as to what action or behaviour is required. Within any plan, there is likely to be a set of sub-plans to be achieved on the way: you may plan to read this text as part of a plan to pass the Organisational Behaviour paper as part of a plan to become a Chartered Secretary as part of a plan to get a job as company secretary etc.

27. Exactly how we go about making and conducting our plans depends on how well we are able to:

    (a) draw on knowledge, skills and procedures that we have learned;

    (b) adjust our plans according to the success or failure of plans we have attempted in the past; and

    (c) adapt our successful plans to altered circumstances.

    Information about the results of our plans in any given situation – ie *feedback* – is clearly vital to the learning, adapting and controlling process.

28. There are different types of feedback.

    (a) *Concurrent* feedback – as in a 'real time' computer process – comes while the action is in process ie. in time to influence and control it as it proceeds. For example, the brain and eye provide concurrent feedback when judging distances, so that you can reach accurately for an object, aim a punch, stop before you bump into people etc. Concurrent feedback is necessary for much human functioning.

(b) *Delayed* feedback is an evaluation of an already completed action, and can only affect future behaviour. Eg: school reports, performance reviews, complaint forms etc. This type of feedback is essential for learning: if people fail or succeed without knowing or being told why, they will never know how to reproduce or change that state of affairs next time round.

(c) *Intrinsic* feedback comes from within the body itself: eg. so that we pant when our bodies need air, perspire when we are overheated, maintain our balance as we sit or walk etc.

(d) *Extrinsic* feedback comes from the environment, including other people, through the senses.

29. The science of 'cybernetics' ('communication in the animal and in the machine') involves the control of the performance of a system through feedback. The feedback control loop can be illustrated as a 'black-box' system diagram (so called because the workings of the system itself are not shown, only inputs and outputs) as follows:

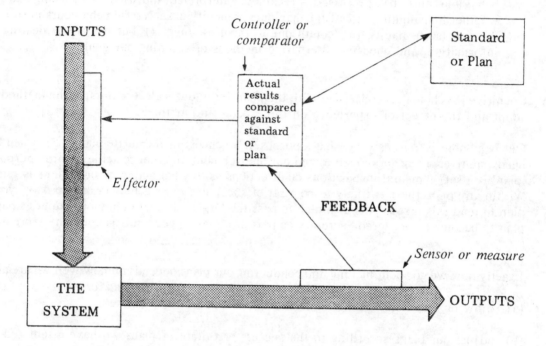

(a) A *sensor* is the device by which information (or data) is collected and measured - eg. a thermometer in a central heating system, or, in an organisational context, a management report compiled by computer.

(b) A *comparator* is the means by which the actual results of the system are measured against the pre-determined plans or system objectives. A manager may be a comparator, setting the production report against targets, and making judgements on the necessary control action.

(c) An *effector* is the device or means by which control action is initiated - eg. the manager's instruction and the subordinate's corrective action.

30. Cybernetics has been used as an analogy for the information processing, and use of feedback for control, that goes on in human learning. The sensor is the senses. The comparator is the mental process through which we perceive and interpret the sensory data in pursuit of our plans, and learn from experience. The standard is our own motives, purposes and objectives. The output is behaviour. This is called the *'cybernetic analogy'*.

Learning about the organisation

31. When an individual joins a work organisation, he is required to learn:

    - the knowledge and skills required to perform his particular tasks and responsibilities; and also
    - the expected and accepted standards, behaviours, values and beliefs that have evolved within the organisation, ie its 'culture'.

32. The socialisation process is usually informal: new recruits come to absorb the culture of the organisation through experience, as they 'learn the ropes', although brief 'induction courses' may also be given by the organisation.

    Correct behaviour is rewarded informally by acceptance and encouragement from colleagues, and perhaps more formally by praise, pay or promotion from superiors.

    Undesirable or non-conforming behaviour may be 'punished' informally by sanctions such as ridicule or 'being sent to Coventry' (ie. ignored), or more formally by fine, suspension or dismissal.

    Continual feedback will be received, and behaviour adjusted accordingly.

33. The particular standards of behaviour will vary from organisation to organisation and within each. There may be strong cultural differences between the behavioural norms of, say, an American company, where everyone is on first name terms (particularly with their superiors) to foster team spirit, and, say, an (un-Americanised) British company, where a certain formality and deference to superiors prevail.

    The recruit may also encounter conflicting norms. For example, the kind of behaviour reinforced by the organisation may be effort, loyalty, high output etc., while the work group - whose acceptance the recruit also desires - may have set a below-optimum norm of achievement: if one member works noticeably faster and better than others, the standards used for management control might become stiffer, productivity bonuses harder to achieve etc.

34. You can probably think of lots of 'norms' that you would wish to know about on your first day in a new organisation, in order to 'fit in'. They may include:

    - the degree of familiarity in relationships, especially with superiors;
    - dress and general appearance;
    - activities and lifestyle outside work;
    - timekeeping and work performance;
    - attitudes - to work, the organisation, unions, workers, management, customers etc.

Learning theory and job training

35. *Job training* is usually a formal educational process, whereby the individuals are taught the knowledge and skills necessary to carry out their specific function in the organisation. This may be done through formal courses (internal and external), or studying for a professional qualification, on-the-job training or group learning.

There are various practical difficulties to be overcome in job training of this sort.

(a) An individual will not benefit from formal training, in particular, unless he/she *wants* to learn. The individual's superior may need to provide encouragement in this respect.

(b) If the subject matter of a course does not relate to an individual's job, the learning will quickly be forgotten. Many training managers provide internal courses without relating their content to the needs of individuals attending them. Equally, professional examinations often include subjects in which individuals have no job experience, and these are usually difficult to learn and quickly forgotten afterwards.

(c) Individuals may not be able to accept that what they learn on a course applies in the context of their own particular job. For example, a manager may attend an internal course on management which suggests a participatory style of leadership, but on returning to his job he may consider that what he has learned is not relevant in his case, because his subordinates are too young or inexperienced.

(d) On-the-job training will not be successful if the assignments do not have a specific purpose from which the trainee can gain experience and immediate, relevant feedback. It will also be frustrated if the organisation is not prepared to be tolerant of the trainee's initial mistakes: these are inevitable at the start of training, and negative reinforcement will prove a disincentive to learning and the element of 'risk-taking' that it involves.

36. Learning psychology can be applied to such training programmes, to try to ensure maximum effectiveness. For example:

(a) *the individual should be motivated to learn.* The advantages of training should be made clear, according to the individual's motives - money, opportunity, valued skills etc.;

(b) *there should be clear objectives and standards set*, so that each task has some 'meaning'. Each stage of learning should present a challenge, without overloading the trainee or making him lose confidence. Specific objectives and performance standards for each will help the trainee in the planning and control process that leads to learning. It is insufficient to state as the objective of a course 'to give trainees a grounding in...' or 'to give trainees a better appreciation of...', as actual achievements cannot be measured quantifiably against such goals;

(c) *there should be timely, relevant feedback on performance and progress.* This will usually be provided by the trainer (ie. extrinsic feedback), and should be concurrent - or certainly not long delayed. If progress reports or performance appraisals are given only at the year end, for example, there will be no opportunity of behaviour adjustment or learning in the meantime;

(d) *positive and negative reinforcement should be judiciously used.* Recognition and encouragement enhances the individual's confidence in his competence and progress: punishment for poor performance - especially without explanation and correction - discourages the learner and creates feelings of guilt, failure and hostility. Helpful or 'constructive' criticism, however, is more likely to be beneficial.

37. *Programmed learning* - an application of operant conditioning theory - is a common method of technical training. It can be provided on a computer terminal, but is most often associated with printed booklets which provide information in easy-to-learn steps. From time to time, simple questions are asked: if the trainee answers correctly, he is asked to carry on with more learning, but if the questions are answered wrongly, the booklet gives an alternative set of instructions to go back and learn again. The advantages are that:

    (a) a trainee can work through the course in simple stages and reach defined objectives;

    (b) at each stage, there is opportunity for confidence-enhancing reinforcement by giving the correct answers;

    (c) a trainee can continually check whether he is going wrong, and can modify his responses accordingly - ie. there is frequent, relevant feedback;

    (d) a trainee can work at his own pace (unlike during classroom training), so the demands on him will not outstrip his motivation or ability.

38. *Group learning* is not common in industry, but is more common in organisations such as social services departments of local government authorities. Its purpose is:

    (a) to give each individual in a training group (or 'T group') a greater insight into his own behaviour;

    (b) to teach an individual how he 'appears' to other people, as a result of responses from other members of the group;

    (c) to teach an understanding of intra-group processes, ie. how people inter-relate, how leaders emerge etc.;

    (d) to develop an individual's skills in controlling such intra-group processes.

    T-groups can therefore be used to develop human relations skills. The underlying concept of T-groups is that sessions of guided discussion will generate concurrent feedback about the individual's perceptions, attitudes, roles and behaviour within a group: the group will in effect study its own behaviour.

Continuous learning

39. Peter Drucker ('Management') argues that there are three basic requirements, if workers are to become productive and responsible:

    ● productive work;

    ● feedback information ('workers on all levels will manage their own performance if only they are being informed immediately what their performance actually is'); and

    ● continuous learning.

40. Drucker sees 'continuous learning' as supplementary to the process of training for new skills, but of equal importance.

> " Above all, it satisfies the need of the employee to contribute what she herself has learned to the improvement of her own performance, to the improvement of her fellow worker's performance, and to a better, more effective, but also more rational way of working... It is also the one way to come to grips with two basic problems: the resistance of workers to innovation, and the danger that workers will become 'obsolete'. "

This 'continuing challenge to the worker', says Drucker 'need not be organised as a formal session, but it always needs to be organised'.

ABILITIES, APTITUDES AND INTELLIGENCE

Points to be covered

- Abilities and aptitudes
- The use of ability assessment
- Intelligence
- Intelligence tests
- Intelligence and leadership ability

Introduction

1. The terms abilities, aptitudes and intelligence have been variously defined (or ill-defined) and used interchangeably in a variety of contexts. We will look at abilities and aptitudes first, and will then go on to discuss intelligence as it may be considered to overlap with 'ability' generally, and in its narrower definition as 'IQ'.

Abilities and aptitudes

2. There have been many attempts to make a useful distinction between:

    (a) *abilities*, largely believed to be inherited; and
    (b) *aptitudes*, the capacity to learn and develop abilities or skills.

    There is, however, not always an observable dividing line between ability and aptitude, which may also be bound up with interest, motivation, experience and other factors influencing behaviour.

3. A further issue has been whether abilities or aptitudes are unitary or complex. Can 'single' abilities be separated out and measured, or are they complexes of various other aptitudes and influences? The exercise of 'athletic ability', for example, may partly display abilities in spatial visualisation, reasoning or manual dexterity, as well as experience, perseverance etc.

    Abilities are commonly *treated* as units for the sake of assessment.

4. Abilities have been broadly grouped and categorized as follows.

    - Reasoning - verbal, numerical and abstract
    - Spatio-visual ability - practical intelligence, non-verbal ability and creative ability
    - Perceptual speed and accuracy - clerical ability
    - 'Manual' ability - mechanical, manual, musical and athletic

The use of ability assessment

5. Abilities are a focus of attention in many spheres, as organisations such as schools, colleges and employers attempt to assess the *sphere* of individuals' abilities, and the *level* of required abilities which different individuals possess. It seems obvious that people are 'naturals' at music, drawing, football etc.; some people have 'the gift of the gab' while others are good with numbers; some people are thinkers, while others are 'good with their hands'.

6. If a certain ability or aptitude category is required or desirable for an individual to perform his job, or to perform it better, then it would be useful to test for and measure that ability or aptitude in the individual, so that:

    (a) the right person can be selected and/or trained for the job (or the task delegated to a person with suitable ability or aptitude)- ie. "Ask Bloggs: *he's* good at...." ; and

    (b) the likely quality of an individual's performance can be predicted - ie. "That won't be a problem: Bloggs is *good* at..."

7. Unfortunately, the relationship between assessments of ability and performance is not as useful as a manager might hope. Knowing what abilities a person has can help in employee selection and task allocation ((a) above), using the broad recognition that ability does influence performance, and a person with, for example, 'musical aptitude' will make a better linguist than someone whose 'forte' is elsewhere.

8. However, ability is only one factor of performance in a work context. As such, it is an indicator of *potential* (which may not be utilised or fulfilled) rather than a predictor.

    Ability may be *essential* to successful performance in a particular job - but it is unlikely to be *sufficient*.

    - Willingness and motivation to perform is likely to be crucial.
    - Experience may also be relevant.
    - The design of the task itself, and the work environment, may hinder or enhance performance.

9. The only ability which has been found to relate positively to the performance of managers in business organisations is the so-called 'helicopter ability'. This is a spatio-visual ability which enables individuals to rise above the particulars of a situation, to see the whole picture, to sift out the important elements, and to conceive strategies.

    The helicopter ability is related to the psychological construct 'field independence', into which research has been conducted. Its opposite, 'field dependence', is characterised by poor conceptual skills, inability to isolate issues, and generally 'not seeing the wood for the trees'.

    Field independence is believed to be at its peak in individuals between the ages of 15 and 35, and its subsequent decline may help to account for 'mid-career' crises, and the emergence of 'whiz-kid' young managers.

Intelligence

10. Intelligence is a wide and complex concept. Theorists disagree on whether it is separate from, or a facet of, personality. The more 'Artificial Intelligence' is explored and developed, the more it is appreciated just how complex the nature and processes of human intelligence is.

Victor Serebriakoff, president of the British Mensa organisation (for members of high-IQ), writes of the nature of intelligence:

> "Surely the whole point about anything that we think of as an intelligent entity is that it has free will, the freedom to invent any crazy scheme or model and test it for its concurrence with the world. It is the freedom to believe anything and act on any belief that enables us to learn, and the ability to learn is the one unifying aspect of anything to which we would give the name intelligence. Present day computers are very much better and faster than we are at syllogistic logic, but they are not intelligent. It is our ability to be wrong and learn from error that distinguishes us." (*Mensa Magazine*, May 1987)

11. The terms 'intelligence' and 'ability' have often been used interchangeably, and have been rather narrowly defined to denote the analytical abilities such as 'mental dexterity', 'verbal fluency' or 'logic'.

Educational theory in the first half of this century tended to assume that most of a child's 'ability' is based on intelligence, and is innate and inherited. It is only in more recent years that:

(a) 'ability', as defined by educational 'success' or 'failure', has been redefined to include concepts other than so-called 'intellectual ability';

(b) family environment and social factors have been put forward as having a stimulating or restricting influence on the development of ability. This is part of a great debate on the effects of heredity and environment on intelligence (and personality), known as the 'nature-nurture' debate.

12. Cyril Burt, an early psychologist, wrote in 1933 that (italics ours):

> "By intelligence, the psychologist understands *inborn, all-round intellectual ability*. It is inherited, or at least innate, *not due to teaching or training*; it is intellectual, not emotional or moral, and remains *uninfluenced by industry or zeal*; it is general not specific, ie. it is not limited to any particular kind of work, but enters into all we do or say or think. Of all our mental qualities, it is the most far-reaching; fortunately it can be *measured with accuracy and ease*."

13. Charles Handy notes that the development of this approach (IQ tests etc.) concentrates on analytic intelligence, and downgrades other facets, or 'mental qualities'. He refers to recent work in America which has confirmed the commonsense observation that 'intelligence (or ability)' takes many forms which do not necessarily correlate with each other, including:

- *analytic* intelligence - measured by IQ tests, and on which most attention has been centred;
- *spatial* intelligence - the ability to see patterns and connections, most obvious in the creative artist or scientist;
- *musical* intelligence - the 'good ear' observable in musicians, mimics and linguists;
- *physical* intelligence - more usually called 'ability', obvious in athletes, dancers etc.;
- *practical* intelligence. Some people can make and fix things without theoretical knowledge;
- *intra-personal* intelligence - the ability to know, be sensitive to, and express oneself, observable in artists, poets, mystics etc.;
- *inter-personal* intelligence - the ability to relate to and work through others; essential in leaders.

14. Further complication to the concept of 'intelligence' comes from research into the processes directed by the different hemispheres of the brain. It has been suggested that the logical, analytical, intellectual functions of the brain are performed in the left-hand hemisphere - ie. those commonly thought of as intelligence (IQ). The right-hand hemisphere was found to be the locus for less 'rational' processes - intuition, vision, imagination, emotion, creativity.

Henry Mintzberg, in a 1976 article about perceptions of management in relation to the processes of the human brain, argued that many perceptions of the management task and management ability were equated exclusively with 'left-hand' processes. In fact, he suggested, experience and observation indicated the supreme importance of 'right hand' processes, particularly in non-routine or ambiguous situations.

15. The trouble with these wider definitions of 'intelligence' is that many of the abilities they embrace are difficult or impossible to measure or assess accurately. Analytical intelligence, however, was something that psychologists believed could be 'measured with accuracy and ease': this is the kind of intelligence that is still most frequently used as a measure of 'ability' in children and adults alike.

Intelligence tests

16. On the basis of the definitions of intelligence put forward by Burt and others, a scale of measurement for 'Intelligence Quotient' (IQ) was devised, with a range of tests used to 'rate' the logical powers of individuals. Those who performed badly in such tests were considered to be individuals of 'low ability': this was the basis of segregation of British pupils into grammar, technical and modern schools. Abilities were inherited in a fixed amount at birth, impervious to influence by subsequent education, and 'streaming' was therefore possible. Abilities were also easily identified and predicted (at the age of eleven, by the '11 plus' examination): all that remained was to choose the type of school to fit the ability level of the child.

17. One major criticism of IQ testing is the narrow and unproblematic use of the concepts 'intelligence' and 'ability', which almost come to be defined solely by the individuals' response to such tests. 'High IQ' should perhaps not be synonymous with 'intelligent': education, experience, wisdom, judgement and even emotional stability might also be taken into consideration.

18. Research has been performed into the assumptions behind, and effectiveness of, IQ testing. The tests are supposedly scientifically rigorous and neutral, but there is considerable debate centred on:

(a) *the reliability and sufficiency of results.* Although the tests appear to rely on sound principles, social and emotional factors affecting performance are not taken into account. Moreover, research has demonstrated that experience of completing IQ tests improves performance - ie. 'practice makes perfect': where does 'intelligence' end and memory or habit take over?;

(b) *the cultural neutrality of the tests.* Research by sociologists has suggested that the basis of the questions is the experience of white, Anglo-Saxon, middle-class individuals, and that results which show other groups to have 'low ability' are therefore subject to this bias. One quoted example is a classic 'odd man out' question from an old '11 plus' paper:

MEASLES, STEAMER, LEAVE, OMELETTE, COURAGE

(The odd man out is 'steamer' - because the others have national connotations: German measles, French leave, Spanish omelette and Dutch courage!)

19. H J Eysenck, in his introduction to the best-selling *Check Your Own IQ*, expresses his own serious criticisms of IQ measurement - but at the same time his conviction that the selection process of 11-plus testing is surprisingly accurate and valid. He makes the following comments (italics ours).

(a) "The measurement of intelligence obviously requires certain *fundamental elements of knowledge*, motivation, habit, and experience in common among testees. Obviously you could not begin to do the problems in this book if you could not read, did not know how to hold a pencil, were blind, did not know the meaning of elementary English words, or were not motivated to undergo the task at all. All these points present problems in comparing the intelligence of one social, national or ethnic group with another." Eysenck recognises that "no intelligence test is universally valid, but applies only to a given subsection of the population".

(b) However, "*given a fairly homogeneous group*, it has been shown that knowledge is a direct function of IQ, as determined by tests not involving specific items of knowledge. Simple vocabulary tests for instance have been found to be the single best index of intelligence, and indeed it does not seem unreasonable that knowledge of a person's native language should be related to his intellectual ability; after all, the chances of acquiring a good vocabulary are limited more by lack of intellectual ability than by outside restrictions." Do you agree with this last point?

(c) Eysenck admits that "intelligence tests are subject to practice and coaching effects". It being impossible to keep everyone in uniform ignorance of the nature of the tests until occasion for testing arises, he declares his desire to give everyone a comparable *familiarity* with testing, so that the effects of practice on *comparison* are reduced to a minimum.

20. On the nature of intelligence itself, Eysenck comments as follows.

(a) "When we analyse performance on intelligence tests in some detail, we find that there is one outstanding characteristic which more than any other determines success or failure. This characteristic is mental *speed*....This all-pervasive mental speed, I would say, is the fundamental inherited basis for intellectual differences among people."

Insofar as IQ is a purely intellectual measure, it may be a measure of speed, but:

(b) "In any particular IQ test various *non-intellectual personality factors* also come into play... The two main personality features which have been experimentally studied and identified in this connection may be called by their popular names, *carelessness* and *lack of persistance*."

Poor marks may therefore be caused by:

(i) slow speed of mental functioning;

(ii) lack of persistance, ie impatience; or

(iii) malfunction of the 'error-checking mechanism'. Original, creative and extravert people are prone to careless errors in 'closed' (ie. pick the one correct solution from various alternatives) tests - although they are good at 'open' (ie. find a solution independently) tests.

You might like to try these examples of questions in IQ tests.

Visuo-spatial ability

Find the odd man out

Numerical ability

Insert the missing number

Verbal ability

Find the word-ending which can be prefixed by all of the following

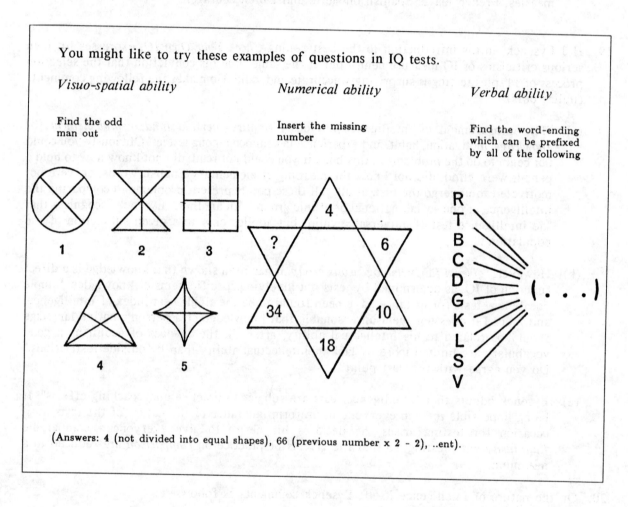

(Answers: 4 (not divided into equal shapes), 66 (previous number x 2 - 2), ..ent).

Intelligence and leadership ability

21. The equation of intelligence with IQ test success is, as we have suggested, not a good basis for the assessment of 'ability' in all contexts. Mintzberg, Peters and Waterman and others have stressed the importance of 'vision' and 'flair' to successful management.

22. The 'trait' approach to leadership – which we will cover in a later chapter – has attempted to distinguish the personal characteristics that are possessed by successful leaders, to create a model of the leader 'type'. Most studies single out intelligence as a required trait, observing that it should be above average, while not of genius level. Recent studies also single out the helicopter ability.

23. John W Hunt notes that while most top managers do possess above average intelligence, and most middle managers average or above average intelligence, no study has been able to show a positive correlation between intelligence *per se* and 'better' management. On the contrary, some 'super intelligent' individuals have been shown to be 'distinctly untalented' managers.

MOTIVATION

Points to be covered

- The nature of motivation
  - Needs, drives and motives
- Motivation theories: some broad classifications
- Maslow's hierarchy of needs: ERG theory
- Two-factor theory: Herzberg
- Expectancy theory: Handy's motivation calculus
- Dissonance: psychological contracts
- Systems and contingency approach to motivation

The nature of motivation

1. As we suggested earlier, human behaviour is *purposive*: we have goals, aims, wants, desires, needs etc. Moreover, we exercise *choice* in the purpose of our behaviour, and in the way we behave to further our ends – whether we actually stop and think about it or not. It is important to us to ascribe meaning to our own behaviour and that of others. We want to know *why* we behave as we do: 'motiveless' crimes frighten us; 'aimless' or 'senseless' actions baffle us.

   Obviously, it is in an organisation's interests to know the reasons or motives behind people's behaviour. In particular, if the organisation finds reasons why people might perform well at work, it can utilise that knowledge to encourage them.

2. The words 'motives' and 'motivation' are commonly used in different contexts to mean:

   (a) goals, or outcomes that have become desirable for a particular individual. These are more properly 'motivating factors' - since they give people a reason for behaving in a certain way (ie. in pursuit of the chosen goal): thus we say that money, power or friendship are 'motives' for doing something;

   (b) the mental process of choosing desired outcomes, deciding how to go about them (and whether the likelihood of success warrants the amount of effort that will be necessary etc.) and setting in motion the required behaviours. Our motivation to do something will depend on this 'calculation' of the relationship between needs/goals, behaviour and outcome;

   (c) the social process by which the behaviour of an individual is influenced by others. 'Motivation' in this sense usually applies to the attempts of organisations to get workers to put in more effort. It also applies to the influence of the family and society in general in teaching individuals to value and seek certain rewards - status, money, or family - through certain behaviours, ie. productive work, marriage etc.

We 'are motivated' by our goals, the expected outcomes of certain behaviours.

We 'are motivated' when we decide to behave in a way that we believe will fulfil our goals.

We 'are motivated' by other people to behave in a way that they desire.

Motivators and motivation

3. In the most basic terms, an individual has needs which he wishes to satisfy. The means of satisfying his needs are 'wants'. For example, an individual might feel the need for power, and to fulfil this need, he might want money and a position of authority. Depending on the strength of his needs and wants, he may take action to achieve them. If he is successful in achieving them, he will be satisfied.

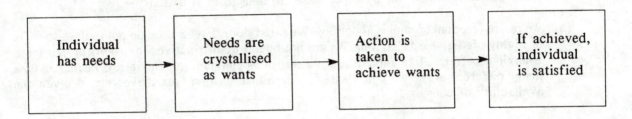

| Individual has needs | → | Needs are crystallised as wants | → | Action is taken to achieve wants | → | If achieved, individual is satisfied |

4. *Motivators* can be established which act as the 'wants' of the individual. For example, the position of sales director might serve as a 'want' to satisfy an individual's need for power, or access to the senior executives' dining room might serve as a 'want' to satisfy a need for status; a chartered secretarial qualification might serve as means of satisfying the need for prestige.

    Motivators may exist which are not directly controllable by management; for example, an individual might want to be accepted by his work-mates, to satisfy his need for friendship and affiliation with others, and he might therefore choose to conform to the norms and adopt the attitudes of the work group - which are not necessarily shared by the 'organisation' as a whole.

5. 'Motivation' is then the urge or drive to take action to *achieve* wants. For example, an individuals might want to be promoted, but he might not be sufficiently motivated to work harder or more efficiently in order to win the promotion: he might also want leisure, or he may not believe that the company really will promote him if he does work harder etc. Management has the problem of creating or 'manipulating' motivators which will actually motivate employees to perform in a desired way.

Needs, drives and motives

6. We will be talking more specifically about 'worker goals' in the following chapter, but here we will discuss the nature of 'goals' themselves, as being central to motivation.

    Are the goals that human beings pursue *innate*, genetically inherited, and basically unalterable? Or are they *learned*, socially transmitted and therefore susceptible to manipulation?

7. Some of our behaviour is directed or influenced by human biology, which dictates the basic 'essentials' of continuing life: self-preservation, oxygen, warmth, food, water, sleep, etc. When the body is deprived of these essentials, innate biological forces called *needs* or *drives* are activated, and determine the behaviour necessary to end the deprivation – eat, drink, flee etc.

8. We never learn to have these drives, we cannot make them go away, and many are overpowering. However, our behaviour is not entirely a slave to our biology, because:

    (a) apart from the need for oxygen (and food and water, after a period of time), the mind is able to over-ride our physical drives, if they are displaced by other goals. The mind has ultimate control over behaviour, and may decide to satisfy intellectual and emotional needs before (or instead of) 'biogenic' or 'primary' needs. Religious orders, for example, may require disciplines such as celibacy or long periods of fasting. People give up much-needed sleep for all sorts of reasons. The self-preservation drive may be overcome by concern for other people (altruism) or by other goals, in dangerous situations;

    (b) we retain freedom of choice about how we satisfy our drives: they do not dictate specific or highly predictable behaviour. We are not bound by instinctive, environment-triggered behaviour patterns, like animals: our patterns of behaviour are flexible. Consider in how many different ways we could satisfy our hunger, thirst, sex drives etc. – given the availability of choice;

    (c) we also behave in ways that make no direct contribution to our physical survival and health. There seem to be other goals which influence behaviour – such as pleasure, knowledge, fulfilment of personal potential etc. (although these things may influence the ways in which we satisfy our drives, and also arguably contribute to our general 'competence' to survive in the world).

9. Apart from 'biogenic needs' or 'drives' ie. biological determinants of behaviour, activated by deprivation, there are *psychogenic needs* – emotional or psychological needs. The American psychologist Abraham Maslow argued that man has seven innate needs – of which only the first two include primary needs such as we have described. Maslow's categories are:

    - physiological needs

    - safety needs — freedom from threat, but also security, order, predictability

    - love needs — for relationships, affection, sense of belonging

    - esteem needs — for competence, achievement, independence, confidence and their reflection in the perception of others, ie. recognition, appreciation, status, respect

    - self-actualisation needs — for the fulfilment of personal potential: 'the desire to become more and more what one is, to become everything that one is capable of becoming'

- freedom of inquiry — for social conditions permitting free speech and
  and expression needs   encouraging justice, fairness and honesty.

- knowledge and understanding — to gain and order knowledge of the environment, to
  needs   explore, learn, experiment etc.

According to Maslow, the last two needs are the channels through which we find ways of satisfying all the other needs, ie. they are the basis of satisfaction. The first two needs are essential to human survival. Satisfaction of the next two is essential for a sense of adequacy and psychological health. Maslow regarded self actualisation as the ultimate human goal, although few people ever reach it. We will discuss the 'hierarchy' into which Maslow put his needs when we come to work-related theories of motivation, later in this chapter.

10. Roethlisberger and Dickson add on to physiological and safety needs:

- Friendship and Belonging Needs
- Needs for Justice and Fair Treatment
- Dependence-Independence
- Needs for Achievement

11. David McClelland, writing in the 1950s, identified three types of motivating needs:

(a) *the need for power.* People with a high need for power usually seek positions of leadership in order to influence and control;

(b) *the need for affiliation.* People who need a sense of 'belonging' and membership of a social group tend to be concerned with maintaining good personal relationships;

(c) *the need for achievement.* People who need to achieve have a strong desire for success and a strong fear of failure.

12. How far are these goals of human behaviour *innate*, however?

We must recognise that some 'innate needs' may in fact be what Buchanan and Huczynski call '*motives*' - ie. 'learned influences on human behaviour that lead us to pursue particular goals because they are socially valued'.

' Our society or our culture influences our motives through the values, ideals, standards and modes of behaviour of other people.'

13. Hence, though our ego 'needs' bolstering through status and recognition, it is attitudes handed down through society that make 'status' and 'recognition' valuable and desirable: it is only by reference to society that we know when we have obtained them.

'Self actualisation' similarly depends on our perception of it, and of ourselves, which in turn depends largely on social values and beliefs. People's perception of their own worth and potential is bound up with the expectations and functions imposed on them by their particular culture. In our own society, men are supposed to be 'fulfilled' by productive work, and women, mainly, by child-bearing - although that particular perception is undergoing some change.

The way in which we go about satisfying our innate, primary needs is also influenced by what is socially acceptable. As Buchanan and Huczynski note, "those behaviours that are typical and conventional tend to become socially necessary, as those who do not conform may be shunned, or even imprisoned. Polygamy is a crime to us, but a social norm and a sign of male achievement, wealth and status in parts of the Arab world."

14. Innate, physiological needs are, as we have noted, activated by deprivation: they are aimed at *satisfaction* or *avoidance*, and when this is achieved, they cease to determine behaviour. Once hunger and thirst, for example, are sated, they are no longer motivating factors.

Those needs or 'motives' that are not wholly innate or physiological, however, tend to be aimed at *stimulation*: they are 'on-going' motivators. If we once fulfil our desires for friendship, recognition, new experience or new information, we do not usually feel satisfied until the need comes upon us again: the desire is aroused for other, or further, experience.

15. We will go on to look at how all these needs, drives and motives work together to determine behaviour, and how all the various goal theories are relevant to motivation (in its 'mental process' and 'social process' senses), by looking at some of the major work-related theories of motivation.

"If we could understand, and could then predict, the ways in which individuals were motivated we could influence them by changing the components of that motivation process. Is that manipulation - or management?"

Charles Handy - Understanding Organisations

Motivation theories: some broad classifications

16. The kind of theory that we subscribe to, about what motivation is and what can be 'done' with it, will influence all our attitudes to management and individuals in organisations. There are various ways of looking at motivation. Handy groups early motivation theories under three headings:

(a) *satisfaction theories*. These theories are based on the assumption that a 'satisfied' worker will work harder, although there is little evidence to support the assumption. Satisfaction may reduce labour turnover and absenteeism, but will not necessarily increase individual productivity. Some theories hold that people work best within a compatible work group, or under a well-liked leader;

(b) *incentive theories*. These theories are based on the assumption that individuals will work harder in order to obtain a desired reward - ie positive reinforcement - although most studies are concentrated on money as a motivator. Handy notes that incentive theories *can* work, if:

- the individual perceives the increased reward to be worth the extra effort;
- the performance can be measured and clearly attributed to that individual;
- the individual wants that particular kind of reward; and
- the increased performance will not become the new minimum standard;

(c) *intrinsic theories*. These theories are based on the belief that higher-order needs are more prevalent in modern man than we give him credit for. People will work hard in response to factors in the work itself - participation, responsibility etc.: effective performance is its own reward.

17. Another way of grouping the major theories of motivation is by distinguishing between:

(a) *content theories*; and

(b) *process theories*.

Content theories assume that human beings have a 'package' of motives which they pursue ie. they have a set of needs or desired outcomes. Maslow's need hierarchy theory and Herzberg's two-factor theory are two of the most important approaches of this type.

Process theories explore the process through which outcomes *become* desirable and are pursued by individuals. This approach assumes that man is able to select his goals and choose the paths towards them, by a conscious or unconscious process of calculation. Expectancy theory and Handy's 'motivation calculus' are theories of this type.

Maslow's hierarchy of needs

18. We have already mentioned Abraham Maslow's classification of man's innate needs. In his motivation theory, Maslow put forward certain propositions about the motivating power of these needs.

(a) Man's needs can be arranged in a 'hierarchy of relative pre-potency'.

(b) Each 'level' of need is dominant until satisfied; only then does the next level of need become a motivating factor.

(c) A need which has been satisfied no longer motivates an individual's behaviour. The need for self-actualisation can never be satisfied.

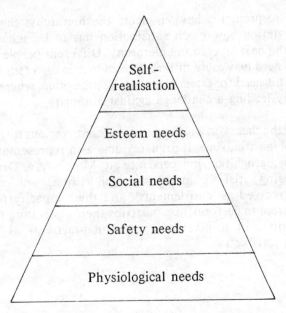

19. There is a certain intuitive appeal to Maslow's theory. After all, you are unlikely to be concerned with status or recognition while you are hungry or thirsty - primary survival needs will take precedence. Likewise, once your hunger is assuaged, the need for food is unlikely to be a motivating factor.

Unfortunately, research does not bear out the proposition that needs become less powerful as they are satisfied, except at the very primitive level ie. of 'primary' needs, hunger and thirst etc.

20. Maslow himself said that the various levels of the need hierarchy overlap to some extent, and an individual may still be motivated by needs at a lower level when he acquires needs at a higher level. For example, a manager might want something which fulfils his need for esteem, but he might also be concerned about reducing the threat of redundancy, which would take away the satisfactions afforded by his job with regard to social needs and safety needs. At any time, therefore, a person might have needs at differing levels in the hierarchy. Even so, there is a general progression upwards as some needs are at least partially satisfied, and others gain importance.

21. It is also worth noting that Maslow did not intend his views to be applied to the specific context of behaviour at work: needs can be satisfied by aspects of a person's life outside work. However, since work provides a livelihood and takes up such a large part of a person's life, it is obviously going to play an important part in the satisfaction of his needs.

22. There are various problems associated with Maslow's theory.

    (a) Empirical verification for the hierarchy is hard to come by. Physiological and safety needs, as we mentioned before, are *not* always uppermost in the determination of human behaviour. It is still not clear, either, whether the higher order needs are innate or learned: it would be pleasant to believe, with Maslow, that they are innate, but, as Buchanan and Huczynski suggest: "Maslow may simply have reflected American middle class values and the pursuit of the good life, and may not have hit on fundamental universal truths about human psychology."

    (b) It is difficult to predict behaviour using the hierarchy: the theory is too vague. It is impossible to define how much satisfaction has to be achieved before the individual progresses to the next level in the hierarchy. Different people emphasise different needs. Also, the same need may cause different behaviour in different individuals: one person may seek to satisfy his need for esteem by winning promotion, whereas another individual might seek esteem by leading a challenge against authority.

    (c) Application of the theory in work contexts presents various difficulties. The role of money or 'pay' is problematic, since it arguably acts as a representative or 'stand in' for other rewards - status, recognition, independance etc. Moreover, as Drucker notes, a want changes in the act of being satisfied: 'incentives' such as remuneration, once regularly provided, come to be perceived as 'entitlements', and their capacity to create dissatisfaction, to become a deterrent to performance, outstrips their motivatory power. Self actualisation, in particular, is difficult to offer employees in practice - as we will consider later, in relation to job satisfaction.

(d) The 'ethnocentricity' of Maslow's hierarchy has also been noted - ie. it does seem broadly applicable to Western English-speaking cultures, but is less relevant elsewhere. In 1963, in a cross-cultural survey of 3,500 managers from 14 countries, Haire, Chiselli and Porter found that 'the theoretical classification of the five types of need according to their priority of prepotency exactly fits the pattern of results for the United States and England, but not for any other group of countries' (although there was substantial agreement between countries about the relative importance of any given 'need').

ERG theory

23. Alderfer simplified Maslow's need hierarchy down to three categories, along the same lines:

    * the need for existence;
    * the need to relate to others; and
    *) the need for personal growth.

    He called this the 'existence-relatedness-growth' (ERG) model.

24. ERG is also a hierarchical model, but Alderfer points out that each individual may have different levels of each kind of need: thus avoiding the difficulties associated with Maslow's idea that needs become less powerful as they are satisfied.

Two-factor theory: Herzberg

25. In the 1950s, the American psychologist Frederick Herzberg interviewed 203 Pittsburg engineers and accountants and asked two 'critical incident' questions: The subjects were asked to recall events which had made them feel good about their work, and others which made them feel bad about it. Analysis revealed that the factors which created satisfaction were different from those which created dissatisfaction. Herzberg called this a 'two factor theory of motivation'.

NB. The ICSA examiner frequently complains of candidates' inability to spell the names of writers they cite in their answers - especially the name of Herzberg. Test yourself from time to time to ensure that you are getting the names right.

---

26. Herzberg in his book *Work and the nature of man* identifies the elements which cause job dissatisfaction, and those which can cause job satisfaction. He distinguished between 'hygiene factors' and 'motivator factors'.

27. Factors which can cause dissatisfaction at work are:
    * company policy and administration;
    * salary;
    * the quality of supervision;
    * interpersonal relations;
    * working conditions;
    * job security.

28. 'When people are dissatisfied with their work it is usually because of discontent with the environmental factors'.

    Herzberg calls such factors 'hygiene' or 'maintenance' factors; hygiene because they are essentially preventative. They prevent or minimise dissatisfaction but do not give satisfaction, in the same way that sanitation minimises threats to health, but does not give 'good' health.

29. Maintenance factors are so called because they have to be continually renewed. Satisfaction with environmental factors is not lasting. In time dissatisfaction will occur. For example:

    (a) an individual might want a pay rise which protects his income against inflation. If he is successful in obtaining the rise he wants, he will be satisfied for the time being, but only until next year's salary review;

    (b) an individual who is newly recruited into a job might want to establish good personal relations with his colleagues. If he is successful, he will be satisfied at first, but in time he will get used to working with them, and may start to get fed up with seeing the same familiar faces day after day.

30. The important concept is that motivation through the above mentioned factors is a necessary but thankless task. It is never-ending. Even if effective it will still not motivate the employee to work well (at a higher than usual level of performance) except for a short period of time.

31. On the other hand, if the environment is deficient in some way the subordinates are likely to become annoyed and to show their displeasure by industrial conflict, decreased productivity, grumbling etc. Yet, if the deficiency is corrected the best that can be expected is that the output/effort will return to 'normal'.

32. *Motivator factors* create job satisfaction and are effective in motivating an individual to superior performance and effort. These factors give the individual a sense of self-fulfilment or personal growth, and consist of:

    • status (although this may be a hygiene factor as well as a motivator factor);
    • advancement;
    • gaining recognition;
    • being given responsibility;
    • challenging work;
    • achievement;
    • growth in the job.

33. Herzberg's original findings have been repeated in several studies since. Collating information based on 12 different studies involving over 1,600 employees in a variety of jobs and countries, Herzberg shows that the overwhelming majority of factors contributing to job satisfaction (81 per cent) were motivators concerned with growth and development. A large majority of factors in job dissatisfaction (69 per cent) were to do with environmental maintenance.

34. Herzberg saw two separate 'need systems' of individuals.

    (a) There is a need to avoid unpleasantness. This need is satisfied at work by hygiene factors. Hygiene satisfactions are short-lived: individuals come back for more, in the nature of drug addicts.

    (b) There is a need for personal growth, which is satisfied by motivator factors, and not by hygiene factors.

    A lack of motivators at work will encourage employees to concentrate on bad hygiene (real or imagined) eg to demand more pay. Some individuals are not mature enough to want personal growth: these are 'hygiene seekers' because they can only ever be satisfied by hygiene factors.

35. Herzberg suggested means by which motivator satisfactions could be supplied. Stemming from his fundamental division of motivator and hygiene factors, he encouraged managers to study the job itself (ie. the type of work done, the nature of tasks, levels of responsibility) rather than conditions of work.

    If there is sufficient challenge, scope and interest in the job, there will be a lasting increase in satisfaction and the employee will work well; productivity will be above 'normal' levels. The extent to which a job must be challenging or creative to a motivator-seeker will depend on each individual ie. his ability and his tolerance for delayed success.

36. Herzberg specified three typical means whereby work can be revised to improve motivation:

    (a) *job enrichment*, or 'the planned process of up-grading the responsibility, challenge and content of the work'. Typically, this would involve increased delegation to provide more interesting work and problem-solving at lower levels in the organisation;

    (b) *job enlargement*, the process of increasing the number of operations in which a worker is engaged and so moving away from narrow specialisation of work. Herzberg says that this is more limited in value, since a man who is required to complete several tedious tasks is unlikely to be much more highly motivated than a man performing one continuous tedious task;

    (c) *job rotation*, or the planned operation of a system whereby staff members exchange positions with the intention of breaking monotony in the work and providing fresh job challenge.

    We will look at these methods, and the validity of Herzberg's assumptions about job satisfaction and motivation in the next chapter.

Expectancy theory

37. The expectancy theory of motivation is a process theory, based on the assumptions of cognitive psychology that human beings are purposive and rational, ie. aware of their goals and behaviour.

    Essentially, the theory states that the strength of an individual's motivation to do something will depend on the extent to which he *expects* the results of his efforts, if successfully achieved, to contribute towards his personal needs or goals.

38. This theory was formulated to apply to human behaviour in general, but has since been applied to work motivation by several American organisational psychologists.

    Georgopoulos, Mahoney and Jones (who called their theory a 'path-goal' approach) made a study in 1957 of more than 600 household appliance assemblers. They argued that productivity is, for the worker, a path to his or her own valued goals: the motivation to behave in a certain way (ie. productively) arises from:

    - the individual's needs, or valued outcomes; and
    - the expectation that productive behaviour will result in the fulfilment of those needs, or the achievement of those outcomes.

    If the individual wants or needs a particular reward (eg. money, praise, promotion), and expects to get it through hard work, then he is likely to work hard. If the individual *doesn't* expect to be rewarded (or to be rewarded in desired way), then he is not likely to put in the extra effort.

39. Georgopoulos found that the valued goals among the assemblers were:

    (a) making more money in the long run;
    (b) getting along well with the work group; and
    (c) being promoted to a better wage rate.

    He found also that workers who expected these goals to be achieved through high productivity were in fact more productive than those who felt that eg. goal (b) would be achieved through *lower* productivity.

40. In 1964 Victor Vroom, another American psychologist, worked out a formula by which human motivation could actually be assessed and measured, based on an expectancy theory of work motivation.

    Vroom suggested that the strength of an individual's motivation is the product of two factors:

    - the strength of his preference for a certain outcome. Vroom called this '*valence*'. It may be represented as a positive or negative number, or zero - since outcomes may be desired, avoided or considered with indifference; and

    - his expectation that the outcome will result from a certain behaviour. Vroom called this '*subjective probability*': it is only the individual's 'expectation', and depends on his perception of the probable relationship between behaviour and outcome. As a probability, it may be represented by any number between 0 (no chance) and 1 (certainty).

41. In its simplest form, the 'expectancy equation' therefore looks like this.

Force or strength of motivation to do something	=	**V**alence ie strength of his preference for a certain outcome	x	**E**xpectation that behaviour will result in desired outcome

42. This is what you would expect: if either valence or expectation have a value of zero, there will be no motivation.

    (a) If an employee has a high expectation that productivity will result in a certain outcome eg. promotion, but he is indifferent to that outcome (eg. doesn't want the responsibility), $V = 0$, and he will not be motivated to productive behaviour.

    (b) If the employee has a great desire for promotion - but doesn't believe that productive behaviour will secure it for him, $E = 0$, and he will still not be highly motivated.

    (c) If $V = -1$, (eg. because the employee fears responsibility and doesn't want to leave his work group), the value for motivation will be negative, and the employee may deliberately under-produce.

43. Expectancy theory attempts to measure the strength of an individual's motivation to act in a particular way. It is then possible to compare 'F' values for a range of different behaviours, to discover which behaviour the individual is most likely to adopt. It is also possible to compare 'F' values for different individuals, to see who is most highly motivated to behave in the desired (or undesirable) way.

44. Are human beings really so predictable, however? Are we as 'rational' as expectancy theory implies? Do we carry out such an analysis and calculation before behaving in a given way, whether consciously or unconsciously?

The expectancy theory has been useful in organisational practice (and also in further research) because it does make room for the subjectivity of human perceptions, the limited nature of rationality. In its most complex form, where a number of alternative expected outcomes are taken into account, the expectancy equation can be a fair reflection of the various influences on behaviour. We do not, after all, tend to take *all* eventualities into account in our decision making, and we are able to draw on substantial past experience for most routine responses.

45. Another advantage of the theory is that, in comparison with Herzberg's ideas, a better distinction is made between an individual's goals and the organisation's goals. An individual may not seek self-realisation through his job; his goals might be unrelated to his job. The outcomes to which 'V' and 'E' values attach may, of course, still be those put forward by content theories of motivation: the two approaches are not mutually exclusive. Expectancy theory, however, goes on to suggest how experience makes some goals desirable to individuals, and to what extent.

46. Experience within the organisation is the main influence on the 'E' and 'V' values of the equation.

    (a) The value attached to an outcome will partly reflect what is valued generally (and especially by the individual's colleagues or career models) in a particular organisation.
    (b) The expectancy will reflect the individual's experience of what can be achieved in the organisation, what rewards he and others like him have received in the past for certain behaviours etc.

47. The particular factors which influence valence and expectation will be those which management will want to identify and change, in order to increase 'F' or motivation in employees.

Charles Handy: the motivation calculus

48. Charles Handy (*Understanding Organisations*) puts forward an 'admittedly theoretical' model not unlike the expectancy model. He suggests that it should be regarded "as the way the individual deals with *individual* decisions, to do or not to do something... to apportion or not to apportion his time, energy and talents. This approach is based on the idea that man is a self-activating organism, and can, to some degree, control his own destiny and his own responses to pressures, that he can select his goals and choose the paths towards them."

49. Handy suggests that for any individual decision, there is a conscious or unconscious 'motivation calculus' which is an assessment of three factors:

    (a) the individual's own set of needs (these may be defined in any of the ways suggested by Maslow, Herzberg, McClelland and others);

    (b) the desired results - ie what the individual is expected to do in his job;

    (c) 'E' factors. Handy suggests that motivational theories have been too preoccupied with 'effort'. He notes that there seems to be a set of words, coincidentally beginning with 'e', that might be more helpful. As well as effort, there is energy, excitement in achieving desired results, enthusiasm, emotion, and expenditure (of time, money etc.).

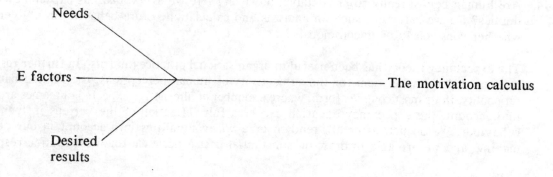

50. The 'motivation decision' - ie how strong the motivation to achieve the desired results will be - will depend on the individual person's judgement about:

    (a) the strength of his needs;
    (b) the expectancy that expending 'E' will lead to a desired result; and
    (c) how far the result will be 'instrumental' in satisfying his needs.

    A man may have a high need for power. To the degree that he believes that a particular result, eg. a well-performed task, will gain him promotion (*expectancy*) *and* that promotion will in fact satisfy his need for power (*instrumentality*) he will expend 'E' on the task.

51. Handy notes that the 'act of calculation' itself may be unconscious or 'instinctive', or may be conscious or 'calculating' to any degree. As we have already discussed, instinctive motivation reacts to immediate needs, triggered by deprivation. Many reactions are also dictated by past experience, ie. based on precedent rather than the activation of the calculus which works for 'new' decisions. More calculating motivation can take into account results or satisfactions covering much longer time spans - where the calculus becomes more complicated, as other needs intervene.

Handy suggests that psychological maturity, as we mentioned earlier, shows up in:

(a) a more conscious calculus; and

(b) a lengthening time span for 'pay-off' from the expenditure of 'E'.

52. In terms of organisation practice, Handy suggests that several factors are necessary for the individual to complete the calculus, and to be motivated.

(a) *Intended results* should be made clear, so that the individual can complete his 'calculation', and know what is expected of him, what will be rewarded and how much 'E' it will take.

(b) Without knowledge of *actual results*, there is no check that the 'E' expenditure was justified (and will be justified in future). *Feedback* on performance - good or bad - is essential, not only for performance but for confidence, prevention of hostility etc.

53. Handy's calculus helps to explain various phenomena of individual behaviour at work.

(a) Individuals are more committed to specific goals - particularly those which they have helped to set themselves. Kay, French and Myer found that, in job appraisal, 62.5% of *specific* goals for self-improvement were achieved by their interviewees, as opposed to 27.3% where no specific goals were set.

(b) If an individual is *rewarded* according to performance tied to standards (ie. 'management by objectives'), however, he may well set lower standards for himself: the 'instrumentality' part of the calculus (ie. likelihood of success and reward) is greater if the standard is lower. Individuals with a high need for 'achievement' frequently set only moderately high standards. Row and Russell set up an experimental game and found that continual *failure* to reach targets eventually made individuals set lower targets, which they were able to achieve. At the same time, continual *success* increases the level of aspiration, and also increases the desirability of the goal itself: the individual feels that it is 'all worthwhile', the strengh of need is increased and a higher expense of E is indicated.

(c) Inertia, withdrawal or even breakdown can occur where the possible variables in the calculus (amount of 'E', obtainable results, time-span etc.) become too many for the individual to cope with (usually in emotionally insecure, or highly analytical individuals). Reducing the available alternatives, or the time-span under consideration, may enable the calculus to function again: a holiday, for instance, is often beneficial.

Dissonance

54. 'Dissonance' is the discomfort or stress which occurs when there is a discrepancy between:

(a) the situation that exists, and the situation an individual would like to exist; or

(b) actual results and the results that an individual expected from his efforts; or

(c) an attitude that an individual would like to express, and the attitude he feels he ought to express because of his position at work (eg his position of authority).

55. In terms of Handy's motivational calculus, dissonance occurs when an individual expends energy and effort to achieve a certain result and fails to achieve it, or achieves it - but does not receive the expected satisfaction of his needs. The dissonance, or stress, needs to be removed, and the individual has a choice of:

   (a)   increasing his efforts to achieve the desired results;

   (b)   lowering his target results; or

   (c)   deciding that his original need did not really exist.

Psychological contracts

56. A psychological contract exists between individuals in an organisation and the organisation itself. An individual belongs to many organisations - ie his/her work organisation, a trade union, club, church or political party, and his/her family. The individual has a different psychological contract with each organisation to which he/she belongs.

57. A psychological contract might be thought of as a set of expectations.

   (a)   The individual expects to derive certain benefits from membership of the organisation and is prepared to expend a certain amount of effort in return.

   (b)   The organisation expects the individual to fulfil certain requirements and is prepared to offer certain rewards in return.

58. Three types of psychological contract can be identified.

   (a)   *Coercive contract.* This is a contract in which the individual considers that he is being forced to contribute his efforts and energies involuntarily, and that the rewards he receives in return are inadequate compensation. Although a prison would be an example of an organisation in which there is a coercive psychological contract with prisoners, such contracts would exist in any work organisation which does not have the voluntary acquiescence of individual members to the terms and conditions of work. For example, if an individual believes that he does not receive enough pay for the work he does, or if he is forcibly transferred to another job he does not like, there would be a coercive psychological contract between the individual and the organisation. Motivation to work would be low, non-existent, or even negative.

   (b)   *Calculative contract.* This is a contract, accepted *voluntarily* by the individual, in which he expects to do his job in exchange for a readily identifiable set of rewards (eg pay, status, or simply having a job of work to keep him occupied). This form of contract is the most frequent in industrial and commercial organisations. With such psychological contracts, motivation can only be increased if the rewards to the individual are improved (eg extra pay, further promotion). If the organisation attempts to demand greater efforts without increasing the rewards, the psychological contract will revert to a coercive one, and motivation may become negative.

(c) *Co-operative contract.* This is a contract in which the individual identifies himself with the organisation and its goals, so that he/she actively seeks to contribute further to the achievement of those goals. Motivation comes out of success at work, a sense of achievement, and self-fulfilment. A co-operative psychological contract must be voluntarily entered into. The individual will probably want to share in the planning and control decisions which affect his work, and co-operative contracts are therefore likely to occur where employees *participate* in decision-making. Since these contracts are likely to result in high motivation and high achievement, the lesson for management would be that employee participation in decision-making is the most desirable way to structure manager-subordinate relations at work - but only if subordinates *want* participation.

59. 'Motivation' happens when the psychological contract, within which the individual's motivation calculus operates for new decisions, is viewed in the same way by the organisation and by the individual.

Systems and contingency approach to motivation

60. Stemming from the early research work of Mayo and the Hawthorne experiments (described in a later chapter), a systems and contingency approach to motivation has been developed by a number of writers, notably Kurt Lewin. A systems and contingency approach means that:

(a) the motivation of an individual cannot be seen in isolation. It depends on the system within which he operates, his work group and his environment;

(b) the motivation of the individual will also depend on circumstances. Different people react to the same environment in different ways, and a person's motivation is likely to vary from day to day, according to his mood, events at work, his fatigue as well as 'hygiene' and 'motivator' factors in his work.

61. Writing in 1938, Lewin developed his 'field theory' in which he compared an individual's environment to a magnetic field, with various forces in that field pulling him in different directions and affecting his attitudes from day to day. His formula for human behaviour was:

$B = (P,E)$ where

B is a person's behaviour, which depends on
P the person himself/herself and
E his or her environment.

62. This means that an individual's motivation, varying over time, could be illustrated on a graph as follows:

Amount or
degree of
motivation
of individual

63. The systems and contingency school of thought is that if a manager wishes to improve the motivation of subordinates, he must take all the circumstances of the particular situation into account, differences between individuals, the external environment, individuals' expectations, work groups, variations in circumstances from day to day or month to month etc.

64. One conclusion from this approach might be that motivation depends on so many interrelated factors that a manager wishing to improve motivation is faced with a complex problem for which there may be no obvious ready-made solution.

Carrot or stick?

65. You might have noted that 'motivation' can be a negative process (ie. appealing to an individual's need to *avoid* unpleasantness, pain, fear etc.) as well as a positive one (ie. appealing to the individual's need to attain certain goals).

   (a) Negative motivation is 'wielding the big stick' - threatening dismissal or demotion, reprimand etc. - ie. negative reinforcement.

   (b) Positive motivation is 'dangling the carrot', and may be achieved by:

      (i) the offer of 'extrinsic' rewards, such as pay incentives, promotion, working conditions etc.
      (ii) 'internal' or psychological satisfaction for the individual, ie. 'virtue is its own reward', a sense of achievement, a sense of responsibility and value etc.

"Have managers outsmarted motivational theory, and become cynical about carrots, world-weary about sticks?" (*Ray Proctor: Finance for the perplexed executive*)

---

66. We discussed in the chapter on Learning how positive reinforcement is generally more effective in eliciting desired behaviours than negative reinforcement.

    Peters and Waterman ('In Search of Excellence') discuss the central importance of positive reinforcement in any method of motivation. "Researchers studying motivation find that the prime factor is simply the self-perception among motivated subjects that they are in fact doing well ... Mere association with past personal success apparently leads to more persistence, higher motivation, or something that makes us do better."

> At Mars Inc. in America, Peters and Waterman observed that every employee - including the president - received a 10% pay bonus for each week in which he got to work on time every day. "That's an... example of creating a setting in which virtually everybody wins regularly... When the number of awards is high, it makes the perceived possibility of winning something high as well. And then the average man will stretch to achieve. [cf. expectancy] Many companies do believe in special awards, but use them exclusively to honour the top few (who already are so highly motivated they would probably have done their thing anyway)."

67. The observations of Peters and Waterman on the 'culture' and motivational environment of 'excellent' companies in the USA may seem slightly eccentric to British managers, but part of the writers' profile of an excellent company is that 'excellent companies require and demand extraordinary performance from the average man'.

    Positive reinforcement - whether in the form of bonuses, prizes, 'reaffirming the heroic dimension' of the job itself, identifying workers with the company's success, or enhancing self-image in the workforce - is the method Peters and Waterman observed succeeding, although, as we noted in the chapter on learning, some research has shown that 'tough' managers, applying sanctions on undesirable behaviour, can also get improved performance out of their subordinates.

68. Peter Drucker suggested that in replacing the carrot of monetary rewards and the stick of fear with more 'enlightened' methods of motivation, appealing to needs for self-fulfilment, creativity etc., what was actually being created was a different kind of equally strict control: psychological despotism. Workers are "controlled - not by fear of hunger and incentive of material rewards but through fear of psychological alienation and through the incentive of 'psychological security'."

> Using psychology to control, dominate, and manipulate others is self-destructive abuse of knowledge. It is also a particularly repugnant form of tyranny. The master of old was content to control the slave's body. (Drucker)

JOB SATISFACTION AND WORKER GOALS

Points to be covered

- The nature and assessment of job satisfaction
- Worker goals: intrinsic and extrinsic factors
- The job as motivator: job design
- Participation as a means of motivation
- Motivation through participation in practice
- Responsibility as a source of job satisfaction
- Pay as a motivator
- Equity
- Culture
- Motivation, satisfaction and performance

The nature of job satisfaction

1. We have already talked about job satisfaction in connection with the work of Frederick Herzberg. He conducted a survey of employees in Pittsburgh and analysed their accounts of times when they 'felt good' about their jobs: this was taken to be a sign of 'job satisfaction' (as opposed to 'job *dis*satisfaction', arising from events which made them 'feel bad' about their jobs).

2. Five factors stood out as factors in job satisfaction:

    (a) achievement;
    (b) recognition;
    (c) the attraction of the work itself;
    (d) responsibility; and
    (e) advancement.

    These are the 'motivator' or growth factors, whose presence will cause satisfaction, according to Herzberg. Herzberg's other job 'hygiene' factors are not the key to greater achievement and satisfaction, merely to the reduction or elimination of *dis*satisfaction.

3. The famous Hawthorne experiments started out to find a relationship between fatigue and output, by improving conditions and introducing other variables in the work environment. In fact, the improvements in productivity that were observed were traced to factors *other* than lighting, rest periods, hours of work etc. The Hawthorne researchers (of whom, more later) decided that: "attitudes to people, as people, may be more important than such factors as rest periods, benefits, money etc. People are not merely instruments'.

4.   Drucker, writing before Herzberg, suggested that 'employee satisfaction' was a vague and ill-defined idea, and should be defined more constructively, before it could become a useful concept. He suggested that satisfaction is the result of increased responsibility.

> "Dissatisfaction arises from environment factors – satisfaction can only arise from the job." (*Herzberg*)

The assessment of satisfaction

5.   Some points to note about the assessment of 'job satisfaction' are that:

(a)   there is little evidence that a satisfied worker actually works harder – so increased productivity *per se* will not imply 'satisfaction' on the part of the work force. They may be motivated by fear, work methods may have been improved etc.;

(b)   there is, however, support for the idea that satisfied workers tend to be loyal, and stay in the organisation.

(i)   *Labour turnover* (ie. the rate at which people leave an organisation) may therefore be an indication of dissatisfaction in the workforce – although there is a certain amount of 'natural' loss (eg. through retirement) in any case, as well as loss due to relocation, redundancy etc.

(ii)   *Absenteeism* may also be an indication of dissatisfaction, or possibly of genuine physical or emotional distress;

(c)   there is also evidence that satisfaction correlates with mental health – so that symptoms of stress, psychological failure etc. may be a signal to management that all is not well.

Worker goals

6.   John Hunt ('Managing People at Work') notes that "to avoid the complication of need theories, it has become more fashionable to talk about goals, values or even work orientations – ie., to acknowledge that people have a tendency to return to similar ends or goals that seem to be (sufficiently) important to them to suggest an underlying theme, pattern or goal behind their behaviour."

7.   We have already discussed the main theories of what it is that workers need, want and aim their efforts towards. There remain two important points to make.

(a)   Each individual has a different set of goals.
(b)   The relative importance or 'hierarchy' of goals may vary with time, circumstances etc.

8. The goals of any one individual at a given time may be influenced by many things, including:

   (a) *genetic inheritance and childhood environment*. As we have discussed, aspiration levels, career models etc. are formed in early stages of development;

   (b) *education*. Again, as we have mentioned, social and career models may be adopted through formal or informal education, as well as habits of exploration, experience of success etc.;

   (c) *experience*. Needs not satisfied at any earlier, appropriate life stage may remain dominant in later life (eg. the play needs of an adolescent in a strict family). Hunt says that our 'tendencies to behave in certain ways are deeply embedded in past experiences', that 'the backgrounds of individuals provide us with themes or patterns which reappear in values, beliefs and goals and then overtly in behaviour';

   (d) *age* and *position*. There is usually a gradual process of 'goal shift' with age, as well as more radical re-evaluations, in cases of eg. illness, redundancy, death of spouse, birth of child etc. Recognition may be high priority for a child, while relationships and exploration may be the preoccupation of teenagers. Career and family goals may then conflict in the 20-40 age group: career launch and 'take-off' may have to yield to the priorities associated with forming permanent relationships, having children etc. Power and autonomy goals may be felt to be essential to the individual's self image in mature years, or 'career peak' time. Retirement usually forces a reappraisal of relationships, purpose in life (which may so far have been bound up in work), security etc.;

   (e) *culture*. Compared to European worker goals, for example, Japanese goals show a greater concern for relationships and a lesser for power and autonomy. Swedish industry, on the other hand, has invested great energy in work groups and collectives. The motivations of a Zen Buddhist will be fundamentally different to those of a Western materialist etc.;

   (f) *self-concept*. All the above factors are bound up with the individual's own self image, which is based on learning, models in the family and interactions with society at large. The individual's assessment of his own capabilities, place in society and orientation to different spheres of activity ('I'm *that* sort of person...') will affect the relative strength and nature of his needs and goals.

Intrinsic and extrinsic factors

9. We have already mentioned that the 'rewards' offered to the individual at work may be:

   (a) *extrinsic rewards* - ie. valued outcomes that are not within the control of the individual but are at the disposal of others. These are the tangible goals which lead most people to work in the first place - eg. wage or salary, bonuses and prizes, working conditions, car etc.; or

   (b) *intrinsic rewards* - ie. valued outcomes which are within the control of the individual himself: feelings of companionship, comfort, sense of achievement, enjoyment of status and recognition, interest in tasks, responsibility, pride in the organisation's success etc. These are the rewards which are often referred to collectively as 'job satisfaction'.

10. Which system of rewards is used in an organisation will largely depend on the assumptions the managers make about their subordinates and what they want from working life. We shall discuss managerial models of the worker in the next section of this text.

Research (Mayo, Herzberg, Lawler etc.) does suggest that *intrinsic* rewards are more closely related to performance, and are more effective motivators.

11. We will go on to look at some of the 'satisfactions' that may be offered to the individual as a worker, including:

(a) job enrichment, enlargement and rotation;
(b) participation;
(c) responsibility;
(d) pay (or equity).

Factors such as leadership style, the work group, and the design of the work environment will be considered in appropriate chapters later in the text.

Katz carried out a study in 1978 of whether job satisfaction was influenced by the length of time an individual had been in the job. He found that the felt 'significance' of the task, and the feedback given on performance, in the early months produced overall satisfaction. Later on, however, individuals became more concerned about the variety of skills needed, autonomy, and having a 'proper' task with a beginning and an end. After five years in the job, the only factors that seemed to influence satisfaction were things like pay, benefits, colleagues and compatibility with supervisors!

Do individuals get *bored* with self-actualisation?

The job as motivator

12. The job itself can be interesting and exciting. It can satisfy the desire for a feeling of 'accomplishing something', for responsibility, for professional recognition, for advancement and the need for self-esteem.

(Even if it does offer any or all of these satisfactions, of course, there is no guarantee that performance will be improved. As with any possible factors in job satisfaction, it is important not to take too simplistic and 'utopian' a view.)

13. The extent to which a job *must* be challenging or creative to a motivator seeker will depend on each individual, ie

(a) his ability; and
(b) his tolerance for delayed success, or delayed gratification of his needs.

14. As we described in the previous chapter, Herzberg specified three typical means whereby job design can be revised to improve motivation. These are:

- *job enrichment*;
- *job enlargement*;
- *job rotation*.

Job enrichment

15. Job enrichment is planned, deliberate action to build greater responsibility, breadth and challenge of work into a job. A job may be enriched by:

    (a) giving it greater variety (although this could perhaps also be described as job enlargement);

    (b) allowing the employee greater freedom to decide for himself how the job should be done;

    (c) encouraging employees to participate in the planning decisions of their superiors;

    (d) ensuring that the employee receives regular feedback on his performance, comparing his actual results against his targets.

16. Job enrichment attempts to add further responsibilities to a job by giving the job holder decision-making capabilities of a 'higher' order. It should not be tackled as a project or a 'one-off' technique; it can only be effective as part of the continuing management process.

17. An example of job enrichment could be seen where an accountant's responsibilities for producing quarterly trading accounts ended at the trial balance stage. These duties were then extended so that he prepared the actual trading accounts and submitted them under his name, to the board. This alteration in responsibilities not only enriched his job but also increased his work-load. This in turn led him to delegate certain responsibilities to clerks within the accounts department. These duties were in themselves job enrichment to the clerks and so a cascading effect was obtained.

18. This highlights one of the basic elements of job enrichment, ie that tedious, mundane detail at high level can represent significant job interest and challenge at a lower level in the organisation where a person's experience and scope are much less.

19. Some experiments have been made whereby *work groups* were given collective job enrichment. Child (in *Organisation: A Guide for Problems and Practice*) cited the example in the UK of Phillips. A work group responsible for manufacturing black and white television sets carried out the entire assembly operation and also had authority to deal directly with purchasing, stores and quality control, without a supervisor acting as intermediary. There were savings, therefore, in supervisory costs, but the change in work organisation meant that the company had to incur additional costs in re-equipment and training.

20. Perhaps a more well-known example is the case of Volvo in Sweden, where a new factory was built so as to facilitate greater flexibility for work groups, with considerable responsibilities for major stages of manufacture, to organise their jobs as they considered best. Once again, job enrichment necessitated large capital expenditure, although the *quality* of work was found to be considerably enhanced.

21. It would be wrong, however, to suppose that job enrichment alone will automatically make employees more productive.

> 'Even those who want their jobs enriched will expect to be rewarded with more than job satisfaction. Job enrichment is not a cheaper way to greater productivity. Its pay-off will come in the less visible costs of morale, climate and working relationships'. (*Handy*).

If jobs are enriched, employees will expect to be paid fairly for what they are doing. It might be more correct therefore to say that job enrichment might improve productivity through greater motivation, but only if it is rewarded fairly.

Job enlargement

22. Job enlargement is frequently confused with job enrichment though it should be clearly defined as a separate technique. Job enlargement, as the name suggests, is the attempt to widen jobs by increasing the number of operations in which a job holder is involved.

23. This has the effect of lengthening the 'time cycle' of repeated operations: by reducing the number of repetitions of the same work, the dullness of the job should also be reduced. Job enlargement is therefore a 'horizontal' extension of an individual's work, whereas job enrichment is a 'vertical' extension.

24. Arguably, job enlargement is limited in its ability to improve motivation since, as Herzberg points out, to ask a worker to complete three separate tedious, unchallenging tasks is unlikely to motivate him more than asking him to fulfil one single tedious, unchallenging task.

25. Job enlargement might succeed in providing job enrichment as well, provided that the nature of the extra tasks to be done in the bigger job gives the employee a greater challenge and incentive.

    (a) When work is organised as a production line, with each employee responsible for just a small part of the total work, the dullness and monotony of the employee's work will be exceptionally high. Just by giving an employee a task which spans a larger part of the total production work - ie by enlarging the job - the dullness and monotony are likely to be reduced.

    (b) Enlarged jobs can provide a challenge and incentive. For example, a trusted employee might be given added responsibilities for:

        (i) checking the quality of output. There is a view that concern for manufacture of manufactured goods is a major reason for the success of Japanese industry. An employee who is allowed to monitor his own work quality, as well as the work of others, might easily see a challenging responsibility in such a job;
        (ii) training new recruits.

    (c) Enlarged jobs might also be regarded as 'status' jobs within the department, and as stepping stones towards promotion.

26. Participation by employees in decision-making is a form of both job enlargement and job enrichment. Drucker (in *The Practice of Management*) quoted the example of IBM where the final details of the design of the first electronic computers by the company were worked out on the factory floor in consultation with the work force. Workers were able to offer suggestions based on their experience and practical know-how for the improvement of the computer design. The effects of this innovation in job design were found by IBM management to be:

    (a) better product design;
    (b) lower production costs;
    (c) greater speed of production;
    (d) greater worker satisfaction.

Job rotation

27. Job rotation might take two forms.

    (a) An employee might be transferred to another job after a period of, say, 2-4 years in an existing job, in order to gain new interest and challenge, and to bring a fresh person to the job being vacated.

    (b) Job rotation might be regarded as a form of training. Trainees might be expected to learn a bit about a number of different jobs by spending 6 months or 1 year in each job before being moved on. The employee is regarded as a 'trainee' rather than as an experienced person holding down a demanding job.

28. No doubt you will have your own views about the value of job rotation as a method of training or career development. It is interesting to note Drucker's view: 'The whole idea of training jobs is contrary to all rules and experience. A man should never be given a job that is not a real job, that does not require performance from him.'

    It is generally accepted that the value of job rotation as a motivator is limited.

Participation as a means of motivation

29. Present social and education trends show that people's expectations rise above the basic requirement for money. The current demand (even in times of high unemployment) is for more interesting work and to have a say in decision-making. These expectations are a basic part of the movement towards greater participation at work.

30. The methods of achieving increased involvement have largely crystallised into two main streams. These can be described as:

    (a) industrial action towards greater day-to-day involvement and participation in the process of management;

    (b) political action towards industrial democracy.

    These two streams have been described by Strauss and Rosenstein as 'immediate' and 'distant' participation.

31. *Immediate participation* is used to refer to the involvement of employees in the day-to-day decisions of their work group. Typical examples of this type of participation in the last decade have come from Scandinavia, eg Volvo, Saab, etc.

    Distant participation, on the other hand, refers to the process of including company employees at the top levels of the organisation which deal with long-term policy issues including investment and employment. Typical examples of this type of participation would be found in any major West German company with the two-tier board structure. (In 1951, a German law was passed which requires labour representatives on the supervisory board and executive committee of certain large companies. The executive committee should include one labour representative as a director.)

32. There is a theory that if a superior invites his subordinates to participate in planning decisions which affect their work, if the subordinates voluntarily accept the invitation, and results about actual performance are fed back regularly to the subordinates so that they can make their own control decisions, then the subordinate will be motivated:

    (a) to be more efficient;
    (b) to be more conscious of the organisation's goals;
    (c) to raise his planning targets to reasonably challenging levels;
    (d) to be ready to take appropriate control actions when necessary.

33. Participation will only be feasible if the superior is willing to apply it, and for this reason the work of writers such as McGregor and Likert is discussed in a later chapter on leadership. It may be helpful at this stage, however, to introduce an example of participation theory.

34. Argyris applied a behavioural approach to the investigation of the process of budgeting and budgetary control. He identified four 'human' problems with budgeting.

    (a) The budget is a pressure device, used by management to force 'lazy' employees to work harder. The intention of such pressure is to improve performance, but the unfavourable reactions of subordinates against it 'seem to be at the core of the budget problem'.

    As an illustration, suppose that a factory operates at 70% efficiency. Pressure to achieve this level of efficiency is exercised through formal budget procedures, criticism of poor results and adverse variances, a sense of failure if the budget is not met, etc. On the other hand, there is resistance to management pressure, arising from resentment, fear of job loss if efficiency levels rise, informal 'group' agreements or trade union organisation etc.

    If management now intends to raise the level of efficiency to, say, 80%, there will be pressure for a 'tighter' budget and higher standards. This pressure may be successful, but at the same time resistance will also increase. 'People and groups are now trying harder (consciously or unconsciously) to keep production at this new level and prevent it from rising again.... Tension begins to mount. People become uneasy and suspicious. They increase the informal pressure to keep production at the new level'. Management must work harder to keep up the new level of efficiency, whereas employees are more inclined to work slowly as soon as the pressure is eased. New ideas by management to raise production further will be met by even greater resistance.

A side effect of management pressure is the creation of close-knit informal work groups where members of the group are united by their common feeling of resentment against management.

(b) The accounting department is usually responsible for recording actual achievement and comparing this against the budget. Accountants are therefore 'budget men'. Their success is to find significant adverse variances and identify the managers responsible (eg a production supervisor). The success of a 'budget man' is the failure of a factory supervisor (or other manager) and this failure causes loss of interest and declining performance. The accountant, on the other hand, fearful of having his budget criticised by factory management, obscures his budget and variance reporting and deliberately makes it difficult to understand.

(c) The budget usually sets targets for each department. Achieving the departmental target becomes of paramount importance, regardless of the effect this may have on the overall company performance. 'And then, particularly in plants which make forceful use of budgets with the supervisors trying to blame someone else so that their departments are not the ones to be penalised, the conflict begins.' Top management therefore has the wasteful task of settling disputes and keeping budget-inspired conflicts under control.

(d) Fourthly, budgets are used by managers to impress their character and patterns of leadership on subordinates. Subordinates, resentful of their leader's 'style', blame the budget rather than the leader.

35. Argyris argued that participation by employees in budget setting and the encouragement of a 'human' approach to man management would remove these drawbacks to effective budgeting. He also criticised many 'participation' schemes as not offering real participation and consequently having little or no value. In particular, he suggested that:

(a) management should not regard subordinates as drones who must be pressured into working;
(b) budgetary control schemes should provide measures for guidance, and not for policing.

> 'Participation does correspond to a number of basic motivators. It is a means of recognition. It appeals to the need for affiliation and acceptance. And, above all, it gives people a sense of accomplishment.'
>
> *Koontz, O'Donnell & Weihrich*

36. It is important to remember, however, that a manager who encourages participation in decision-making by his subordinates does not abdicate his responsibility. He is responsible for the eventual decisions which are taken: the purpose of participation is to reach better planning decisions and to achieve higher targets, with a well-motivated work team. The manager himself gains from participation; he is not leaving his problems to others to sort out for him.

Why is participation desirable?

37. Why might participation be a good thing? Does it really contribute to efficiency?

'Participation is sometimes regarded as a form of job enlargement. At other times it is a way of gaining commitment by workers to some proposal on the grounds that if you have been involved in discussing it, you will be more interested in its success. In part, it is the outcome of almost cultural belief in the norms of democratic leadership. It is one of those 'good' words with which is is hard to disagree.'

Handy

38. The advantages of participation should perhaps be considered from the opposite end - ie what would happen if there were *no* participation? The answer to this is that employees would be told what to do, and would presumably comply with orders. However, their compliance would not be enthusiastic, and they would not be psychologically committed to their work. This might affect the quality, if not quantity, of output, and the 'longevity' of the workforce.

39. Participation can involve employees and make them committed to their task, but only if:

(a) *participation is genuine*. It is very easy for a boss to pretend to invite participation from his subordinates but end up issuing orders. If subordinates feel the decision has already been taken, they might resent hypocrisy of 'discussing' the decision;

(b) *efforts to establish participation are made consistently* over a long period and with energy. However, 'if the issue or the task is trivial, or foreclosed, and everyone realises it, participative methods will boomerang. Issues that do not affect the individuals concerned will not, on the whole, engage their interest'. (Handy);

(c) *the purpose of participation is made quite clear*. If employees are consulted to make a decision, their views should carry the decision. If, however, they are consulted for advice, their views need not necessarily be accepted;

(d) *the individuals really have the abilities and the information* to join in decision-making effectively;

(e) *the manager believes in participation*, and does not suggest it because he thinks it is the 'done thing'.

In an experiment, researchers gave their subjects puzzles to solve, with a background of loud, random, distracting noise. One group was simply told to get on with it, while another was given switches which would shut off the noise. This group solved five times the number of puzzles that the other group solved. The twist was, however, that none of the subjects ever *used* the off switch: the mere knowledge of having a modicum of apparent control over the situation was enough.

40. Anthony Hopwood (*Accounting and Human Behaviour*) believes that arguments in favour of participation are too general and sweeping. Whilst it is probably true that participation raises employee *morale*, he argues, its effect on *productivity* is uncertain. In some cases, it will fail, depending on the circumstances prevailing. "The practical problem is in trying to identify which conditional factors determine the wider impact of a particular type of participative management programme'.

41. Hopwood develops his argument with several suggestions.

   (a) The success of participation will depend on the character of the individuals involved, the technology of the industry, and the social atmosphere at work.

   - Some individuals want and expect authoritarian managerment.

   - In advanced technology industries, where unanticipated problems arise frequently, participation is likely to be more successful than in situations where the work is predictable.

   - Participation will only succeed if the social atmosphere at work is conducive to its implementation. 'Inauthentic' attempts by management to impose participation will not succeed.

   (b) There is no certain evidence that group participation will result in decision-making of a higher quality than decisions made by a capable manager acting on his own. However, participation does appear to improve the *transmission of information* (horizontally and vertically) within an organisation, so that where decisions are made in conditions of change or uncertainty in the business environment, it is likely that decisions made through group participation will be more informed and therefore of a higher quality.

   (c) The degree of participation will vary with the *nature of the decisions* taken. A study by Heller (1971) of 260 senior managers in 15 successful US companies revealed that the degree of participation invited depended on four factors.

   - Participation is more likely in decisions affecting personnel below the participating subordinates in the hierarchy (ie. managers are less likely to ask subordinates to share decisions which will affect their superiors, which could be 'awkward').

   - General managers and personnel managers use participation more successfully than production and finance managers, because of the nature of decisions involved.

   - Participation is more common where subordinates are fewer in number, and have a greater level of ability.

   - Senior managers allow greater participation as they gain experience in their job. Junior managers tend to restrict participation more, the longer they remain in the same job (perhaps because they become frustrated, and jealously guard their own authority).

   (d) Participation may be better for choosing the best out of several available options, than for identifying what decision options actually exist in the first place.

"It is simply naive to think that participative approaches are always more effective than authoritarian styles of management or vice versa. The critics as well as the advocates of participative management would therefore be wise to direct their energies towards identifying the situations in which a variety of decision-making styles are effective, rather than towards universalistic claims for the applicability or otherwise of any single approach." (*Hopwood*)

Responsibility as a source of job satisfaction

42. Drucker suggested that employee satisfaction comes about through encouraging - if need be, by 'pushing'- employees to accept 'responsibility'. There are four ingredients to this:

    (a) *careful placement of people in jobs.* The selection or recruitment process is an important one, because the person selected should see the job as one which provides a challenge to his abilities. There will be no motivation for a university graduate in the job of shop assistant, whereas the same job can provide a worthwhile challenge to someone of lesser academic training and intelligence;

    (b) *high standards of performance in the job.* Targets for achievement should be challenging. However, they should not be imposed in an authoritarian way by the employee's bosses. The employee should be encouraged to expect high standards of performance from himself;

    (c) *providing the worker with the information he needs to control his own performance.* The design of a reporting system is important in this respect. Being told how you're doing by a boss comes as a praise or reprimand, and the fear of reprimand may inhibit performance: access to information as a matter of routine overcomes this inhibition;

    (d) *opportunities for participation in decisions that will give the employee managerial vision.* Participation means the employee having some say and influence in how his work is organised and targets set.

Pay as a motivator

43. You may have noticed that none of the well-known catalogues of human needs mentions money - yet it is often assumed to be a means of satisfying any or all of the other needs. Attitudes to money and the things it can buy vary from individual to individual, from culture to culture, and even over time. A young, independent person may 'despise' money ('money isn't everything', 'the best things in life are free' etc.), but in later life, with a family and mortgage to support, it may take on a greater significance. The value of money as a motivator will therefore depend on its *perceived* value for the individual, but, on the other hand, it can usefully be offered as an incentive because it is instrumental in satisfying so many different needs.

44. We must remember, however, that an employee needs income to live. The size of his income will affect his standard of living, and although he would obviously like to earn more, he is probably more concerned:

    (a) that he should earn *enough* pay; and

    (b) that his pay should be *fair*, in terms of

    • equity - ie a fair rate for the job; and
    • *relativity*, or fair differentials, ie justified differences between the pay of different individuals.

45. Wages and salaries must be considered as:

    (a) a cost, which appears in the cost of the product or service to the market;

(b) an investment, ie money spent on one factor of production (labour) in the hope of a return; and

(c) a potentially crucial environmental variable - ie in incentivating and motivation, as a source of job satisfaction or dissatisfaction, political status, conflict etc.

46. The assumption behind most payment systems is that pay is the prime motivating factor. As Herzberg, among others, suggested, however, it is more likely to be a cause of dissatisfaction. In either case, management must 'assess what level and type of inducements it is able to offer in return for the contributions it requires from its workforce'. (Armstrong - *A Handbook of Personnel Management Practice*).

47. Apart from established pay or salary structures, *incentive schemes* of various sorts are thought to add the required link between effort and reward. These include:

(a) *measured day work*. Under this system, there is an 'incentive level of performance': the rate of pay is fixed on the understanding that a specified level of performance (set by work measurement) is maintained. Unfortunately, the incentive is not directly related to individual effort, and encourages an 'enough and no more' level of performance;

(b) *payment by results*. Pay (or part of it) is related to output (in terms of the number of items produced, or time taken to produce a unit of work), with bonuses. Theoretically, people work harder because there is a direct connection to greater reward. However, research projects (eg by Lupton) suggest that PBR systems are not effective in increasing output. There may be work group pressure because of fears of high output becoming a new norm, and bonuses being cut; there may be insecurity about illness, holidays etc; there may be conflict between competing groups etc;

(c) *bonus schemes* may be effective where pay is a prime motivator, if they:

- offer 'real' incentives, after tax
- relate bonuses to criteria over which the individual has control
- make clear the basis on which bonuses are calculated (remember Handy's 'motivation calculus');

(d) *group schemes* have similar effects to PBR schemes with regard to group manipulation of output. It is also difficult to design a scheme that is 'felt fair' by all individuals;

(e) *profit-sharing schemes*. These offer all employees an end-of-year bonus, perhaps in the form of shares in the company, related directly to profits. This will only be effective if:

- a perceivedly significant sum is made available to employees
- there is a clear and not overly delayed link between effort/performance and rewards
- forecasts indicate a reasonable chance of achieving the above: potential for disappointment is great.

48. There are a number of difficulties associated with profit-sharing schemes, some of which also apply to other incentive schemes.

(a) Increased earnings simply may not be an incentive to some individuals. An individual who already enjoys a good income may be more concerned with increasing his leisure time. For some years now in the UK employee representatives have argued that improved conditions and longer holidays should be the aim of their campaigning, rather than merely higher pay.

(b) Workers are unlikely to be in complete control of the company's profitability. External factors, such as the general economic climate, interest rates and exchange rates may play a part. In these cases, the relationship between an individual's efforts and his reward may be indistinct.

(c) Greater specialisation in production processes means that particular employees cannot be specifically credited with the success of particular products. This may lead to frustration amongst employees who think their own profitable work is being adversely affected by inefficiencies elsewhere in the organisation.

Limitations of pay as a motivator

49. It should be apparent that pay as a motivator is commonly associated with payment by results, whereby a worker's pay is directly dependent upon his output. If pay increases don't immediately follow improved performance, or completed tasks, they lose their 'connection' with results and become accepted as the consequence of age, experience, etc. This is less effective as a factor in the motivation calculus.

50. All such schemes are based on the principle that people are willing to work harder to obtain more money. However, the work of Elton Mayo and Tom Lupton has shown that there are several constraints which can nullify this basic principle. For example:

(a) the average worker is generally capable of influencing the timings and control systems used by management;

(b) workers remain suspicious that if they achieved high levels of output and earnings then management would alter the basis of the incentive rates to reduce future earnings;

(c) generally, the workers conform to a group output norm. The need to have the approval of their fellow workers by conforming to that norm is more important than the money urge;

(d) high taxation rates mean that workers do not believe that extra effort produces an adequate increase in pay.

51. There are other drawbacks to the use of money as a form of motivation:

(a) Rates of pay are perhaps more useful as a means of keeping an organisation adequately staffed by competent, qualified people, rather than as a means of getting them to work harder.

(b) In most large companies, salary levels and pay levels are usually structured carefully so as to be 'equitable' or fair. Managers and workers will compare their pay with that of others and will be dissatisfied if the comparison is unfavourable. Pay is therefore more likely to be a 'hygiene' factor at work than a motivator. Lawler suggested that in the absence of information about how much colleagues are earning, individuals guess their earnings and usually over-estimate; this in turn leaves them dissatisfied because they will then resent earning less than they *think* their colleagues are getting.

(c) When employees expect a *regular* annual review of salary, increases in pay will not motivate them to work harder. Indeed, if the increase is not high enough, it may be a source of dissatisfaction.

Pay as a motivator: conclusions

- Money *can* be a motivator, depending on the individual's perceived need for it. It is not usually an end in itself, but it provides the means of buying the things an individual wants to satisfy his needs.

- . It is generally agreed that pay will be a more effective incentive if there is a clear, short-term and direct link between extra effort, results and higher pay. However, Drucker suggested that pay is an incentive to produce better output only where a *willingness* to perform better already exists.

- It has become clear from the experiences of many companies that profit sharing schemes, incentive schemes (productivity bonuses) and joint consultation machinery do not in themselves improve productivity or ease the way for work to get done. Company-wide profit sharing schemes, for example, cannot be related directly to extra effort by individuals.

Equity

52. We mentioned 'equity' briefly above. It is worth emphasising the point that pay is *comparative*, since it can be measured precisely against past levels, other peoples' levels (within and outside the organisation) etc.

Money itself is not usually the source of dissatisfaction, but an unfavourable comparison with others' remuneration, or with the individual's expectations, may be.

53. If pay is to be an incentive to worker behaviour, *differentials* in pay will have to be meaningful. If 'results' or 'success' are ambiguous or subjective in a certain type of job, or individual contributions to group effort cannot be isolated, it is extremely difficult for an organisation to justify significant pay differentials. It will usually:

(a) shroud pay levels in secrecy. This can be self-defeating, as individuals will over-estimate the pay of others in relation to their own. Speculating and worrying about differentials may absorb a lot of the 'E' factors that might more profitably be expended on the task;

(b) strive for *equity* - ie. usually, paying a rate for the *job*, objectively assessed by various methods (job definition and evaluation systems, graded structures, competitors' rates etc.). Job evaluation is mainly based on the skill content of job tasks, but Elliott Jaques developed the concept of '*time span of discretion*' - the idea that the relative importance of a job is implicitly evaluated mainly according to the time span between the decision taken by an individual, and the checking and evaluation of it. A low level employee is frequently checked up on by superiors - in so far as his tasks are discretionary at all - while the effectiveness of higher level decisions may not emerge for some years.

54. Equity implies that:

(a) pay is no longer an incentive or reward, related to individual performance, but 'fair compensation', part of the conditions of work;

(b) other incentives - eg. promotion up the corporate ladder, or job satisfaction - must be devised, otherwise 'satisficing' behaviour will be established: ie. individuals will only do enough to get their entitled compensation, and no more.

Since most individuals are not willing to work without recognition for very long, promotional rewards may cause some instability in the organisational structure and personnel. Promotion as a reward for performance also has the drawback of elevating people *above* the level at which they have demonstrated ability - ie. the 'Peter Principle' that people are promoted to the level of their incompetence. Job satisfaction, as we have suggested, is not a lastingly effective reward on its own.

Culture

55. We will be discussing the 'culture' or shared value system of organisations in a later chapter, but we must mention briefly the way in which the psychological climate of an organisation affects motivation. Drucker speaks of the 'spirit of performance', which is the 'creation of energy' in the organisation.

Peters and Waterman argue that employees can be 'switched on' to extraordinary loyalty and effort if:

(a) the cause is perceived to be in some sense great - ie. 'reaffirming the heroic dimension' of the work. Commitment comes from believing that a task is inherently worthwhile. Devotion to the *customer*, and his needs and wants, is an important motivator in this way.

> "Owing to good luck, or maybe even good sense, those companies that emphasise quality, reliability, and service have chosen the *only* area where it is readily possible to generate excitement in the average down-the-line employee. They give people pride in what the do. They make it possible to love the product."

Shared values and 'good news swapping' - a kind of folklore of past success and 'heroic' endeavour - create a climate where intrinsic motivation is a real driving force;

(b) they are treated as winners. "Label a man a loser and he'll start acting like one." Repressive control systems and negative reinforcement break down the employee's self-image. Positive reinforcement, 'good news swapping', attention from management etc. enhance the employee's self-image and create positive attitudes to work and to the organisation;

(c) they can satisfy their dual needs to:

(i) be a conforming, secure part of a successful team; and
(ii) be a 'star' in their own right.

This means applying control (through firm central direction, and shared values and beliefs) but also allowing maximum individual autonomy (at least, the *illusion* of control) and even competition between individuals or groups within the organisation. Peters and Waterman call this 'loose-tight' management. Culture, peer pressure, a focus on action, customer-orientation etc. are 'non-aversive' ways of exercising control over employees.

Motivation, satisfaction and performance

56. You may be wondering whether motivation is really so important. It could be argued that if a person is employed to do a job, he will do that job and no question of motivation arises. If the person doesn't want to do the work, he can resign. The point at issue, however, is the *efficiency* with which the job is done. It is suggested that if individuals can be motivated, by one means or another, they will work more efficiently (ie. productivity will rise) or they will produce a better quality of work. There is some debate as to what the actual effects of improved motivation are, efficiency or quality, but it has become widely accepted that motivation is beneficial to the organisation.

57. The link between motivation (and effort etc.) and performance is not a clear one, and various writers have tried to explain what it is. Porter and Lawler designed a *performance/satisfaction model* as follows.

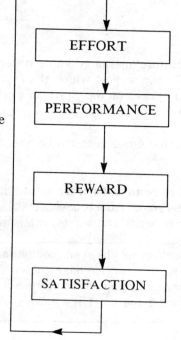

Factors which will influence employee's attitudes

The employee puts in effort to achieve a desired standard of performance.....

provided that he receives some reward (pay), promotion, recognition, status etc)...

and the reward satisfies some of his needs.

This in turn will lead to renewed efforts.

What is the individual's role? To what extent can his effort affect performance?

Is there likely to be some reward as a direct consequence of performance?

Is the reward fair? Is the reward of any worthwhile value to the person?

58. The case for 'job satisfaction' as a factor in efficiency is not proven. You should be clear in your own minds that although it seems obviously a 'Good Thing' to have employees who enjoy their work and are interested it it, there is no reason why the organisation should want a 'satisfied' work force unless it makes the organisation function better: it is good for 'human' reasons, but it is not necessarily relevant to organisational efficiency or effectiveness.

59. Pasmore reviewed the research data available in 1984. His conclusions were as follows.

- Involving employees does not guarantee improved performance – and neither does increased motivation. Ability, job design and other variables may intervene.

- Motivation depends on employees being involved in decisions about changes to the work itself.

- The whole organisation needs to change, to improve motivation and performance - not just isolated aspects.

- Managerial resistance to conditions which would facilitate success is often more of a problem than employee resistance.

"Programs for people - incentive programs, training programs or simple hoopla - undergo continuous tuning... No practice is expected to have impact forever, and programs for people have life cycles just as products do, may be even shorter ones."

Peters and Waterman "In Search of Excellence"

PERSONALITY

Points to be covered

* Personality
* Informal approach
* Nomothetic approach
  * Types and traits: Hans Jurgen Eysenck
* Idiographic approach
* Psychological adjustment
* Personality differences and work behaviour

Introduction

1. Individuals are unique. In order to explain, describe and identify the differences between people, psychologists use the concept of *'personality'*. This is a term which is used in common speech as well as in psychology, and the assumptions behind its use in a given context must be clearly understood.

2. Personality has been defined as "the total pattern of characteristic ways of thinking, feeling and behaving that constitute the individual's distinctive method of relating to the environment."

   This raises several points which are important to our understanding of the concept of personality.

   (a) *It is an integrating, comprehensive concept.* The term usually describes properties, or features, of the individual that determine how he relates to his environment - ie. his current personality - but all the processes of learning and motivation, which we have already discussed, are also part of the development of personality.

   (b) *However, it focuses on consistent or stable properties* - those that are 'characteristic' of a certain individual in different situations and at different times. Occasional or random behaviours do not demonstrate a 'tendency' which is useful to the consideration of personality. You should be able to recognise consistent responses in your own behaviour: you 'always' react badly to criticism, arrive late for lectures, like animals etc.

   (c) *It focuses on the 'distinctive' behaviour patterns of individuals*, those which may be variable from individual to individual, which can be identified and used consistently in comparisons between them.

76

PERSONALITY

3. Psychologists themselves disagree on exactly what should be included in the term 'personality'. Narrower definitions than the one given above exclude intellectual and observable physical qualities. There is a considerable controversy over whether intelligence should be regarded as a separate characteristic, or as a facet of personality. (We have followed the syllabus, and dealt with it as a separate topic, but this is not the only position.)

Personality: common usage

4. Everyday use of the term personality is faulty, according to the more precise psychologists' usage, because:

    (a) it tends to be defined by a single, key characteristic of behaviour eg. 'a shy personality', 'a happy personality' etc.

    (b) it tends to get confused with charisma and social success, and therefore adds a notion of 'quantity' which the psychologists' definition does not possess: 'showbiz personalities' by implication have 'lots of personality', while other individuals are said to 'lack personality'.

The source and nature of personality

5. As with intelligence, there is a 'nature-nurture' debate about whether or how far the factors of heredity and environment influence personality. Theorists disagree on the relative importance of each factor, and how (if at all) they relate to each other.

    (a) Some psychologists believe that personality is part of an individual's genetic endowment - ie. is inherited from his parents, fixed by cerebral biochemistry and not significantly alterable by experience.

    (b) Others suggest that as an individual experiences life and interacts with other people, his personality is shaped. Behaviour is influenced by environmental, cultural and social factors: individuals become 'socialised', to fit in with their environment. Personality is *adaptive* and flexible: a 'well adjusted' individual is one who can adapt facets of his personality to suit the changing environment.

6. There are two main, fundamentally different approaches to the study of personality:

    * the *nomothetic* approach. This means 'law setting or giving'. The approach generalises, to emphasise 'laws' or regularities in human behaviour: it isolates separate, identifiable elements in personality which are the same from individual to individual. Personality is determined by heredity and unalterable by experience, so its 'regularities' are stable and useful for comparisons;

    * the *ideographic* approach. This means 'writing about individuals'. The approach individualises, starting from a detailed, complex picture of the individual personality: it describes personality as a unified whole, and in terms of a person's own image and understanding of himself. Personality is determined by social and cultural processes, and is adaptive, changing with experience.

Assessment of personality: informal approach

7. The ability to assess the personality of others - with very little information - is an essential part of social behaviour, enabling individuals to interact with each other effectively in any number of contexts. A reasonably swift and accurate appraisal of personality consciously or unconsciously precedes any attempt at communication: to whom you are talking, what they will want (or not want) to hear, how they will react etc.

    We use our informal assessments of personality to explain and predict the behaviour of other individuals and to regulate the way in which we ourselves behave towards or around them.

8. We mainly do this by a process of simplification and generalisation, called *stereo-typing*. Our perception of other people (as we will discuss in the next chapter;) is highly selective; on the basis of those characteristics that are most 'transparent', we form a generalised picture or 'stereotype' of their personalities, which is simple enough to be of immediate use in social interaction.

    Behaviour, appearance, dress, manner of speech - or simply age or sex - are sufficient to create stereotypes eg. the man with the honest face, the dimwitted Irishman, the helpless woman etc.

9. Some people's stereotypes are more accurate than others, according to selectivity of perception, prejudice or simply poor judgement. Research shows, however, that most attempts at personality assessment are at best over-simplified, and at worst wildly inaccurate. We must admit, on reflection, that there are intelligent Irishmen and strong-minded, competent women: we probably know people whose cherubic expression conceals Machiavellian subtlety.

10. The reason why we are able to succeed in relating to other people despite our demonstrable lack of ability to assess personality accurately is that interaction generally works within a limited range of possible or permissable behaviours. In other words, individuals do behave in a 'simplified' way, according to the 'role' they are in - ie. the expectations, shared with the others concerned, of how a person in that social position or relationship should behave.

    When we interact, we are only faced with selected facets of the other individual's personality: we do not have to be accurate judges of the 'whole' person. Indeed many areas of the personality may not be 'visible' at all, ie. they may not emerge in the observable behaviour of the individual, or may do so only indirectly. Psychological complexes and 'scars' may be buried deep in the subconscious of the individual, coming identifiably to light only under the probing of a clinical psychologist.

Assessment of personality: nomothetic approach

11. The 'scientific' approach to personality assessment is, of course, more rigorous. The nomothetic 'law setting' approach proceeds as follows. (Notice the assumptions made at each stage, and how they are crucial to the methods used and the results obtained.)

    *   Identify the main areas or 'dimensions' in which personality can vary - eg. introversion, extraversion, emotional stability or instability - *assuming* that these are constants ie. qualitatively the same in any individual.

- Test the personalities of groups of individuals, using questionnaires, which are usually completed by the individuals themselves. The questionnaires usually ask 'forced choice' questions - ie they give a number of possible alternative answers - which are *assumed* to be a true reflection of the individual's actual behaviour. (You may have seen simple versions of such tests in journals or magazines: choosing 'the nearest' answer to your actual response may involve considerable compromise with the truth.) The answers are scored for the personality dimension under analysis.

- Construct a personality profile for the individual. Scores on each dimension are compared with averages, to identify 'average' personalities and any pronounced deviation from the norm (in a statistical rather than judgemental sense) in particular characteristics.

- Further analysis. Sub-group results (eg. according to age, sex or social class) provide new 'norms' for each sub-group, and also allow comparison and contrast between sub-groups. General laws about personality and behaviour can be formulated - *assuming* that personality is largely inherited and impervious to environmental factors.

Types and traits

12. *Type* theories of personality divide people into categories, which are defined as possessing common behaviour patterns.

    Ancient and mediaeval theories of personality were based on individuals fitting a recognisable type, which was then considered to be determined by body chemistry ie. the relative proportions of 'humours' or fluids in the body. We still use the terms 'phlegmatic' (phlegm), 'sanguine' (blood), 'choleric' (bile) and 'melancholic' (black bile) in much the same way as Hippocrates or Chaucer, though the four-type, chemistry-determined theory has been discredited.

13. The trouble with 'types' is that they are too general, and do not do justice to the complexity and subtlety of individual personality.

14. *Trait* theories of personality, on the other hand, identify dispositions to behave in a particular way, or any consistently observable behaviour. If you say someone is 'always late', or is 'sweet-tempered', 'nervous', 'emotional', 'undemonstrative' etc. you are identifying traits in their personality.

    This assumes that there is a range of common traits which may be identified and compared, as like to like, in different individuals, but it also admits that:

    (a) different individuals possess different traits; and
    (b) different individuals possess different strengths of the same traits.

    This is a more accurate reflection of the complexity of personality.

Hans Jurgen Eysenck

15. Eysenck's explanation of personality and individual differences is one of the most influential current theories. His books of personality tests have been best sellers. There are three elements to the theory:

- *personality traits*. Eysenck uses personality test questionnaires to identify a number of traits in individuals;

- *trait clusters*. Individuals who possess one particular trait are likely to possess certain other 'compatible' traits;

- *types*. The pattern or cluster of traits forms an identifiable personality type.

Personality is inherited, fundamentally unalterable, and physiologically based – ie. associated with the nervous system and other genetic and biological factors.

16. Eysenck's research has identified two major areas in which variations in individual personality can occur.

   (a) *The 'E' dimension*. Human beings are divided into two types (the terms for which were coined by the German psychologist Carl Jung):

   - Extravert   Traits: expressiveness, impulsiveness, risk-taking, sociability, practicality, irresponsibility, activity

   - Introvert   Traits: inactivity, carefulness, responsibility, control, reflectiveness, unsociability, inhibition

   Most people lie somewhere on the line or continuum between these two extremes. Where do you fit in?

   (b) *The 'N' dimension*. There is a similar continuum between:

   - Neuroticism (emotional instability)   Traits: Anxiety, guilt, obsessiveness, hypochondriasis (imaginary illness), unhappiness, lack of autonomy, low self esteem

   - Stability   Traits: calm, freedom from guilt, casualness, sense of health, happiness, autonomy, self esteem

17. A standard questionnaire asks mainly 'yes or no' questions for each dimension (plus some 'lie scale' questions to test the subject's overall honesty in answering questions). The scores on 'E' and 'N' are not correlated directly ie. you could be introverted and *either* neurotic *or* emotionally stable.

18. Questionnaires attempt to find those questions that *discriminate* between individuals (ie. not using those that everyone answers in the same way) and that *correlate* (ie. appear to be measuring the same thing). Despite the statistical method, however, there is a certain amount of human subjectivity involved in the wording of questions and the interpretation of the results.

19. There are other limitations to the use of such personality tests.

   (a) The hypothetical yes/no question may be irrelevant to an individual's experience, and inaccurate as a reflection of complex thought processes. It filters out all self-expression, which many would say is an integral part of personality.

(b) The data are not in any case designed for predicting individual behaviour (such as might be most useful to a manager), but for comparison. General tendencies in specified groups and sub-groups may be observed, however, and *extreme* scores may indicate an individual with psychological imbalance of some kind.

(c) The conditions of 'being tested' may falsify the response. Most subjects of such tests are willing and interested enough to try to be honest, but may be:

(i) hostile to unqualified 'yes or no' questions, with no room for self-expression or middle ground;

(ii) inclined to give what they think is the 'normal', desirable or expected response (particularly in view of the value judgements commonly attached to character analysis);

(iii) inclined to give 'neutral', or alternatively 'extreme' responses (according to personality).

(d) It is easy to cheat or falsify the data deliberately. W H Whyte writes: "you should try to answer as if you were like everyone else is supposed to be." Even the lie scale questions are easy to spot and answer 'correctly'.

Idiographic approach

20. The aim of the idiographic approach is to build up a 'true' picture of the individual personality in all its complexity and uniqueness. Normal and abnormal individuals are subjected to in-depth study, with data drawn from interviews, observation, letters, diaries, life histories etc. Information about the individuals *from the individuals themselves* is very important.

    The approach concentrates on the *development* of the 'self': personality is the product of the processes through which an individual learns to be what and who he is.

21. Idiographic theory assumes that hereditary factors are only part of our make-up, and that behaviour is influenced by experience, reasoning, and social processes as well. We behave according to a self-image or self-understanding which we learn and develop through social interaction: ie. through our evaluation of:

    (a) the effect of our behaviour on other people; and
    (b) their expectations of, attitudes and behaviour towards, us.

    Our personality is capable of adjustment, as the self-concept is reorganised with each new experience.

22. Most people learn and accept as part of their personality the stock of attitudes, values, knowledge and 'norms' of the society in which they live. The cry 'I just want to be myself' is never wholly accurate: we all need to some extent to be accepted, and continuing, routine interactions with other people are only possible on the basis of certain shared perceptions of reality.

    George Herbert Mead, noting that despite the acceptance of generalised, socially desirable behaviours, man still displays originality, individuality and a drive towards variety and change, argued that 'self' has two components:

- 'I' - the unique, active, impulsive part of the individual, which rises above conformity to the social process; and

- 'Me' - the mental process which reflects objectively on the 'self', measuring it against the social norms, values and expectations which have been 'internalised' or accepted by the individual.

23. Sigmund Freud's psychological constructs were based on a similar tension between man's individual nature and social 'regulation'.

    (a) The '*id*' is the original system of personality, and the source of its primary energy and drive (which Freud took to be the libido, or sexual energy, though other psychologists have disagreed with this emphasis). All innate, essentially pleasure-seeking, drives and impulses originate from the id.

    (b) The '*super-ego*' is the internal representative of the values, rules and ideals of society, as learned by reflection from social interaction and institutions ie. a socio-moral influence. Social mores in the areas of sexuality and aggression, according to Freud, are particularly rigid.

    (c) The '*ego*' is the system of psychological forces which resolves this conflict, by redirecting the impulses of the id so that they can be gratified in the real world. It is the 'executive' of the personality, integrating the demands of the id, super-ego and external environment, for the psychological health of the individual.

Psychological adjustment

24. Psychological 'adjustment' depends on the flexibility of the self-image in relation to experience and environment. If an individual's perception of his own qualities, abilities, attitudes etc. is accurate, coherent and consistent with his experience, and adaptable to change as it occurs, the individual will be 'well-adjusted'.

    People usually behave in ways that are consistent with the self-image they have built up: faced with feelings or experiences that are *not* consistent (cf. distortion, mentioned earlier), a well-adjusted individual will try to re-integrate the two elements. A 'maladjusted' individual will feel threatened by the inconsistency, and will experience psychological tension: he will deny or distort reality in an effort to 'dodge' the inconsistency.

Personality assessment

25. Various techniques have been established to evaluate an individual's self-understanding. (Questionnaires, such as Eysenck's, reflect more the understanding of the researchers - who determine the questions and answers in advance.) The individual is given complete freedom of expression, and the researcher's task is to identify themes which indicate the direction of the subject's thought processes.

    Some approaches include:

    (a) getting subjects to write or talk about themselves (ie. the famous 'couch' of the clinical psychologists, or 'analysts');

(b) free association of words or images. Such tests allow strong needs, interests, obsessions and motives to find expression. The famous Rorschach inkblot test - where subjects are invited to find images in random inkblots - is one such test;

(c) the interpretation of dreams;

(d) analysis of imagination. One example of a systematic application of this is the 'thematic apperception test'. The subject is invited to write short imaginative stories in response to pictures: he is given the opportunity to 'project' his personality onto the pictures, through the stories. He is then scored according to the presence or absence of certain themes and images in his stories: eg. David McClelland developed the test to support his need theory, looking for images of achievement, power, affiliation etc.

26. Again, many of these methods are subject to the risk that, for one reason or another (eg. as Whyte suggests, getting a 'safe' score in tests set by the work organisation) the individual might falsify the data. If the subject knows what the researcher is after, it is not difficult to give it to him. The subject in a thematic apperception test as part of a management training programme, for example, might fill his stories with what he regards as themes and images of high achievement, success, authority, perseverence, dominance etc. - and, without knowing exactly how the test is scored, gain a moderately high rating as leadership material.

Personality differences and work behaviour

27. Whichever approach to personality we adopt, it is clear that the context in which individual and social behaviours emerge or develop is, for very many individuals, a work organisation, which takes much of an adult's waking time. In such an organisation, the individual will be confronted by rules, norms and expectations that others have of him; he will interact with other individuals; he will perform tasks and make decision in ways that are consistent with the character 'traits' he possesses; he will suffer frustration or stress, or will be motivated and satisfied at work.

We have discussed how individual differences in personality arise, and in what 'dimensions' people differ. What difference does it make to behaviour at work, and to the management of individuals?

28. In general terms, organisations will make certain generalised assumptions about the personalities of the individuals they employ, about the 'type' of individuals they would wish to employ and to whom they would wish to allocate various tasks and responsibilities. They may have an idea of the character traits or type that are considered desirable in whatever business they are in, or in whatever role the individual is to fill. You have only to look in job advertisements to see the recurrence of the desired characteristics: extravert, steady, lively, responsible, hard-working etc.

(There are various 'models' of the worker - his personality, attitudes, needs, motivations etc. - which have been adopted by management as a basis for policies on recruitment, remuneration and incentives, management style, and other aspects of handling individuals. We discuss these as part of the 'social context of work' in a later chapter.)

29. W H Whyte (*The Organisation Man*) suggests that there is an emerging 'social ethic' in America, which aims to submerge the individual in the group, and particularly in the Organisation, which, he says, attempts to select those who will fit in, who have no disturbingly exceptional characteristics. In his appendix on 'How to cheat on Personality Tests', he suggests that in order to portray oneself as the personality most sought after by the Organisation, one merely has to tell oneself:

" (a) I loved my father and my mother, but my father a little bit more [for men]
(b) I like things pretty well the way they are
(c) I never worry much about anything
(d) I don't care for books or music much
(e) I love my wife and children
(f) I don't let them get in the way of company work. "

Do you know any 'organisation clones' like this?

30. You may also recall Argyris' view that there are 'basic incongruities' between the requirements of the organisation and the psychological needs of the individual as his personality develops. But how is the organisation to be more sensitive?

> "Managers, if one listens to the psychologists, will have to have insights into all kinds of people. They will have to be in command of all kinds of psychological techniques. They will have to understand an infinity of individual personality structures, individual psychological needs, and individual psychological problems... But most managers find it hard enough to know all they need to know about their own immediate area of expertise, be it heat-treating or cost accounting or scheduling."
>
> (Drucker: *Management*)

31. We have already suggested that psychological testing is of uncertain usefulness in assessing personality accurately, let alone predicting individual behaviour. The question "What type of person - possessing what traits - will make a successful ....?" is naive. As we have indicated, experience, ability, motivation, job design, sex, age, opportunity and other factors may also be significant influences on job performance. Research has not been able to show significant correlation between personality (on the basis of test results) and performance.

32. It has not, for example, been possible to prove frequent organisational assumptions that extravert, stable personalities (to use Eysenck's approach) are more successful in particular occupations than any other type of individual.

(a) The extravert may be active, cheerful, social and not averse to risk - but may also be unreliable, easily bored, irresponsible and fickle.

(b) Neurotics tend to be depressive, anxious, obsessive and emotional, and take too many days off sick - but they may also be conscientious, highly disciplined, and do not fret under authority. Moreover, the ability to display and share emotion can be a healthy and desirable quality.

33. Nonetheless, if we assume broad consistency in traits or types of personality, we *can* make some useful observations about individual differences and work behaviour - at least enough to be going on with in the real world.

The syllabus specifically mentions:

(a) authoritarianism;
(b) the need for achievement; and
(c) self esteem.

We will look briefly at these and other aspects of personality that might give a manager a 'handle' on individuals' work behaviour.

Authoritarianism

34. 'Control' and 'control systems' in organisations (ie. systems by which performance is measured, compared to standard, and corrected as necessary) may conjure up pictures of the repression or manipulation of the individual by the organisation (as represented by management), for purely economic and political ends.

However, the concept of control can also be seen as necessary to create conditions of stability and predictability, which enable people to work effectively and are also psychologically necessary.

35. People might *want* to be controlled in a work situation because control processes:

(a) provide feedback on the individual's performance, which may be essential for learning, satisfaction, motivation and the confirmation or adjustment of self-image;

(b) give the task itself definition and structure, standard methods and levels of performance. This is reassuring to most individuals, and essential to those with high security or 'structure' needs;

(c) encourage dependency, which is particularly welcome to a personality type known as the *authoritarian personality*. [Note: authoritarianism is not just 'bossiness'!]

36. The authoritarian personality is an extreme type, first identified by researchers during the Second World War. It is related mainly to the process of socialisation in early childhood, and is associated with a pattern of personality traits such as:

- conservatism or conventionalism
- submissiveness, and an uncritical attitude to idealised moral authorities
- fatalism
- rigid thinking - including scorn for subjectivity, imagination and 'softness'
- preoccupation with authority, power figures, strength etc.

37. It has been argued that such traits lead individuals to large, highly structured organisations, such as the armed services, which provide secure, ordered, controlled environments. Authoritarian individuals 'fit in' so well that they rise to responsible positions, yet their rigid thinking and uncritical adherence to convention, as well as their leader-follower

preoccupation in interpersonal relations, makes them disastrous decision-makers and leaders. This has been demonstrated in the military, but may well be true of large bureaucracies in other spheres.

38. There is, however, a danger of reading too much into simple obedience and adherence to rules. This may not be due so much to a need for control, routine, conformity and directive leadership (ie. personality determining job), but rather due to socialisation at work (ie. job determining personality). Obedience and conformity equals promotion etc., and gradually those who rise to responsibility, having been subjected to tight control themselves, adopt the accepted 'control' approach to leadership.

Need for achievement

39. One of the main uses of the Thematic Apperception Test, as developed by McClelland, is to measure the strength of individuals' need for achievement. McClelland identified the need for achievement as a prime motivator for people who have a strong desire for success (in relation to standards of excellence, and in competition with others) and a strong fear of failure. Such people tend to want work which offers:

   (a) personal responsibility;

   (b) moderately difficult tasks and goals, which present a challenge and an opportunity to display their abilities - but not excessively difficult, since that might increase the possibility of failure. We have already mentioned how strong achievement needs can lead a person to lower his personal targets or aspirations, in order to increase the likelihood of success;

   (c) acceptable, realistic levels of risk-taking - but not gambles, again because of the fear of failure;

   (d) clear, frequent feedback on performance - so that they can improve their performance, or have their success confirmed.

40. Other personal characteristics associated with this type include:

   (a) perfectionism, and a dislike of leaving tasks incomplete;
   (b) a sense of urgency, always being in a hurry, and an inability to relax; and
   (c) unsociability, if people seem to be getting in the way of performance.

   Low scorers on need for achievement worry more about security and status, their own ideas, feelings and self-presentation - ie. are not performance-orientated in the same way.

41. McClelland's researches suggested that:

   (a) entrepreneurs tend to rank high on need for achievement;

   (b) chief executives of large companies, having fulfilled their ambitions, tend to rank low on need for achievement;

   (c) successful 'up and coming' managers rank high on need for achievement; and

(d) a need for achievement can be *taught* to managers on training courses, by getting them into the habit of thinking in achievement terms, and using achievement imagery.

42. The need for achievement is thought to be related to early socialisation. Children whose parents expect them to gain early independence, and impose few restrictions on them, who positively reinforce independent behaviour, and who foster an atmosphere of competitiveness, aspiration and achievement at home, are more likely to develop high achievement needs than children whose parents dominated, restricted or 'molly-coddled' them.

Self esteem

43. Argyris, among others, has suggested that an individual continually seeks to increase his *self esteem*, to make his self-concept more gratifying, or to get closer to his ideal self-concept, or ego-ideal. The experience of 'psychological success' is one aspect of this, making the individual feel more competent and more secure.

Psychological success is experienced when an individual sets himself a challenging goal which is in some way related to his self-concept, and determines his own methods of achieving it. (This obviously relates to our discussion of job satisfaction and motivation.)

44. The main aspects of self esteem, as they effect behaviour at work, are that:

(a) an individual's confidence in his competence, or in his ability to do something, contributes to the successful demonstration of that competence or ability. The 'self-perception' of success is a motivating force, and a secure basis for further action: people with low self-esteem tend to be demoralised and stressed by their perception that their actions and decisions are inferior, likely to fail etc. The expectation of failure will tend to breed failure, and people with low self-image who *do* succeed tend to want to 'quit while they're ahead';

(b) a sense of competence is a secure basis for risk-taking in important personal areas. The self-concept is not felt to be under threat, and the individual does not feel the need to protect it by lowering his aspirations or goals, or by surrounding himself with familiar, non-threatening and undemanding people and environments. People with high self-esteem are therefore likely to be more competent in social interaction with a variety of people, more creative in their thinking, more confident in decision-making, and more ready to accept the challenge of new tasks and responsibility.

45. The self-concept is, as we suggested earlier, formed through social interaction and experience. Individuals will tend to develop a 'positive' self-image, which they find satisfying, if other people have responded warmly and favourably to them, if positive rather than negative reinforcement has been part of their development etc.

46. Few work organisations could afford to tolerate the unrestricted range of behaviours that would result from an attempt to create an atmosphere of 'unconditional acceptance' such as might encourage high self esteem in all individuals.

Nevertheless, as we discussed in the chapter on motivation, enhancement of individuals' self image can encourage behaviour that will be of use to the organisation. This can be achieved through:

    (a)   positive reinforcement;

    (b)   identification of the individual with group or organisational success;

    (c)   a sense of 'significance' in the task; and

    (d)   opportunities to experience psychological success by participating in goal-setting etc.

47. We ought to add, however, that although *lack* of self esteem may be a demoralising and inhibiting characteristic, an overly enhanced self-image may have its drawbacks for work behaviour, eg:

    (a)   over-confidence: taking on too much work or responsibility, risk-seeking, unwillingness to consult or take advice from others etc;

    (b)   'superiority': personal relations in the work place may suffer from patronising or arrogant attitudes to others;

    (c)   inflexibility: although high self esteem is better able to handle criticism, or challenges to the self-concept, it may also tend to ignore them eg. by simply rejecting the source ('Why should I listen to *him*, anyway?').

You will no doubt be able to add your own observations from experience.

Dualism in the individual

48. The psychologist Ernest Becker has argued that man is driven by an essential 'dualism', the need:

    (a)   to be part of something, a conforming member of a winning team (ie. security instinct); and at the same time

    (b)   to stick out as an individual in his own right, to 'shine' in some way (ie. self-expression instinct).

The implication of this for work behaviour affects the way in which individuals can be motivated and managed. As Peters and Waterman argue, a strong 'central faith', which binds the organisation together as a whole, should be combined with a strong emphasis on individual self-expression, contribution and success: individuals should be given at least the 'illusion of control' over their destinies, while still being given a sense of belonging, and a secure, perceived meaningful framework in which to act.

Decision-making psychology

49. An interesting article by L Shaw and F Bamber in 'The Administrator' journal (October 1987) outlines the effects of personality on decision-making, including the following.

    ●   People who tend towards 'dependency' on others will

        - be more optimistic about outcomes
        - evaluate fewer potential alternative outcomes
        - be less rational in considering alternatives

    ●   People with high security needs (eg. desire for certainty) and who experience high emotional arousal will make more extreme judgements about the desirability and likelihood of outcomes.

50. The same article outlines the results of a study by Argyris of 165 managers. It was found that they:

    (a)   rarely expressed feelings. The open expression of sentiments during decision-making meetings in particular was felt to be a sign of immaturity;

    (b)   were averse to risk and experimentation;

    (c)   rarely behaved in a way that would support others' individuality, and rarely encouraged others to be open or to take risks;

    (d)   suffered from tension, stress and frustration, due to the suppression of feelings.

The study concluded that personality should be allowed free expression in the decision-making process. Instead it tends to be suppressed, in the interests of 'objectivity', or on the grounds of the 'irrelevance' of personal values to organisational objectives. In fact, this conflict between the perceived demands of personality and organisation causes tension, dissatisfaction and inefficiency.

PERCEPTION, SOCIAL INFLUENCE AND ATTITUDES

Points to be covered

- The perceptual process
- Attribution Theory
- Social perception
- Social influence and self concept development
- Reference groups
- Role theory
- Attitudes

Introduction

1. 'Perception' is the psychological process by which stimuli or in-coming data are selected and organised into patterns which are meaningful to the individual.

    Different people 'see' things differently: human beings behave in (and in response to) the world *as they see it* - not 'as it really is'.

2. You may have noticed that the processes of learning, motivation and personality development are based on the way in which the individuals concerned *perceive* themselves, other people and the world around them. For example, the motivation calculus depends heavily on the perceived likelihood of achieving certain goals, and the perceived (highly subjective) desirability of those goals: the individual's self concept may be formed and adapted to his perception of himself, the world, and other people's responses to him.

3. In this chapter, we will be looking at two major aspects of perception as it is relevant to organisational behaviour, ie:

    (a) perception as the interpretation of information and events, including reasons why people *mis*interpret them;

    (b) social perception and social influence: ie. the ways in which perception affects our attitudes to and interrelations with other people. Role theory and the influence of reference groups are two aspects of this.

    Communication processes - which are also closely related to perception - are discussed in the following chapter.

90

The perceptual process

4. The sensory apparatus of humans has certain limitations which serve to filter out certain pitches or volumes of sound (eg. a dog whistle), types of light (eg. infra-red) etc. The process of *perception* acts as another screen for stimuli: we are constantly bombarded by sensory data of all kinds, not all of which is interesting or useful to us. We would not be able to function effectively if we had to deal with every sound, sight, smell etc.

   If you make a real effort to listen to all the sounds in the room where you are sitting now, you will realise that they were only 'background', or that you hadn't noticed them at all, while your attention was focused elsewhere (hopefully on this text).

5. This process of '*perceptual selectivity*' means that the 'world picture' that our brains actually hold is not a whole or accurate one. It may be determined by:

   (a) *the context in which it is formulated*, ie. what is necessary or relevant in the situation in which the individual finds himself. People are often said to 'see what they want to see' in situations;

   (b) *the nature of the stimuli*. Advertisers use this to make their designs attention-grabbing. Our attention tends to be drawn to large, bright (or loud), unfamiliar, moving and repeated (but not repetitive) stimuli;

   (c) *internal factors* ie. characteristics of the individual - personality, motivation, past experience etc. - which shape his *expectations* about the world, and what goes on in it. Those expectations tend to form the context in which information and events are perceived. The 'perceptual set' of the individual is his readiness to respond to some stimuli more than others, and in different ways.

6. A complementary process of '*perceptual organisation*' deals with the *interpretation* of information and events, ie. groups and patterns stimuli to make them recognisable, intelligible and useful to the mind. Sound waves become music, patterns of light become vision etc.

7. The mind also tends to fill in gaps in partial or confusing information, according to its expectations. This is called 'closure'. It is partly why speed reading is possible: the mere shape of a familiar word, as the eye skims over it, together with its context, which creates an expectation of the kind of word it must be, is enough for the mind to make the connection, without having focused on all the information available.

8. This interpretative element of perception is also a source of inaccuracy, of course. The children's game of 'whispers' demonstrates how half-heard phrases can be distorted beyond recognition as they pass from person to person. The same process may account for the 'grapevine' in organisations: as rumours fly, gaps in the story get filled by incorrect assumptions and inferences, becoming less and less accurate. There is another famous story of a victorious (but unhealthy) French general who was heard to cry: "Ma sacrée toux!" (My 'wretched' cough!) by his aides, who had been on their way to ask him what he wanted done with all the prisoners taken in battle that day. They heard "Massacrez tous!" (Kill them all!) and did...

Attribution theory

9. We mentioned in the previous chapter how 'maladjusted' individuals perceive as threatening any feelings or experiences that are not part of the image they have of themselves, and how one defence mechanism for dealing with this threat is to deny or distort the experience, perhaps by putting the blame on 'other' factors.

   The experience of 'psychological failure' may also activate a similar defence mechanism, in particular the transference of responsibility from the self to another person, 'the way things are', the System, the organisation structure, 'Fate' etc.

   This disowning of unpleasant or threatening experience is called *Attribution Theory* - because failure is attributed to causes other than self. (You may recall that, as an opposite effect, psychological success depends on the individual's awareness that it was due to his *own* efforts and abilities that his goal was achieved.)

10. It is therefore possible for individuals to keep 'reality' at a distance, by means of the interpretation of events: their own perception of the reality of a situation may, for defensive reasons, become not only highly selective, but distorted.

    The way in which information, and in particular the actions and characters of other people, are interpreted may be distorted by an individual's own prejudices, expectations, pre-occupations and all kinds of attempts to defend or reinforce a self-concept which is perceived to be under threat.

Social perception

11. The way in which we perceive other people is obviously going to be crucial to how we will relate to them and communicate with them in any context. It is the root of all attempts to motivate and manage people at work, and the basis from which individuals develop themselves (ie. by comparison with others as they perceive them).

12. There are two important forms of *bias* in the perception of other people that tend to operate in any situation:

    - the 'halo effect'; and
    - 'stereotyping'.

13. The *halo effect* was a term coined by the psychologist Edward Thorndike, to describe the way that our first highly selective judgements about people - based on immediately obvious characteristics eg. dress, manner or facial expression - colour our later perception of other features of those people, whether to positive or negative effect. Information subsequently gathered that does not agree with the first assessment tends to be filtered out - even though the characteristics on which that first assessment was based may be largely:

    (a) irrelevant to the kind of judgement we may later wish to make; and/or

    (b) highly superficial, and usually the characteristics that we possess ourselves - since these are most readily recognisable and generally sought after.

14. The halo effect operates, favourably or unfavourably, in all sorts of situations, such as job interviews, where 'first impressions count'. You have probably been told at some point that well-groomed, smiling people with firm handshakes do well in interviews. Attractive women are more often discriminated against at work than unattractive ones, because the first 'halo' of femininity and 'sex-appeal' filters out following signals of competence, ambition etc.

15. *Stereotyping* can have the same practical implications as the halo effect, but operates through perceptual organisation rather than selectivity. We group together people who share certain characteristics, and then attribute traits to the group as a whole, which are (illogically) therefore assumed to belong to each individual member.

16. The grouping may be done according to nationality, occupation, social position, age, sex or physical characteristics. The traits may be based on personal experience of particular individuals, common misconceptions, pure prejudice etc.

So, for example, in a recent survey to find the most boring group of people in Britain, accountants 'won' by a large majority! Dumb blondes, mean Scotsmen and other stereotypes are frequently spread and perpetuated by jokes and other cultural communication methods. Exceptions in our own experience may be dismissed as 'proving the rule', and inconsistencies are passed over (if accountants are boring and blondes have more fun, what are we to think of blonde accountants?)

Stereotypes are obviously over-generalisations, and although, as we suggested earlier, they may be a convenient shortcut to personal relations, they should be consciously checked for accuracy in each case.

Social influence and self-concept development

17. As we discussed briefly in the previous chapter, self-concept is partly developed through interaction with other people - or, as we now know, with other people as we perceive them to be. The main sources of social influence on individual self-concept and behaviour are:

- role models, and self-comparison with other individuals;
- peer groups or 'reference groups';
- social experience in general, and the 'roles' the individual is expected to play in various contexts.

Selection of role models

18. Individuals consciously or unconsciously select and adopt *role models* for themselves, for the various roles that are relevant to their lives, and these become part of their developing self-concept.

Parents are likely to be the earliest and most influential models, moulding the child's aspirations and expectations with regard to education, career, life-style, and generally the 'type of person' the child should be. Research has shown that highly ambitious individuals tend to have highly motivated parents for whom status is important: managerial and professional positions tend to 'run in the family', and lower socio-economic groups also tend to reproduce themselves in the next generation.

Individual teachers at school may also be a powerful formative influence. Particular colleagues at work, or bosses, may become 'mentors' or 'gurus' to an individual who takes them as a model of success or other valued qualities.

19. Adolescence and the early adult years are often times when models are re-evaluated. Parents may – temporarily or permanently – be discarded as models, perhaps out of conscious rebellion. Friends may take on greater influence (cf. peer groups, below). People whose social environment is fairly constant in early years - eg. if they have grown up in a small town, in a local school etc. – will have a fairly consistent set of models, and a secure self-concept on that basis. The increasing flexibility of society, however, tends to present young people with a variety of fluctuating models.

It has been noted that a working-class child whose intelligence has taken him into a grammar school environment may even use two different accents in his speech - ie. at home and at school – because he is torn by the influence of two sets of models, and desires acceptance by both.

20. The selection of models may also be related to what Festinger, in 1951, called 'social comparison theory'. People most seek to evaluate their own performance through comparison with other individuals - not by using absolute standards. Comparative performance information can be a strong motivator, as can peer reviews and even internal competition (eg. between teams, or brands) in organisations.

21. The source of an individual's attraction as a model may come from an (often idealised) perception of his:

   (a) charisma, or personal magnetism, charm;
   (b) expertise, or knowledge - the appeal of the parent, teacher, boss, guru;
   (c) demonstrated success - as with a manager, 'hero' or 'famous person'; or
   (d) moral or physical ascendancy, strength or personal domination.

Reference groups

22. 'Reference groups' are groups with which an individual closely identifies himself and which have a significant influence on his behaviour, by providing him with models and 'norms'. The individual need not be a member of the group itself: any group to which he *aspires* to attain membership is also a reference group.

23. Reference group theory was formulated in the 1940s by Herbert Hyman, to describe the way in which an individual uses groups as a point of reference for his own judgements, beliefs and behaviour.

The theory has since been investigated particularly in relation to consumer decision-making, response to marketing etc. It has been suggested that buyers of certain products tend to conform to the group norm or collective opinions of those with whom they identify themselves: this is particularly true of high-profile, 'symbolic' products - such as clothing, cars, furniture or drinks - which are badges of social or group identity and acceptability.

24. There are various inter-related factors on which reference group influence depends.

    (a) Individuals must be aware of the reference group, and of its norms and values - otherwise they will have nothing concrete to model their behaviour on.

    (b) Individuals must identify themselves to a lesser or greater extent with the particular group - otherwise there will be no impulse towards conformity with that group's norms. The degree of identification is known as 'affectivity'.

    (c) The group must impose sanctions - whether positive or negative - to encourage conformity. In fact, few individuals wish to be complete conformists, and there is usually a range of acceptable alternatives within given norms: in consumer terms, for example, the group might dictate the product (eg. personal organiser) or even the brand (eg. Filofax), but the sense of independence will be maintained by the choice of size, colour etc.

25. Reference groups influence behaviour by:

    (a) affecting aspiration levels - eg. the junior manager who wants to get his golf up to the standard of his colleagues, who are members of the local country club; or the worker who does *not* want to produce as much as he is capable of, because the work group has set lower standards for itself, and does not want to be 'shown up' to management;

    (b) affecting the type or direction of behaviour, by establishing conventions, norms and taboos. Styles of clothing, manner of speech, and voiced attitudes are examples of areas in which conformity may be expected.

26. The mass media and various marketing strategies contribute to put forward pictures of various sections of society, with which individuals are intended to identify - thus creating a 'group' where none naturally existed. 'Peer groups' for young people are natural reference groups, based on shared values, problems and tastes - but 'youth culture' itself is partly a creation of media and consumer projections. 'Yuppies', 'Eastenders' and 'Martini drinkers' are similar groups with which people desire or are encouraged to identify themselves.

It has been suggested that we adopt different reference groups for different areas of our lives. Miles carried out a study of adolescent girls, and found that the peer group (other girls) was most influential in, for example, the choice of clothes, books etc. while in more important matters eg. the choice of boy friends, their parents' opinions were more valued. Reference groups may even conflict: the member of a shop-floor work team who also aspires to managerial status and lifestyle may face a dilemma over the kind of behaviour that will gain acceptance in either circle or both.

Role theory

27. Role theory is concerned with the roles that individuals act out in their lives, and how the assumption of various roles affects their attitudes to other people.

28. An example may help to explain what is meant by 'roles'. An individual may consider himself to be a father and husband, a good neighbour and an active member of the local community, a supporter of his sports club, an amateur golfer, a conscientious church-goer, a man of certain political views, an academic and a research scientist. Each organisation to which he belongs provides him with one or several such roles to perform. His perceptions of other people and interactions with other people will be influenced by his varied roles, although in any particular situation one role is likely to have a stronger immediate bearing than others on what he thinks and does.

29. A *role set* is a term to describe the individuals or group of people who relate to a 'focal' person in one of that person's roles. For example, in his role as research scientist, an individual may be surrounded by a role set consisting of:

   (a) his research director;
   (b) his research assistants;
   (c) fellow research scientists in the department;
   (d) other employees in the department;
   (e) members of other departments (eg product design and development) with whom he works;
   (f) members of other scientific institutions with whom he corresponds.

30. The role of the individual will be shaped by the *expectations* that each of the various groups in his role set have of the role he is in, ie he will tend to assume a role that others expect of him (although these other groups might in fact have conflicting expectations). It can be argued that professors are often scatter-brained and absent-minded because there is a popular myth, held by students and university workers in their role set, that professors *should* be absent minded.

31. Individuals give expression to the role they are playing at any particular time by giving *role signs*. An example of role signs is clothing or uniform, for example:

   (a) a businessman will wear a suit at work, in his role as executive, but when he returns home in the evening, he may change into casual wear, to reflect his new role as father and husband;

   (b) a white coat indicates that an individual is performing his role as a hospital doctor, a rosette indicates that an individual is acting in the role of a football team supporter, and a college scarf is a sign that a person is in the role of student.

In a recent advertising campaign, a major high street bank exploited stereotypical perceptions of roles and role signs. A young, fresh-faced, 'trendily' dressed man is seen entering a bank. The scene switches to the Manager's office, where a forbidding, sombrely suited older man is seen shaking hands with the youngster. Which is the Bank Manager? *Not* as you'd expect...

---

32. *Role ambiguity* is a term which describes a situation when the individual is not sure what his role is, or when some members of his role set are not clear what his role is. The causes of role ambiguity for a worker might be:

(a) uncertainty about the responsibilities of his job. Job descriptions/definitions should help to remove such uncertainties, but an individual may still be unclear as to what the boundaries of his work-load are;

(b) uncertainty about other people's expectations of him. For example, a manager may not be certain whether his superiors expect him to be an innovator, challenging accepted practices and ideas, or whether he should be a company 'yes-man'. He may also be uncertain whether his subordinates expect him to show a close, supportive interest in their work, or whether they expect him to be stand-offish and authoritarian. He may be unsure whether people in other departments welcome his advice, or whether they would regard any suggestions from him as 'busy-bodying';

(c) a lack of clarity about how performance is evaluated. For example, is the sole criterion of a manager's performance meeting budget targets, or will he be judged by his social responsibility, or his contribution to the longer-term interest of the organisation?

(d) uncertainty about the potential for promotion and advancement.

33. *Role incompatibility* occurs when different groups have different expectations about what an individual should be doing, which may also differ from the individual's own role expectations. For example, management might be expected to run a profitable operation and to achieve certain financial targets through efficient management. The employees and unions might expect management to involve them in planning decisions, and to co-operate with them to protect the future of the industry. The management, aware of these conflicting expectations of their role, might also place greater emphasis on their duty to provide a satisfactory service to the general public.

34. *Role conflict* occurs when an individual, acting in several roles at the same time, finds that the roles are incompatible. A businessman who receives a telephone call from his wife, who wants him to leave work and go home, will experience conflict in his roles as businessman and family man. Similar conflict might be experienced by a working woman, who must reconcile her roles as a businesswoman and a mother. A trade union member may be reluctant to obey a strike call, because he disapproves of its reasons.

35. Many organisations might benefit from a greater awareness of roles and their influence on individual attitudes. For example, suppose that a company is suffering heavy losses, and the departmental managers meet to discuss a solution to their problem.

- The production manager might recommend the purchase of new equipment to increase productivity.

- The accountant might recommend the shutdown of unprofitable departments or products.

- The marketing manager might recommend methods of boosting sales.

- The research and development manager might suggest the speedy implementation of some new product ideas.

- The personnel director might suggest a pay freeze, or some redundancies.

- The trade union representative might suggest a reform of middle management attitudes.

- The data processing manager might recommend the computerisation of certain aspects of work.

Each manager would be guilty of *selective perceptions* ie seeing the problem, and the solution, from the viewpoint of his/her own position and role, and not necessarily from a company-wide point of view.

Attitudes

36. An *attitude* is the position that an individual has adopted in response to a theory or belief, an object, event or other person.

A more technical definition is: 'a mental and neural state of readiness, organised through experience, exerting a directive or dynamic influence upon the individual's response to all objects and situations with which it is related'. (*Allports*)

Attitudes are our general 'standpoint' on things. They are therefore linked to perception, personality, goals etc. as part of the developing 'package' of assumptions and beliefs that each individual brings to his behaviour, decision-making and interactions with other individuals. They are subjective ie. dependent on perception and personal experience, rather than wholly objective, although reasoned opinions may be part of the individual's attitudinal position.

37. Attitudes are thought to contain three basic components:

- *cognition*: knowledge, perception, belief or disbelief;
- *affectivity*: feelings, desires etc - positive or negative;
- *conation*: volition, the desire to perform an action.

This implies that attitudes are not only part of how we perceive and feel about our environment, but also predispose the individual to behave in a certain way: ie if a relevant situation presents itself, the individual is likely to react with a particular mode of behaviour.

This is of interest to the work organisation. Attitudes such as job satisfaction, class antagonism etc may create a tendency to behave in ways which the organisation will wish to anticipate and control.

38. Behaviour in a work context will be influenced by:

(a) attitudes *at* work: ie all sorts of attitudes which individuals may have about other people, politics, education, religion etc., and which they bring with them into the work place; and

(b) attitudes *to* work: ie. the position the individual has adopted about work itself - a necessary evil, an interesting sideline, a life goal etc. This will be discussed in the chapter on 'work and non work'.

Attitudes and work behaviour

39. The influence of attitudes on work behaviour is something that we have in effect already been discussing: motivation and job satisfaction, for example, are in a sense the product of attitudes to work, to rewards and incentive schemes, to money and other goals, to work conditions, to management, to participation, to other workers etc.

The central conclusion of the Hawthorne experiments, which we mentioned earlier, was that many problems of worker-management co-operation were the results of the emotionally-based attitudes of the workers, rather than of objective difficulties in the situation.

40. Positive, negative or neutral attitudes to other workers, or groups of workers, to the various systems and operations of the organisation, to learning - or particular training initiatives - to communication in the organisation etc. will obviously influence performance at work. In particular, they may result in:

   (a)   varying degrees of co-operation or conflict between individuals and groups, or between departments;

   (b)   varying degrees of co-operation or conflict between different levels in the organisational hierarchy ie. worker resistance to managerial tactics and the 'machinery' imposed by them eg. payment schemes, training schemes, plans and controls;

   (c)   varying degrees of success in communication - interpersonal and organisation wide. Negative attitudes to particular people, 'types' or classes of people, or to communicating at all ('what's the point of saying anything?') can create almost insuperable barriers.

41. The main elements of a positive attitude to work itself might be described as a willingness to:

   (a)   commit oneself to the objectives of the organisation, or adopt personal objectives that are compatible with those of the organisation;
   (b)   accept the right of the organisation to set standards of acceptable behaviour;
   (c)   contribute to the development and improvement or work practices and performance;
   (d)   give a fair day's work for a fair day's pay;
   (e)   take advantage of opportunities for personal development.

   (Of course, this is a 'positive attitude' within the mainstream social culture of work: radical viewpoints - or attitudes - which do not recognise the legitimacy of organisational attempts to direct and control behaviour, and to buy labour, would disagree.)

Non work factors

42. *Non work* factors that might influence attitudes to work, or affecting work, include:

   (a)   *class and class-consciousness:* attitudes about the superiority or inferiority of others, attitudes to money, or 'working class morality', as well as attitudes to work itself (economic necessity, duty, exploitation, career etc.);

   (b)   *age.* Attitudes about all sorts of issues may be formed by experience, and therefore by the era in which the they were formed: attitudes to sexual equality, morality, education etc. have varied widely from one generation to the next. Attitudes also tend to become less flexible with age, as experience is perceived to confirm them;

   (c)   *race, culture or religion.* Attitudes *about* these areas will again affect the way in which people regard each other - with tolerance, suspicion or hostility - and their willingness to co-operate in work situations. Culture and religion are also strong influences on attitudes to work: the 'Protestant work ethic', Japanese concepts of the organisation family;

(d) *lifestyle and interests*. Again, attitudes about these areas - where someone lives, what car he drives, whether he has a family, what he does in his spare time - affect interpersonal relations, and the self concept of each individual. Is he 'fulfilled' and successful? Do other people *think* he is? Attitudes to work itself are, again, also affected by attitudes to the things money can buy, and whether they are worth striving for, to work and leisure, and the relative importance of each in the individual's life;

(e) *sex*. Attitudes to the equality of the sexes, and their various 'roles' at work and in society, may be influential in:

   (i) interpersonal relations at work (especially where women are in positions of authority over men: sexist attitudes may come into painful conflict with imposed power structures);

   (ii) the self concept of the individual: women at work may be made to feel inferior, incompetent or simply unwelcome, while men working for female managers might feel their masculinity threatened; and

   (iii) attitudes to work itself. Stereotypical role profiles ('a woman's place is in the home', 'the man has to support the family') may be held by both sexes and may create feelings of guilt, resentment, or resignation about wanting or having to work.

Attitude change

43. Charles Handy suggests that "getting people to change their behaviour is relatively easy compared with changing their attitudes." Apart from systematic and powerful ways of changing attitudes, such as brain-washing or indoctrination, Handy refers to 'socialisation' as a process of attitude change (or development).

We have already mentioned socialisation as the process by which society - or, in our context, the organisation - seeks to influence the individual to adopt its values and customs, ie to 'condition' the individual so that he 'joins' the group psychologically as well as physically. Peters and Waterman refer to organisations with strong cultures: the individual has to "buy in or get out".

44. Socialisation is achieved in organisations through:

   (a) schooling - ie. instruction, or 'induction' in the methods and traditions;

   (b) apprenticeship - ie. providing individuals with models or mentors to learn from;

   (c) co-option - ie. progressively initiating individuals into 'inner' groups, of which membership is desirable, and to which conformity is required;

   (d) mortification - ie. forcing the individual into conformity, by punishment, ridicule etc., robbing the individual of his own identity until he closely identifies with the group (eg. in army training).

45. Handy also uses his concept of 'dissonance' (discussed briefly earlier) to study how attitudes can be changed. Dissonance is the discomfort or stress that occurs when two 'inputs' to the mental process conflict. If an individual thinks, for example, that promotion will bring him fulfilment - but his closest, most admired friends despise management and regard promotion as betrayal of class values - he will experience dissonance. This will only be alleviated by his:

    (a) changing his own attitude to promotion (although this creates another dissonance - the discrepancy between his past and current attitudes);

    (b) changing his attitude to his friends - down-grading them so that their dissonant input need no longer concern him. (This will obviously be easier where the source of dissonant information is less important to the individual and more easily dismissed. In such a case, it has been shown that the dissonance originally experienced will in any case be less, so that the individual may not feel the need to change his views at all);

    (c) not exposing himself to dissonant information, or seeking only information which confirms his attitude. The individual may conform to his friends' attitudes, and then choose to recall what he 'always said' about promotion being a curse etc.

46. The implications of this for an organisation wishing to change attitudes is that:

    (a) if the source of dissonant information (ie. a conflicting attitude) is not highly regarded, the individual will experience less discomfort, and will not be moved to change his attitudes. 'Expert' power, position and personal authority will therefore be required by the change agent so that he can create dissonance in non-conforming individuals;

    (b) if you *pay* people to change their attitudes, they may change their behaviour - but they will be able to explain away the dissonance created by acting contrary to their attitude (ie. by justifying their actions with the reward): again, they will suffer less discomfort, and will not need to change their views. In other words, power through money creates *compliance*, but not *internalisation*, or inner acceptance. This is one of the important behavioural implications of monetary incentive schemes;

    (c) public commitment to, or admission of 'ownership' of, an attitude or course of action makes it very difficult to renounce without painful dissonance. In research studies, those who had to instruct others in a new viewpoint changed their own attitude more than those who simply listened. The persuasive power of communication in general - lectures, memos etc. - is overrated.

In other words, an individual will only change his attitude if:

- the topic is of little importance to him; or
- the topic is of great importance to him, and there is no other way of reducing the dissonance between his original and his new behaviour or belief.

---

47. Note that a change in *behaviour* (ie compliance) does not imply a change in *attitude*. The latter is harder to achieve, but lasts much longer.

Attitude surveys

48. *Attitude surveys* are a technique used frequently in market research. When data collected from a survey concerns customer attitudes, it is necessary to use some method of recording differing attitudes for analysis and evaluation.

    Attitudes are measured by means of *attitude* scales, and there are three common types used in market research:

    (a) *Thurstone scales.* A Thurstone scale contains 7, 9 or 11 statements which appear to cover a range of attitudes in equal intervals. Respondents are then asked to select the statement which most closely reflects their own attitude.

    (b) *Likert scales.* A respondent is asked to indicate his measure of agreement or disagreement with a series of statements put to him - ie strongly agree, agree, uncertain, disagree, strongly disagree.

    (c) *Semantic differential scales* are based on extreme objectives (strong-weak, good-bad, always-never etc) with perhaps intermediate attitudes as well (eg extremely good, very good, fairly good, neither good nor bad, fairly bad, very bad, extremely bad).

49. Attitude surveys can also be used to obtain information about the attitudes and motivation of employees. Information about employees might be considered useful when management believes that:

    (a) operational efficiency depends to some extent on employees' attitudes towards their work;

    (b) when organisational changes are planned, attitudes towards the change should be monitored closely. When resistance to change is found to be strong, action would need to be taken to prevent industrial unrest, or the failure of the change-over plan;

    (c) communications between employees and their managers might be inadequate, and there might be considerable frustration within the organisation. An attitude survey might help to reveal the full extent of any such frustration, and how it affects relationships between superiors and subordinates;

    (d) finding out more about what employees want and think will help senior management to plan pay and reward schemes which are better suited to employees' interests.

50. Attitude surveys can be carried out by means of interview or questionnaire, and a 'scoring' or 'marking' system can be used to give quantitative values to attitudes, if these are thought useful. In the UK, attitude surveys are not nearly as widely used as they are in the USA.

COMMUNICATION

Points to be covered

- Communication processes and problems
- The need for communication
- Communication in practice

Introduction

1. There are two main contexts in which organisational communication may be viewed.

   (a) The organisation as an entity communicating with the people who come into contact with it. Each organisation has an 'identity' or 'corporate image' in its dealings with individuals or other organisations: employees, customers, clients, suppliers, government, the Press, the general public etc. People form generalised but often quite strong views about the organisation as a whole, according to how it communicates itself to them: 'an old-fashioned company', 'a go-ahead outfit', 'an exploitative employer' etc. A company may inspire loyalty, commitment and a sense of belonging in its employees, by the image that it projects of itself as a whole 'package'.

   (b) The individuals within an organisation communicating with each other. An organisation is by definition a collection of individuals co-ordinating their efforts towards shared goals: the individuals benefit from the increased power and sense of identity that the 'group' gives them, but the organisation should never be allowed to seem an 'inhuman' entity apart from the people that create it. Particularly in the context of communication, it is important to remember the individuality of the participants: if 'something must be done to improve communication in the company' the responsibility is ultimately *yours*, whatever policies the organisation as a whole might design to guide you.

2. A very basic definition of communication might be the transmission or exchange of information.

   Information may be the main focus of the communication - eg. if you are simply telling someone something, or *about* something - but may also be a means of achieving other desired effects. You may want:

   (a) to initiate some action;
   (b) to make your needs understood;
   (c) to share ideas, attitudes and beliefs, perhaps persuading others to embrace them; or
   (d) to establish and maintain links with other people, possibly to entertain them.

COMMUNICATION

Communication processes

3. Effective communication is a two-way process, perhaps best expressed as a cycle. Signals or 'messages' are 'sent' by the communicator and 'received' by the other party, who 'sends' back some form of confirmation that the 'message' has been received and understood. This is enormously complicated in practice, especially in face-to-face communication: you may send a letter and receive an acknowledgement back, which would correspond to a single cycle of communication, but face-to-face, the workings of two or more minds *and* bodies (eg. nodding understanding, gesturing etc) complicate the picture.

    A basic interpretation of the process of communication might be as follows:

A	IMPULSE TO COMMUNICATE	
B	ENCODING OF MESSAGE	sender activity
C	RELAY OF MESSAGE	
D	DECODING OF MESSAGE	receiver activity
E	'FEEDBACK'	

4. Deciding (a) *to communicate* and (b) *what to communicate* is the first stage of the process.

    Messages may be conceived as the result of an impulse, a feeling, a train of thought (which may be more or less coherent) or an external stimulus of some kind, and the decision to communicate the 'idea' may then be taken, consciously, unconsciously, or not at all. For example, you might:

    (a) conceive an idea, chew over it for a while, and then decide to set it out for someone else in a logical way;

    (b) see or feel something which causes you to send a totally involuntary message - a cry for help, a groan, an exclamation of delight;

    (c) 'blurt out' something you feel without thinking too much about it.

5. Words, gestures and expressions are the articulation of the idea in the brain; they make it into a message for communication. The idea/feeling/opinion has to be put into a form which can be transmitted, a form which the sender and receiver must *both* understand, if the sender's message is to be correctly interpreted by the receiver. This is like a 'code', because the words, pictures and gestures we use are only symbols representing our ideas.

    We have to bear in mind that a word or gesture we use and understand may be ambiguous or mean something else to a person of different age, nationality, experience, beliefs etc. Just because *we* understand what we mean, it does not necessarily follow that someone else will.

6. The code or 'language' of a message might be:

    (a) verbal:

        (i) spoken words;
        (ii) written words;

    (b) non-verbal:

        (i)   pictures, diagrams, symbols;

        (ii)   numbers;

        (iii) facial expression, gestures, body posture - eg. a look of surprise, a nod of agreement, a threatening way of standing;

    (c) a mixture of verbal and non-verbal.

7.   Once the idea has been 'encoded' as a message, the sender needs to choose how to 'transmit'. The particular route or path via which the message is sent, connecting the sender and receiver, is called the 'channel of communication'. Examples would include postal, telecommunication or computer systems. The tool or instrument used is the 'medium', eg gesture, picture, letter, report, telephone conversation etc.

The choice of medium will depend on such factors as:

    (a) the time necessary to prepare and transmit the message, considering its urgency;

    (b) the complexity of the message: what channel will enable it to be most readily understood;

    (c) the distance the message is required to travel and in what condition it must arrive;

    (d) the need for a written record eg. for confirmation of transactions, legal documents;

    (e) the need for 'interaction' or immediate exchange eg. question and answer, instant 'feedback' etc.;

    (f) the need for confidentiality or, conversely, the dissemination of information widely and quickly;

    (g) sensitivity to the effect of the message on the recipient: the need for tact, personal involvement, or impersonality;

    (h) cost, considered in relation to all the above, for the best possible result at the least possible expense.

8.   The first step in communication from the receiver's point of view is the 'decoding' of the message, ie. understanding what it says. This involves:

    (a) grasping the meaning of the words or symbols used by the sender. The 'key' to the code is, as we have said, not always shared by the receiver eg. if the word is unfamiliar, the picture is not recognisable in the receiver's experience etc.;

    (b) interpreting the message as a whole. 'What it says' is not necessarily 'what it means', and 'reading between the lines' may be necessary to establish the underlying meaning of the message.

        The meaning may be deliberately disguised by a sender using sarcasm, innuendo or double-meanings. In other situations, both sender and receiver will have to be aware that the underlying meaning may have to be interpreted according to the context, the relationship between the parties, tone of voice etc.

9. 'Feedback' is the reaction of the receiver which indicates to the sender that the message has (or has not) been successfully received, and enables him or her to assess whether it has been understood and correctly interpreted. This is a very important and sometimes neglected aspect of communication: feedback creates a *two-way* process or cycle, rather than a simple send–receive relationship.

Feedback may consist of:

Positive	*Negative*
Action being taken as requested	No action or wrong action being taken
A letter/note/memo being sent confirming receipt of message, and replying to question/invitation etc.	No written response at all, or written request for more information, clarification of message, repetition etc.
Accurate reading-back of message	Failure to repeat message correctly
Smile, nod, murmur of agreement, etc.	Silence, gesture or sound of protest, blank look shrug etc.

Communication problems

10. You can see what a complicated process this is, with many variable factors at each stage. Feedback is vital to success in communication precisely because there are so many potential barriers and breakdowns to guard against. Two terms used to describe problems or breakdowns which occur in communication are:

- distortion; and
- noise.

11. *Distortion* refers to the way in which the meaning of a communication is lost in 'handling'. It occurs largely at the encoding and decoding stages of communication, where:

(a) the precise intention of the sender ie. what he wants to communicate, fails to translate itself accurately into language, so that the 'wrong' message is being sent; or

(b) the language used is not translated into proper understanding by the receiver, ie. the wrong message is received.

12. The basic problem is 'language'. It is extremely difficult to describe and explain in language exactly what is intended: words, gestures and pictures may convey different meanings or no meaning at all to different people, according to their nationality, region, education, age, interests and attitudes etc.

A foreign language, incorrect use of a language, technical or otherwise obscure words, unfamiliar and unexplained pictures or diagrams, or words/pictures with more than one possible interpretation can all be sources of distortion, even when both parties are *trying* to understand and make themselves understood. Each party may simply have failed to take into account (a) who they were talking to, and (b) the context or situation within which they were talking.

In addition, differing opinions and attitudes, lack of concentration or co-operation can set up barriers to understanding: either party may deliberately make a meaning unclear, or choose to understand only what they want the message to say.

Information
Ideas, attitudes ──→ Code ⟩⟩ ──→ Message ──→ Decode ──→ ⟩⟩
Desired Action

Incorrect information
Misinterpretation
Wrong or inadequate action

13. *Noise* refers to distractions and interference in the environment in which communication takes place, obstructing the process by affecting the accuracy, clarity or even the 'arrival' of the message. For example:

   (a) physical noise, such as other people talking in the room, passing traffic or the clatter of machinery, can prevent a message from being heard, or heard clearly;

   (b) 'technical noise' involves a failure in the channel of communication while information is being transmitted. A breakdown in a computer printer, a crackle on a telephone line or bad handwriting may prevent an effective exchange of information from taking place;

   (c) 'social noise' is a failure in communication created by differences in the personality, culture and outlook of the communicator of a message and its intended recipient. When two people do not get on well together, there will almost inevitably be some barrier to full and open communication. Social noise includes difficulties experienced by members of different social classes, old and young, male and female, boss and subordinate. *Watch people*, and learn to recognise the signs of and reasons for such problems;

   (d) 'psychological noise', such as excessive emotion (anger, fear etc), prejudice or nervousness can also interfere with the effective transmission of a message: the meaning may get clouded by irrelevant expressions of emotion or attitude, or the message may reach the recipient in a garbled state (because of a nervous stammer, angry spluttering etc.).

14. The problem of noise can be overcome, or at least reduced, by using the principle of *redundancy*, that is by using more than one channel of communication, so that if a message fails to get through by one channel, it may succeed by another. For example, a spoken comment might be confirmed by an appropriate gesture, an agreement or decision made by telephone or at a meeting can be backed up by issuing a letter, or minutes. Communicators must generally be aware of possible sources of noise in their situation: a bustling office is not the place for a confidential discussion; a computer printer which produces poor quality graphics should not be used for important presentation diagrams; a hot-tempered person with known racial and sexual prejudices should not be appointed to conduct job interviews.

15. The choice of medium and channel will be an important factor in reducing the risk of noise and distortion. A vital exchange of complex information might best be made in writing, rather than over a crackling telephone line; a tricky negotiation requiring tact, trust and persuasive skill on both sides is more likely to succeed in a face-to-face context than through an exchange of letters which would be impersonal and slower to respond to changing factors.

16. The fault in a failure of communication may be with the message itself. The wrong message may be transmitted if the sender fails to encode his 'idea' precisely and accurately, but in other circumstances the message *intended* by the sender may itself be faulty, if:

(a) the idea itself is ill-conceived, muddled, ambiguous or illogical;

(b) the sender has omitted some vital item of information without which the communication will not be effective – ie. the desired understanding or action will not be achieved;

(c) the sender has 'thrown in' superfluous information which obscures the important item, or simply makes the message 'too much to take in'.

Summary

17. Communication problems, then, can be caused by:

(a) *not* communicating. It is worth mentioning that silence – broody, hostile or forgetful – is not likely to be helpful, and even 'tactful' or 'thoughtful' silences are open to misinterpretation, and should be a prelude and aid to communication, rather than an end in themselves;

(b) sending the wrong message, ie. one that is meaningless, irrelevant or unsuitable;

(c) paying little or no attention to the context in which communication takes place, or to the intended recipient of the message; this increases the risk that the 'wrong' message will be received;

(d) encoding or decoding a message wrongly, ie. distortion;

(e) choosing an unsuitable medium and/or channel of communication;

(f) failing to take into account possible sources of noise;

(g) failing to seek or offer feedback, or ignoring feedback offered.

18.

19. We may say that communication has been *effective* if the sender gets the intended or desired response from the recipient, in which case feedback will indicate understanding, agreement or performance of the required action.

Oral and non-verbal communication

20. 'Oral communication' means communication by speech, or word of mouth. Face-to-face oral media include:

    (a) conversations;
    (b) interviews;
    (c) meetings;
    (d) public addresses or briefings.

    Oral communication can also take place despite the remoteness of sender and receiver, through:

    (a) telephone calls;
    (b) intercom;
    (c) audio or video tape recordings.

21. The advantages of oral communication include the following.

    (a) It is a swift and direct medium. There is little or no time lapse between the sending and receiving of the message.

    (b) It is therefore suitable for 'interactive' communication, the exchange of ideas, opinions, attitudes. Decisions can be arrived at and action taken more swiftly than eg. with a lengthy correspondence. All parties present are able to contribute.

    (c) This creates greater flexibility: circumstances and attitudes can be changed more easily, especially since the personality, voice and manner of the parties involved can be employed in persuasion and motivation.

    (d) Instant feedback is obtainable to overcome doubts or misunderstandings. The sender will be able to ascertain immediately whether his message has been received and correctly interpreted.

    (e) In face to face oral communication, there is the added advantage of being able to see as well as hear the other party. Verbal meaning may be reinforced and feedback given by facial expression, bodily gesture etc.

    (f) Face to face communication allows for the sensitive handling of personal messages, eg. bad news, a reprimand or 'clear the air' discussion. Parties can respond flexibly to the situation, offering support, sympathy, encouragement, directness etc. as required.

22. The disadvantages of oral communication compared to written include the following.

    (a) 'Technical noise' eg. background sounds or bad telephone lines, can interfere with effective transmission.

    (b) Memory is untrustworthy, and perceptions differ. A written confirmation and record of an oral event will be required, so that both parties can check that they agree on what has been decided, can recall the details later, and can produce evidence if necessary.

(c) Less time is usually available for planning the message's general content, let alone the exact wording. Inferior decisions may be made, because they had to be thought through 'on the spot' in a meeting. Time may be wasted and misinterpretation caused by ill-conceived utterances.

(d) Face to face, strong personalities may 'swamp' and overrule weaker ones, however valid their respective ideas. A louder voice on the telephone may hinder the two-way process. Clash of personalities may become a crippling barrier to effective communication.

(e) Where a large number of people are involved, it is even more difficult to control the process, and ensure that it is effective.

23. The same stages apply in oral communication as in written: a message is conceived, encoded, transmitted, decoded, interpreted and acknowledged. In face to face oral communication, however, you are sending and receiving messages at the same time, or very close together. You switch rapidly between speaking and listening, and all the time your relationship with the other person, your tone of voice, your expressions and gestures, are modifying, qualifying or confirming the messages you are sending and your response to messages received.

24. 'Non-verbal communication' is, as its name implies, communication without words, or other than in words. The way we stand, where we position ourselves in relation to other people, our tone of voice, gestures and facial expressions all communicate something.

We may use them deliberately:

(a) instead of words, eg. storming from a room, or pointing something out; or

(b) to confirm or add to the meaning of our words eg. nodding and saying 'yes', pointing something out and saying 'look!'.

We may also *unconsciously* be confirming or even undermining our spoken messages by our non-verbal ones eg. banging the table to reinforce a point; a grim expression belying an assertion that 'Really - everything's fine'; a shaking hand revealing the truth behind 'Oh, I'm quietly confident, you know'. (You have probably heard someone say: 'Well, she didn't *sound* very happy...': the verbal message received is being interpreted in the light of other factors.)

'Metacommunication' ('Meta' = beyond, in addition to) is a form of 'supercommunication' where all the elements over and above the actual words are taken into account in interpreting the true meaning of the message, or 'reading between the lines'.

'Paralanguage' ('Para' = beside, beyond) occurs when spoken language is used in a way that conveys a meaning greater or other than its surface one. For example, a sarcastic tone of voice conveys the opposite meaning to the words themselves: 'That's just *great*, then, isn't it?' (It isn't).

---

25. We can fruitfully control and *use* non-verbal communication in order to:

    (a) provide appropriate 'physical' feedback to the sender of a message (eg. yawn, applause, clenched fist, fidgeting);

    (b) create a desired impression (eg. smart dress, no fidgets, firm handshake) ;

    (c) establish a desired atmosphere or conditions (eg. friendly smile, informal dress, attentive posture, respectful distance);

    (d) reinforce our spoken messages with appropriate indications of how our interest, seriousness and feelings are engaged (eg. emphatic gesture, sparkling eyes, disapproving frown).

26. If we can learn to *recognise* non-verbal messages, we can also:

    (a) receive feedback from a listener and modify the message accordingly;

    (b) recognise people's real feelings when their words are constrained by formalities (eg. an excited look, nervous tic, close affectionate proximity);

    (c) recognise existing or potential personal problems (the angry silence, the indifferent shrug, absenteeism or lateness at work, refusal to look someone in the eye);

    (d) 'read' situations in order to modify our own communication and response strategy. Is the potential customer convinced? (Go ahead.) Is the complaining customer on the point of hysteria? (Be soothing.)

The need for communication

27. In any organisation, the communication of information is necessary:

    (a) for management, to make the necessary decisions for planning, co-ordination and control; managers should be aware of what their departments are achieving, what they are not achieving and what they *should* be achieving;

    (b) between departments, so that all the interdependent systems for purchasing, production, marketing and administration can be synchronised to perform the right actions at the right times to co-operate in accomplishing the organisation's aims;

    (c) by individuals. Each employee should know what is expected from him and how his work fits into the work of his department (at least). Otherwise, he may be off-target, working without understanding, interest or motivation, and without any sense of belonging and contributing to the organisation.

28. Communication in the organisation may thus take the form of:

    (a) giving instructions;
    (b) giving or receiving information;
    (c) exchanging ideas;
    (d) announcing plans or strategies;
    (e) comparing actual results against a plan;
    (f) laying down rules or procedures;

(g) job descriptions, organisation charts or manuals, ie. communication about the structure of the organisation and individual roles.

The management problem of communication

29. Rosemary Stewart reported a survey of 160 managers in British companies (1967) in which it was found that 78% of their time was spent communicating. (Talking took up 50% and reading and writing 28% of their time.)

30. Good communication is essential to getting any job done: co-operation is impossible without it. Difficulties occur for the usual reasons:

   (a) distortion or omission of information by the sender;

   (b) misunderstanding due to lack of clarity or technical jargon;

   (c) non-verbal signs contradicting the verbal message, so that its meaning is in doubt;

   (d) 'overload' ie. a person being given too much information to digest in the time available;

   (e) differences in social, racial or educational background, compounded by age and personality differences creating barriers to understanding and co-operation;

   (f) perceptual bias or selectivity - ie. people hearing only what they want to hear in a message.

31. There may also be particular difficulties in a work situation:

   (a) a general tendency to distort a message in its re-telling from one person to another;

   (b) a subordinate mistrusting his superior and looking for 'hidden meanings' in a message;

   (c) the relative status in the hierarchy of the sender and receiver of information. A senior manager's words are listened to more closely than a subordinate's;

   (d) people from different job or specialist backgrounds (eg. accountants, marketing managers, engineers) having difficulty in talking on the same wavelength;

   (e) people or departments having different priorities or perspectives so that one person places more or less emphasis on a situation than another;

   (f) subordinates giving superiors incorrect or incomplete information (eg. to protect a colleague, to avoid 'bothering' a superior); a senior manager may in any case only be able to handle edited information because he does not have time to sift through details;

   (g) managers who are prepared to make decisions on a 'hunch' without proper regard to the communications they may or may not have received;

   (h) information which has no immediate use tending to be forgotten;

   (i) lack of opportunity, formal or informal, for a subordinate to say what he thinks or feels;

(j) conflict in the organisation. Where there is conflict between individuals or departments, communications will be withdrawn and information withheld.

32. Each individual does not communicate, formally or informally, with every other individual in their organisation (except in very small organisations). The way in which information is channelled between individuals forms a communication 'pattern' or 'network'. We will discuss this later in detail, in the chapter on 'Groups'.

Communication between superiors and subordinates

33. In a well known 'real-world' study into three companies in the USA (1962) W Read showed how the mobility aspirations of subordinates in a large organisation strongly affect the amount of communication that takes place.

34. The more a subordinate wants promotion, the less likely he will be to transmit 'negative' aspects of his work performance. This relationship was conditioned or modified by the degree of inter-personal trust that existed between the superior and the subordinate.

35. O'Reilly and Roberts (1974) developed this argument in a laboratory study from which they concluded about the upward flow of communication that 'If the information is important but unfavourable to the sender it is likely to be blocked. This has implications for top-level decision-making and policy formulation because it may mean that organisational resources are often committed in a vacuum of relevant (particularly non-favourable) information'.

Communication in practice

36. In early 1986, a survey was carried out by Vista Communications, an employee consultancy company. 222 large UK companies were asked to complete questionnaires on their methods of internal communication.

37. The most popular methods of communication proved to be internal memos, circulars and notice boards (used by 92% of companies who completed the questionnaire), followed by team or line briefings (86%) and the company newspaper (81%). Lower down the list came management conferences (65%), employee reports (63%) and communication via trade union representatives (62%).

38. The most discouraging finding of the survey was that few companies made any systematic efforts to find out the views of their own workers on the quality of communications within the firm (although most respondents claimed that communications in their firm were good or very good). Asked how they checked the effectiveness of their communications with employees, most said by feedback through line management. (A smaller proportion mentioned the state of their industrial relations as a good indicator).

39. Commenting on this, the managing director of Vista Communications said: 'That is like asking the salesman what he thinks of the product he is selling, rather than asking the consumer'.

Informal communication

40. The formal system of communication in an organisation is always supplemented by an informal one: talks in the canteen, at the pub, on the way home, on the telephone etc.

    The danger with informal communication is that it might be malicious, full of inaccurate rumours or wild speculation. This type of gossip in the organisation can be unsettling, and make colleagues mistrust one another.

41. Formal communication systems do, however, need the support of a good - accurate - informal system, which might be encouraged by:

    (a) setting up 'official' communications to feed information into the informal system, eg house journals or briefings, (though these will have to earn the attention and trust of employees); or

    (b) encouraging 'networking': 'a collection of people, usually with a shared interest, who tend to keep in touch to exchange informal information'. (Nancy Foy, 1985)

42. The *'grapevine'* or 'bush telegraph' is one aspect of informal communication. A well-known study into how the grapevine works was carried out by K Davis (1953). The recipient of some information, A, was asked to name the source of his information, B. B was then asked to name his source, C etc until the information was traced back to its originator. His research findings were that:

    (a) the grapevine is fast;

    (b) the working of the grapevine is selective: information is not divulged randomly;

    (c) the grapevine usually operates at the place of work and not outside it;

    (d) perhaps suprisingly, the grapevine is only active when the formal communication network is active: the grapevine does not fill a gap created by an ineffective formal communication system;

    (e) it was also suprising to discover that higher level executives were better communicators and better informed than their subordinates. 'If a foreman at the sixth level had an accident, a larger proportion of executives at the third level knew of it than at the fourth level, or even at the sixth level where the accident happened';

    (f) more staff executives were in the know about events than line managers (because the staff executives are more mobile and get involved with more different functions in their work).

43. Davis concluded that since the grapevine exists, and cannot be got rid of, management should learn both to accept it and to use it, ie harness it towards achieving the objectives of the organisation.

Brainstorming

44. Brainstorming sessions are problem-solving conferences of 6-12 people who produce spontaneous 'free-wheeling' ideas to solve a particular problem. Ideas are produced but not evaluated at these meetings, so that originality is not stifled in fear of criticism. Brainstorming sessions rely on the ability of conference members to feed off each other's ideas. They have been used in many organisations and might typically occur, for example, in advertising agencies to produce ideas for a forthcoming campaign.

45. In the 1950s W J Gordon of the Arthur D Little company, a consulting firm in Massachussets, developed the *Gordon technique*. The company offered, among its other business lines, the services of an invention design group which could invent a product to order. The Gordon technique relies on brainstorming sessions with the unique difference that only the conference leader knows the nature of the problem and it is his task to steer the ideas of the group towards a solution 'in the dark.' This prevents any member from getting addicted to a single idea, which is an inherent danger in a normal brainstorming session.

Koontz, O'Donnell and Weihrich (*Management*) reproduce "'Ten commandments' of good communication" published by American Management Associations Inc.

1. Clarify ideas before attempting to communicate.

2. Examine the purpose of communication. The purpose of the communication may affect the way in which the message should be conveyed.

3. Understand the physical and human environment when communicating. Choices can then be made about where and how the message is conveyed.

4. In planning communication, consult with others to obtain their support as well as the facts. The consultation may produce helpful additional information or a new insight on how to approach the communication.

5. Consider the content and the overtones of the message. The content may be distorted by non-verbal factors, or the choice of language.

6. Whenever possible, communicate something that helps, or is valued by, the receiver. Effective communication depends partly on action performed by the person receiving the message: the reaction of the receiver is therefore important.

7. Communication, to be identified as effective, requires feedback and follow-up.

8. Communicate messages that are of short-run and long-run importance. One of the difficulties that may arise in communication is conflict between long-term and short-term objectives.

9. Actions must be congruent with communications. Subordinates will not act in accordance with communications unless their superior is seen to be doing so.

10. Be a good listener. Understanding other people's viewpoints is an important element in communicating effectively.

---

46. Bear in mind, however, that communication is one of those things that may be 'necessary' for good performance, but is not 'sufficient'. Improved vertical communication (upwards or downwards in the hierarchy) and lateral communication will undoubtedly be a good thing, if only in human terms. It will not be a guarantee of improved effectiveness, productivity etc.

USE OF INFORMATION ABOUT PEOPLE: PERSONNEL SELECTION

Points to be covered

- Staffing
- Personnel specification
- Interviews
- Psychological testing
- Group selection methods

Introduction

1. Throughout this text, we suggest ways in which organisations and their managers might use information and judgements about people at work: that is what the study of 'Organisational Behaviour' is all about. We will be considering how such information is used in the structuring of the work environment, the design of jobs and systems, the functioning of work groups, and the control of conflict and cooperation in organisations.

2. One particular area of interest that we might highlight, however, is how information about people - such as we have covered in this section of the text - is used in the selection of personnel for the organisation. What aspects of the individual as a worker is the organisation particularly interested in?

Staffing

3. Staffing is the managerial function of recruiting, selecting, placing, appraising, training and developing people to carry out the jobs or roles in the organisational structure. Staffing is therefore closely related to organising. Organising involves creating a formal structure of departments and positions: staffing involves filling the positions with people.

4. Staffing is important both to the organisation and to the people it employs.

    (a) Employees are human assets of an organisation, and as such they have a value to the organisation. An employee's value will be higher if he has more basic abilities, and it will grow higher as he gains experience. When an organisation loses an employee, it loses the experience and abilities of that person, and these might be difficult or costly to replace.

117

An organisation should try to apply a staffing policy which provides:

(i)   the recruitment of the right numbers of people;

(ii)   the selection of people of the required basic abilities;

(iii) the training and development of people to fill senior vacancies when these arise.

(b) Employees often have career ambitions, and might be motivated by:

(i)   concern for their career development (through an appraisal scheme or training and development programme);

(ii)   the prospects of promotion.

It is therefore important to employees that their organisation should have a policy of filling vacancies in more senior positions, to some extent at least, by internal promotions instead of recruiting staff on the external jobs market whenever a vacancy arises.

Personnel specification

5.   A personnel specification identifies the type of person the organisation should be trying to recruit - ie their character, aptitudes, educational or other qualifications, aspirations in their career etc.

6.   A personnel specification is an all-purpose selection assessment plan for recruiting younger people in fairly large numbers into a fairly junior grade. Research has been carried out into what a personnel specification ought to assess. Two designs of specification which you should be aware of are:

- Rodger's Seven Point Plan (1951);
- J Munro Fraser's Five Point Pattern of Personality (1966).

The Seven Point Plan and Five Point Pattern

7.   Professor Rodger was a pioneer of the systematic approach to recruitment and selection in Britain. He wrote that:

'If matching (*ie of demands of the job and the person who is to perform it*) is to be done satisfactorily, the requirements of an occupation (or job) must be described in the same terms as the aptitudes of the people who are being considered for it.'

This was the basis for the formulation of the personnel specification as a way of matching people to jobs on the basis of comparative sets of data, ie defining job requirements and personal suitability along the same lines.

8.   The personnel specification includes job requirements in terms of a candidate's:

(a) capacities (ie what he is capable of); and

(b) inclinations (ie what he will do).

In other words, behavioural versatility must be accounted for, by considering not only the individual's mental and physical attributes, but his current attitudes, values, beliefs, goals and circumstances - all of which will influence his response to work demands. It is not merely 'traits' that the recruitment officer should be interested in: they can only give a static and inflexible portrait of a dynamic process, and the interaction of the individual and his (work and non-work) environment.

9. The Seven Point Plan of Professor Rodger draws the selector's attention to seven points about the candidate:

    (a) physical attributes (neat appearance, ability to speak clearly and without impediment etc);
    (b) attainment (educational qualifications etc);
    (c) general intelligence;
    (d) special aptitudes (eg neat work, speed and accuracy etc);
    (e) interests (practical and social);
    (f) disposition (or manner, eg friendly, helpful);
    (g) background circumstances.

    Of these, (a) to (d) may be considered as capacities, and (e) to (g) as inclinations.

10. The five fold grading system of Munro draws the selector's attention to:

    (a) impact on others, including physical attributes, speech and manner;
    (b) acquired knowledge or qualifications*, including education, training and work experience;
    (c) innate ability, including mental agility, aptitude for learning;
    (d) motivation, ie individual goals, demonstrated effort and success at achieving them; and
    (e) adjustment, ie emotional stability, tolerance of stress, human relations skills.

    This similarly considers the dynamic aspects.

    * Most personnel specifications include achievements in education, because there appears to be a strong correlation between management potential and higher education.

11. Of the two systems, the seven-point plan is more comprehensive, while the five-fold system is simpler and concentrates more closely on the dynamic aspects of the applicant's career: motivation, in particular, will be a crucial indication of potential (although not necessarily, therefore, performance).

    Both provide a useful interview framework, as a kind of 'identi-kit' picture of the suitable candidate.

Interviews

12. The interview is the second stage of the selection process. Interviewing is a crucial part of the selection process because it:

    (a) gives the organisation a chance to assess the applicant directly; and
    (b) gives the applicant a chance to learn more about the organisation, and whether or not he wants the job.

13. The interview is a two-way process, but the interviewer must have a clear idea of what the interview is setting out to achieve, and he must be in sufficient control of the interview to make sure that every candidate is asked questions which cover the same ground and obtain all the information required.

14. The interview should be conducted in such a way that the information required is successfully obtained during the interview.

   (a) The interview should be conducted in such a way that the information should be planned carefully. Most interviewers wish to put candidates at their ease, and so it would be inadvisable to put the candidate in a 'hot seat' across a table from a large number of hostile-looking interviewers. On the other hand, some interviewers might want to observe the candidate react under severe pressure, and deliberately make the layout of the room uncomfortable and off-putting.

   (b) Normally, however, the interviewers do want to put the candidate at his ease, and to make the candidate feel able to talk freely to the interviewers. The manner of the interviewers, the tone of their voice, and the way their early questions are phrased can all be significant in establishing the tone of the interview.

   (c) Questions should be put carefully. The interviewers should not be trying to confuse the candidate, but should be trying to obtain the information about him that they need.

   (d) The best way of finding out about a candidate is to encourage him to talk. It is necessary to ask relevant questions, but the time of the interview should be taken up mostly with the candidate talking, and not with the interviewers asking questions. Questions should therefore discourage short answers. The more a candidate talks, the easier it should be to assess his suitability for the job.

   (e) The candidate should be given the opportunity to ask questions. Indeed, a well-prepared candidate should go into an interview knowing what questions he may want to ask. His choice of questions might well have some influence on how the interviewers finally assess him.

The limitations of interviews

15. Interviews have often been criticised because they fail to select suitable people for the job vacancies. The criticisms occur because recruits turn out to be unsuitable for the job, and questions are asked about how it could happen that they should be employed at all in the first place. The main criticisms of interviews are:

   (a) Unreliable assessments. The opinion of one interviewer may differ from the opinion of another. They cannot both be right, but because of their different opinions a suitable candidate might be rejected or an unsuitable candidate offered a job.

   (b) They fail to provide accurate predictions of how a person will perform in the job.

   (c) The information obtained about a candidate might not be relevant to whether or not the candidate would do the job well. After all, what information can be obtained from answers to questions at an interview which accurately assesses a person's general intelligence, motivation or disposition?

   (d) The interviewers are likely to make errors of judgement even when they agree about a candidate. There might be:

(i)   *a halo effect* (discussed in the chapter on Perception);

(ii)   *contagious bias* – a process whereby an interviewer changes the behaviour of the applicant by suggestion. The applicant might be led by the wording of questions or non-verbal clues from the interviewer to change what he is doing or saying, to tell the interviewers more of what they want to hear. For example, questions which begin: 'Don't you think that....' are an obvious way in which applicants might be led by the interviewer;

(iii)   a possible inclination by interviewers to *stereotype* candidates on the basis of insufficient evidence, eg on the basis of dress, hair style, accent of voice etc;

(iv)   *incorrect assessment of qualitative factors*, such as motivation, honesty or integrity. It has already been suggested that abstract qualities are very difficult to assess in an interview;

(v)   *logical error* – in other words, an interview might draw conclusions about a candidate from what he says or does when there is no logical justification for those conclusions. For example, an interviewer might decide that a person who is articulate must be intelligent, when this is not the case;

(vi)   *incorrectly used rating scales*. For example, if interviewers are required to rate a candidate on a scale of 1–5 for a number of different attributes, there might be a tendency to:

    (1)   mark candidates in the middle range when they are not sure what opinion they have obtained;

    (2)   mark candidates consistently above or below average for every attribute, because a general impression about the candidate clouds the interviewer's assessment of particular attributes.

16. It might be apparent from the list of limitations above that a major problem with interviews is the skill and experience of the interviewers themselves. Any interviewer is prone to bias, but a person can learn to reduce this problem through training and experience. The problems with inexperienced interviewers are not only bias, but:

(a)   inability to evaluate properly information about a candidate;

(b)   inability to compare a candidate against the requirements for a job or a personnel specification;

(c)   badly planned interviews;

(d)   a tendency to talk too much in interviews, and to ask questions which call for a short answer;

(e)   a tendency to act as an inquisitor and make candidates feel uneasy.

USE OF INFORMATION ABOUT PEOPLE: PERSONNEL SELECTION

Psychological testing

17. In some job selection procedures, an interview is supplemented by some form of selection test. The interviewers must be certain that the results of such tests are reliable, and that a candidate who scores well in a test will be more likely to succeed in the job. The test will have no value unless there is a direct relationship between ability in the test and ability in the job.

18. Psychological tests may be used:

    (a) in the initial selection of new recruits;
    (b) in the allocation of new entrants to different branches of work;
    (c) as part of the process of transfer or promotion.

19. There are four types of test commonly used in practice:

    (a) intelligence tests;
    (b) aptitude tests;
    (c) proficiency tests;
    (d) personality tests.

    Sometimes applicants are required to attempt several tests (a *test battery*) aimed at giving a more rounded picture than would be available from a single test.

20. *Intelligence tests* aim to measure the applicant's general intellectual ability. They may test the applicant's memory, his ability to think quickly and logically and his skill at solving problems.

21. *Aptitude tests* aim to measure the extent of an applicant's existing skills and his ability to acquire new skills.

22. *Proficiency tests* are perhaps the most closely related to an assessor's objectives, because they measure ability to do the work involved. An applicant for an audio typist's job, for example, might be given a dictation tape and asked to type from it.

23. *Personality tests* may measure a variety of characteristics, such as an applicant's skill in dealing with other people, his ambition and motivation or his emotional stability. They usually consist of questionnaires asking respondents to state their interest in, or preference for jobs, leisure activities etc. To a trained psychologist, such questionnaires may give clues about the dominant qualities or characteristics of the individuals tested, but wide experience is needed to make good use of the results.

24. All such tests should be administered to groups in a uniform way. Instructions, timing and scoring procedures should be standardised for all candidates. Comparison of a candidate's score with the scores achieved by a typical group of similar candidates will then provide a good basis of assessment.

25. These kinds of tests must be used with care, as they suffer from several limitations.

    (a) It was mentioned above that there must be a direct relationship between ability in the test and ability in the job. One way of assessing a test is to try it on existing employees whose capabilities are already known. It is very unlikely that tests alone will be sufficient to assess an applicant's suitability. They should be supplemented by other information, eg that derived from interview.

    (b) The interpretation of test results is a skilled task, for which training and experience is essential.

    (c) Particular difficulties are experienced with particular kinds of test. For example, an aptitude test measuring arithmetical ability would need to be constantly revised; otherwise, its content might become known to later applicants. Personality tests can often give misleading results, as discussed in the chapter on Personality.

    (d) It is difficult to exclude bias from tests. Many tests are tackled less successfully by women than by men, or by immigrants than by locally-born applicants. This is a particular problem in countries, such as the UK, where equal opportunities legislation makes it illegal to discriminate in employment on the basis of sex or race.

26. An interesting article on recruitment and staff selection procedures was written by Dr Ivan Robertson and Peter Makin in May 1986. It was summarised in the Financial Times of 9 June 1986.

27. The authors referred to a scale constructed by psychologists to describe how reliable various techniques are at predicting who will do well. The scale ranges from 1 (meaning a method that is right every time) to 0 (meaning a method that is no better than random chance). On this scale, interviews have been found to score only 0.2 - little better than tossing a coin. IQ tests score better at 0.4, and a similar level is achieved by the use of the so-called *biodata technique*. This refers to a questionnaire which applicants complete with details of their life-style and attitudes.

28. Despite these results, Robertson and Makin found that the great majority of the large companies they circularised used only interviews and references in their recruitment procedures. Only 4% of companies responding to their questionnaire said that they made use of the comparatively sophisticated technique of personality tests.

Group selection methods

29. Group selection methods might be used by an organisation as the final stage of a selection process for management jobs. They consist of a series of tests, interviews and group situations over a period of two days, involving a small number of candidates for a job. Typically, six or eight candidates will be invited to the organisation's premises for two days. After an introductory chat to make the candidates feel at home, they will be given one or two tests, one or two individual interviews, and several group situations in which the candidates are invited to discuss problems together and arrive at solutions as a management team.

30. Applicants for a job might be expected to submit an application form and be called to a first interview before they are invited to a group selection gathering. These group sessions might be thought useful because:

(a) they give the organisation's selectors a longer opportunity to study the candidates;

(b) they reveal more than application forms, interviews and tests alone about the ability of candidates to persuade others, negotiate with others, and explain ideas to others and also to investigate problems efficiently. These are typically management skills;

(c) they reveal more about the candidates' personalities - eg stamina, interests, social interaction with others (ability to co-operate and compete etc), intelligence, energy, self confidence etc.

31. Since they are most suitable for selection of potential managers who have little or no previous experience and two days to spare for interviews etc, group selection methods are most commonly used for selecting university graduates for management trainee jobs.

32. The drawbacks to group selection methods are:

(a) the time and cost;

(b) the lack of experience of interviewers/selectors;

(c) the rather false and unreal nature of the group situations in which candidates are expected to participate. Candidates might behave differently in a contrived situation than they would given a real-life problem.

CONFLICT, STRESS AND CHANGE

Points to be covered

- Frustration and aggression
- Stress at work
- The individual and change
- Resistance to change at work

Introduction

1. We have already had cause to mention some forms of what the syllabus calls 'individual forms of conflict' - in the sense of 'intra-personal' conflict, ie within the individual. The experience of psychological failure, dissonance and incompatible goals or needs, are psychological conflicts of this kind.

    Conflict is also sometimes used to refer to stress and frustration, ie the consequence of conflict between the individual and his environment. In this chapter we look at:

    (a) frustration and aggression;
    (b) various kinds of stress; and
    (c) the effect of change and innovation at work.

Frustration

2. 'Frustration' is defined in the Oxford dictionary as 'discontent through inability to achieve one's desires'. As we know, individuals have many different desires and goals which they bring to their work situations, so there are many ways in which an individual might feel balked, neutralised - frustrated - at work. For example:

    (a) if the individual desires to expand his skills, or utilise to the full his intellectual capacity, but his job is designed to be purely routine, mechanical, 'fool-proof' and repetitive - e.g. copy-typing, assembly work etc. - he will be frustrated in his desire for self-actualisation. You may recall Argyris' suggestion that the demands of a typical, formal, efficiency-seeking organisation frustrate the individual's development - especially in positions low in the hierachy, where opportunities for self-actualisation are more limited;

    (b) if the individual desires promotion, but is always by-passed when decisions are made and communicated, and is always 'overtaken' by others - perhaps younger or less experienced - he will be frustrated in his desire to 'get somewhere' in the organisation;

(c) if the individual desires to express his feelings - but is unable to do so because of behavioural norms designed to preserve objectivity, stifle argument etc. - he will suffer repression;

(d) if the individual simply desires to 'do his job' properly, but 'the system' seems to hamper him at every turn, he will experience frustration. He may be 'responsible' for some area of operation - but may have been given:

    (i) no position of authority from which to get things done; or
    (ii) insufficient manpower or financial resources for the task; or
    (iii) insufficient, irrelevant or untimely information, which was necessary for the task.

Budgets may therefore be a source of frustration, as may a variety of organisational policies, operating systems, and politics: staffing, management style and structure, communications, inter-personal and interdepartmental relations etc.

3. Elliott Jaques led a study for the Tavistock Institute of Human Relations into worker and management activities in the Glacier Metal Company in London. The study started to 'work through' (by discussion involving investigator and group) specific problems of payment methods, co-operation etc. - but came to focus on fundamental frustrations and stresses.

One of the major findings of the 'Glacier investigations' is the felt need of individuals to have their role and status acceptably and clearly defined. If there is confusion of role boundaries between individuals, or the multiple roles occupied by one individual, insecurity and frustration result. Lack of clarity in the definition of the powers exercisable by the individual or group was highly disturbing to them.

This is the classic organisational dilemma of the middle manager, who has his decisions and plans imposed on him from above, and is frequently by-passed in both 'upward' and 'downward' communication in the organisation, in situations where the proper channels are not observed.

4. Since frustration is the *perceived incapacity* to fulfil an aim or desire, for whatever reason, its symptoms will tend to be:

(a) a sense of *powerlessness*, or helplessness - even if the blocking factor is the individual himself, eg when he feels frustrated and cross with himself because he 'just can't get something right', or 'wishes he hadn't...'. The feeling is that the situation is not - or is no longer - under his control;

(b) *insecurity*. With a set of demands being made on one side, and a perceived inability to meet them on the other, the individual's self-image of competence is under threat - even if the blocking factor is *not* within his control;

(c) defensive responses:

- reduce the salience of the need or desire, e.g. by withdrawing commitment, feeling apathy, fatalism etc., in order to alleviate the dissonance or frustration;
- transfer the need or desire to other objects;
- bolster the self-image e.g. with displays of power - often negative ('throwing a spanner in the works') - or aggression, blaming others etc.;
- leave the situation altogether, ie *avoidance:* get another job; get promoted; take time off - legitimately or by absenteeism; day-dreaming; poor time-keeping etc.

Aggression

5. 'Aggression', in many species of living creature, is a standard response to the threat (or perceived threat) of attack. It is defined as 'hostile or destructive tendency or behaviour'.

    Anthony Jay *(Corporation Man)* sees the organisation as a direct descendant of the primitive tribe, and notes that aggression is still a basic instinct. He suggests that *group* aggression can be a powerful binding force, and that this can be exploited if an 'aggression focus' can be found, ie another group or factor that is perceived to be a threat to survival - the competitor, management, the workers, Blacks, Whites or whatever it may be.

6. You can see how the idea of an aggression focus can be used by the organisation to create indignation against competitors, for example, with an aggressive, highly-motivated response. Jay also suggests, however, that the organisation may itself become the aggressive focus of the labour force - eg as the entity which who could terminate their employment (the most real 'threat to survival') - with disastrous effects for labour relations, and general attitude to work ('let's get everything out of Them while we can').

7. Individual aggression may also focus on personal factors which are perceived as a threat to physical or psychological security. Frustration, for this reason, often issues in angry outbursts, unco-operative or even destructive behaviour. The forms of 'attack' open to individuals in a work situation are generally limited by the range of 'acceptable' behavioural norms: most people will find ways of venting aggression that will not involve the risk of losing either their jobs, or the acceptance of their peers, which may be perceived as even greater threats to security.

8. Occasionally, however, uncontrolled aggression may erupt - e.g. in 'spoiling' behaviour, defacing work or damaging machinery, in vandalism, even in physical violence between individuals.

> Charles Handy reports an incident at an automobile assembly plant, where one of the workers waited until the foreman was not looking, and then put his wrench into the conveyor belt that drove the line. Everything came to a (literally) grinding halt. And all the other workers cheered.

9. Obviously, the problem for management is how to prevent or control hostile or destructive behaviour in its employees. 'Conflict' in certain senses - e.g. as competition or argument - can be healthy and constructive, but as hostility, it may create:

    (a) poor communication; the distortion or withholding of information;
    (b) inter-personal (or inter-group) friction, jealousies etc.;
    (c) denigration of others; tale-telling etc.;
    (d) low morale and commitment;
    (e) displays of 'negative power' ie the power to annoy, disrupt etc.

10. Management attempts to control 'negative' forms of conflict tends to focus on:

(a) *obtaining consensus between individuals* - by arbitration, the negotiation of rules and procedures, the creation of 'liaison/co-ordination' positions to improve communication, constructive confrontation, role negotiation etc.;

(b) *emphasising the group nature of organisational life*, ie selling the idea of the 'team', the 'family' etc.;

(c) *separation where possible* - ie removing the offending element. Purely inter-personal clashes may be handled in this way - by simply separating the people concerned - and disruptive individuals may, as a last resort, have to be removed from the organisation altogether, but some of the root causes of harmful behaviour may be widespread and deep-seated. Class-consciousness, attitudes, the changing nature of work (new technology etc.), the design of jobs and many other factors might cause hostile behaviour - and may not be susceptible to change by the organisation.

Stress at work

11. 'Stress' is a term which is often loosely used to describe feelings of tension or exhaustion - usually associated with too much, or overly demanding, work. In fact, stress is the product of demands made on an individual's physical *and mental* energies: psychological dissonance, psychological failure etc. are sources of stress, as much as the conventionally-considered factors of 'pressure', 'overwork' etc.

It is worth remembering, too, that demands on an individual's energies may be *stimulating* (ie people work well under pressure) as well as harmful (causing strain). Many people require some form of stress to bring out their best performance: excessive stress, however, can be damaging.

Symptoms of stress (strain) and methods of coping

12. Harmful stress, or 'strain', can be identified by its effects on the individual and his performance. Symptoms usually include:

(a) *nervous tension*. This may manifest itself in various ways: irritability and increased sensitivity, preoccupation with details, a polarised perspective on the issues at hand, sleeplessness, etc. Various physical symptoms - e.g. skin and digestive disorders - are also believed to be 'stress-related';

(b) *withdrawal*. This is essentially a defence mechanism which may manifest itself as unusual quietness and reluctance to communicate, or as physical withdrawal ie absenteeism, poor time-keeping, or even leaving the organisation;

(c) *low morale:* low confidence, dissatisfaction, frustration etc.

13. Individuals have various methods of coping with stress:

    (a) *withdrawal;*

    (b) *repression,* ie refusal to admit the existence of the problem. Forced cheerfulness, playfulness, excessive drinking, drugs, etc. may indicate that this is occurring, as may exhibitions of irritability etc. outside work, if the problem has been transferred elsewhere;

    (c) *rationalisation,* ie deciding simply to endure, or come to terms with, the situation, if it is inevitable. Stress can be contained, so that its harmful effects may be alleviated. Nervous tension can be reduced by the creation of opportunities for rest, recreation and generally 'getting things into perspective', ie areas of stability and non-work stimulation. The organisation may be able to help by offering time, facilities or counselling.

14. We will look at the causes and control of stress as it relates to:

    • role theory;
    • insecurity;
    • personality variables; and
    • management style.

Role stress

15. The kinds of 'role problems' discussed in the earlier chapter on perception and social influence - ie role ambiguity, role incompatibility and role conflict - all lead to stress. Two other problems we might include here are:

    (a) role *overload,* when an individual has too many roles to cope with, and feels out of his depth - e.g. on moving from an executive to a management position; and

    (b) role *underload,* when an individual moves into a role or set of roles which he perceives as being below his capacity (ie out of line with his self-concept). In the current employment market, for example, graduates or skilled people may find themselves in 'limiting' or routine roles - e.g. as typists, or quality inspectors. Delegation may also make a manager feel un-needed and insecure. Monotony may be as stressful as constant change and challenge.

16. The stress in such situations can be resolved by:

    (a) the individual taking his own unilateral action to redefine his role, the scope of his job, the roles which are most important to him and those which can be downgraded etc. He will then have to force his expectations on the the others involved - which may aggravate stress in inter-personal relations; or

    (b) the individual co-operating with other members of his role set, to try and classify or resolve his role(s) relative to the other demands made on him. This may be a matter of redrafting job-descriptions, boundaries of authority or timetables (e.g. to make room for conflicting demands).

Only role underload offers no possibility of a co-operative solution, such as those in (b) above. It can only be alleviated by the exercise of 'nuisance' power - which increases the individual's perceived importance, if only in a negative sense - or by encroaching on someone else's role (ie job enlargement - but this is rarely a solution that employees feel able to *ask* for and it is more likely to lead to inter-personal conflict, or effort wasted in duplicated tasks).

Insecurity

17. Other situations in which stress may be particularly acute involve uncertainty, and therefore insecurity, together with a sense of responsibility for their outcome.

    (a) A manager may find himself having to initiate change or growth: attempts at innovation may be highly stressful, especially if there is an element of risk. (This may partly be a role problem - if, for example, there is a political conflict in the organisation between the supporters of the status quo and the supporters of change, usually the 'Planning and Development department'.)

    (b) Career change, end or uncertainty. Worrying about 'burn-out' or redundancy or retirement - or even about ability to cope with promotion - can be a source of stress. The pace of change in technology and markets adds to the uncertainties which now attach to the work environment.

Personality

18. Most people experience stress of some kind, at some time: there are simply some individuals who 'handle' it better than others, and it is important for organisations to identify those individuals. Pincherle did a study of 2,000 UK managers at a medical centre, and found that physical symptoms of stress were related to age, and to the level of responsibility - especially for other people. But are there *types* of people who are more prone to stress than others?

19. People have been divided into two types (first, by Friedman and Rosenheim):

    • 'type A' - competitive, 'thrusting', dynamic, impatient, restless, tense, and sensitive to pressure; and

    • 'type B' - 'laid back', patient, calm, etc.

    Type A individuals are the 'get-up-and-go' individuals in the organisation, the self-starters and innovators - but their behaviour has been associated by several research studies with a range of unhealthy symptoms (high blood pressure, cholesterol, smoking and drinking). One national study in America showed that Type A men in their forties had 6.5 times the incidence of coronary heart disease of Type B men!

20. Some people seem to *feel* less stress than others. Others, like Type A managers, may feel it acutely, but try to *overcome* it - with consequent risk to health. Personality traits which might affect one's ability to cope with stress, in either fashion, include:

(a) *sensitivity*. Emotionally sensitive individuals are pressured more by conflict and doubt, which insensitive people are more able to shrug off (although in extreme cases, insensitivity may prove such a barrier to satisfactory relationships with others, that another source of stress may be created);

(b) *flexibility*. Individuals who are seen to give in to pressure tend to invite further pressure from those who seek to influence them: intractable, 'stubborn' individuals may suffer less from this, although, when they *are* subjected to pressure, they tend to 'snap' rather than 'bend', as there is more dissonance involved in their giving way;

(c) *inter-personal competence*. The effects of stress may be handled better from a basis of strong, supportive relationships with others, and indeed many role problems may be solved by maintaining and fostering relationships and reaching co-operative solutions. The individual who turns his back on others in times of stress, like a wounded animal, is unlikely to find a satisfactory resolution;

(d) *sense of responsibility*. Some individuals have an 'easy come, easy go' outlook - where their own affairs are concerned, as well as those of others that are affected by their actions. Others have a more acute sense of 'owing' other people something, or of their accountability to others for the consequenses of their decisions, actions etc. The burden of perceived *guilt* can be a very painful source of stress.

Management style

21. In an article in the 'Administrator' (Jan 1987), Sarah Rookledge describes the findings of an American report entitled: 'Working Well: Managing for Health and High Performance'.

The report pointed out particular management traits that were held responsible by workshop interviewees for causing stress and health problems (e.g. high blood pressure - hyper-tension - insomnia, coronary heart disease and alcoholism). These included:

- *unpredictability*. Staff work under constant threat of an outburst;
- *destruction of workers' self esteem* - making them feel helpless and insecure;
- *setting up win/lose situations* - turning work relationships into a battle for control;
- *providing too much - or too little - stimulation*.

22. In British research, according to the same article, managers are criticised for:

- not giving credit where it is due;
- failing to communicate policy or involve staff in decisions;
- supervising too closely; and
- not defining duties clearly enough.

The most 'harmful' style of management is said to be *'leave alone and zap'* - where the employee (frequently young and inexperienced) is given a task, left without guidance, and then 'zapped' with a reprimand or punishment when mistakes are discovered. This simply creates a vicious circle of anxiety and guilt.

The individual and change

23. Change may affect individuals in several areas.

    (a) There may be *physiological* changes in a person's life, both as the natural product of development, maturation and ageing, and as the result of external factors: a change in the pattern of shift-working, for example, may temporarily throw the individual's eating, waking and sleeping routine out of sync. with the body's 'clock', or sense of time. A change of location may have physical side effects, related to different drinking water, levels of pollution in the air, altitude etc. A change in routine or location may affect the amount of exercise and fresh air an individual is able to get: the stress resulting from unfamiliarity may cause physical symptoms, as we have seen.

    (b) *Circumstantial* changes - living in a new house, establishing new relationships, working to new routines etc. - will involve letting go of things, perhaps 'unlearning' old knowledge, and learning new ways of doing things.

    (c) Above all, change affects individuals *psychologically*.

        (i) It may create feelings of disorientation before new circumstances have been assimilated: you may have felt this on waking up in an unfamiliar room, or performing familiar tasks in an unfamiliar setting at college or at work.

        (ii) Uncertainty may lead to insecurity, especially acute in changes involving work, where the pressures for continuity - ie staying in employment, or progressing smoothly - and/or fast acclimatisation - ie short learning curve - can be very great ('What if I can't pick up the technology?' 'What if the new supervisor doesn't like me?'). Individuals who are not averse to risk, who have handled uncertainty before, are more likely to adapt than risk-averse people. Similarly, people whose goals are more 'open' (usually younger ones, and those without parental or peer pressure to perform in a particular way) are more flexible.

        (iii) The secure basis of warm, accepting relationships may be up-rooted and the business of forging new inter-relations can be fraught with personal insecurity, risk of rejection, the feeling of being an outsider.

24. Change can affect the individual's self-concept quite radically.

    (a) A new 'psychological contract' may result from the change, bringing with it new expectations, challenges and pressures, in the face of which the self-image may have to be revised - perhaps, initially, with an uncomfortable experience of dissonance.

    (b) A new set of models may have to be confronted, if the change involves a new role set, new 'milieu', new relationships. The forging of new relationships will also involve putting the self-concept 'on the line', risking challenge and rejection.

    (c) The individual's uncertainty of being able to cope with new circumstances - because of their sheer unfamiliarity - can shake his sense of competence. Many people feel guilty and inadequate as 'beginners' or 'new boys', even though they know, and are told, that it is perfectly natural and acceptable, that their performance will improve as they get used to it, etc.

(d)   Change can be particularly threatening if it is perceived as an outside force or agent, against which the individual is powerless: it is *he* who must adapt to the 'caprices of Fate', or 'the system' (or whatever), rather than imposing his will upon events. This may be a blow to the concept of self as the agent, the controller of its destiny etc.

Resistance to change at work

25.   Resisting change means attempting to preserve the existing state of affairs - the status quo - against pressure to alter it. Despite the possibly traumatic effects of change *per se*, as discussed above, most people do *not* in fact resist it on these grounds alone. Many people - think of your own study or work situation - long for change, and have a wealth of ideas about how it should be achieved.

26.   Sources of resistance to change itself may include age and inflexibility, strong needs for security, emotional instability etc.

Sources of resistance to particular proposed changes - e.g. in location, methods of working, pay structure - may include:

(a)   *attitudes or beliefs*, perhaps arising from cultural, religious or class influences (e.g. resistance to change in the law on Sunday trading);

(b)   *loyalty to a group and its norms*, perhaps with an accompanying rejection of other groups, or 'outsiders' (e.g. in the case of a relocation so that two departments share office space). Groups tend to close ranks if their independent identity is threatened;

(c)   *habit, or past norms.* This can be a strong source of clinging to old ways, whether out of security needs, respect for tradition, or the belief that 'you can't teach an old dog new tricks' (e.g. resistance to the introduction of new technology);

(d)   *politics* - ie in the sense of resisting changes that might weaken the power base of the individual or group, strengthen a rival's position etc. Changes involving increased delegation may be strongly resisted by senior management, for example. In the same way, the introduction of automation, or new methods, may be seen by the workforce as an attempt to devalue their skills and experience in the job market: they will be superfluous, or will be 'starting at the bottom again', and will have lost their position of strength as suppliers of labour in demand;

(e)   the *way* in which any change is put forward and implemented - as we will discuss later.

27.   Arthur Bedeian cites four common *causes* of resistance:

*   *self-interest:* ie if the status quo is perceived to be comfortable, or advantageous to the individual, or the group with which he identifies himself;

*   *misunderstanding and distrust:* ie if the reasons for, or the nature and consequences of, the change have not been made clear: this aggravates uncertainty and suspicion, ie the perceived threat;

*   *contradictory assessments:* ie different individuals' evaluations of the likely costs and benefits of some change. Resistance arises from individuals' perceptions of the undesirability of change;

- *low tolerance of change itself:* ie differences in tolerance of ambiguity, uncertainty, challenge to self-concept etc.

28. Reactions to proposed change may range from:

- *acceptance* - whether enthusiastic espousal, co-operation, grudging co-operation or resignation; to

- *indifference* - usually where the change does not directly affect the individual: apathy, lack of interest, inaction etc.; to

- *passive resistance* - refusal to learn, working to rule etc; to

- *active resistance* - deliberate 'spoiling', go-slows, deliberate errors, sabotage, absenteeism or strikes.

29. John Hunt highlights a number of responses that may not *look* like resistance on the face of things, but are behaviours aimed at reinforcing the status quo. Apart from the 'behind the scenes' political manoeuvres - withholding or distorting information, gossip, undermining the authority of management, blaming the agents of change for small failures etc - there are a number of responses that the manager should learn to recognise, e.g.:

(a) pleas of ignorance ('I need more information');

(b) delayed judgement ('let's wait and see...'), perhaps stalling for time with comparisons ('there are other ways...');

(c) defensive stances - ('This isn't going to work', 'It'd be too expensive', 'It's the wrong time to...');

(d) the display of various personal insecurities: ('I won't be able to cope', 'I won't see my team anymore', 'We won't have control over our planning any more', 'Why can't we just go on as we are?'); fear, anxiety, resentment at the manner of change, frustration at perceived losses etc.;

(e) withdrawal, or disowning of the change: ('Oh, well. On their heads be it', 'I'm not interested in flexitime anyway').

'Most of us are all in favour of progress so long as it doesn't involve change'.

Ray Proctor.

Overcoming resistance to change

30. Three factors which might be helpful to managers in overcoming resistance to change include:

- the pace of change;
- the manner of change; and
- the scope of change.

31. Changes ought generally to be introduced slowly. Apart from 'people problems', there may be a long planning and administrative process and/or financial risks to be considered, e.g. in a relocation of offices or a factory: a range of alternatives will have to be considered, information gathered etc. Change is, however, above all a 'political' process: relationships are changed, and must be reformed, old ways have to be unlearned and new ways learned, (cf. attitude change, discussed earlier).

32. The more gradual the change, the more time is available for questions to be asked, reassurances to be given and retraining (where necessary) embarked upon. People can get used to the idea of new methods - can get acclimatised at each stage, with a consequent confidence in the likely success of the change programme, and in the individual's own ability to cope.

Presenting the individuals concerned with a *fait accompli* ('Let's get it over with - they'll just have to get used to it!') may short-circuit resistance at the planning and immediate implementation stages. But it may cause a withdrawal reaction (akin to 'shock'), if the change is radical and perceived as threatening, and resistance is likely to surface later, as the change is consolidated - probably strengthened by resentment.

Timing will also be crucial: those responsible for change should be sensitive to incidents and attitudes that might indicate that 'now is not the time'.

33. The *manner* in which a change is put across is very important: the climate must be prepared, the need made clear, fears soothed, and if possible the individuals concerned positively motivated to embrace the changes as their own.

(a) Resistance should be welcomed and confronted - not swept under the carpet. Talking through areas of conflict may lead to useful insights and the adapting of the programme of change to advantage. Repressing resistance will only send it underground, into the realm of rumour and covert hostility.

(b) There should be free circulation of information about the reasons for the change, its expected results and likely consequences. That information should appear sensible, clear, consistent and realistic: there is no point issuing information which will be seen as an attempt to 'pull the wool over the eyes' of the people concerned, or to 'blind them with science' - or which is a blatant misrepresentation of the situation. Competent experts should be used. Expectations should not be inflated - otherwise disappointment will be inevitable if the plan doesn't succeed as far or as fast as expected.

(c) The change must be 'sold' to the people: ie people must be convinced that their attitudes and behaviours *need* changing. Objections must be overcome - but it is also possible to get people *behind* the change in a positive way.

(i) Pure 'position power' (ie of individual managers or powerful groups or functions in the organisation) is often used to force people to accept changes: this makes the change *look* more unreasonable than it may really be, and resistance may increase. The same kind of power will constantly have to be applied to ensure continuing compliance.

(ii) If the reason for the change can be put across, there will be less need for 'position power' to push it through. If those involved understand that there is a problem, which is real, and poses a threat to the organisation and themselves, *and* that the solution is a sensible one and will solve that problem, there will be a firm rational basis, at least, for implementing change. If the people can be positively committed to the change - e.g. by emphasising the threat which the problem poses, or the advantages of the solution, *to them* - so much the better. Changes in *crisis* often face less resistance than changes of a *routine* nature.

(iii) The people should also be reassured that they have the learning capacity, the ability and the resources to implement the plan. It may even be possible to get them really *excited* about it - by, again, 're-affirming the heroic element' ie the challenge and opportunity, by injecting an element of competition perhaps (ie who can get their system running better, faster?) or simply offering rewards and incentives. Games, videos, group exercises may be used to 'fire' people to change - as long as they do not become 'pure entertainment' in themselves, losing sight of their objective.

(d) Individuals must be helped to learn - ie to change their attitudes and behaviours.

(i) Very few individuals will really be able to 'figure all the angles', to 'see the big picture' in a proposed programme of change. In order to put across the overall objective, the organisation should use visual aids - pictures, models, charts etc. - to help people conceptualise. (Professional outside consultants, who specialise in conceptualising, may be useful.)

(ii) Learning programmes for any new skills or systems necessary will have to be designed according to the abilities, previous learning experience etc. of the individuals concerned. This will include not only the style and content of the programmes, but the pace at which they proceed, and the techniques for consolidating learning which are used e.g. workshops, team-building games, feedback seminars etc. The time available, the nature of what has to be learned, and the capacity of the people must all be considered.

(e) The effects of insecurity, perceived helplessness, and therefore resentment, may be lessened if the people can be involved in the planning and implementation of the change, ie if it is not perceived to have been imposed from above. *Persuasion* will depend on the political forces in the organisation - the position or personal power of the change agent, the importance of his function in the organisation structure, any influential support he has been able to gain, the backing of 'experts' etc. Encouragement and rewards at each stage of learning may help in the transitional period. The degree to which *consultation* or *participation* will be possible (or genuine) will depend on management's attitude towards the competence and trustworthiness of its workforce. Successful change will usually be initiated from the top (otherwise the politics are too complicated) but there could certainly be opportunity for those who are, after all, most immediately involved in the changing systems, processes or structures to assess and advise on the 'nitty gritty' of the change programme.

Tell	- the people: clearly, realistically, openly
Sell	- the pressures which make change necessary and desirable
	- the vision of successful, realistically attainable change
Evolve	- the people's attitudes, ideas, capacity to learn new ways
Involve	- the people where possible in planning and implementation

34. The *scope* of change should also be carefully reviewed. Total transformation will create greater insecurity - but also greater excitement, if the organisation has the kind of innovative culture that can stand it - than moderate innovation. There may be 'hidden' changes to take into account: a change in technology may necessitate changes in work methods, which may in turn result in the breaking up of work groups. Management should be aware of how many various aspects of their employees' lives they are proposing to alter - and therefore on how many 'fronts' they are likely to encounter resistance.

Summary

35. In an article in the Financial Times (June 25, 1986), Christopher Lorenz reviews 'The Change Masters' by Rosabeth Moss Kanter, quoting the following list of personal 'dos' and 'don'ts' for the would-be 'change master':

" (1) Tune into the company's external environment much more effectively. Only then will you be
able to identify new needs.

(2) Use 'kaleidoscope thinking' to create new approaches, by combining known facts and fragments to form different patterns. (This is one of the various definitions of creativity). This way of thinking can be stimulated throughout an organisation by encouraging playfulness and irreverence.

(3) Develop the ability to create and communicate a clear vision. The importance of this is underlined by the fact that venture capitalists place more weight on the person behind a project than on the project itself.

(4) Build coalitions, and don't spring new things on people. Moss Kanter uses colourful jargon to describe four phases of coalition-building: planting seeds; 'tin-cupping' around the organisation (getting other people to contribute to the new idea); horse-trading; and 'sanity checking' (final checking of possible problems).

(5) Work through highly-motivated teams. 'Successful change efforts are associated with heightened teamwork.'

(6) Persevere and persist. 'Everything looks like a failure halfway through, which is when the political problems arise.'

(7) Share credit and recognition - 'make everyone a hero.' "

THE SOCIAL AND ORGANISATIONAL CONTEXT
OF WORK

THE NATURE OF WORK ORGANISATIONS

Points to be covered

- Nature of work organisations
- Formal and informal organisations
- Objects and objectives
- Bureaucracy
- Large and small organisations
- Authority, power and influence
- Delegation

Introduction

1. Writings on 'organisations' over the years have taken very many different perspectives and 'angles' on the subject. Organisational metaphors have varied from the primitive tribe with its constituent hunting bands, to the ship with its crew, to the biological organism, according to the emphasis which the writer wished to put on particular aspects of organisational life.

2. Buchanan and Huczynski put forward the following definition of organisation:

    "social arrangements for the controlled performance of collective goals".

    They point out that the difference between organisations (and particularly work organisations) and other social groupings with collective goals (eg. the family, the bus stop queue) is:

    (a) the preoccupation with performance; and
    (b) the need for controls.

3. (a) Organisations are collections of interacting individuals, occupying different roles but experiencing common membership. However, this embraces a wide variety of behaviours; the relationship between them may be co-operative or coercive; their roles may be ill-defined or clearly-defined, overlapping, conflicting etc.

    (b) Organisations are created because individuals need each other in order to fulfil goals which they consider worthwhile. However - as we have seen - one individual's goals may be very different from another's and from those of the organisation as a whole.

(c) Performance must be controlled in order to make best use of human, financial and material resources, for which individuals, groups and organisations compete. The need for controlled performance leads to a deliberate, ordered environment, allocation of tasks (ie. division of labour), specialisation, the setting of standards and measurement of results against them etc. This implies a whole structure of 'power' or 'responsibility' relationships, whereby some individuals control others.

Reasons for organisations

4. In general terms, organisations exist because they can achieve results which individuals cannot achieve alone. By grouping together, individuals overcome limitations imposed by both the physical environment and also their own biological limitations. Chester Barnard (1956) described the situation of a man trying to move a stone which was too large for him:

    (a) the stone was too big for the man (environmental limitation) and
    (b) the man was too small for the stone (biological limitation).

    By forming an organisation with another man, it was possible to move the stone with the combined efforts of the two men together.

5. Barnard further suggested that the limitations on man's accomplishments are determined by the effectiveness of his organisation.

6. In greater detail, the reasons for organisations may be described as follows:

    • *social reasons:* to meet an individual's need for companionship;

    • to *enlarge abilities:* organisations increase productive ability because they make possible both:

        (i) specialisation; and
        (ii) exchange.

    The potential benefits of specialisation were recognised by Adam Smith in his famous book *The wealth of nations* (1776). Specialisation permeates our modern industrial and commercial society;

    • to *accumulate knowledge* (for subsequent re-use and further learning);

    • to *save time:* organisations make it possible for objectives to be reached in a shorter time.

Synergy

7. Organisation can have a synergistic effect. Synergy is explained, briefly, as the principle that $2 + 2 = 5$. In other words, by bringing together two separate and individual 'units of resource' the output of the units combined will exceed the joint output of the separate units so that:

    (a) before their combination, $2 + 2 = 4$; and
    (b) after their combination, $2 + 2 = 5$.

Thus if A can grow 1,000 units of a product on his land, and B can grow 800 units on his land, by combining their resources (perhaps to buy some modern farming equipment and to organise their work more efficiently) they might succeed in growing, say, 2,100 units of the product.

Formal and informal organisations

8. A formal organisation may be defined (Etzioni) as a social unit deliberately constructed to seek specific goals. It is characterised by:

    (a) planned divisions of responsibility;
    (b) power centres which control its efforts;
    (c) substitution of personnel;
    (d) the ability to combine its personnel in different ways.

9. Formal organisations have an explicit hierarchy in a well-defined structure; job specifications and communication channels are also well-defined.

10. An informal organisation, in contrast, is loosely structured, flexible and spontaneous. Membership is gained consciously or unconsciously and it is often difficult to determine the time when a person becomes a member. Examples of an informal organisation are managers who regularly go together for lunch in a local cafeteria, a clique of workmates etc.

11. With every formal organisation there exists, to a greater or lesser extent, a complex informal organisation. The formal organisation is a structure of relationships and ideas; informal organisation, in practice, modifies this formal structure (Blau and Scott 1962).

Personal objectives and organisations

12. Barnard described an organisation as a 'system of co-operative human activities' and it is important to be aware that:

    (a) an organisation consists of people who inter-react with each other;

    (b) the way in which people inter-react is designed and ordered by the organisation structure so as to achieve joint (organisational) objectives. Each individual has his own view of what these organisational objectives are;

    (c) each person in the organisation has his own personal objectives;

    (d) the organisational objectives as gauged by an individual need to be compatible with personal objectives of the individual if he is to be a well-integrated member of the organisation.

13. The task of management is:

    (a) to recognise the personal objectives of individuals and to integrate these with organisational objectives;

(b) to reconcile and integrate the differing views of organisational objectives that are held by different individuals so that a total company objective may be recognised (Argyris);

(c) to make the optimal use of resources (materials, human abilities and efforts etc.) in achieving these integrated personal and organisational objectives.

14. An organisation will be effective only so far as it helps individual members to achieve their own personal objectives, and a large part of the task of management is therefore concerned with this problem.

15. It is important that an individual should consider that the objectives of the organisation (and consequently his own efforts and actions within the organisation) are compatible with his various needs. Some personal needs will be more important than others and an individual will be prepared to sacrifice some of his objectives for his own greater benefit (eg. an individual may be prepared to sacrifice some of his time in order to do a job which earns extra money).

The objects and objectives of an enterprise

16. Every business organisation has its *objectives* - ie its main purpose for being in existence. These may be to make as large a profit as possible for the organisation's owners, in the case of private enterprise, or to provide a service in the case of non-profit-making organisations or government departments and institutions.

17. Every business organisation also has its *objects* - ie every business exists to carry out certain activities such as manufacturing and selling motor cars, providing retail services, providing telecommunications services, etc. In the case of companies, their objects are described in the objects clause of the memorandum of association. Non-profit-making organisations, public corporations and other government institutions might also have formally-stated objects in their constitution, whereas other organisations such as sole traderships do not have any formally-stated objects (even though they will still have objects of some description). As an example, a partnership of solicitors might be formed with the *objective* of making profits but with the *object* of providing legal services.

18. Business organisations differ from each other partly because they have different objects, despite similar objectives. A hairdressing business and a manufacturer of armoured tanks have the same profit objective, but radically different objects. The objects of a business also help to dictate what sort of organisation structure the business requires.

19. To integrate individual and organisational objectives it is necessary to formulate organisational objectives which are understood by all members as well as compatible with their personal goals.

> 'Organisational objectives should give the organisation meaning to man... and man meaning to the organisation.' (*Davis*)

Bureaucracy

20. A bureaucracy exists when the officials of an organisation are physically separated from the 'real work' of the organisation. To a layman, the word 'bureaucracy' has unpleasant associations; however, the German writer, Max Weber (1864-1920) who is the organisational theorist most closely associated with the analysis of bureaucracy, was inclined to regard bureaucracy as the ideal form of organisation, which is 'from a purely technical point of view, capable of attaining the highest degree of efficiency and is in this sense formally the most rational means of carrying out imperative control over human beings.'

21. Weber regarded an organisation as an authority structure. He was interested in why individuals obeyed commands, and he identified three grounds on which legitimate authority could exist:

    (a) *charismatic leadership:* in such an organisation, a leader is regarded as having some special power or attribute; decision-making is centralised in him and delegation strictly limited. The leader expects personal, sycophantic devotion from his staff and followers. Decisions are frequently irrational;

    (b) *traditional, or patriarchal leadership:* in such organisations, authority is bestowed by virtue of hereditary entitlement, eg the family firm, the lord of the manor. Tradition is glorified. Decisions and actions are bound by precedent;

    (c) *bureaucracy:* authority is bestowed by dividing an organisation into jurisdictional areas (production, marketing, sales etc) each with specified duties. Authority to carry them out is given to the officials in charge, and rules and regulations are established in order to ensure their achievement. Leadership is therefore of a 'rational-legal' nature.

22. Weber specified several general characteristics of bureaucracy, which he described as 'a continuous organisation of official functions bound by rules':

    • *hierarchy:* each lower office is under the control and supervision of a higher one;

    • *specialisation and training:* there is a high degree of specialisation of labour. Employment is based on ability, not personal loyalty;

    • *impersonal nature:* employees work full time within the impersonal rules and regulations and act according to formal, impersonal procedures;

    • *professional nature of employment:* an organisation exists before it is filled with people. Officials are full-time employees, promotion is according to seniority and achievement; pay scales are prescribed according to the position or office held in the organisation structure;

    • *rationality:* the 'jurisdictional areas' of the organisation are determined rationally. The hierarchy of authority and office structure is clearly defined. Duties are established and measures of performance set;

    • *uniformity* in the performance of tasks is expected, regardless of whoever is engaged in carrying them out;

    • *technical competence* in officials, which is rarely questioned within the area of their expertise;

- *stability*: the reward for employees who do their jobs well is stability, regular pay, a retirement pension, the chance of promotion etc.

23. Compared with other types of organisation the potential advantages of bureaucracy may seem apparent. Weber was impressed with the development and accomplishments of bureaucracy, and especially with the role of technical knowledge in bureaucratic administration which he regarded as the primary source of the superiority of bureacracy as an organisation. He was also ready to acknowledge the failures of bureaucracy and deplored an organisation of 'little cogs, little men, clinging to little jobs and striving towards bigger ones.'

24. Koontz, O'Donnell and Weihrich suggest that the principles of formal organisations are:

   (a) the conscious attainment of a common goal by organised, collective effort;

   (b) unity of objective: the formal organisation should ensure that individuals in the organisation find it easy to work towards the common organisation goal. 'If the objective is to make profit over a period of time, then the organisation pattern that helps to accomplish this conforms to the principle of unity of objective';

   (c) efficiency: an organisation structure is efficient if it facilitates the achievement of organisational and personal goals by individuals with the 'minimum unsought consequences or costs.' However, efficiency may be difficult to measure or gauge.

Criticisms of bureaucracies

25. Many criticisms of bureaucracies may already be familiar. Weber acknowledged their existence but did not discuss them. However ideal bureaucracy may appear in theory, there are many inefficiencies in practice which need to be overcome. The very strength of some of the characteristics of bureaucracy may in some cases be turned into a cause of weakness.

26. Responsibility may be avoided by using the rule-book, although the rules are established to enable efficient decisions and actions. By sticking to the letter of the law, the spirit of the law may be lost. Bureaucratic red tape may prevail, and risk-averse officials become 'sticklers' for the rules.

27. There is frequently a tendency to 'pass the buck'.

   (a) In giving orders to subordinates, an official will go by the rule book and will blame someone else for the existence of the rules where his decision appears inappropriate. He may also act on the principle that 'things have always been done this way' and justify his actions accordingly.

   (b) A manager who wishes to resist change will pass the buck by saying that customary habits and methods have always worked in the past.

28. A formal bureaucratic structure, by creating a well-defined awareness of areas of authority and responsibility, may lead to 'empire building' - ie hoarding authority to prove competence and ability.

29. Other influences commonly found in bureaucracies are:

  (a) The complexity of decision-making (eg to obtain the go-ahead for new projects etc) slows down the decision-making process, causing unwanted delays.

  (b) Conformity creates ritualism, formalism and 'organisation man'.

  (c) Personal growth of individuals is inhibited.

  (d) Innovation is discouraged; there is a school of management thinking which believes that too much bureaucracy represses creativity and initiative in moulding organisation man.

  (e) Control systems are frequently out of date.

30. Weber suggested that certain general social consequences of the development of bureaucracy would arise. These are:

  • a tendency to 'levelling' (eg recruitment based on competence);

  • a tendency to plutocracy, ie rule by the wealthy (based on the interest in long-term training before qualification);

  • a spirit of 'formalistic impersonality, without hatred or passion, and hence without affection or enthusiasm'.

31. Various writers have written about the inefficiencies or 'dysfunctions' of bureaucracy.

Merton suggested that there is a rigidity of behaviour in a bureaucracy, due to:

  (a) the reduction in the amount of personalised relationships (officials work with officials, not people with people);

  (b) the internationalisation of the rules of the organisation. Rules originally designed for efficiency take on a significance which is totally unrelated to any organisational goal;

  (c) the increase in the use of categorisation of situations in order to reach decisions; decision-making is simplified (based on precedents);

  (d) the development of an 'esprit de corps'. In spite of impersonalised relationships, there is a propensity amongst members of an organisation to defend each other against outside pressures.

32. Rigidity of behaviour, Merton argued, has three consequences.

  • It creates reliability, thus meeting an important maintenance need of the system.

  • It creates defensibility of individual action (due to categorisation for decision-making purposes).

  • It increases difficulties with clients.

Client pressure (eg complaints from members of the public) creates a felt need for defensibility of individual actions, which in turn encourages further rigidity of behaviour.

33. Selznick suggested a further dysfunction in bureaucracy. As a result of increasing specialisations and technical competence, delegation of authority has increased. With delegation, however, comes the 'bifurcation of interests'. What one expert sees as the organisational goals are different from the views of another expert.

This in turn raises conflict between sub-units of the organisation and there is a tendency for individuals to identify with the sub-goals of their sub-unit to the detriment of the organisation as a whole.

Selznick concluded that delegation achieves a necessary purpose, as specialisation increases, but that it carries problems with it, ie it is both functional and dysfunctional at the same time.

34. Gouldner argued that rules are both functional and dysfunctional in a bureaucracy.

   (a) *Rules are functional*: they take away from a subordinate the feeling that his superior, in issuing orders, holds power over him. This in turn reduces the interpersonal tensions which otherwise exist between superiors and subordinates, and for this reason the 'survival of the work group as an operating unit' is made possible by the creation of rules.

   (b) *Rules are dysfunctional*: employees use rules to learn what is the minimum level of behaviour expected from them, and there is a tendency for employees to work at this minimum level of behaviour. This, in turn, suggested Gouldner, creates a requirement for close supervision. Greater pressure from supervisors will make subordinates more aware of the power the supervisor holds over him, thereby increasing tension within the work group.

Overcoming the disadvantages

35. The financial and technical advantages of bureaucratic organisations usually outweigh the disadvantages, which need to be reduced to acceptable proportions. Arguably therefore:

   (a) bureaucratic managers need to believe that all employees are individuals and that the individuals matter;

   (b) the content of subordinates' jobs should be increased as far as possible (by decentralisation);

   (c) the organisation should be arranged:

   (i)   into small working groups (to promote group loyalty and purpose);
   (ii)   into small working establishments (for the same reasons);
   (iii) with as little centralisation as possible (to give junior management more scope);
   (iv)   with good communications;

   (d) culture may be used to increase the flexibility and humanity of the organisation: eg. the 'loose-tight' properties of Peters and Waterman's excellent companies.

36. A bureaucracy, on balance, promotes efficiency in larger organisations, but it must achieve a balance whereby rules are impersonal but not inhuman, the structure is organised but not rigid, and employees are loyal without being unthinking conformists.

Many large organisations are structured in the main as bureaucracies, although other formal organisation structures may be designed, at least for a part of the organisation.

Large and small organisations

37. It is wrong to confuse 'bureaucracy' with 'large' organisations, because the features of bureaucracy can be found in many small and most medium-sized organisations. It might be useful, however, to consider the advantages and disadvantages of *large* size in this chapter.

38. The advantages of a large organisation are as follows:

   (a) A large-scale organisation should have access to sufficient resources to command a significant market share. This in turn will enable it to influence prices in the market so as to ensure continuing profitability.

   (b) A large organisation can provide for greater division of work and specialisation. Specialisation, and the development of a wide range of products or customer services, should enable the organisation to attract continuing customer support and market shares. In contrast, a small or medium-sized business will require greater competence and versatility from its top management, because they will not have the benefits of support from functional specialists which are available to the top managers of large organisations.

   (c) A large organisation with a wide variety of products or customer services should be able to offer an attractive career to prospective employees, and it is therefore likely to receive job application requests from very talented people. This in turn should enable the large organisation to recruit and develop high-quality personnel for future top management positions.

   (d) Specialisation brings with it the ability to provide expert services at a relatively low cost to the customer. A large organisation is also able to make use of the advantages of efficient 'large-scale' equipment (eg advanced computer systems or manufacturing equipment). For these (and other) reasons, large organisations are able to achieve *economies of scale* in the use of resources. Cheaper costs in turn mean either lower prices for customers or higher profits for the organisation.

   (e) A large organisation is more likely to provide continuity of goods or services, management philosophy, customer relations etc than a smaller organisation. A smaller organisation might be prone to sudden policy changes or changes of product when a new management team takes over.

39. The disadvantages of a large organisation are as follows:

   (a) There is a tendency for the management hierarchy to develop too many levels. The more management levels there are, the greater the problem of communication between top and bottom, and the greater the problems of control and direction by management at the top.

(b) An organisation might become so widely diversified in the range of products or services it offers that it becomes difficult, if not impossible, for management to integrate all of the organisation under a common objective and within a single 'management philosophy' and culture.

(c) Top management might spend too much time in maintenance of the organisation (ie with problems of administration) and lose sight of their primary tasks of setting objectives and planning for the future.

(d) There is a tendency of top management in large organisations to become 'ingrown and inbred, smug and self-satisfied'. The tendency towards 'group-think' – an acceptance by all managers of a common attitude towards problems - might introduce an unconscious resistance to necessary changes and developments.

(e) The sheer size of an organisation may provide management with problems of co-ordination, planning policy and effective control. For example, a junior manager might find the organisation so large that he has relatively little influence. Decisions which he regards as important must be continually referred up the line to his superiors, for inter-departmental consultations etc. At the same time, the top management might find the organisation so large and complex, and changes in policy and procedures so difficult and time-consuming to implement, that they also feel unable to give direction to the organisation. The organisation is therefore a 'monster' which operates of its own accord, with neither senior nor junior managers able to manage it effectively.

(f) In a large organisation, many of the tasks of junior management are routine and boring. Even middle management might be frustrated by the restrictions on their authority, the impersonal nature of their organisation, the inability to earn a just reward for their special efforts (owing to the standardisation of pay and promotion procedures) and the lack of information about aspects of the organisation which should influence their work.

Problems of large organisation

1.   **Organisation structure**

1.1   Sharing out tasks and responsibilities. Who does what?
1.2   How much specialisation/functionalisation should there be?
1.3   What span of control is suitable? And so how tall/flat will the organisation be? There is a tendency for the management hierarchy to develop too many levels. The more management levels there are, the greater the problem of communication between top and bottom, and the greater the problems of control and direction by management at the top.
1.4   To what extent should authority be delegated? How much centralisation/decentralisation should there be? Can junior/middle managers be trusted to exercise discretion and make decisions? How should managers be trained and developed?

2. **Planning and control**

2.1 How should the organisation identify its objectives and set targets for achievement? In the case of large diversified 'conglomerate' corporations, can the organisation have a major objective other than a financial one (eg profit maximisation)?

2.2 Developing formal management information systems to enable managers to plan and control properly. Communication problems.

2.3 The problem of making managers accountable, monitoring performance and setting up effective control systems.

2.4 The difficulties of co-ordinating the efforts of managers: problems of conflict (line versus staff; interdepartmental rivalries etc).

2.5 Difficulties of setting up a system of rewards that is directly linked to performance appraisal and the achievement of objectives.

3. **Adapting to change**

3.1 Large organisations might be slow to adapt to change because of a bureaucratic system of operating and decision-making that stifles ideas for innovation.

4. **Motivation**

4.1 It is difficult for individuals to identify themselves with the objectives of a large organisation. The organisation's objectives and their personal objectives will differ.

4.2 Difficulties for individuals to see how their efforts contribute to achieving the organisation's objectives (due to narrow specialisation of jobs etc).

4.3 Possible problems in getting employees to enjoy working in a large organisation, where a bureaucratic 'role culture' predominates.

4.4 Decision-making might be slow, with managers not allowed the authority and discretion they would like.

40. These difficulties of large organisations can, to some extent, be overcome by:

(a) *decentralisation and delegation of authority*. The aim of decentralisation should be to encourage decision-making at lower levels of management 'closer to the action'. Management motivation, but also management efficiency in target-setting, planning and control should improve;

(b) *pay policies* which provide for just rewards (individual or team bonuses) for outstanding effort, achievements and innovation;

(c) the introduction of comprehensive management and employee *information systems* which enable all managers and employees:

(i) to understand their planned contribution towards achieving organisational objectives;
(ii) to compare their actual achievements against their targets;

(d) *a task structure* within the organisation which stimulates employee commitment. Peters and Waterman advocate what they call 'chunking' - breaking organisational structures down into small, task-centred units.

Small organisations

1. Organisation structure, planning and control

1.1 Less rigid definition of jobs than in large organisations, and less specialisation.

1.2 Authority often centralised, although the management hierarchy will be small and all managers should feel quite close to the decision-making process.

1.3 Planning, control and communication (management information systems) will be less formal than in larger organisations.

1.4 Fewer people than in large organisations, and so lesser problems of co-ordination. Greater sense of teamwork but greater risk of disaster through personality clash.

1.5 Not so much bound by formal rules and procedures as large organisations.

1.6 Decision-making procedures are relatively fast. Decisions can be taken quickly.

2. Adapting to change

2.1 Small organisations are usually staffed by individuals who are more innovative in their ideas, and more responsive to change. Ideas for innovation and adapting to change are more accepted by the small organisation culture.

2.2 However, resources are likely to be limited for R & D, personnel, marketing etc.

3. Motivation

3.1 Individuals have a wider range of duties, and are often able to contribute more to the achievements of the organisation, compared with the achievements of individuals in large organisations.

3.2 Individuals might develop a closer sense of identity with the organisation - eg through personal association with the owner-managers.

3.3 Pay and reward systems are usually more personalised than in large organisations.

3.4 Management training and development are not encouraged as much as in large organisations.

3.5 The 'culture' in small organisations is unlikely to be bureaucratic.

4. Resources

4.1 Small businesses are considered risky investments and a small organisation's borrowing capability might be limited.

4.2 Limited resources may restrict capacity for developing new product ideas on which the organisation may have been founded.

Informal organisation

41. The structure of an organisation is affected by the people working within it, and an informal organisation exists side by side with the formal one.

The informal organisation of a company is so important that a newcomer has to 'learn the ropes' before he can settle effectively into his job, and he must also become 'accepted' by his fellow workers.

42. When people work together, they establish social relationships and customary ways of doing things, ie they:

   (a) form social groups, or cliques (sometimes acting against one another);
   (b) develop informal ways of getting things done - ie. norms and rules which are different in character from the 'organisational manual' rules which are *imposed* by the formal organisation.

   Social groups, or cliques, may act collectively for or against the interests of their company; the like-mindedness which arises in all members of the group strengthens their collective attitudes or actions.

   Whether these groups work for or against the interests of the company depends to some extent on the type of supervision they get. If superiors involve them in decision-making, they are more likely to be management-minded.

43. The informal organisation of a company, given an acceptable social atmosphere:

   (a) improves communications by means of a 'bush telegraph' system;
   (b) facilitates the co-ordination of various individuals or departments and establishes 'unwritten' methods for getting a job done.

44. Certain individuals can have an important informal influence in an organisation. To take an illustrative example, the managing director of XY Company is a very remote individual and the production and sales directors have difficulty in communicating and working with him effectively. The financial director, however, has a remarkably good personal understanding with the managing director and can approach him readily in all matters at work. The sales and production directors therefore often ask the financial director to put their views informally to the managing director and to sound out his opinion before they approach him formally.

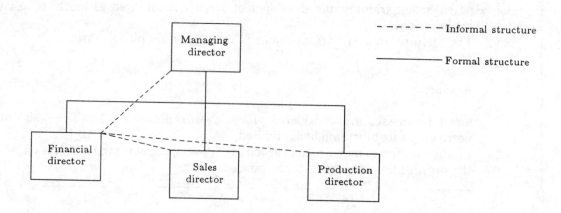

The formal organisation structure is therefore supplemented by an informal structure which improves the way in which top management sets about its job.

45. The informal structure of a company may 'take over' from the formal organisation when the formal structure is slow to adapt to change.

46. When employees are dissatisfied with aspects of formal organisation (eg they dislike the work they do or the person they work for) they are likely to rely more and more heavily on an informal organisation at work to satisfy their personal needs in their work situation. When this happens, it has been argued (by Argyris and others) that the informal organisation of the individual will act against the efficiency of the formal organisation. Informal organisations always exist within a formal organisation, and if employees are properly motivated, these informal organisations should operate to the advantage of the formal organisation's efficiency and effectiveness.

47. A conclusion might therefore be that management should seek to harness the informal organisation to operate to the benefit of the formal organisation. In practice, however, this will be difficult because unlike formal organisation, which does not change even when individual employees move into and out of jobs (by promotion, transfer, appointment, resignation or retirement etc) most informal organisations depend on individual personalities. If one member leaves, the informal organisation is no longer the same, and new informal organisations will emerge to take its place.

Authority, power and control

48. If an organisation is to function as a co-operative system of individuals, some people must have authority or power over others. Authority and power flow downward through the formal organisation.

49. By one set of definitions:

(a) authority is the right to do something, ie in an organisation it is the right of a manager to require a subordinate to do something in order to achieve the goals of the organisation. Managerial authority thus consists of:

   (i)   making decisions within the scope of one's own managerial authority;
   (ii) assigning tasks to subordinates;
   (iii) expecting and requiring satisfactory performance of these tasks from subordinates;

(b) power is distinct from authority, but is often associated with it. Whereas authority is the right to do something, power is the ability to do it.

50. Three aspects of authority developed by Hicks and Gullet ('Management') are as follows.

(a) *Responsibility and accountability* are coupled with managerial authority. When a manager is given the authority to do something, it is automatically presupposed that he has the ability to do it, the facilities that he needs and that the desired results will be achieved.

The manager is responsible for the actual results achieved, and he is held *accountable* because information about his achievements will be fed back to his superiors, and they can then call him to account to explain his performance.

(b) *Authority is subjective.* Amitai Etzioni made a study of authority and motivation in differing environments. He found that the way in which authority and power are exercised will differ according to the environment, relationships and type of subordinates.

(c) *Sources of authority.* The authority of a manager might come from one or more sources.

    (i) *Top down authority* refers to the authority conferred on a *manager* because of the position he holds in the organisation's hierarchy and the extent to which authority has been delegated. It is the official authority 'traditionally' associated with management, which goes down the scalar chain. In most organisations, top down authority combines with departmentalisation and the division of work, and does not cross departmental or sectional boundaries.

    (ii) *Bottom up authority* refers to the authority conferred on a *leader* from the people at lower levels in the organisation. Elected leaders, such as politicians and many trade union officials, have such authority, which they will be expected to exercise in the interests of the electors/members.

    (iii) *Rank.* In some organisations such as the armed forces, rank is a clear expression of authority, and orders gain credibility because they come from someone of higher rank.

    (iv) *Personal authority or charisma.* Some managers acquire authority through their personal charisma, and as a consequence are capable of influencing the behaviour of others.

    (v) *Tradition.* Some individuals acquire authority by tradition. In old established family firms, the elder members of the family might continue to be obeyed and held in respect, even after they have officially retired.

Power and influence

51. Influence is the process by which one person in an organisation, A, directs or modifies the behaviour or attitudes of another person, B. Influence can only be exerted by A on B if A has some kind of power from which the influence emanates. Power is therefore the ability to influence, whereas influence is an active process.

52. Power and influence are clearly important factors in the structure and operations of an organisation. They help to explain how work gets done. In addition, it has also been suggested that:

(a) most individuals in an organisation would like to have more influence over their work;

(b) an individual who believes he exerts some influence is likely to show greater interest in his work. The research of writers, such as Likert, who support the principle of management by participation suggests that employees may be more productive when they consider that they have some influence over planning decisions which affect their work;

(c) some individuals are motivated by the need for power (McClelland) and show great concern for exercising influence and control, and for being leaders.

53. Charles Handy (*Understanding Organisations*) identified six types of power:

- *physical power* - ie the power of superior force. Physical power is absent from most organisations (except the prison service and the armed forces), but it is often evident as an under-current in industrial relations (eg violence on the picket line or bullying on the shop floor);

- *resource power* - ie the control over resources which are valued by the individual or group to be influenced. Senior managers may have the resource power to grant promotion or pay increases to subordinates; trade unions possess the resource power to take their members out on strike;

- *position power* - ie the power which is associated with a particular job in an organisation. Handy noted that position power has certain 'hidden' benefits:

  (i)   access to information;

  (ii) the right of access: eg entitlement to membership of committees and contact with other 'powerful' individuals in the organisation;

  (iii) the right to organise conditions of working and methods of decision-making;

- *expert power* - ie the power which belongs to an individual because of his acknowledged expertise. This power can only belong to a person if others acknowledge him to be an expert. Many staff jobs in an organisation (eg computer systems analysts, organisation and methods analysts, accountants, lawyers or personnel department managers) rely on expert power to influence line management. If the expert is seen to be incompetent (eg if an accountant does not seem to provide sensible information) or if his area of expertise is not widely acknowledged (which is often the case with personnel department staff) he will have little or no expert power;

- *personal power*, or *charisma* - ie the popularity of the individual. Personal power is capable of influencing the behaviour of others, and helps to explain the strength of informal organisations;

- *negative power* is the use of disruptive attitudes and behaviour to stop things from happening. It is associated with low morale, latent conflict or frustration at work. A subordinate might refuse to communicate openly with his superior, and might provide false information; a colleague might refuse to co-operate; a typist might refuse to type an urgent letter because she is too busy; a worker might deliberately cause his machine to break down. Negative power is destructive and potentially very damaging to organisational efficiency.

54. Influence, the act of directing or modifying the behaviour of others, may then be achieved through:

  (a) the application of force, eg physical or economic power;

  (b) the establishment of rules and procedures - enforced through position and/or resource power;

  (c) bargaining and negotiation - depending on the relative strengths of each party's position, (expert, resource or personal power etc);

    (d)   persuasion, again associated with various sources of power.

55. Handy identified two further, 'unseen' methods of influence.

    (a)   *Ecology*, or the environment in which behaviour takes place. The physical environment can be altered by a manager, who may be able to regulate noise levels at work, comfort and security of working conditions, seating arrangements, the use of open-plan offices or segregation into many small offices, the physical proximity of departments as well as individuals.

> 'The design of work, the work, the structure of reward and control systems, the structure of the organisation, the management of groups and the control of conflict are all ways of managing the environment in order to influence behaviour. Let us never forget that although the environment is all around us, it is not unalterable, that to change it is to influence people, that ecology is potent, the more so because it is often unnoticed.' (*Handy*)

    (b)   *Magnetism*, ie the unseen application of personal power. 'Trust, respect, charm, infectious enthusiasm, these attributes all allow us to influence people without apparently imposing on them.'

The authority of trade union officials

56. One of the great organisational problems concerning trade unions is that of 'dual authority'. An employee works for an organisation, but may also be a member of a trade union. The employee therefore see his involvement in a union, or support for his union, to be the best means of securing his personal objectives (eg through extra pay or shorter working hours) or the employee may consider that his own goals would be furthered better by loyalty to senior managers in the organisation and acceptance of the organisation's goals.

57. Another feature of a trade union is the nature of authority of its leaders.

    (a)   Union officials are elected by the members (although some full-time officials, such as economic advisors, will be appointed from outside) and therefore derive their authority 'bottom up'.

    (b)   In some unions, officials may then exert position power and give instructions to members or junior officials.

    (c)   Shop stewards very occasionally may rely on physical power to 'bully' members on the shop floor; most shop stewards hope that members will accept their guidance as industrial relations 'experts' and therefore exert influence through expert power.

    (d)   In negotiations with management, union officials may feel compelled to resort to the threat of industrial action (a strike, 'blacking' certain work practices, a work-to-rule or go-slow etc ie to use resource power in the form of their control over the labour force, ie the support of their members). It might also be called a form of 'negative power' - ie the power to disrupt.

Delegation

58. It is generally recognised that in any large complex organisation, management must delegate some authority because:

    (a) there are physical and mental limitations to the work load of any individual or group in authority;

    (b) routine or less important decisions are therefore passed 'down the line' to subordinates, and the superior is free to concentrate on the more important aspects of the work (eg planning), which only he is competent (and paid) to do;

    (c) the increasing size and complexity of organisations calls for specialisation, both managerial and technical. This is the principle of division of work.

    However, by delegating authority to subordinates, the superior takes on the extra tasks of calling the subordinates to account for their decisions and performance, and also of co-ordinating the efforts of different subordinates.

59. When authority is delegated, the relationship between subordinate and superior is critically important. Drucker has argued that although authority is passed down to subordinates, the relationship between subordinates and superiors, and their responsibilities, have three dimensions.

    (a) Every manager has the task of contributing towards what his superior's section must do to achieve its objectives.

    (b) Every manager has a responsibility towards the organisation as a whole, and must define the activities of his own unit so as to contribute towards achieving the organisation's objectives.

    (c) Every manager has a responsibility towards his subordinates (ie to make sure they know what is expected of them, to help them set their own objectives, to help them attain their objectives, to offer counsel and advice etc).

    > 'The vision of a manager should always be upward-towards the enterprise as a whole. But his responsibility runs downwards as well to the managers on his team'. (*Drucker*)

60. Jaques (the 'Glacier investigations') found that even a *well-defined* role in the organisation posed problems for the person expected to fill it with regard to the exercise of authority. In particular, he found that in an organisation committed to consultative management, a superior may become more and more reluctant to exercise his authority. Mechanisms for *avoiding* responsibility and authority included:

    (a) the exercise of a *purely* consultative relationship with others while ignoring roles involving line authority;

    (b) misuse of formal joint consultation processes - ie. using contact between higher management and workers' representatives as an excuse to ignore responsibility for immediate subordinates. Consultation must not by-pass intervening roles in the chain of command;

    (c)   pseudo-democracy - eg. a superior, senior member on a committee asserting "I'm just an ordinary member".

One of the most important conclusions of the Glacier studies was that there is a distinctive leadership role in groups, and that members (in their roles as participants) *expect* it to be properly filled.

61. In practice many managers are reluctant to delegate and attempt to do many routine matters themselves in addition to their more important duties. Amongst the reasons for this reluctance one can commonly identify:

- low confidence and trust in the abilities of the subordinates, ie the suspicion that 'if you want it done well, you have to do it yourself';

- the burden of responsibility and accountability for the mistakes of subordinates, aggravated by (a) above;

- a desire to 'stay in touch' with the department or team - both in terms of workload and staff - particularly if the manager does not feel 'at home' in a management role, and/or misses aspects of the subordinate job, camaraderie etc;

- an unwillingness to admit that subordinates have developed to the extent that they could perform some of the manager's duties. The manager may feel threatened by this sense of 'redundancy';

- poor control and communication systems in the organisation, so that the manager feels he has to do everything himself, if he is to retain real control and responsibility for a task, and if he wants to know what is going on;

- an organisational culture that has failed to reward or recognise effective delegation by superiors, so that the manager may not realise that delegation is positively regarded (rather than a 'shirking of responsibility');

- lack of understanding of what delegation involves - ie *not* giving the subordinates total control, making the manager himself redundant etc.

62. Handy writes of a 'trust-control dilemma' in a superior-subordinate relationship, in which the sum of trust + control is a constant amount; ie

$$T + C = Y$$

where $T =$ the trust the superior has in the subordinate, and the trust which the subordinate feels the superior has in him;
          $C =$ the degree of control exercised by the superior over the subordinate;
          $Y =$ a constant, unchanging value;

Any increase in C leads to an equal decrease in T, ie if the superior retains more 'control' or authority, the subordinate will immediately recognise that he is being trusted less. If the superior wishes to show more trust in the subordinate, he can only do so by reducing C, ie by delegating more authority.

63. To overcome the reluctance of managers to delegate, it is necessary to:

    (a) provide a system of selecting subordinates who will be capable of handling delegated authority in a responsible way. If subordinates are of the right 'quality', superiors will be prepared to trust them more;

    (b) have a system of open communications, in which the superior and subordinates freely interchange ideas and information. If the subordinate is given all the information he needs to do his job, and if the superior is aware of what the subordinate is doing:

        (i)   the subordinate will make better-informed decisions;
        (ii) the superior will not 'panic' because he does not know what is going on.

    Although open lines of communication are important, they should not be used by the superior to command the subordinate in a matter where authority has been delegated to the subordinate; in other words, communication links must not be used by superiors as a means of reclaiming authority;

    (c) ensure that a system of control is established. Superiors are reluctant to delegate authority because they retain absolute responsibility for the performance of their subordinates. If an efficient control system is in operation, responsibility and accountability will be monitored at all levels of the management hierarchy, and the 'dangers' of relinquishing authority and control to subordinates are significantly lessened;

    (d) reward effective delegation by superiors and the efficient assumption of authority by subordinates. Rewards may be given in terms of pay, promotion, status, official approval etc.

64. We will discuss further aspects of authority and delegation in our chapter on the structures and cultures of organisations. First, however, we will get a brief overview of organisation theory.

INTRODUCTION TO ORGANISATION THEORY

Points to be covered

- Scientific management
- Human relations or 'behaviouralist' school of thought
- Systems approach
- Socio-technical systems approach
- Other approaches

Introduction

1. We shall consider the development of management and organisation theory. We will look at three main schools of thought on this subject:

   (a) the 'classical school' of management thought, which arose out of the industrial revolution and the age of the great industrial barons in the United States;

   (b) the 'behaviouralist' school;

   (c) the systems school.

   Each school of thought contributed to an understanding of the nature of organisations and the management of them.

2. The history of management thinking must be studied with a clear idea in your mind about what it was primarily trying to achieve. Writers on management and organisation hold the view that if certain principles of management or organisation are put into practice, then the management will be more successful in ensuring that the objectives of the organisation are achieved, and in an efficient manner. Their aim was (and still is) effectiveness and efficiency in the use of resources to achieve organisational goals.

3. The different schools of thought had different ideas as to how this aim could be achieved:

   (a) The scientific management or classical school believed that the solution would be achieved by:

      (i) a scientific analysis of the work done and the development of improved methods by the application, perhaps, of management techniques (work study etc); or by

      (ii) applying certain principles of organisation to create the organisation's structure, and applying certain principles of management.

(b) The human behaviour school of thought emerged out of the belief that scientific management did not properly recognise the potential of individual employees. The work given to employees, in their view, usually failed to make use of their talents. Employees are the greatest potential source of improvements in organisational efficiency and effectiveness because they are capable of putting their talents to much better use. Motivating employees to use their talents fully, and giving them work which will give them ample scope to express these talents, is therefore the key to better organisational performances.

(c) The systems school of thought emerged out of the belief that not enough consideration was being given to the importance of:

(i) proper *co-ordination* between different people within an organisation;

(ii) the relationships between an organisation and its *external environment*.

Efficient work methods and the effective motivation of employees will not create a successful organisation if either:

(i) the work done by one person or department is not consistent with the work done by others, so that the efforts of people within the organisation pull in different directions and there is 'sub-optimisation'; or

(ii) the organisation fails to respond to changes in its environment. For example, it must respond to changes in the needs of its customers, the activities of competitors, the supply of raw materials and labour.

4. Each school of thought has provided a valuable contribution to the practice of management, although there is still a long way to go before the different theories are successfully consolidated, and theory applied universally in practice.

Scientific management and FW Taylor

5. Frederick W Taylor (1856 - 1917) pioneered the *scientific management* movement. He argued that management should be based on 'well-recognised, clearly defined and fixed principles, instead of depending on more or less hazy ideas'.

6. His purpose was to maximise efficiency and he suggested that by offering workers more money for being efficient, both the workers and employers would benefit. Instead of arguing about how profits should be divided between them, workers and employers together should work for greater efficiency and productivity, so that there are more profits to share out.

7. Productivity would not be improved by the offer of more money alone, and Taylor argued that a radical change of attitudes, on the part of both management and workers, was essential if his system were to be successful.

'The great mental revolution that takes place in the mental attitude of the two parties under scientific management is that both parties take their eyes off the division of the surplus as the all-important matter, and together turn their attention toward increasing the size of the surplus until this surplus becomes so large that it is unnecessary to quarrel about how it should be divided. They come to see that when they stop pulling against one another, and instead both turn and push shoulder to shoulder in the same direction, the size of the surplus created by their joint effort is truly astounding. They both realise that when they substitute friendly co-operation and mutual helpfulness for antagonism and strife, they are together able to make this surplus so enormously greater than it was in the past that there is ample room for a large increase in wages for the workmen and an equally great increase in profits for the manufacturer.'

8. His famous four principles of scientific management were:

(a) the development of a true science of work: all knowledge which had hitherto been kept in the heads of workmen should be gathered and recorded by management. 'Every single subject, large and small, becomes the question for scientific investigation, for reduction to law.' Very simply, he argued that management should apply techniques to the solution of problems and should not rely on experience and 'seat-of-the-pants' judgements;

(b) the scientific selection and progressive development of workmen: workmen should be carefully trained and given jobs to which they are best suited. Although 'training' is an important element in his principles of management, 'nurturing' might be a more apt description of his ideas of worker development;

(c) the bringing together of the science and the scientifically selected and trained men: the application of techniques to decide what should be done, using workmen who are both properly trained and willing to maximise output, should result in maximum productivity;

(d) the constant and intimate co-operation between management and workers: 'the relations between employers and men form without question the most important part of this art.'

9. The four principles should be applied together; unfortunately, it is possible to apply 'scientific management' techniques in order to improve productivity, without training the workforce or paying them for the improvement in output. This resulted in great hostility from trade union leaders, who condemned scientific management as a means of overworking the labour force and reducing the number of jobs. Taylor was eventually obliged to defend his ideas before a committee of the US House of Representatives in 1912.

10. It is useful to consider an application of Taylor's principles. In testimony to the House of Representatives Committee, Taylor used as an example the application of scientific management methods to shovelling work at the Bethlehem Steel Works:

(a) Facts were first gathered by management as to the number of shovel loads handled by each man each day, with particular attention paid to the relationship between weight of the average shovel load and the total load shifted per day. From these facts, management was able to decide on the ideal shovel size for each type of material handled in order to optimise the speed of shovelling work done. Thus, scientific technique was applied to deciding how work should be organised.

(b) By organising work a day in advance, it was possible to minimise the idle time and the moving of men from one place in the shovelling yard to another. Once again, scientific method replaces 'seat-of-the-pants' decisions by supervisors.

(c) Workers were paid for accepting the new methods and 'norms' and received 60% higher wages than those given to similar workers in other companies in the area.

(d) Workers were carefully selected and trained in the art of shovelling properly; anyone falling below the required norms consistently was given special teaching to improve his performance.

(e) 'The new way is to teach and help your men as you would a brother; to try to teach him the best way and to show him the easiest way to do his work. This is the new mental attitude of the management towards the men....'

(f) At the Bethlehem Steel Works, Taylor said, the costs of implementing this method were more than repaid by the benefits. The labour force required fell from 400 - 600 men to 140 men for the same work.

11. A summary of scientific management, in Taylor's own words, might be:

- 'The man who is fit to work at any particular trade is unable to understand the science of that trade without the kindly help and co-operation of men of a totally different type of education.'

- 'It is one of the principles of scientific management to ask men to do things in the right way, to learn something new, to change their ways in accordance with the science and in return to receive an increase of from 30% to 100% in pay....'

It should now be clear why Taylor is regarded as a pioneer in the work study techniques described in an earlier chapter.

Other writers of the scientific management movement

12. Early supporters of the principles of scientific management included the following writers:

(a) *Frank and Lillian Gilbreth.* A husband and wife team, they did much work in advancing the techniques of time and motion study (work study). As an example, Frank Gilbreth made a study of 'wasted motions' ie physical movements which are unnecessary to get a job done – and he was able in one case to reduce the number of motions in bricklaying from 18 to 5, thereby doubling productivity without the need for an increase in effort. Lillian Gilbreth was an industrial psychologist, and her interest in human attitudes at work was blended with her husband's concern for efficiency.

(b) *Harrington Emerson* was a leading advocate of standards and standardisation.

(c) *Henry Gantt*, as associate of Taylor, did much work on the scientific selection of workmen, their training and development, and the formulation of incentive bonus schemes. Gantt is best-known for his development of the bar chart (Gantt chart) in which the time-relationship of activities in an overall project are depicted and time-critical activities can be identified. This was a fore-runner of network and critical path analysis and project evaluation and review techniques (PERT).

(d)   *Carl Georg Barth*, also an associate of Taylor, developed many mathematical techniques and formulae for application in management.

13.   The areas of interest of these writers/management consultants may help to give some indication as to the nature and emphasis of scientific management.

Henri Fayol (1841-1925)

14.   Fayol, a French industrialist, was another early writer associated with the classical school of management thought, and popularised the concept of 'universality of management principles'. He was a pioneer of *modern operational management theory* although his work was not published in the USA until 1949.

15.   His 'principles' allowed for flexibility in their application: 'Seldom do we have to apply the same principle twice in identical conditions; allowance must be made for different changing circumstances'.

16.   Fayol argued that as managers rise up the 'scalar chain', or organisation hierarchy, they need to show an increasing amount of managerial ability. For top executives, management ability is of paramount importance; however, when he wrote, there were no accepted theories or principles of management and there was no concept of training to be a manager. This was a gap which Fayol set out to close.

17.   Applying the principles of management is a 'difficult art requiring intelligence, experience, decision and proportion'. Among these principles, he listed the following:

(a)   *division of work* ie specialisation. The object of specialisation is to produce more and obtain better results;

(b)   *authority and responsibility*: Fayol distinguished between a manager's official authority (deriving from his office) and personal authority (deriving from his experience, moral worth, intelligence etc).

'Authority should be commensurate with responsibility', in other words the holder of an office should have enough authority to carry out all the responsibilities assigned to him.

He also suggested that 'generally speaking, responsibility is feared as much as authority is sought after, and fear or responsibility paralyses much initiative and destroys many good qualities'.

A good leader should encourage those around him to accept responsibility;

(c)   *discipline*: 'the state of discipline of any group of people depends essentially on the worthiness of its leaders'. A fair disciplinary system, with penalties judiciously applied by worthy superiors, can be a chief strength of an organisation;

(d)   *unity of command*: for any action, a subordinate should receive orders from one boss only. 'This rule seems fundamental to me...' Fayol saw dual command as a disease, whether it is caused by imperfect demarcation between departments, or by a superior $S2$ giving orders to an employee, E, without going via the intermediate superior, $S1$.

(This 'principle' immediately gives rise to problems concerning the role of 'staff' as opposed to 'line' management.)

(e) *unity of direction*: there should be one head and one plan for each activity. Unity of direction relates to the organisation itself, whereas unity of command relates to the personnel in the organisation;

(f) the interest of one employee or group of employees should not prevail over that of the general interest of the organisation;

(g) remuneration of personnel should be fair, satisfying both employer and employee alike;

(h) *scalar chain*: the scalar chain is the term used to describe the chain of superiors from lowest to highest rank. Formal communication is up and down the lines of authority, eg E to D to C to B to A. If, however, communication between different branches of the chain is necessary (eg D to H) the use of a 'gangplank' of horizontal communication saves time and is likely to be more accurate.

Scalar chains:

ABCDE
ABJL
ABJM
AFGHI
AFKN
AFKOP

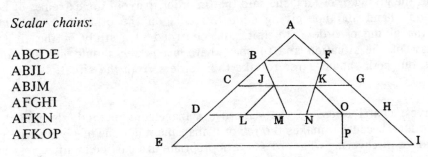

Fayol criticised government departments for making insufficient use of the 'gangplank'. By this, he meant that subordinates refer too many problems up the scalar chain to their boss because the problem involves a person in another section or department. Instead, the subordinate could contact the other person directly and ask for a joint solution to the problem. In the diagram here, if C has a problem which affects G, instead of referring it up to B (who might then refer it to A) C could cross the 'gangplank' - ie communicate horizontally - with G. The problem might then be solved jointly by C and G;

(i) *stability of tenure of personnel*: 'It has often been recorded that a mediocre manager who stays is infinitely preferable to outstanding managers who merely come and go';

(j) *esprit de corps*: personnel must not be split up. 'In union, there is strength.' Verbal communication is preferable to written communication which is frequently abused, causing friction between departments;

(k) *initiative*: 'it is essential to encourage and develop this capacity to the full';

(l) *centralisation*: although he did not use the term 'centralisation' of authority, Fayol argued that circumstances would dictate whether overall efficiency would be optimised by concentrating or by dispersing authority.

18. Fayol considered the main elements of management to be planning, organising, commanding, co-ordinating and controlling. His writings were based on his own experience as a top manager in industry, and he spent some thirty years as managing director of a large French mining and engineering combine.

19. He himself would probably not have accepted the view, held by many other people who have adopted his principles, that there is such a thing as a universal manager who can manage any type of organisation with equal success. While he said that the need for technical knowledge decreases with a rise in the management hierarchy, he felt that even top managers could not depend on administrative skills alone. In fact, in discussing the qualities needed by top management, he gave administrative ability a weight of only 50% in the case of a manager of a very large firm, and only 25% in the case of a small firm top executive.

Mary Parker Follett (1868 - 1933)

20. Mary Parker Follett saw management as a continuous process rather than a series of discrete events.

21. She suggested that in any industrial organisation everyone in the organisation should have a rational appreciation of what is required by the situation. When applying the idea to one aspect of management, the giving of orders, she said that in order to avoid the extremes of being too bossy on the one hand and not giving enough orders on the other, 'My solution is to depersonalise the giving of orders, to unite all concerned in a study of the situation....to discover the law of the situation and to obey that....*one person* should not give orders to another *person*, but both should agree to take their orders from the situation.'

22. One of the largest contributions of the scientific management method, she added, was to depersonalise orders, because it makes the job of management not one of giving orders, but of devising methods of discovering what orders are appropriate to a particular situation – and both managers and employees must then follow the dictates of the situation they find revealed. She postulated four fundamental principles of organisation:

    (a) co-ordination by direct contact;
    (b) co-ordination in the early stages;
    (c) co-ordination as the 'reciprocal relating' of all factors in a situation;
    (d) co-ordination as a continuing process.

23. She believed that differences could be made to contribute to the common cause. The leader must regard his job as being concerned with drawing out the abilities and contributions of individual members. He must know how to create a group power rather than express a personal power. Her work is illustrative of a growing interest in industrial psychology and 'personnel management'.

Refinements to the scientific management school of thought

24. Perhaps in response to the development of the human relations school of management thought (see later) proponents of scientific management continued to develop their ideas.

25. L F Urwick based much of his analysis on the work of Taylor, Follett and, particularly, Henri Fayol. From these early writers, Urwick has created a number of principles of good organisation:

    (a) *the principle of specialisation*: as far as possible, each individual should perform a single function only;

(b) *the principle of authority*: there should be clear lines of authority from the top to each individual;

(c) *the principle of definition*: the duties, authority and responsibility of each position, and its relationships with other positions, should be defined in writing and made known to everyone concerned;

(d) *the principle of correspondence*: authority should be commensurate with responsibility;

(e) *the principle of span of control*: managers should not control more than five or six subordinates with interlocking responsibilities.

26. Urwick considers that a leader has four basic functions:
    (a) he embodies and represents the organisation he serves;
    (b) he initiates thought and action;
    (c) he administers routine;
    (d) he interprets to others the purpose or meaning of what is done.

The contribution of scientific management to management theory

27. The 'classical' school of management thought is associated mainly with the work of Taylor and Fayol. Their contributions were:

    (a) to introduce techniques in order to study the nature of work and solve the problem of how to organise work better (Taylor, Gantt, Gilbreth etc);

    (b) to suggest a theory of organisation and management, based largely on formal structures, ie clear lines of authority, distinguishing line and staff management, organisation charts etc. (Fayol).

28. Their concept of organisation was essentially a mechanistic one; workers were to be given instructions, and no choice in their method of working. Nevertheless, the classical school provided theories where none had hitherto existed, and they provided a basis from which subsequent theories were able to proliferate.

> 'By the end of the scientific management period, the worker has been reduced to the role of an impersonal cog in the machine of production. His work became more and more narrowly specialised until he had little appreciation for his contribution to the total product... Although very significant technological advances were made....the serious weakness of the scientific approach to management was that it de-humanised the organisational member who became a person without emotion and capable of being scientifically manipulated, just like machines'. (*Hicks*)

Conclusion: scientific management

29. The preceding paragraphs have introduced scientific management theory. Many of the ideas, described briefly, will be re-introduced in greater detail in later chapters. For the moment, the scientific management approach may be summarised as follows.

(a) An organisation should be an alliance of management and workers, to increase efficiency and productivity, so as to improve profitability.

(b) Management should contribute towards this greater efficiency by the application of scientific techniques, and certain principles of management.

(c) The attitude of workers should not be ignored, and attention must be given to industrial psychology. Human attitudes began to attract increasing attention from management theorists, so that a sociological approach to management and the behavioural school of thought began to emerge as an alternative to scientific management.

The human relations school or behaviouralist school of management thought

30. In the period from about 1930 a school of management thought developed, emphasising the importance of human relationships in organisations. In many ways, it was a reaction against the de-humanising aspects of the scientific management school of thought. (Note: 'de-humanising' refers not so much to the thinking of Taylor himself, but to the tendency of scientific management techniques to be introduced without the co-operation and approval of the workforce.)

31. Elton Mayo was perhaps the most important contributor to this school of thought, as a result of his experiments at the Hawthorne plant of Western Electric Company (known as the 'Hawthorne experiments'). These experiments will be described in a later chapter, but it is worth mentioning Mayo's conclusions here.

32. He found that when a group of workers were consulted by management, and participated in the determination of working methods and conditions, their productivity increased. Motivation to work was greatly influenced by social relations among the workers and their relationship with their supervisor. These factors were more important than those on which scientific management theorists would lay emphasis, such as improved lighting and more comfortable working conditions.

> 'We have failed to train students in the study of social situations; we have thought that first-class technical training was sufficient in a modern and mechanical age. As a consequence we are technically competent as no other age in history has been; and we combine this with utter social incompetence. This defect of education and administration has of recent years become a menace to the whole future of civilisation. The administrator of the future must be able to understand the human-social facts for what they actually are, unfettered by his own emotion or prejudice. He cannot achieve this ability except by careful training - a training that must include knowledge of relevant technical skills, of the systematic ordering of operations, and of the organisation of co-operation.' (*Mayo*)

33. Human attitudes and behaviour have been investigated in great detail by many subsequent writers, notably McGregor, Likert, Blake and Mouton, Maslow, Herzberg and Fiedler. The contributions of these theorists are described elsewhere in this text.

Drucker's comparison of scientific management and the human relations school of thought

34. Drucker made some very interesting and useful comments on both the scientific management and human relations schools of thought. Remember, however, that since he wrote his comments further work has been carried out, and new ideas have emerged.

35. His comments about scientific management are as follows.

   (a) Scientific management has contributed a philosophy of worker and work. 'As long as industrial society endures, we shall never lose again the insight that human work can be studied systematically, can be analysed, can be improved by work on its elementary parts. Like all great insights, it was simplicity itself'.

   (b) However, it is capable of providing solutions to management problems only up to a certain point, and it seems incapable of providing significant further developments in future. 'Scientific management....has been stagnant for a long time....During the last thirty years, it has given us little but pedestrian and wearisome tomes on the techniques, if not on the gadgets, of narrower and narrower specialities....The reason for this is that scientific management, despite all its worldly success, has not succeeded in solving the problem of managing worker and work. As so often happens in the history of ideas, its insight is only half an insight'.

   (c) One major weakness of scientific management is that by breaking work down into its elementary parts, and analysing a job as a series of consecutive 'motions', the solution to management problems often provided is that each separate 'motion' within the entire job should be done by a separate worker.

   This is a mistake. It is correct to analyse work into its constituent parts, but it is wrong to create jobs for each different part. 'It is possible that Taylor himself saw the need to integrate...But practically all other writers - and all practitioners - see in the individual motion the essence of good work organisation'.

   The boring nature of assembly-line work is the most obvious example of Drucker's criticism - and one which you are no doubt familiar with. It is much more satisfying to assemble a whole motor car than to be given a single part of the overall job, eg paint spraying. Scientific management therefore assumes that the human being, organised in a specific way to specific tasks, is a (poorly designed) 'machine tool'.

   Drucker concluded that in doing a work task 'every one of the operations should be analysed by means of scientific management to the point where they can be done by unskilled people. But the operations must be integrated again into a job'.

   (d) A further criticism of scientific management is that it divorces planning work from doing the work. 'The divorce of planning from doing reflects a dubious and dangerous philosophical concept of an elite which has a monopoly on esoteric knowledge entitling it to manipulate the unwashed peasantry'.

   It is perfectly correct to realise that a job will be done better if it is properly planned beforehand. This is a significant contribution of scientific management. Drucker's objection was that the people who do the planning beforehand should be the people who later do the job itself. 'Planning and doing are separate parts of the same job; they are not separate jobs'.

36. Drucker concluded that his criticisms of scientific management explain the resistance to change in work practices which is often found amongst workers. 'Because the worker is supposed to do rather than to know - let alone to plan - every change represents the challenge of the incomprehensible and therefore threatens his psychological security'.

37. In contrast, the human relations theory of management starts out with the right basic concepts - that people want to work; management's task is therefore to get the best out of them; and to do so, work must not be organised as a series of unrelated activities. However, at the time of writing (1955) Drucker argued that:

    (a) 'Human relations, at least in the form in which it exists thus far, is primarily a negative contribution. It freed management from the domination of viciously wrong ideas, but it did not succeed in substituting new concepts'.

    (Note: the work of theorists such as Herzberg and Likert came later).

    (b) Human relations thinking, whilst recognising the importance of work groups (Roethlisberger and Dickson pioneered this work) did not properly recognise that some groups might have their own separate interests and objectives. The most significant reason for Drucker's criticism was the failure to recognise the 'political' and 'visionary' interests of trade unions.

    (c) Human relations thinking tends to emphasise the importance of work to the workers without properly considering the economic advantages of their recommended approach to the organisation itself. There is still no *clearly proven* link between motivation and either productivity or the effective achievement of organisational goals.

    (d) In practice, human relations thinking might be used to 'manipulate' employees, and Drucker believed that there was a possibility that it would be used as 'a mere tool for justifying management's action, a device to 'sell' whatever management is doing. It is no accident that there is so much talk in human relations about 'giving workers a sense of responsibility' and so little about their responsibility, so much emphasis on the 'feeling of importance' and so little making them and their work important. This criticism was later echoed by McGregor in his analysis of Theory X and Theory Y management.

    The difficulty of applying human relations ideas in practice remains an apparently insuperable practical problem for many managements, which are simply reluctant to do anything more than pay lip service to the principles.

38. It might also be added that the principles of human relations thinking have not yet been successfully introduced in the *management* 'hierarchy' of many organisations, and yet they are intended to apply to *workers* as well as to junior managers. Clearly, there is still a long way to go, even today.

The systems approach

39. There is no universally accepted definition of a 'system', although Ludvig von Bertalanffy, a pioneer of general system theory in the 1930s, said it is 'an organised or complex whole' and 'organised complexity'. Alternatively, it is 'an entity which consists of interdependent parts', so that system theory is concerned with the attributes and relationships of these inter-acting parts.

40. General system theory makes a distinction between open and closed systems.

    (a) A *closed system* is a system which is isolated from its environment and independent of it, so that no environmental influences affect the behaviour of the system - ie. the way it operates (nor does the system exert any influence on its environment).

    (b) An *open system* is a system connected to and interacting with its environment. It takes in influences (or 'energy') from its environment, ie. inputs (and outputs from other systems) and through a series of activities, converts these inputs into outputs (or inputs into other systems). In other words it influences its environment by its behaviour. An open system is a stable system which is nevertheless continually changing or evolving. All social systems are open systems.

    Inputs to the organisation include labour, finance, raw materials, components, equipment and information. Outputs include information, services provided, goods produced etc.

41. The organisation 'open system' must remain sensitive to its external environment, with which it is in constant interaction: it must respond to threats and opportunities, restrictions and challenges posed by markets, consumer trends, competitors, the government etc. Changes in input will influence output.

42. A system might keep an unchanging state, or it might change. A 'homeostatic' system is one which remains static, but in order to do so, has to react to its own dynamic elements and also to a dynamic environment. It must make internal adjustments so as to remain the same. A 'dynamic' open system is one which transforms inputs from the environment so as to be continually changing (growing or shrinking).

43. For a business, homeostasis would not mean keeping an absolutely steady state, but would mean that the business has a 'dynamic or moving equilibrium', so that it is continually adjusting (eg. to changes in customer demand or raw material supply), without necessarily growing in size or changing radically in character.

44. An organisation is not simply a structure: the organisation chart reflects only one sub-system of the overall organisation. Trist and his associates at the Tavistock Institute have suggested that an organisation is a 'structured sociotechnical system', ie. it consists of at least 3 sub-systems:

    • a structure;

    • a technological system (concerning the work to be done, and the machines, tools and other facilities available to do it); and

    • a social system (concerning the people within the organisation, the ways they think and the ways they interact with each other).

45. The systems model therefore emphasises the interdependence of the component parts comprising the system: one facet can rarely be changed without impacting on another.

46. Systems may also be classified according to a hierarchy of 'levels' or properties.

    (a) A *deterministic* system is one in which various states or activities follow on from each other in a completely predictable way. A fully-automated production process is one example.

    (b) A *probabalistic* or *stochastic* system is one in which, although some states or activities can be predicted with certainty, others will occur with varying degrees of probability.

    (c) A *self-organising* system is one which adapts and reacts to a stimulus. The way in which it adapts is uncertain and the same input to the system will not always produce the same output (response). Social and psychological systems come within this category; an example within a company would be the subsystem of management/trade union relations.

The contribution of the systems approach

47. General systems theory can contribute to the principles and practice of management in several ways, not least by enabling managers to learn from the experience of experts and researchers in other disciplines.

    (a) It draws attention to the *dynamic* aspects of organisation, and the factors influencing the growth and development of all its sub-systems.

    (b) It creates an awareness of sub-systems, each with potentially conflicting goals which must be integrated. *Sub-optimisation* (ie. where sub-systems pursue their own goals to the detriment of the system as a whole) is a feature of organisational behaviour.

    (c) It focuses attention on interrelationships between aspects of the organisation, and between it and its environment, ie. the needs of the system as a whole: management should not get so bogged down in detail and small political arenas that they lose sight of the overall objectives and processes.

    (d) It teaches managers to reject the deterministic idea that A will always cause B to happen. 'Linear causality' may occur, but only rarely, because of the unpredictability and uncontrollability of many inputs.

    (e) The importance of the *environment* on a system is acknowledged. One product of this may be customer orientation, which Peters and Waterman note is an important cultural element of successful, adaptive companies.

48. Like any other approach, managers should take what they find useful in practice in the systems view, without making a 'religion' of it.

49. Systems theory has been developed over the years, and still contributes greatly to management science. Katz and Kahn are leading researchers into social systems (such as business organisations). They wrote:

> 'Social structures are essentially contrived systems. They are made by men and are imperfect systems. They can come apart at the seams overnight, but they can also outlast by centuries the biological organisms which created them. The cement which holds them together is essentially psychological rather than biological. Social systems are anchored in the attitudes, perceptions, beliefs, motivations, habits and expectations of human beings. Such systems represent patterns of relationships in which the constancy of the individual units involved in the relationships can be very low. An organisation can have a very high rate of turnover and still persist. The relationship of items, rather than the items themselves, provides the consistency.'

50. The systems school has developed and extended the views of the behaviouralists, and suggests that:

    (a) the efficiency or inefficiency of an organisation depends on the structure of the system or organisation, rather than on the characters of individual people who work in the system;

    (b) an organisation should be viewed as a complex whole of inter-acting parts, and as isolated units or groups wherein human attitudes prevail.

51. In addition to emphasising the importance of co-ordination through planning and control as a management task, the systems school of thought also drew attention to the influence of the organisation's environment on the way in which the organisation operates. Management, when making their planning, co-ordinating and control decisions, must have regard to the way in which changes in the business environment might affect:

    (a) their sources of supply for resources such as materials, labour, machine technology and money (finance);

    (b) the way in which they carry out their operations; or

    (c) the way in which the objectives of the organisation can best be achieved (eg the type of products or services it sells or the markets where it tries to sell them might need to change; or the rewards to shareholders might need to be reduced so as to provide greater rewards to employees).

The socio-technical systems approach

52. An important development of the systems school of thought has been the socio-technical systems school. This will be described more fully in the next chapter. Briefly, however, the approach is normally associated with the work in Britain in the 1950s of Eric Trist of the Tavistock Institute.

53. Trist put forward the view that the behaviour of groups or individuals within an organisation is significantly affected by the technology employed within the organisation (ie the equipment used, and the methods of working which follow on from the use of this equipment). The technology

of the organisation interacts with the social system and human behaviour within the organisation. (In systems theory, both the technology and also the social inter-relationships between employees, employees and management etc are sub-systems of the overall system - ie the organisation. Their inter-relationships should therefore be studied and co-ordinated in a way which ensures the most efficient and effective use of the organisation's resources).

Other approaches to management and organisation theory

54. Three basic approaches to organisation theory and management theory have now been described, ie the scientific management school, the behaviouralist school and the systems school of thought. A wider variety of approaches to management theory could be listed, and Koontz, O'Donnell and Weihrich identified eleven approaches:

  (a) *the empirical, or case approach*: management is studied from past experience in individual case histories. Generalisations are then drawn from the individual cases. This being so, the empirical approach is often used to support a more theoretical approach;

  (b) *the interpersonal behaviour approach*: this is the study of human interactions within the organisation, and is based on the belief that a knowledge of interpersonal relations will help managers to motivate their subordinates to do their work better. The approach can be criticised as narrow-minded, and cannot explain all of organisation behaviour nor can it provide a comprehensive theory or science of management;

  (c) *the group behaviour and organisation behaviour approach*: this is a form of interpersonal behaviour theory which concentrates on the attitudes and motivation of work groups. The importance of work groups has already been described;

  (d) *the co-operative social systems approach*, as conceived by Barnard;

  (e) *the systems approach* is a development from the early work of Barnard, but places greater emphasis on the properties of 'systems' and rules of systems behaviour. General systems theory (GST) was pioneered by a biologist, von Bertalanffy, but the later work of Katz and Kahn has already been mentioned;

  (f) *the socio-technical systems approach*;

  (g) *the decision theory approach, or 'behavioural' decision theory*. Writers such as March and Simon emphasised the importance of the inter-reaction and co-ordination between organisational units (ie an organisation is a complex web of interlocking structures). Decision theorists may analyse the person or groups who make decisions, the decision process, or the decision itself;

  (h) *the mathematical or 'management science' approach*: this approach takes the view that management is a task which can be aided by mathematical formulae and models (eg operational research, simulation). This approach is concerned with techniques, and does not provide an overall concept of management or organisation theory;

  (i) *the contingency or situational approach*: this approach to organisation theory is an important one, supported by writers such as C B Handy. Essentially, it takes the view of 'different horses for different courses' - ie what managers should do in practice will depend on the particular circumstances or situation he is in; similarly, the optimal organisational structure will depend on the individual circumstances or situation of the organisation.

Size is not the only factor which will affect the optimal structure of the organisation. Handy identified history and ownership, technology, goals and objectives, the environment and the people involved as other contributory factors.

This approach is an important one because it rejects the belief, which is inherent in scientific management especially, that there is a universally correct answer to a given problem in every case whenever and wherever it crops up. The problem which follows on from this rejection of a universally correct answer, however, becomes one of identifying what solution would appear to be the best one to solve an organisation or management problem in given circumstances. Contingency theory draws heavily on the contributions of other schools of thought to develop solutions to specific problems in specific circumstances.

Conclusions may be drawn from a study of general principles, about what type of organisation or style of management appears to be best for different situations, but specific conclusions should be reached with care and caution;

(j) *the managerial roles approach* is to observe what managers actually do, and from this draw conclusions about what their jobs (or roles) are. Mintzberg moved away from the traditional view that the functions of management are planning, organising, co-ordinating and controlling, and suggested that management fills ten roles:

   (i) *inter-personal roles*:

      1 the role as figurehead (to perform ceremonial and social duties as the organisation's representative);
      2 the role as leader (of men);
      3 the role of liaison, especially with people outside the organisation;

   (ii) *informational roles*:

      4 receiving information about performance of the organisation's operations;
      5 passing on information (to subordinates etc);
      6 transmitting information outside the organisation;

   (iii) *decision roles*:

      7 taking entrepreneurial decisions;
      8 handling disturbances;
      9 allocating resources to get jobs done;
      10 negotiating (with persons or groups of people);

   Koontz, O'Donnell and Weihrich criticise Mintzberg's view of management as being incomplete, since it excludes various key management tasks, such as those of structuring the organisation, determining strategies and selecting and appraising managers;

(k) *the operational approach* to the study of management draws on the ideas of all ten preceding approaches, but takes the view that management theory should be formulated by looking at the operational tasks which are carried out by managers - ie planning, organising, staffing, leading, controlling and co-ordination.

THE STRUCTURE AND CULTURES OF ORGANISATIONS

Points to be covered

- Centralisation and decentralisation
- Line and staff management
- The span of control
- Departmentation
- The contingency approach to organisation structure
- Matrix organisation
- Culture
- The cultures/structures approach to organisation
- The adaptive organisation
- The socio-technological systems approach to organisation: Trist, Woodward

Introduction

1. In this chapter we shall briefly look at *formal* organisation structure and consider a variety of views of how this structure might be established so as to optimise the efficiency of the organisation. An efficient organisation may be defined as:

    (a) a 'high-performing' organisation; or

    (b) an organisation whose structure lends itself most readily to ensuring that employees work effectively for the achievement of their own and the organisation's goals.

Centralisation and decentralisation

2. Centralisation and decentralisation refer to the degree to which authority is delegated in an organisation - and therefore the *level* at which decisions are taken in the management hierachy.

3. Complete centralisation would mean that no authority at all was exercised by subordinates; complete decentralisation would mean that *all* authority was exercised by subordinates. It is doubtful whether any organisation approaches to either of these extremes.

    In the following paragraphs, we shall use the term 'centralisation' to mean a greater degree of central control, and 'decentralisation' to mean a greater degree of delegated authority.

The advantages and disadvantages of centralisation

4. The advantages of centralisation are as follows.

    (a) Senior management can exercise greater control over the activities of the organisation and co-ordinate their subordinates more easily.

    (b) Procedures can be standardised throughout the organisation.

    (c) Senior managers can make decisions from the point of view of the organisation as a whole, whereas subordinates might tend to make decisions from the point of view of their own department or section.

    (d) Centralised control enables an organisation to maintain a balance between different functions or departments, eg. where a company has only a limited amount of funds available.

    (e) Senior managers are theoretically more experienced and skilful in making decisions, so centralised decisions should be better in 'quality' than decentralised decisions by less experienced subordinates.

    (f) Centralised management will often be cheaper, in terms of managerial overheads. When authority is delegated, there is often a duplication of management effort at lower levels of the hierarchy. To avoid such costs some specialised departments (eg data processing or personnel) may remain centralised.

5. Some delegation is necessary in all large organisations because of the limitations to the physical and mental capacity of senior managers. A greater degree of decentralisation, ie over and above the 'minimum' which is essential, has the following advantages.

    (a) It reduces the stress and burdens of senior management.

    (b) It may provide subordinates with greater job satisfaction by giving them more say in decision-making which affects their work.

    (c) Subordinates may have a better knowledge of 'local' conditions affecting their area of work and may therefore be capable of informed decision-making.

    (d) Delegation should allow greater flexibility, a quicker response to changing conditions, and speedier decision-making: problems do not have to be referred up a scalar chain of command to senior managers for a decision.

    (e) Management at middle and junior levels are 'groomed' for eventual senior management positions, because they are given the necessary experience of decision-making.

Alfred Sloan

6. Sloan's ideas were first developed in General Motors and Du Pont in the United States. He recognised the interaction of technical, financial and personal factors in the management of large enterprises and the value of having an organisational structure that took account of this interaction. He also recognised that the major problem which faces any large multi-operational enterprise is the appropriate degree of centralisation or decentralisation of decision-making authority.

7. Sloan recognised that centralisation and decentralisation are not mutually exclusive, but that an organisation should find the right combination between freedom for its divisions and control over them. He considered his executives needed motivation and opportunity, and chose decentralisation wherever possible, provided *co-ordination* remained intact.

> 'From decentralisation we get initiative, responsibility, development of personnel, decisions close to the facts, flexibility – in short, all the qualities necessary for an organisation to adapt to new conditions. From co-ordination we get efficiences and economies. It must be apparent that co-ordinated decentralisation is not an easy concept to apply'.

8. Sloan's solution to the problem in General Motors was related to committee work and good communications. A continuous series of meetings took place in the organisation with the objectives of:

- agreeing long-term plans;
- agreeing short-term plans;
- comparing achievement with plans;
- setting objectives and goals.

Information was designed to flow up and down the organisation to ensure that all decentralised objectives were compatible with, and a part of, the total corporate objective.

9. This communication system removed one of the principal organisational dilemmas. Group directors and national directors were committed to the same goals. Decentralisation did not create confused objectives.

Divisional managers made all decisions affecting the operations of their own divisions, but:

(a) their decisions had to be in conformity with the organisation's general policies;

(b) they had to report their results to central managers;

(c) they had to 'sell' changes in operating policy to central management, and had to be prepared to accept advice from the 'general officers' at headquarters about desirable changes.

10. Whatever system is set up, it is of paramount importance that all managers at all levels should clearly know where they fit into the organisation. They should know the nature and extent of their authority and responsibility and that of fellow managers at all levels. Managers can then exercise as much authority and carry as much responsibility as possible within the constraints of the policies set by the organisation and the commitments they have made to their own superior executive.

The contingency theory of delegation

11* The contingency theory states that the degree of centralisation or decentralisation which would be most appropriate for an organisation will depend on the particular situation of that organisation.

12. The *market environment* of the organisation is an important variable. If the organisation is faced with rapid change, and therefore uncertainty in decision-making, there will be a greater reliance on local knowledge of events and 'on-the-spot' decisions, so there should be greater decentralisation than in a relatively static organisation in a stable environment. ✳

13. The *culture* and *personnel* of the organisation - ie the skill, knowledge and attitudes of subordinates, and the philosophy and psychological security of superiors, will help to determine how much delegation will be desired by the subordinates, and how far superiors will feel that they can trust the people below them.

14. It has been suggested that the *technology* of an organisation will help to determine its structure, and also the degree of centralisation of authority. (The work of Eric Trist and Joan Woodward on this subject will be discussed later.) For example, it is possible to exercise better and cheaper central control by means of a centralised computer information system for management. However, developments in computer technology (eg micro-computers linked to a larger central computer or networked micros) may also have made decentralised management control easier and cheaper. ✳

15. Where a high level of *uniformity* is required throughout the organisation, and where effective co-ordination of different parts of the organisation is essential, there is likely to be more centralisation of authority. Examples of organisations requiring such uniformity might be the armed services, or some government departments (eg those dealing with the payment of social security, supplementary benefits, pensions etc).

16. *Environmental factors* (eg geography, socio-cultural conditions, the legal and political environment etc) may pull towards delegation *or* centralisation, for example:

   (a) geographical dispersion of an organisation increases the pressure for decentralisation of authority to regional or area managers;

   (b) on the other hand, the growth in the exercise of power by trade unions has resulted in a tendency to by-pass lower and middle management, and union representatives may insist on dealing with top officials. This creates greater centralisation of decision-making.

Line and staff management

17. There are two ways of looking at the distinction between line and staff management.

   (a) The terms can be used to denote functions in the organisation. Line management consists of those managers directly involved in achieving the objectives of an organisation (ie all production and sales managers in a manufacturing company). Every other manager is staff (eg accounting, marketing, research and development).

> 'Line functions are those which have direct responsibility for achieving the objectives of the company. Staff activities are those which primarily exist to provide advice and service.'
> *Rosemary Stewart*

(b) The terms can also be used to denote relationships of authority. A line manager is one who has direct authority over a subordinate: by this definition, any manager, whether he works in an operations department or an advisory department, will have line authority over his subordinates. Thus, in the (staff) personnel department the manager in charge of recruitment and training will be subordinate in a line relationship to the personnel director.

18. Another popular distinction between line and staff is that:

- staff managers are thinkers and advisors;
- line managers are doers.

19. Staff departments exist in many organisations where there is a need for specialisation of management. Accountants, personnel administrators, economists, data processing experts and statisticians are all experts in a specialised field of work. Where this expertise is 'syphoned off' into a separate department, the problem naturally arises as to whether:

(a) the experts exist to *advise* line managers, who may accept or reject the advice given; or

(b) the experts can step in to *direct* the line managers in what to do - ie to assume line authority themselves.

20. No organisation of substantial size can avoid operating problems unless there is a clear understanding as to the structure of the tasks and relationships of an organisation, ie where authority and responsibility rest. This means that managers must know whether they are 'line' or 'staff'. Unfortunately, this is an aspect of organisation which causes enormous friction. Line managers are thought of as 'first class citizens' and staff are relegated in status to the second rank as expensive 'overheads', who are not contributing anything of worth to the organisation. Staff managers are therefore constantly trying to acquire line functions.

Functional staff

21. A development in more recent years has been the recognition that some 'staff' management has become highly specialised in areas of work which form a fundamental part of line management, eg in the fields of industrial relations and capital expenditure. In these areas the line manager would allow the staff manager to assume some of his responsibilities, while still retaining final authority and responsibility. A typical example would be where the personnel manager specified the rules for disciplining and dismissal of employees.

The line manager recognises that the staff manager has greater knowledge and expertise on this subject and acquiesces in the carrying out of the prescribed steps of the procedure. (This obviously requires a degree of communication and co-operation, an acceptance of 'expert' as opposed to 'position' power, which is not so essential in the purely 'legal' relationships of line structures.)

22. This is clearly different to the role of the traditional staff manager (eg work study, organisation and methods, 'personal assistant to' positions etc). Urwick and Dale have defined it as 'functional staff' as opposed to 'general staff'. General staff positions, as in the Army context, are seen as purely advisory positions.

Implications of line and staff for organisational design

23. There are drawbacks to using staff, awareness of which should enable management to use staff functions more effectively. The problems are as follows.

   (a) There is a danger that staff experts may, intentionally or not, undermine the authority of line managers. Subordinates might respect the 'expert power' of the staff man, and show less willingness to accept the judgement of their line boss.

   (b) Friction may also occur when staff managers report to a higher authority in the scalar chain of command. For example, a management accountant may submit reports about a line manager's performance to the production director or the managing director. The line manager might resent the perceived interference.

   (c) Staff managers have no line authority and therefore no responsibility for what actually happens. If they give advice, which is acted on but fails to achieve desired results, staff men can blame the line managers for not carrying out their plan properly.

   (d) Staff managers may attempt to usurp line authority. Any change in the boundaries of authority should be the result of conscious planning, and not surreptitious empire- building.

24. The solutions to these problems are easily stated, but not easy to implement in practice.

   (a) Authority must be clearly defined, and distinctions between line authority and staff advice clearly set out (eg in job descriptions).

   (b) Senior management must encourage line managers to make positive efforts to discuss work problems with staff advisors, and to be prepared to accept their advice. The use of experts should become part of the organisational culture - with emphasis on the building of expert teams if possible, (ie 'two heads are better than one').

   (c) Staff managers must be fully informed about the operational aspects of the business on which they are theoretical experts. By providing them with detailed information they should be less likely to offer impractical advice.

   (d) When staff advisors are used to plan changes the business, they must be kept involved during the implementation, monitoring and review of the project, so that they share responsibility for outcomes. ✳

25. Drucker argues that the traditional view of staff specialists as 'advisors with some authority' is a poor approach to organisation design. He suggests that 'as far as I have been able to grasp the concept, to be 'staff' means to have authority without having responsibility. And that is destructive'. It is much better that (support) functional departments, which are necessary in any large organisation:
   (a) should have their own clear objectives;
   (b) should have clearly stated areas of authority;
   (c) should be responsible and accountable for their exercise of that authority.

Span of control

26. Span of control or 'span of management', refers to the number of subordinates responsible to a superior. In other words, if a manager has five subordinates, the span of control is five.

27. Various writers of the classical school, such as Fayol, Graicunas and Urwick, argued that the managerial span of control should be limited to between three and six. Their arguments were based on the twin beliefs that:

- there should be tight managerial control from the top of the organisation; and
- there are physical and mental limitations to any single manager's ability to control people and activities.

To ensure effective control, the number of subordinates and tasks over which a manager has supervisory responsibilities should therefore be restricted to what is physically and mentally possible.

28. The French writer V A Graicunas devised a formula to show how the number of possible relationships between members of an organisation increases geometrically in proportion to the number of members:

$$N = n(\frac{2^n}{2} + n - 1)$$

where N is the total number of possible relationships and n is the number of members.

29. In any given organisational unit, therefore, as the number of subordinates increases, the supervisor finds himself managing a mushrooming number of organisational relationships (where n = 1, N = 1, and where n = 7, N = 490). This exploding complexity of larger and larger units must impose some limitations on the capabilities of management, ie the span of control is limited by the number of inter-relationships that one person can manage.

30. A narrow span of control offers:

- tight control and close supervision; better co-ordination of subordinates' activities;
- time to think and plan; managers are not burdened with too many day-to-day problems;
- better communication with subordinates, who are sufficiently few in number to allow effective 'networking'.

> *James Worthy* reported in 1950 that the policy of the American Sears Roebuck company was to have as wide a span of control as possible between stores managers and their subordinates, the merchandising managers. A wide span of control forced stores managers to delegate authority: the consequences, Worthy claimed, were improved morale and greater efficiency of merchandising management.
>
> *Lyndall Urwick* put forward a counter-argument that a wide span of control had been possible in this example because the work of the merchandising managers did not interlock, and so the need for co-ordination and integration was not present: this reduced the burdens of supervision and made a wider span of control feasible. Urwick concluded that the maximum management span of control should be six, when the work of subordinates interlocks.

31. On the other hand, a wide span of control offers:

- a greater decision-making authority for subordinates;
- fewer supervisory costs;
- less control, but perhaps greater motivation through job satisfaction.

32. It is reasonable to accept the view that there is a limit to a supervisor's capabilities and that the span of control should therefore be limited. However, the span of control is now thought to be dependent on:

    (a) the amount of time a supervisor has to spend with his subordinates, taking into account the demands of his own superiors, other departments and operational/non-managerial work;

    (b) the geographical distribution of subordinates;

    (c) the responsibilities and diversity of work done by superiors and subordinates. This will determine the amount of delegation that is possible, and the amount of control required, the suitability of team working etc;

    (d) the ability of superiors to deal with interruptions to the work they may be doing and the number of problems which arise and need to be dealt with;

    (e) the degree to which staff management relieves line management of aspects of their work, leaving them free to exercise supervision;

    (f) the quality of lateral communications, which may enable subordinates to get jobs done without constant reference back to their superior;

    (g) the technology of the organisation. (This view emerged from the work of Joan Woodward, described later in the chapter); and

    (h) the extent to which subordinates need to be controlled and supervised, and in particular the strength of the 'central faith' or culture of the organisation, which provides an alternative means of control over employees.

Tall and flat organisations

33. The span of control concept has implications for the 'shape' of an organisation. A *tall organisation* is one which, in relation to its size, has a large number of management hierarchies, whereas a *flat organisation* is one which, in relation to its size, has a smaller number of hierarchical levels. A tall organisation implies a narrow span of control, and a flat organisation implies a wide span of control.

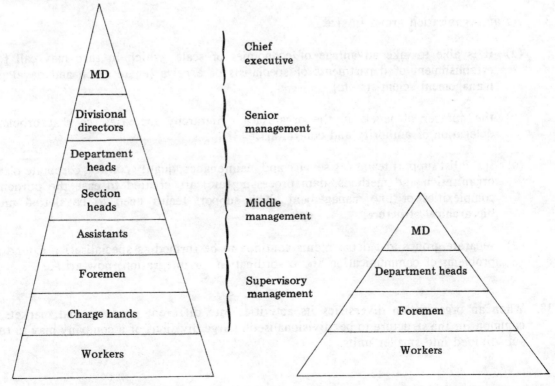

34. Some classical theorists accepted that a tall organisation structure is inefficient, because:

    (a) it increases overhead costs;

    (b) it creates extra communication problems, since top management is more remote from the work done at the bottom end of the organisation, and information tends to get distorted or blocked on its way up or down through the organisation hierarchy;

    (c) management responsibilities tend to overlap and become confused as the size of the management structure gets larger. Different sections or departments may seek authority over the same territory of operations, and superiors find it difficult to delegate sufficient authority to satisfy subordinates;

    (d) the same work passes through too many hands;

    (e) planning is more difficult because it must be organised at more levels in the organisation.

35. Behavioural theorists add that tall structures impose rigid supervision and control and therefore block initiative and ruin the motivation of subordinates.

36. Nevertheless, not all researchers favour flat organisation structures. Carzo and Yanouzas suggested that if work is organised on the basis of small groups or project teams (therefore narrow spans of control and a tall organisation structure) group members would be able to plan their work in an orderly manner, encourage participation by all group members in decision-making and monitor the consequences of their decisions better, so that their performance will be more efficient than the work of groups in a flat structure with a wide span of control. Peters and Waterman also observe the success of 'chunking' - breaking the organisation into small, task-centred units.

Departmentation

37. As an organisation grows in size:

    (a) it is able to take advantage of economies of scale, which in turn may call for the establishment of departments of specialists or experts (eg research and development, management scientists etc);

    (b) the number of levels in the organisation hierarchy increases, so that problems of delegation of authority and control arise;

    (c) specialist support teams (eg service and maintenance, quality control, corporate planning, organisation and methods, data processing etc) are created to ease the burdens and complexities of line management. Such support teams need to be slotted into the hierarchical structure;

    (d) separate groups and departments continue to be formed as specialisation extends; new problems of communication and co-ordination (or integration) now arise.

38. When an organisation diversifies its activities into different products and markets, it is common for the structure to be 'divisionalised'. Large divisions of a company may in turn be sub-divided into smaller units.

39. The creation of departments and divisions is known as *departmentation*. Different patterns of departmentation are possible, and the pattern selected will depend on the individual circumstances of the organisation. Various methods of departmentation are:

    (a) *by numbers:* when menial tasks are carried out by large numbers of workers, supervision can be divided by organising the labourers into gangs of equal size. Departmentation by numbers alone is rare; an example might be the organisation of a conscript army of infantrymen into divisions, and battalions etc;

    (b) *by shifts:* with shift-working employees organised on the basis of 'time of day';

    (c) *by function:* this is a widely-used method of organisation. Primary functions in a manufacturing company might be production, sales, finance, and general administration. Sub-departments of the production function might be manufacturing (machining, finishing, assembly etc), production control, quality control, servicing and purchasing. Sub-departments of sales might be selling, marketing, distribution and warehousing. Government departments include the Treasury, Home Office, Foreign Office, Department of Trade, Department of Industry, Ministry of Defence, etc.

    Functional organisation is logical and traditional and accommodates the division of work into specialist areas. Apart from the problems which may arise when 'line' management resents interference by 'staff' advisors in their functional area, the drawback to functional organisation is simply that more efficient structures might exist which would be more appropriate in a particular situation;

    (d) *by territory:* this method of organisation occurs when similar activities are carried out in widely different locations. The telecommunications service, for example, is divided into regions which in turn are sub-divided into Telephone Areas. Some authority is retained at Head Office (organised, perhaps, on a functional basis) but day-to-day service problems are handled on a territorial basis. Within many sales departments, the sales staff are organised territorially.

    The *advantage of territorial departmentation* is better local decision-making at the point of contact between the organisation (eg a salesman) and its customers. Localised knowledge is put to better use and in the right circumstances it may be less costly to establish area factories/offices than to control everything through Head Office (eg costs of transportation and travelling may be less).

    The *disadvantage of territorial departmentation* might be the duplication of management effort. For example, a national organisation divided into ten regions might have a customer liaison department at Head Office. If the organisation did all customer liaison work from head office it might need fewer managerial staff. In a similar way, there would be a tendency for regions to duplicate planning management, personnel and training management, accountancy management etc, thus increasing overhead costs and problems of co-ordination and integration;

    (e) *by product:* some organisations group activities on the basis of products or product lines. Some functional departmentation remains (eg manufacturing, distribution, marketing and sales) but a divisional manager is given responsibility for the product, product line or brand, with authority over the personnel of different functions involved in its production, marketing etc.

Advantages of product departmentation are that:

    (i)   individual managers can be held accountable for the *profitability* of individual products;

    (ii)   specialisation can be developed. For example, salesmen and/or engineers will be trained to sell and/or service a specific product in which they may develop technical expertise and thereby offer a better sales and after-sales service to customers;

    (iii)   the different functional activities and efforts required to make and sell each product can be co-ordinated and integrated by the divisional/product manager.

The disadvantage of product departmentation is that it creates a new form of management and therefore increases the overhead costs and managerial complexity of the organisation;

(f)   *by customer or market segment:* a manufacturing organisation may sell goods through wholesalers, export agents and by direct mail. It may therefore organise its functions (particularly marketing) on the basis of types of customer, market segment or distribution channels.

The *advantages of market-oriented organisations* are that:

    (i)   they encourage efficient marketing techniques and PR, which in turn should improve sales and relationships between the organisation and its environment (customers, the government, the general public etc);

    (ii)   they promote a culture whose values are heavily customer-oriented, which may be a strong motivating force (Peters and Waterman).

The *disadvantages of market-orientation* may be that it requires special leadership (a 'bureaucratic' management would fail to achieve the required inter-relationships between the organisation and its customers) and is likely to be costly in terms of staffing and other overheads;

(g)   *by equipment specialisation:* the most obvious example of departmentation based on equipment specialisation is provided by the data processing departments of large organisations. Batch processing operations are conducted for other departments at a computer centre (where it is controlled by DP staff) because it would be uneconomical to provide each functional department with its own large mainframe computer.

The contingency approach to organisation structure

40. The contingency approach states that while a particular structure may create optimum efficiency in an organisation, this ideal structure will vary according to the internal and external conditions of each organisation.

41. The structure which is selected is likely to be a compromise between environmental pressures which pull in opposite directions. For example:

(a)   there are pressures for *uniformity*. ✱
   (i)   Standardisation of methods, rules and procedures might result in economies of scale.
   (ii)   Where uniform procedures exist, it is easier to impose centralised control.
   (iii) The movement of personnel from one part of an organisation to another is made easier.
   (iv)   Specialised skills can be developed and applied throughout the organisation;

(b)   there are also strong pressures for *diversity*. Differences in regional characteristics, markets, customers or products, differences in the technology used in various aspects of the organisation's work, the greater readiness of individuals to identify with smaller work groups than with an entire organisation, and the desire of subordinates to have more authority are all factors which tend towards decentralisation and diversification in different parts of an organisation.

42. The contingency approach suggests that the factors which help to determine the optimal structure in any particular situation include:

(a)   *the environment*. The organisational structure most conducive to high performance depends on whether the environment is stable and simple, or changing and complex. In a stable environment, the pressures for uniformity are strong; any unforeseen events will be rare and can be dealt with by top management.

> Lawrence and Lorsch compared the structural characteristics of a 'high-performing' container firm, which existed in a relatively stable environment, and a 'high-performing' plastics firm which existed in a rapidly changing environment. They concluded that:
>
> - in a stable environment (ie the container firm) the most efficient structure was one in which the influence and authority of senior managers were relatively high and of middle managers low;
>
> - in a dynamic environment (ie the plastics firm) the most efficient structure was one in which the influence and authority of senior managers were somewhat less, and of middle managers correspondingly greater; ✱

(b)   *size*. Contingency theory suggests that although an informal structure is more efficient for smaller firms, in large organisations formalisation and bureaucracy is often the most efficient type of structure available;

(c)   *type of personnel*. Some employees like to be told what to do and prefer a standardised, uniform structure of organisation with authoritarian leadership; other employees (often those with a broader and greater education) prefer to be given responsibilities and to work in teams, and to make decisions in their own ways;

(d)   *the 'culture' of the organisation*. This is described later in this chapter;

(e)   *technology of the organisation*. The socio-technical systems approach to organisation structure is also described later in this chapter.

43. Contingency theory does have its critics, such as John Child:

> 'One major limitation of the contemporary contingency approach lies in the lack of conclusive evidence to demonstrate that matching organisational designs to prevailing contingencies contributes *importantly* to performance.'

44. Lawrence and Lorsch suggested in their research that poor-performing companies have an inappropriate organisation structure for their particular circumstances. However, it could be argued that an organisation is badly structured because it is poorly managed, and even if it were re-structured, poor management would continue to depress the organisation's performance - ie performance may not be attributable only to structure.

   Other factors might contribute more importantly to organisational performance, such as planning and control methods, information systems, leadership and employee motivation.

45. Well-established organisations in non-competitive environments might be able to perform successfully with *any* type of organisation structure, because they are secure within their environment and can ignore contingency factors (eg the Civil Service, perhaps).

Matrix organisation

46. Matrix organisation is a structure which emerged in the USA during the 1950s and 1960s and which is now widely practised in a variety of forms. Basically, a matrix organisation provides for the formalisation of management control across functional boundaries, whilst at the same time maintaining functional departmentation.

   It may be thought of as a reaction against the 'classical' form of bureaucracy (and unity of command - ie one man, one boss) by establishing a structure of *dual command*.

47. Matrix management first developed in the 1950s in the USA in the aerospace industry. Lockheed-California, the aircraft manufacturers, were organised in a functional hierarchy. Customers were unable to find a manager in Lockheed to whom they could take their problems and queries about their particular orders, and Lockheed found it necessary to employ 'project expediters' as customer liaison officials. From this developed 'project co-ordinators', responsible for co-ordinating line managers in solving a customer's problems. Up to this point, these new officials had no functional responsibilities.

48. Owing to increasingly heavy customer demands, Lockheed eventually created 'programme managers', with authority for project budgets and programme design and scheduling. These managers therefore had functional authority and responsibilities, and a matrix management organisation was created. It may be shown diagramatically as a management *grid*; for example:

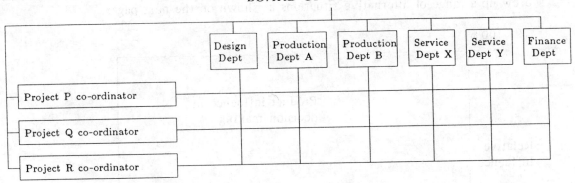

BOARD OF DIRECTORS

49. Authority would be shared between the project co-ordinators and the heads of the functional departments. Functional department heads are responsible for the organisation of the department, but project co-ordinators are responsible for all aspects of the project itself. An employee in a functional department might expect to receive directions/commands from a project co-ordinator as well as from the departmental head - ie there may be dual command.

50. A product management structure may be superimposed on a functional structure in a matrix; product or brand managers may be responsible for the sales budget, production budget, pricing, marketing, distribution, quality and costs of their product or product line, but may have to co-ordinate with the R & D, production, finance, distribution, and sales departments in order to bring the product on to the market and achieve sales targets, ie:

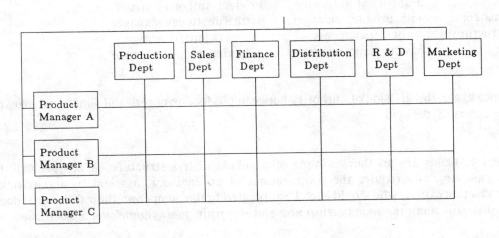

SENIOR MANAGEMENT

* The product managers may each have their own marketing team; in which case the marketing department itself would be small or non-existent.

51. The authority of product managers may vary from organisation to organisation. J K Galbraith drew up a range of alternative situations as shown on the next page:

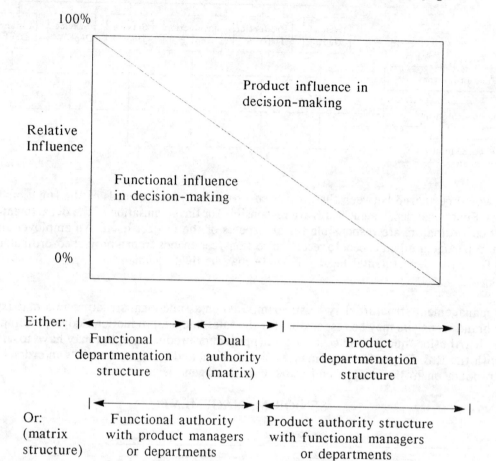

Once again, the division of authority between product managers and functional managers must be carefully defined.

52. Project teams are another example of a simple matrix structure. A project may be inter-disciplinary, and require the contributions of an engineer, a scientist, a statistician and a production expert, who would each be appointed to the team from their functional department, whilst still retaining membership and status within their 'home' department, ie:

Level in departmental hierarchy	Department A	B	C	D	E
1	X	Ⓧ	X	X	Ⓧ
2	Ⓧ	X	X	X	X
3	X	X	Ⓧ	X	X
4	X	X	X	Ⓧ	X

Members of the project team (circled) would provide formal lateral lines of communication and authority, superimposed on the functional departmental structure. Leadership of the project team would probably go to one of the more senior members in the hierarchy, but this is not a requirement of the matrix structure. The team member from department A may be team leader (eg if A was the Production Department, and its member was able to gain an operational overview of the team's activities): he would then be in a subordinate position in the organisation chart to the Head of Department B - but his superior within the project team.

53. Matrix management thus challenges classical ideas about organisation in two ways:

- it rejects the idea of one man, one boss;
- its subverts the bureaucratic ethic of authority based on status in the formal hierarchy.

54. The advantages of matrix structures are said to be that:

(a) they foster greater flexibility:

(i)   in people, by creating a culture of adaptability and readiness to accept change;
(ii) of tasks and structure. The matrix structure may be short-term (as with project teams) or readily amended (eg a new product manager can be introduced by superimposing his tasks on those of the existing functional managers);

(b) dual authority gives the organisation multiple orientation. For example, a functional department may be production-oriented, but the superimposition of product managers will provide market orientation;

(c) they provide a structure for allocating responsibility for end-results. A product manager is responsible for product profitability; a project leader is responsible for ensuring that the task is completed;

(d) they provide for inter-disciplinary co-operation and a mixing of skills and expertise;

(e) the offer employees greater participation in planning and control decisions, which may provide job satisfaction, and perhaps motivation.

(f) they break down departmental monopolies and foster participative management styles based on teamwork, rather than on traditional subordinate-superior relationships (Argyris).

55. The disadvantages of matrix organisation are said to be as follows.

(a) Dual authority threatens a conflict between functional managers and product/project managers. Where matrix structure exists it is important that the authority of superiors should not overlap and areas of authority must be clearly defined. A subordinate must know to which superior he is responsible for a particular aspect of his duties.

(b) An individual with two or more bosses is more likely to suffer stress due to the ambiguity (and potential political problems) of his situation.

(c) Matrix structures are sometimes more costly - eg if product managerment positions are additional jobs, where a simple structure of functional departmentation would suffice.

(d) It may be difficult for the management of an organisation to accept a matrix structure. A manager may feel threatened by the seeming erosion of his authority, or by the uncertainties created by a culture of change and flexibility.

Culture

56. At this point, it is worth discussing in more detail the concept of 'culture' in organisations. It may be defined as the complex body of shared values and beliefs of an organisation.

Peters and Waterman, in their study (*In Search of Excellence*) found that the 'dominance and coherence of culture' was an essential feature of the 'excellent' companies they observed. A 'handful of guiding values' was more powerful than manuals, rule books, norms and controls formally imposed (and resisted). They commented: 'If companies do not have strong notions of themselves, as reflected in their values, stories, myths and legends, people's only security comes from where they live on the organisation chart.'

57. Handy sums up 'culture' as 'that's the way we do things round here'. For Schein, it is 'the pattern of basic assumptions that a given group has invented, discovered, or developed, in learning to cope with its problems of external adaption and internal integration, and that have worked well enough to be considered valid and, therefore, to be taught to new members as the correct way to perceive, think and feel in relation to these problems.'

> 'I believe that the real difference between success and failure in a corporation can very often be traced to the question of how well the organisation brings out the great energies and talents of its people. What does it do to help these people find common cause with each other? And how can it sustain this common cause and sense of direction through the many changes which take place from one generation to another?...I think you will find that it owes its resiliency not to its form of organisation or administrative skills, but to the power of what we call *beliefs* and the appeal these beliefs have for its people.'
>
> Watson (IBM) quoted by
> Peters and Waterman

58. All organisations will generate their own cultures, whether spontaneously, or under the guidance of positive managerial strategy. The culture will consist of:

(a) the basic, underlying assumptions which guide the behaviour of the individuals and groups in the organisation, e.g. customer orientation, or belief in quality, trust in the organisation to provide rewards, freedom to make decisions, freedom to make mistakes, the value of innovation and initiative at all levels, teamworking etc;

(b) overt beliefs expressed by the organisation and its members, which can be used to condition (a) above. These beliefs and values may emerge as sayings, slogans, mottos etc. such as 'we're getting there', 'the customer is always right', or 'the winning team'. They may emerge in a richer mythology – in jokes and stories about past successes, heroic failures or breakthroughs, legends about the 'early days', or about 'the time the boss...'. Organisations with strong cultures often centre themselves around almost legendary figures in their history. Management can encourage this by 'selling' a sense of the corporate 'mission', or by promoting the company's 'image'; it can reward the 'right' attitudes and punish (or simply not employ) those who aren't prepared to commit themselves to the culture;

(c) visible artifacts - the style of the offices or other premises, dress 'rules', display of 'trophies', the degree of informality between superiors and subordinates etc.

The cultures/structures approach to organisation

59. The cultures/structures approach states that the structure of an organisation reflects different varieties of organisation culture. The ideal organisation structure in any particular situation is dependent on the culture which exists. The approach is thus a 'contingency theory' of structure.

60. Handy, following a 1972 article by Roger Harrison, discusses four cultures. An organisation might have a structure which reflects a single culture; on the other hand, different structures reflecting different cultures might exist in separate parts (or departments) of the organisation. (For example, the organisation structure of the marketing division and the computer systems design department might differ, because the culture in the two departments are not the same.)

61. The four cultures discussed by Handy are:

(a) the *power culture:* power and influence stem from a central source, perhaps the owner-directors. The degree of formalisation is limited, and there are not many rules and procedures. Important decisions are made by key people, and other employees tend to rely on precedent in the absence of other guidelines as to what to do. Other characteristics of the power culture are:

(i) the organisation, since it is not rigidly structured, is capable of adapting quickly to meet change; however, the success in adapting will depend on the luck or judgement of the key individuals who make the rapid decisions;

(ii) personal influence decreases as the size of an organisation gets bigger. The power culture is therefore best suited to smaller organisations, where the leaders have direct communication with all employees;

(b) the *role culture* or bureaucracy. These organisations have a formal structure, and operate by well-established rules and procedures. Job descriptions establish a definite task for each person's job, and procedures are established for many work routines, communication between individuals and departments, and the settlement of disputes and appeals. The organisation structure defines authority and responsibility to individual managers, who enact the role expected of their position. Individuals are required to perform their job to the full, but not to overstep the boundaries of their authority. Line management will accept advice from specialist staff experts only when such advice seems necessary or appropriate. Since a wide variety of people of different personalities are capable of doing the same job, the efficiency of this organisation depends on the structuring of jobs and the design of communications and formal relationships, rather than on individual personalities. Individuals who work for such organisations tend to learn an expertise without experiencing risk; many do their job adequately, but are not over-ambitious.

The bureaucratic style can be very efficient in a stable environment and when the organisation is of a large size. Thus the Civil Service, insurance companies and many large well-established companies with long-term products are associated with bureaucratic organisations and the role culture. Unfortunately, bureaucracies are very slow to adapt to change and when severe change occurs (eg an economic depression) many run into financial difficulties or even bankruptcy (eg BL cars, the British Steel Corporation);

(c)   the *task culture*, as reflected in a matrix organisation, in project teams and task forces. In such organisations, there is no dominant or clear leader. The principal concern is to get the job done; therefore the individuals who are important are the experts with the ability to accomplish a particular aspect of the task. Each individual in the team considers he has more influence than he would have if the work were organised on a formal 'role culture' basis.

Such organisations are flexible and constantly changing: they adapt to the environment in order to create or maintain the conditions necessary for success in the task, and do not become a mere part of the machinery as, for example, project teams are disbanded as soon as their task has been completed.

Since job satisfaction tends to be high, owing to the degree of individual participation and group identity, 'behavioural' management theorists might recommend this type of organisation structure as being the most efficient available. Handy would argue that this type of structure might only be successful if the nature of the *work* is suited to matrix organisation or project work, and if the *employees* of the organisation belong to the task culture and therefore want the work organised in this way;

(d)   the *person culture*, formed in an organisation whose purpose is to serve the interests of a person or the individuals within it. These organisations are rare, although an example might be a partnership of a few individuals who do all the work of the organisation themselves (with perhaps a little administrative assistance). It is quite common, however, for individuals to use an organisation to suit their own purposes; for example:

(i)   studio artists look on their job as a means of expressing themselves artistically;
(ii)   university lecturers might use their official position as a springboard from which to launch a wider career.

62.   The factors which help to determine, in any situation, what the predominant culture and therefore organisation structure will/should include:

(a)   *size:* large organisations are more likely to favour a bureaucracy (role culture) as a means of organising the complexity of work;

(b)   *people:* some people like to be told what to do, and would favour an organisation structure based on power culture or role culture. Others enjoy the challenge of a complex job and 'ambiguity' and would therefore prefer (task-culture) project work. People with strong need for security, and people of low intelligence or with poor inter-personal skills, tend to prefer bureaucracies. Personal ambition might be served by a bureaucracy, but is perhaps more associated with power culture and person culture;

(c)   *the age of the organisation:* many businesses and other organisations begin to grow through the efforts of a few individuals (eg owner-directors, or the founder of a political pressure group) and tend to be highly centralised (power culture). As the organisations get older, and the former leaders are replaced by a new 'generation' of managers, systems tend to formalise and bureaucracy develops;

(d) *the predominant goals or objectives of the organisation:* if the main purpose of an organisation is service to the community (eg hospitals, local government, railways, public utilities), a bureaucratic organisation will probably be most suitable for providing, monitoring and controlling the required level of service. If the predominant goal is growth or survival, an organisation based on power culture or task culture would be more efficient and successful;

(e) *the technology of the organisation:* an important school of thought best known through the works of Eric Trist and Joan Woodward suggests that the most efficient structure of an organisation will be one which is suited to the technological conditions of the work (ie the equipment, methods of working, the nature of automation etc). This important theory is described more fully below;

(f) *the environment (economic, competitive, socio-cultural, legal, geographical etc):* examples of environmental influences are:

   (i) economic and market changes. Organisations which adapt best are those structured according to a task culture or power culture;

   (ii) an organisation which is spread over a wide geographical area is likely to decentralise authority on a regional basis, so that different cultures might predominate in different regions;

   (iii) the appointment of worker-directors to the board of a company might betoken a change of attitudes towards decision-making within an organisation, from bureaucracy towards teamwork and group decisions (ie from a role culture to a task culture).

The adaptive organisation

63. Most organisations exist in a changing environment and must adapt in order to survive. Although formalisation and bureaucratic organisation helps a small company to develop into a large one, it may be insufficient to enable the organisation to survive continuing environmental changes. Handy suggests that an organisation adapts to change in one of three ways:

(a) *by deliberation:* the organisation 'seeks to reinforce the formal structure by more formal structures'. Companies or governments might establish committees with powers to investigate, recommend or even to make decisions. Special project teams might be created, or new departments established (eg corporate planning department or economic advisory section);

(b) *by reproduction:* large national organisations might delegate authority ('decentralise') to regional headquarters. Unfortunately, decentralisation of this sort usually results in regional structures which duplicate the former national structure: bureaucracy in the same form, but on a smaller scale. Unless the environment is fairly stable, such adaptation is likely to be inefficient;

(c) *by differentiation:* the organisation employs different structures with different cultures, in separate parts of the organisation, using a contingency approach - ie choosing the most suitable structure for each particular situation:

   (i) stable, routine work will be performed in a formalised bureaucratic manner (*role culture*);

THE STRUCTURE AND CULTURES OF ORGANISATIONS

(ii)   adaptation to change (development of new products and new markets, or meeting environmental 'threats') should be organised on a task basis;

(iii) any sudden crisis might have to be dealt with by key individuals with emergency powers (*power culture*);

(iv)   overall policy decisions of the organisation should be set by a ruling body of key individuals (board of directors, the Cabinet of government ministers, or the supreme policy-making councils of other organisations) (*power culture*).

'One culture should not be allowed to swamp the organisation' (Handy). However, where differentiation, on a contingency basis, is applied in an organisation structure, there is a potential for conflict. Project teams might resent policy decisions of senior managers because they believe them to be inappropriate to the problems of the organisation; line managers might resent 'free-wheeling' 'undisciplined' members of project teams. The management of an organisation must be capable of reconciling differences and integrating the work of all employees towards a common aim.

Organic and mechanistic organisations

64. Burns and Stalker contributed significant ideas about managing organisation growth and change. They identified the need for a different organisation structure when the technology of the market is changing; innovation is crucial to the continuing success of any organisation operating in the market.

65. They recommended an *organic structure* (also called an 'organismic structure') which has the following characteristics.

- There is a 'contributive nature' where specialised knowledge and experience are contributed to the common task of the organisation.

- Each individual has a realistic task which can be understood in terms of the common task of the organisation.

- There is a continual re-definition of an individual's task, through interaction between the individual and others.

- There is a spread of commitment to the concern and its tasks.

- There is a *network* structure of authority and communication.

- Communication tends to be *lateral* rather than vertical.

- Communication takes the form of information and advice rather than instructions and decisions.

66. Burns and Stalker contrasted the organic structure of management, which is more suitable to conditions of change, with a *mechanistic* system of management, which is more suited to stable conditions. A mechanistic structure has the following characteristics.

196

- Authority is delegated through a hierarchical, formal scalar chain.

- Communication is *vertical* rather than lateral.

- Individual tasks are not clearly related to whole projects, or the overall goals of the organisation, owing to specialisation of work.

- Individuals regard their own tasks as something distinct and divorced from the organisation as a whole.

- There is a precise definition of duties in each individual job (eg rules, procedures, job definitions).

67. Mechanistic systems are unsuitable in conditions of change because they tend to deal with change by cumbersome methods. For example:

   (a) the *ambiguous figure system:* in dealing with unfamiliar problems authority lines are not clear, matters are referred 'higher-up' and the top of the organisation becomes over-burdened by decisions;

   (b) *mechanistic jungle:* jobs and departments are created to deal with the new problems, creating further and greater problems;

   (c) *committee system:* committees are set up to cope with the problems. The committees can only be a temporary problem-solving device, but the situations which create the problems are not temporary.

Organisation development

68. It is important to have a good understanding of the term 'organisation development'.

- 'Growth is defined as change in an organisation's size, when size is measured by the organisation's membership or employment; development is defined as change in an organisation's age.' (*Starbuck 1965*)

- 'Development involves policy decisions that change organisational objectives. Growth, on the other hand, involves technical or administrative improvement by which it is possible more effectively to accomplish old objectives.' (*Hicks 1967*)

- Organisation development 'is a complex educational strategy intended to change the beliefs, attitudes, values and structure of organisations so that they can better adapt to new technologies, markets and challenges and to the dizzying rate of change itself'. (*Bennis 1969*)

---

69. From the definition of Bennis, two important points must be emphasised.

   (a) Organisation development is an *educative* process.
   (b) It is based on the prescription that there is no ideal form of organisation design, but that organisations must be *adaptive* in order to survive.

70. It is generally accepted that the 'master and slave' ideology of classical management theory is not properly tenable, (although these beliefs still exist widely today and, to varying degrees, classical management theories are used in practice: bureaucracy and the formal structure of organisations offer security, familiarity and safety which continue to have strong appeal).

    Organisation theorists have begun to emphasise:

    (a) the importance of individuals in organisations: the problems of conflict between individuals or work groups, the psychological importance of the work group, the effect of different styles of leadership, and the problems of motivation;

    (b) the influence of the environment on an organisation; and of the organisation on its environment (open systems theory).

71. Proponents of organisational development programmes would argue that although there are many cases where a bureaucratic organisation might be the appropriate organisational structure to have (eg possibly with routine or repetitive work) it is clearly inappropriate in other cases.

    To adapt to the increasing complexities of modern business life, an organisation cannot afford to be a sluggish bureaucracy.

    (a) Individuals should be motivated to welcome change, and to co-operate with other members of an organisation in achieving change and adapting to it. The problems of employee resistance to change were discussed in the earlier chapter on conflict, stress and change.

    (b) Management styles and organisational culture must be such as to make change and adaptation (development) possible: encouraging innovation, tolerating small errors in the process of experimentation, rewarding new ideas etc.

    (c) An organisation must react to its environment. Management involvement in internal operations and problems must be oriented to the environment, its opportunities and demands.

The socio-technical systems approach to organisation: Eric Trist

72. This approach takes the view that organisation structure (along with the work done by an individual, and the way in which he can relate to fellow-workers) tends to be influenced by the technology of the operations. Organisations are complex social systems, but must be seen in the context of their technology - ie they are *socio-technical systems*.

73. The originators of socio-technical systems theory are reputedly Eric Trist and his colleagues at the Tavistock Institute who (in the early 1950s) studied the effects of technological change on the morale of workers. They based their studies on the coal mines where, owing to increased mechanisation, the miners were merged into larger and larger groups, found it difficult to identify their share of the work within the enlarged groups and suffered low morale: productivity was falling.

    Trist realised that productivity was linked to job satisfaction and the ability of the miner to associate his own extra effort with extra reward. When he introduced a method of organisation where the large shifts were sub-divided into small, identifiable units, morale improved and productivity increased.

74. Trist also believed that the primary task of management was to relate the organisation to its environment. Management must realise that an organisation is a conversion process that converts units of input from the environment into units of output desired by the consumer in that environment. The market is constantly changing and management should monitor these changes and react to them.

75. Trist has consistently developed a systems approach to organisations, in which:

- task requirements and
- individuals' needs

are inter-related as an interdependent 'socio-technical' system.

> 'It is difficult to see how these (organisation) problems can be solved efficiently without restoring responsible autonomy to *primary groups* throughout the system and ensuring that each of these groups has a satisfying sub-whole as its work task, and some scope for flexibility in work-pace. Only if this is done will the stress of the deputy's role be reduced and his task of maintaining the cycle receive spontaneous support from the primary work groups.'
> *Trist and Bamforth*

The research work of Trist

76. The Coal Board had been trying to introduce new mechanical processes into coal mining in order to increase productivity, but the innovation provoked severe industrial unrest. Trist and his colleagues were invited to study the problem and to come up with a solution.

77. Prior to the technical innovations by the Coal Board, miners had been used to working in small autonomous groups or teams. Each team had its own place at the coal seam and was responsible for hewing coal with a pick or drill, loading it into tubs for transportation out of the mine and propping up the roof as they advanced. Each miner in the team was an all-rounder and did not have to specialise in any single activity within the overall task of the group. Each team was paid as a group and the pay was shared out equally between its members.

78. The Coal Board decided to change the work organisation in order to introduce new coal-cutting equipment capable of cutting a long stretch of wall at a time. Their new organisation (known as the *conventional longwall* system) divided the mining work into three separate tasks or shifts.

(a) One group of miners did the cutting.
(b) A second group of miners loaded the loose coal onto a moving conveyor which took it away from the coal face.
(c) A third group moved the coal cutting equipment and conveyor forward, and propped up the roof.

79. The new arrangements proved unsuccessful. Within each specialised task there were some miners more willing and more able than others to carry out the specialised work. There were also problems in co-ordinating the work of the three different groups or shifts. As a result, it was found that closer supervision was required by management to ensure that the work was done properly and that every individual did his fair share.

80. Trist and his colleagues suggested that close managerial supervision was unsuitable to mining work, which was carried out in dangerous conditions.

They agreed that the technical equipment used in operations must influence the type of work organisation for employees: in the case of coal mining, the new cutting equipment and conveyor belts made working in small groups no longer practicable. However, a work group has social and psychological properties and the work organisation should not be arranged in such a way that the advantages of technological improvements are offset by employee resistance and unrest.

81. Trist et al argued that an organisation is a socio-technological system which must attempt to balance

   • economic advantages,
   • technological advantages, and
   • social and psychological advantages

from work organisation.

It is not sufficient to introduce the most up-to-date technology if a cheaper older technology is available or if the new work organisation will create serious employee unrest. Nor is it sufficient to create worker satisfaction if this entails inefficiency and uneconomic working which could be improved by better technological equipment.

82. Their solution to the coal mining problem was to recommend a *composite longwall* method of working. Under this method the new technology was retained, but the workforce was no longer divided for three separate tasks. The team as a whole was given the responsibility for the whole task and for assigning individuals to particular jobs. By this means, the work group was given autonomy, self-regulation, multi-skilled roles and a complete task to perform. As far as possible, the social conditions of the traditional system of mining were restored, while the 'three-task' group was defined as the new primary work group for coal mining operations.

Joan Woodward (1916 - 1971)

83. Joan Woodward developed the socio-technical systems approach with extensive research into difering types of organisations. She discovered that the structure of organisations varied very widely and that technology was a major factor contributing to the variances.

84. Woodward categorised the levels of technology into:

   • unit production, or small batch production;
   • mass production, or large batch production;
   • process production, or continuous flow production.

This categorisation also describes a rising scale of *technical complexity*, ie process production is more complex than mass production, which is more complex than unit production. By 'technical complexity' she meant the extent to which the production process is controllable and its results predictable.

> Woodward described the findings of a survey of firms in Essex.
>
> 'When the firms were grouped according to similarity of objectives and techniques of production, and classified in order of the technical complexity of their production systems, each production system was found to be associated with a characteristic pattern of organisation. It appeared that technical methods were the most important factor in determining organisational structure and in setting the tone of human relationships inside the firm.'

85. Elaborating further on the survey, Woodward noted the following.

   (a) Different objectives of different firms controlled and limited the techniques of production they could use (eg a firm developing prototypes of electronic equipment cannot go in for mass production).

   (b) Analysing the firms into a continuum of ten levels of technical complexity (sub-divisions, slightly overlapping, of the three main levels described above) firms using similar technical methods also had similar organisational structures.

   > 'It appeared that different technologies imposed different kinds of demands on individuals and organisations and that these demands have to be met through an appropriate form of organisation.'

86. Specific findings were that:

   (a) the number of levels in the management hierarchy increase with technical complexity, ie complex technologies lead to 'tall' organisation structures, while simpler technologies can operate with a 'flat' structure;

   (b) the span of control of first-line supervisors was at its highest in mass production, and then decreased in process production, ie

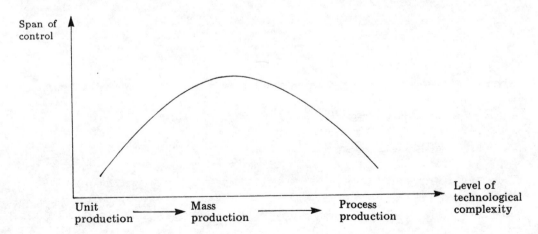

   (c) labour costs decreased, and the ratio of indirect labour increased as technology advanced;

(d)   the span of control of the chief executive widened with technical advance;

(e)   the proportion of graduates in supervisory positions increased with technical advance;

(f)   the organisation was more flexible at both ends of the scale of complexity ie duties and responsibilities were less clearly defined. In mass production, duties and responsibilities are clearly set out, largely owing to the nature of the technology, and this favours a formal, authoritarian structure. As a consequence,

   (i)   the amount of written, as opposed to verbal, communication peaked with mass production, being a feature of bureaucracy and formal structures;

   (ii)   specialisation between the functions of management was most frequent in large batch and mass production companies. The clear-cut demarcation (and resulting conflicts) between line and staff management was also most frequent here;

   (iii)   the administration of production (ie the 'brainwork') and the actual supervision of production work are the most widely separated in large-batch and mass production companies;

(g)   industrial and human relations were better at both extremes of the scale than in large-batch and mass production companies, possibly owing to heavier pressure on all individuals in this type of organisation;

(h)   the size of the firm was not related to its technical complexity, ie it is not possible to attribute the 'faults' of mass production to the size of the firm rather than to the nature of its technology;

THE WORK ENVIRONMENT AND
JOB DESIGN

Points to be covered

- Environment and motivation
- Office layout
- Health and safety
- Fatigue and monotony
- Noise
- Ergonomics
- Hours of work and rest pauses
- Shift work
- Flexitime
- Automation and technology
- Job design

Introduction

1. As we have seen throughout this text study, organisations are composed of individuals. While external environment and internal systems shape and direct the organisation as a whole, it is also relevant to consider the impact of the working conditions under which individuals are called upon to function daily. We will look at general and specific aspects of this, and then go on to consider particular features of the work environment and design of jobs; the human effects of operating systems, conditions and the organisation of work.

Environment and motivation

2. Employers are wise to consider the importance of working conditions and try to make their offices, shop floors etc. pleasant as well as efficient places in which to work. Both the quality and the quantity of work may be affected by tiredness, uneasiness, unhappiness, or distraction. Even if these are considered as 'hygiene', rather than 'motivating' factors, it is generally recognised that dissatisfaction with the work environment may contribute to poor performance.

It is not always possible to please all of the people all of the time: smokers and non-smokers, for example, or people who like studying with background music and people who don't. Still, it is important for employers to consider such matters:
(a) because of a genuine concern for the condition of their employees;
(b) to improve the morale and loyalty of employees; and
(c) because of the sheer cost of reduced productivity, increased staff turnover etc.

THE WORK ENVIRONMENT AND JOB DESIGN

External and internal factors

3. The 'surroundings' of a work place include not only the immediate space in which employees carry out their duties, but also the external environment in which they may shop, bank, eat, commute, park their cars etc. and the overall design and construction of the complex within which their particular office may be placed.

4. The *siting* of buildings is probably the first point to be considered in the acquisition or construction of offices or factories.

    - Particularly, does the business want to be located in an urban area, or out of town? In which case, how far out of town?

    - Are available transport and communication links sufficient to keep up the in- and out-flow of materials/goods/information/people?

    - What about *cost:* could the business take advantage of lower land prices, lower rates and insurance costs, development grants from the government etc. outside urban areas?

    - Where do most of the *employees* live? Could they commute easily? Would they rather move out of town? Or, is there an existing 'pool' of sufficient suitable labour in the area?

    - Are *customers* all based in town? How would the company keep in touch with them? Could it attract new business without an office in town to present a public 'profile'?

5. One consideration in locating the site must be the facilities in the surrounding area. From the point of view of employees and the organisation, the proximity of banks, postal services and transport will be very important. For the employees' well-being, shops, restaurants and perhaps recreation/sport facilities would also be welcome.

6. General design and construction is partly an external factor, although specific aspects eg. space, lighting, lifts in tall buildings, are also internal factors. Size and age of buildings must be taken into account for efficient use of space and possible shortcomings in comfort and safety. Availability of space for employees and equipment (and foreseeable expansion of both) must be assessed, and eg. heating, plumbing, wiring, and general structural soundness should be looked at in old buildings, if only to comply with legal requirements for health and safety.

7. As ever, financial considerations largely determine the organisation's attitudes to such factors. The site, size and age of buildings acquired, and whether they are rented, bought or built, will be determined by their cost and will in turn determine such operating costs as insurance and rates, heating and lighting, maintenance and renovation.

8. Some of the *internal* factors to be considered are:

    - space;
    - heating, lighting and ventilation;
    - decor (colour scheme etc);
    - furniture and equipment;
    - noise and movement;
    - cleanliness.

These factors affect the immediate surroundings of the workforce during their working hours. If they are approached logically and considerately, the result should be an environment which will satisfy most of the people working in it.

Office layout

9. In considering the layout of a new or adapting office, flexibility will obviously be needed to cope with the needs of different individuals and activities, the shapes and sizes of available rooms. But there are some basic features which any office should possess:

    (a) economical use of space;
    (b) arrangement for efficient work flow - ie. movement of people and documents etc.;
    (c) arrangement for ease of supervision;
    (d) provision for security where necessary;
    (e) safety of occupants.

10. There are four general types of office layout.

    (a) *Small closed offices* linked by corridors. These have the advantage of privacy, peace and security, and are desirable for 'status conscious' managers for whom a separate office is an important symbol of authority, but supervision and communication is hindered, and this system is generally not favoured in new office designs.

    (b) *Open plan offices.* These do away with the maze of walls and doors to make better use of the space than small closed offices. It has been estimated that a 33% space saving is possible under this system. Advantages include:

      * easier supervision;
      * freer communication;
      * flexible arrangement of furniture and equipment in the available space;
      * economies on heating and lighting;
      * sharing of equipment, such as photocopiers etc.

      Disadvantages include:

      * lack of privacy;
      * distraction from noise and movement;
      * loss for managers of the status of a separate office, possibly lowering morale;
      * tendency for managers to become unnecessarily involved in routine matters;
      * difficulty of satisfying every individual's needs and preferences.

    (c) *Landscaped offices* are a variation of the open plan system, overcoming some of the latter's problems. They use movable screens of variable height, shape and colour etc., usually 'acoustic' to absorb noise, and flame-proof for safety, to break up the office space. Filing cabinets and large pot plants may also be placed to give staff more privacy in their own areas and to cut down on noise and distractions, while still preserving the communication advantages of the open plan. Equipment and furnishings are generally of good quality, but more space and better furnishings may be given to management to enhance their status and morale.

(d) A mixture of closed and open offices within business premises. In order to allow managers some degree of privacy for meetings or perhaps to give them some sign of status, some organisations provide closed offices for management and site all staff below perhaps junior management level in an open plan office.

11. The factor common to all these systems is the efficient use of space. If there is not enough space for employees and equipment this may lead to dissatisfaction and reduce motivation (Herzberg), not to speak of safety hazards from obstructing movement and exit ways (eg. in an emergency). On the other hand, too much unused space is wasteful and inefficient.

The Offices, Shops and Railway Premises Act, which we will look at later in the chapter, lays down that each person must have at least 40 square feet excluding furniture and equipment. Other studies have suggested that it ought to be about 60 square feet for clerks and typists, 100 square feet for junior/middle management and 200 square feet for senior management.

12. Work study might be used to determine the best layout for sections in an open plan system, based on the amount of contact usually necessary between each section. Within each section, attention should be given to the *proximity* of:

- people regularly working together (eg. the manager and his/her secretary); and
- supervisors and those under their control.

Attention should also be given to the *accessibility* of:

- people whose advice or services are required by the section as a whole (eg. supervisors, typists);

- equipment and facilities regularly used and shared by the section (eg. files, photocopier, coffee machine).

The flow of work could be looked at from the point of view both of staff movements (ie. free passage from one place to another), and the movement of documents.

13. A simple illustration may help to explain. This is the original layout of a purchasing department, showing the routes of staff dealing with an order being made by the company.

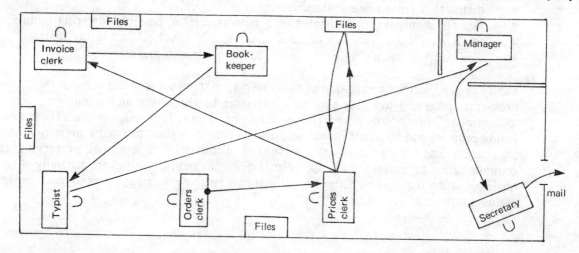

Rearranged to improve the work flow and layout, as suggested above, the department might look like this:

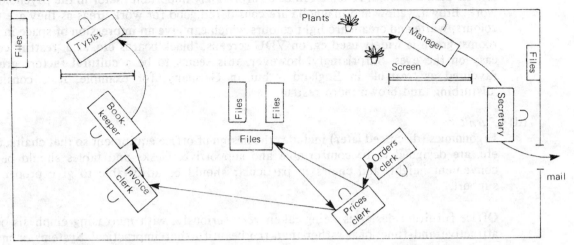

14. Work flow between different departments will depend on the layout of the premises as a whole. The same principles of *proximity* and *accessibility* apply. So, for example, Purchasing and Accounts departments may be located for easy communication with each other; the mail room and office supplies may be centralised, and rest areas, toilets etc. distributed for general use.

Other common sense measures would include:
(a) locating any design, drawing and planning (whether production or advertising etc.) in 'studio'-type accommodation, with plenty of natural light;
(b) locating activities involving the movement of heavy machinery, materials or goods as close to ground level and transport facilities as possible;
(c) ensuring that senior management offices and conference facilities are situated where interruptions and noise are minimal;
(d) keeping dining, drinking, rest and recreation areas (if any) separate from those where concentrated work is taking place.

15. As we saw earlier, there are various factors which combine to affect the physical comfort and (arguably) performance of employees.

(a) *Heating, lighting and ventilation*
The effect of these is fairly obvious, particularly when one or more of them is inadequate. The only law relating to any of these is that of a minimum working temperature of 16° C (60° F). Wherever possible lighting should be natural rather than artificial and strip lighting rather than bulbs because fluorescent tubes emit a light closer to natural light. Ventilation should be provided without causing draughts, and if necessary, steps should be taken to filter smoke and dust out of the air for the sake of equipment and personnel alike.

(b) *Noise*
Strangely enough, we do need noise at work - or at least a certain amount of it. Constant loud noise, or intermittant noise at any volume, is distracting and should be reduced by carpeting, sound-absorbent walls and ceilings; 'acoustic hoods' are used to cover noisy machinery eg. some computer printers, to muffle the noise; soft bleep phones are increasingly used instead of bell-ringing ones. A total absence of any noise, however, causes uneasiness. Some large office blocks have solved this problem by using speakers around the building to give out 'white noise', a low background hiss which is sufficient and suitable noise; some prefer background music.

(c) *Decor.*

A well-planned colour scheme can be a surprisingly important factor in the psychology of work. Brown, yellow and magnolia are considered good for work areas as they are warm colours; white and cream are light colours which can give an impression of space in small rooms; green is widely used eg. on VDU screens, 'black'boards etc. as a 'restful' colour, easy on the eyes. Surprisingly, however, this seems to be a cultural factor: green is favoured as 'restful' in England - but in Germany, for example, it is considered 'disturbing' and brown more restful.

(d) *Furniture*

Ergonomics (discussed later) includes the design of office equipment so that chairs, desks etc. are designed to be comfortable and supportive. Desks and tables should be of a convenient height, and chairs in particular should be adjustable to give proper back support.

Office furniture design is being taken very seriously, with increasing emphasis on the attractive-and-functional rather than the beautiful-but-impractical. Systems or module furniture is being designed, with light, easy to move, linkable desks, cabinets, printer tables etc. for total flexibility and use of available space. Easily cleaned surfaces, and colour/style co-ordination are also taken into account. A 'hi-tech' or traditional *image* may be an important part of the culture of the organisation.

(e) *Cost*

This is not a 'physical factor' in itself, of course, but must be considered together with all of them. The costs of purchasing and maintaining office buildings, furniture and equipment, and the costs of heating, lighting, cleaning etc. must be weighed against all possible benefits to the organisation from employee satisfaction and motivation, enhanced work flow, smart office image etc. The 'perfect' ergonomically-designed office would still have to have questions of cost, durability, and justification asked of it.

Office design consultants are increasingly used to make the work place as a whole more efficient, and a more congenial environment for people.

In an article in the Financial Times (Feb. 1987) it was suggested that workplace design is psychologically important to the individual (and, rather extravagantly, that 'happy bees make more honey').

According to one consultant: 'there is a territorial desire to protect yourself and wrap walls around you, and to a degree it is right that people should be allowed to define and personalise their own area. In traditional cellular offices, they would make their office an extension of their home with plants and pictures of their children...But there is a big change as the nature of work is changing. With a reduction in status consciousness, particularly among senior staff, it is less common to find executive suites separated out from the main body of the workers.'

Health and safety

16. Apart from obviously dangerous equipment in factories and even offices, there are many hazards to be found in the modern working environment. Many accidents could be avoided by the simple application of common sense and consideration by employer and employee; safety consciousness should be encouraged or enforced by a widely acceptable and well-publicised safety policy, advising and warning about safe and unsafe procedures, activities and attitudes.

Common causes of injury include:
- slippery or poorly maintained floors;
- frayed carpets;
- trailing electric leads;
- obstacles (files, books, open drawers etc.) in gangways;
- standing on chairs (particularly swivel chairs!) to reach high shelving;
- staircases used as storage facilities;
- lifting heavy items without bending properly;
- removing the safety guard on a machine to free a blockage.

In factories, most accidents arise from the handling of goods eg. lifting, moving etc.; falls, machinery accidents, fires and explosions are other important sources.

17. In the UK and in most other industrialised countries, the number of work days lost through industrial injury exceeds those lost through industrial disputes and strikes! 'Ill health' also arises from exposure to harmful working conditions. Particular care must be taken with safety procedures where employees work with hazardous materials (eg. radioactive materials, asbestos) or in hazardous places (eg. coalmines) because of potential short-term or long-term effects on health.

18. Health and safety at work are important for three reasons:
   (a) primarily, to protect employees from pain and suffering (obviously);
   (b) because an employer has legal obligations for the health and safety of employees;
   (c) because accidents cost the employer money, eg:
      - time lost by the injured employee;
      - time lost by other employees who choose to or must stop work at the time of the accident or following it;
      - time lost by supervisors, management and technical staff following the accident;
      - cost of employing first aid, medical staff etc.
      - cost of disruption to operations at work;
      - cost of any damage to equipment or necessary modification to equipment;
      - cost of any compensation payments or fines resulting from legal action;
      - costs associated with increased insurance premiums;
      - possible reduced output from the injured employee on his return to work;
      - cost of possible reduced morale, increased absenteeism, increased labour turnover among employees;
      - the cost of recruiting and training a replacement for the injured worker.

19. We will now look in more detail at particular aspects of working conditions, and their effects on work behaviour.

Fatigue and monotony

20. You may not think that 'fatigue' is a product of the working environment. It is more commonly associated with the depletion of an individual's energy resources, ie 'tiredness'.

'Fatigue', however, is merely a useful term to describe a variety of phenomena, e.g.:

   (a) the depletion of 'fuel reserves' ie 'blood sugars';

(b) exhaustion, increased heart rate etc. from over-heating and lack of oxygen in hot, stuffy conditions;

(c) temporary disability, resulting from the build-up of lactic acid in the blood during short bursts of intense activity with insufficient oxygen.

21. Studies of 'industrial fatigue', moreover, have shown that 'fatigue' is part of the conflict between the individual and his environment that we mentioned in an earlier chapter. Performance is at its optimum when the worker is in a 'steady state': interference may create a condition of 'dis-equilibrium', which might render him temporarily unable to continue at the same level of activity, or indeed at all.

Studies of hours of work, rest pauses, lighting, heating, ventilation, individual suitability to particular tasks, posture, physique etc. have been aimed at identifying sources of this dis-equilibrium - whether within the individual himself, or in the relationship between the individual and his job or work environment.

22. Elton Mayo (1880-1949) led the famous investigation of the Hawthorne works of the Western Electric Company in Chicago. His initial interests were in fatigue, accidents and labour turnover, and the effect on them of rest pauses and physical conditions of work. (A previous study had concentrated on lighting conditions). In the end (as we shall see later), Mayo's attention was diverted from purely physical working conditions; the effects of the informal organisation (working attitudes etc.) on performance became the central part of his thesis. But his observations on fatigue are interesting - given his early assumption that physical conditions are responsible for falling production.

Mayo argued that from a purely physical aspect, we are entitled to infer a 'steady state' where organic processes are kept in balance with the required expenditure of energy: in such a state, work could continue indefinitely. Even under such 'internal' biological conditions, however, workers do slow down or stop - so external conditions must be affecting performance.

23. *Monotony* - and the experience of boredom - was early on identified as another form of 'interference' in worker performance.

(a) Specialisation, and the breaking of the job into smaller and smaller tasks, such as were advocated by 'scientific management' theorists, created conditions that gave the worker no mental stimulation: inattention, daydreaming or social conversation were usually the result, with accidents and errors following. It might be argued that repetitive and routine work on assembly lines, in largely automated processes, or in the typing pool, have such an effect. The strain on the worker is even worse, if the social outlet is not available to him - e.g. the typist working in an isolated booth, the assembly worker separated from the group by the layout of machinery.

(b) The extent to which workers suffer boredom - or role 'underload' - depends on the mental capacity (and self-concept) of the individuals. The more intelligent a person is, the more keenly he will *perceive* the monotony of repetitive tasks: some workers will derive satisfaction from a long uninterrupted run of work (however undemanding) - especially if there are good piece rates for the job.

24. Robert Karasek, in studies of Swedish and American workers, found that *stress* was related to work overload and level of discretion in work methods: high workload/low discretion jobs are the most highly stressful. (If both factors are low, the job will require little mental or physical activity, and as long as discretion is high, there will be *some* challenge and opportunity.)

Handy reports on the following situations.

A group of inmates from a mental institution was given jobs on an assembly line. The inmates proved to be highly productive workers in the plant, never getting bored or needing breaks, despite long hours on the job. Their job satisfaction was reckoned to be very high.

A pigeon was trained as an inspector in a drug factory. Human inspectors had been employed to watch thousands of pills pass on a conveyor belt, and to discard rejects: they worked only short spells, and there were high absenteeism and turnover rates. The pigeons, however, worked longer hours - and made fewer errors.

---

25. The general conclusions of studies of monotony have been that it is less likely to arise if:

(a) the activity is changed from time to time, and rest pauses allowed; workers might be trained to alternate jobs, or might simply be allowed to move around a bit - e.g. by fetching their own materials or tools;

(b) work is grouped into whole, self-contained tasks - rather than the repetition of a single part of a job by each individual; completely autonomous work groups have even been set up, with responsibility for the production of whole units - and even in competition with each other;

(c) workers are permitted the outlet of social interaction, ie are allowed to form groups, rather than being isolated by the way the work place is designed; 'chatting' is usually permitted within reason; Volvo, in the 1970s, decided 'to bring people together by replacing the mechanical line with the human work group. In this pattern, employees can act in co-operation, discussing more, deciding more among themselves how to organise the work - and, as a result, doing much more';

(d) payment by results is used - depending on the significance of pay as a motivator to the individual.

26. The application of the above conclusions to the organisation of work, and job design, is discussed later.

Noise

27. Noise can be a particularly stressful form of 'interference'. Continuous, loud, random noise may have to be accepted by workers in some situations - although sound-proofing is increasingly a feature of offices and factories - and perceptual selectivity usually filters it out after a while: you get used to it, and it becomes part of the 'background' to activity.

Elusive but potentially meaningful sounds (which you strain to hear and make sense of), sharp intermittent noises or unexplained variations in noise level can, however, be irritating, distracting or hard on the nerves. Concentration can easily lapse if there is a sound competing with other more relevant sensory information: 'mental blinking' ie the shifting of attention from one sensory input to another, can cause significant lapses. Any work which demands alertness and concentration may suffer.

Ergonomics

28. Ergonomics is taken from the Greek - 'ergos' (work) and 'nomos' (natural laws).

    Ergonomics is usually described as the scientific study of the relationship between man and his working environment. This sphere of scientific research explores the demands that can arise from a working environment and the capabilities of people to meet these demands.

    Through this research, data is made available to establish machines and working conditions which, apart from functioning well, are best suited to the capacities and health requirements of the human body. In old people's homes and hospitals, switches etc. are placed according to measurements of chair height and arm reach. In the same way, computer consoles and controls, office furniture, factory layout etc. can be designed so that the individual expends minimal energy and experiences minimal physical strain in any given task.

29. Both work study and ergonomics are concerned with 'fitting the job to the worker' and ergonomic data is used in establishing workplace layout. The operator's comfort will depend on many factors connected with the particular job, but there are certain general considerations which ensure a comfortable position.

    (a) The operator should be allowed to sit where possible.
    (b) The chair should permit alternate sitting and standing.
    (c) In either case the elbows should be 2-3 inches above the working surface. This often calls for benches to be higher than those normally found.
    (d) There should be room for the operator to put both legs under the bench.
    (e) Work, tools and equipment should be within easy reach.

    If possible, the workplace should be tailored to the requirements of the individual operator.

30. Movements should be natural, rhythmical, and symmetrical.

31. Industrial psychology increasingly enters into this field. Apart from purely mechanical considerations - e.g. in what position should a worker be sitting in order to exert maximum force over a long period of time without physical strain or fatigue? - the ergonomist must now take into account the increasing problems of the worker as information processor. The perceptual limitations of the worker can also be measured, and systems designed which do not make unreasonable demands on the worker's attention span, capacity to absorb information etc. - e.g. the use of sound signals to attract attention to visual displays or equipment.

Hours of work and rest pauses

32. It is generally recognised that personal, family and social commitments must be allowed for in the demands made on workers' time. Role conflict, as we have discussed, may be caused or aggravated if, for example, an individual works late or at weekends when he/she should be with his/her family. A shorter working week, 'preserved' weekends, long weekends, and more holidays are developments towards the promotion of leisure time as the benefit of increased prosperity.

33. Overtime, however, has become an established feature of working life: it is taken for granted in planning and scheduling by many organisations, even though in most spheres it is still considered voluntary, and paid at a premium. Despite common expectations, it has been shown that individuals who regularly work overtime have reasonably good morale, attendance records etc. Pay is considered to be the major incentive, where:

    (a) low basic rates necessitate 'earning a bit extra'; or
    (b) more highly-paid workers also work overtime to preserve differentials between themselves and others.

    High achievement needs may also lead an individual to work extra hours - 'to get the job done', 'tie up loose ends' etc. There may even be political 'points' to be scored with superiors being seen at work beyond the call of duty. Overtime may even be 'addictive', self-sustaining activity, whereby the worker compulsively puts his time and energy into his work, for its own sake, as a substitute for other activities which the individual feels insecure in tackling, or as a means of acquiring more and more luxury goods from the overtime payments.

34. The number of hours in the 'standard' working week have fallen from around fifty to forty, while the hours actually worked have also fallen - though not by so much. Since the Second World War, average hours worked have hovered around forty-seven. As well as overtime hours, some individuals may seek supplementary jobs elsewhere - preferring increased earnings to increased leisure time.

    In fact, average hours worked may well continue to fall, with the influence of new technology reducing man-hours required, unemployment, and a higher proportion of the working population now tending to work part-time or shorter hours ie skilled workers, married women etc.

35. The hours worked by any given individual will depend on many factors, including employment law, domestic and social demands, sex, age etc.

    Rates of pay determine that labourers tend to work longer hours than technicians or craftsmen, manual workers than clerical etc - although this has a confusing effect on pay differentials between skilled and unskilled workers and may (albeit illogically) cause some resentment. *Methods* of payment also affect the hours worked by those who seek cash rewards: piece-rate workers can earn more by increased effort during standard hours, whereas time-paid workers have no way of increasing their take-home pay except through overtime.

36. The value of longer hours worked by a minority is not significant in production terms. Overtime will obviously be desired by management if it enables essential, round-the-clock services to be kept running, or enables them to cope with occasional peaks of activity without the necessity of recruiting new staff.

Long working days, however, almost certainly involve a lower average effort over the hours worked. Also, if overtime is worked unit costs of production will rise - unless increased production results from the practice.

37. Making the best use of the hours worked is perhaps what 'organisational behaviour' is all about. In trial programmes, the institution of natural pauses (ie whenever the work allows, as opposed to fixed, 'off the clock' breaks), and kiosks/safe-smoking areas close to production units was shown to save around 25,000 productive man hours per year. Workers can (generally) be trusted not to abuse the facilities and flexibility - and are able to maintain a steady rate of working more easily under the more congenial conditions.

> 'Most types of continuous or sustained work may lead to a build-up of fatigue. In many jobs there are natural breaks where you can move about to do something different. Jobs should be designed to allow such changes in activity, but if this is not possible, short frequent breaks seem to prevent fatigue. Being able to choose when to take a break is preferable to having fixed rest break schedules.'
>
> *Health & Safety Executive* booklet for VDU users

Shift work

38. Increasing numbers of workers are employed on a *shift* basis. The advantage to the organisation is that overhead costs can be spread over a longer productive 'day', and equipment and labour can be used more efficiently.

There are three main systems in operation:

- *the double-day system* - ie two standard working day (eight hour) shifts, say from 6am - 2pm, and 2pm - 10pm. The physical and social problems of such a system are much less acute than where night-work is required - although the hours may seem somewhat 'anti-social' and hard on the evening social life;

- *the three-shift system* - ie three eight-hour shifts covering the twenty-four hour 'day' (say 6am - 2pm, 2pm - 10pm, 10pm - 6am). The main problem here is the 'unnaturalness' of night-time work, on the third shift. There are physiological, psychological and social effects - which we will discuss below. Most complaints are directed at the so-called 'dead fortnight', when the pattern of afternoon and night shifts interfere most with normal social life;

- *the Continental or 3-2-2 system.* This entails more frequent changes than the traditional system, enabling employees to have 'normal' leisure time at least two or three time per week! Over a four-week cycle, shifts rotate so that workers do 3 mornings, 2 afternoons, 2 nights, 3 rest days, 2 mornings, 2 afternoon etc (see table below). This gets away from the 'dead fortnight', but it may cause confusion initially, and also means that there are no entirely free weekends - which may be important to families.

			3-2-2 system				
Week	Mon	Tue	Wed	Thur	Fri	Sat	Sun
1	6-2	6-2	2-10	2-10	10-6	10-6	-
2	-	-	6-2	6-2	2-10	2-10	10-6
3	10-6	10-6	-	-	6-2	6-2	2-10
4	2-10	2-10	10-6	10-6	-	-	6-2

Average 42 hours per week.

39. The 3-2-2 system is becoming increasingly popular – and is already established in the chemical and iron and steel industries. ICI operate it in two factories, and surveys show 80% of the workforce in favour because:

   (a) shorter, though more frequent, spells on each shift were found to be less fatiguing than longer periods on, say, the night shift;

   (b) the variety was more enjoyable;

   (c) employees felt that they had more time off for social and family life; and

   (d) senior staff found it easier to keep in touch with the shiftworkers.

40. The effects of shiftwork have been well researched. They include:

   (a) *physiological or medical effects* – a disruption of body-temperature, disturbance of digestion, inability to sleep during the day etc. resulting from the disorientation of the body's 'clock', its regular cycle of meals, sleep, energy expenditure etc. Shiftwork tends to conflict with the body's 'circadian rhythms', or 24-hour body cycles. Stress-related ill-health may also be caused. Some people suffer more from the physical disruption than others: in particular, diabetics, epileptics and those prone to digestive disorders should be screened by management, and excluded from shiftwork for health reasons;

   (b) *psychological effects*. The experience of variety can be stimulating. On the other hand, the fatigue and sense of physical disorientation can be stressful. Those with strong security or structure needs may feel threatened by a lack of 'rhythm' in working life. A sense of isolation and lack of variety arising from the social problems of shiftwork may also be threatening – particularly if strain is being put on non-work relationships and roles;

   (c) *social effects*. Some forms of shiftwork involve high social costs, though others – in particular double-day working, very little. In some systems, the normal hours of socialising – ie afternoon and evening – are taken up at work, which may isolate the individual from his non-work social circle. Family problems may be acute – especially where weekends are lost: not only is the worker absent, leaving a role gap in the family, but the routine of the whole family will be disrupted by his sleeping and eating patterns;

   (d) *economic effects*. Overtime is not necessarily eliminated by shiftwork: premiums for double-shift and Sundays are common in practice. Shiftworking itself is inherently unpopular, and its appeal will largely depend on financial incentives.

41. The EEC Commission Report on 'The Problems of Shiftworking', in 1977, proposed to reduce the extent of shiftworking, and to improve conditions by:

(a) giving older shiftworkers, or those with a certain length of shift service, the right to return to day work - to counter negative physical and psychological effects; and

(b) reducing the length of the working week, lengthening rest periods and offering earlier retirement to shiftworkers.

Flexitime

42. There are many 'flexitime' systems in operation providing freedom from the restriction of a '9 to 5' work-hours routine. The concept of flexitime is that predetermined fixed times of arrival and departure at work are replaced by a working day split into two different time zones.

(a) The main part of the day is called 'core time' and is the only period when employees must be at their job (this is commonly 10.00 to 16.00 hours).

(b) The flexible time is at the beginning and the end of each day and during this time it is up to the individual to choose when he arrives and leaves. Arrival and departure times would be recorded by some form of 'clocking in' system. The total working week or month for each employee must add up to the prescribed number of hours, though he may go into 'debit' or 'credit' for hours from day to day, in some systems.

43. A flexitime system can be as flexible as the company wishes.

(a) The most basic version involves flexibility only within the day, with no possibility of carrying forward debit or credit hours into other days (ie. - arrive late, work late). This type of system is used in some factories where transport difficulties make arrivals and departures difficult.

(b) Another system is flexible hours within the span of the week. Hours can be carried forward to the next day. This enables an employee to cope with a fluctuating work load without overtime and gives him some control over his work and leisure time.

(c) Finally, flexitime may be operated by the month. Each employee will have a coded key which can also serve as an identity card, and this will be used on arrival and departure by insertion into a key acceptor, which records hours worked on a 24 hour clock.

44. Flexitime enables workers to plan their lives on a more personal basis, as long as they work their contracted hours in the period. Where the employee works longer hours than necessary, he is usually able to save these hours for holiday or days off.

45. Morale is improved by allowing staff to arrange their days to fit particular needs, leisure pursuits, available transport etc. Stress (related to frustration, monotony, isolation, fears associated with being 'late for work' etc.) is reduced. The temptation to take time off is also reduced: pioneer schemes showed that absenteeism dropped, because trips to the dentist, social visits etc were allowed for, and the idea that 'I'm late for work; I may as well not go in at all' discounted.

> 'Flexible Working Hours not only bring order into this disorder [peak hour travel, traffic strikes etc]; within limits that are clearly defined and acceptable to management, it gives staff a new facility deliberately to vary arrival and departure times for personal reasons, and to do so with candour and dignity'
>
> (M.W Cuming: *Personnel Management*)

46. In Office Magazine (Jan. 1987) it was reported how the Bedford Offices of the Anglian Water Authority implemented a flexitime scheme. With offices on the edge of town, staff had been experiencing annoying traffic delays. However, the Authority was reluctant to incur extra clerical costs in implementing the system, and installed an electronic 'clock-in/clock-out' system to record staff hours. Staff can monitor their own hours, with flexibility up to four hours in debit and eight hours in credit in any one 'settlement' period of four weeks. The Authority has found that attendance has improved, apart from general staff 'satisfaction' with the arrangement.

The influence of automation and technology

47. It has been said that we are in the middle of a 'New Industrial Revolution' based on developments in the field of microchip technology. The effects of this revolution on jobs is largely a matter of the changing relationship between man and machine. Machines have progressively replaced human effort and skills, in the interests of increased efficiency, standardisation, speed and precision. Computers and micro-processors have changed the nature of production and clerical work alike, and we might expect continued changes in:

   - the way we work (eg the electronic office or robotic factory);
   - where we work (with communications bringing remote locations within reach);
   - how we work (with new skills and materials);
   - whether we work or not (the time a job takes and therefore the number of people required to do the work is altered by the new technology);
   - how we live (because IT has extended into the home).

48. The progressive mechanism of production processes can be traced to demonstrate this.

   Initially, engineering tasks were performed by hand, or by hand tool. The initiating source of the activity, the control of the 'machine response', and the power source all resided with the human operator. Towards the end of the 19th century it became possible to 'programme' machine tools to carry out single functions, or even a sequence of functions, automatically. Initiation, control and power source resided within the machine: human skills were, however, required to strip and reset the machines.

   With the beginning of computerisation in the 1950s, the work changed again. Even the task of setting and resetting the tool was performed by electronic - rather than mechanical - means.

49. During the 1970s cheap, reliable microprocessing technology was built into machine tools. Computers can initiate action according to variables in the environment, and can respond to signals (e.g. error detection) or can select from a range of programmed options (e.g. changing speed, position etc. according to measurement data, or segregating/rejecting units according to size etc., or even identifying and initiating appropriate sequences of action). Computers are now even capable of 'adaptive control' - responding to working conditions as they arise (over-

heating, dulling of tools etc.) and modifying their behaviour over a wide range of variables - correcting after, during, or even before the event. Human intervention is reduced even further - to loading and removing workpieces, and replacing dulled tools (although robotics is beginning to encroach on these areas also).

The work of several machines may be scheduled and controlled from a single central computer, which tells the operator, via a VDU (visual display unit), which workpieces to fit on which machines.

50. The systematic reduction of human intervention and control in work has made work less tiring and safer for the worker, and more efficient, less prone to human failings (carelessness, idleness or hostility) from the point of view of the organisation.

However, the American Marxist sociologist Harry Braverman suggests that 'the remarkable development of machinery becomes, for most of the working population, the source not of freedom but of enslavement, not of mastery but of helplessness, and not of the broadening of the horizon of labour, but of the confinement of the worker within a blind round of servile duties...'

51. Robert Blauner carried out a study in America of working conditions in various industries.

(a) Printing - dominated by *craft work* - allows workers to set their own pace, choose their own methods, practice high-status skills and have strong social relationships at work.

(b) Cotton spinning - dominated by *machine minding* - offers textile workers simple, repetitive, non-discretionary work. However, they live in close rural communities, whose 'culture' overcomes the alienation experienced to a degree at work (see below).

(c) Car manufacture - dominated by *process production* - gives assembly workers little control over their work, little perceived 'significance' in their tasks, social isolation in the work place, and no opportunity to develop skills. Alienation is very high.

(d) Chemicals manufacture - dominated by *process production* - gives the process workers an advanced work environment, where manual work is automated. The workers have team work and social contact, and control over their work pace and movements. They have opportunities to learn about the processes they monitor, and also derive satisfaction from a sense of responsibility, achievement and belonging.

52. Blauner identified feelings of *'alienation'* in workers, due to a sense of:

• powerlessness - ie loss of control over work and conditions;
• meaningless - loss of significance of work;
• isolation - ie loss of sense of belonging and relatedness; and
• self estrangement - ie loss of personal identity, of any sense of work as a central life activity.

His conclusion was that *advanced* technology - such as the chemical processing plant - actually eliminated alienation.

53. So is technology 'good' or 'bad' for the worker? Two sides have been argued, ie:

(a) Process operators are victims of management's use of technology to create work that is unskilled – and unlikely to offer any learning opportunities – boring, repetitive, tightly controlled, lacking meaning, and socially isolating. Microelectronic extension of automation may alter the demand for operators' human skills, and may damage the quality of working life: it may replace the exercise of human mental capacity altogether.

(b) Process operators are skilled, knowledgeable decision makers, with responsibility, discretion and prosperous working conditions. Process automation eliminates dirt and hazard, and can offer a motivating work environment with task variety, meaning, learning opportunities and discretion. Electronic controls lack human flexibility and creativity: systems can enhance job skills and interest.

54. Obviously the motivational and political implications must be considered together with the nature of the technology – its capabilities and limitations, and the skills required to operate it effectively.

Computer

"It has a mathematical brain but it is not capable of exercising intuition, discretion or creativity; nor can it make moral or strategical judgements. If a problem can be mathematically posed or if it can be structured in a logical series of questions, then a computer will provide answers with remarkable speed and absolute accuracy. But *real* decisions, particularly those involving social implications, must be made by people. A mathematically viable solution is sometimes not acceptable when account has to be taken of such intangibles as moral attitudes, human and political responses and the vagaries of economic forces."

Ronald Pitfield

Attitudes to advanced technology

55. Buchanan and Huczynski comment that computers have in recent years moved from the 'background' functions of accounting and administration, and into 'foreground' tasks – text production, order processing, product and process design, equipment control etc.

56. Advanced technology therefore has a 'high-profile' image, which in the popular mind may have little basis in fact or experience. Common fears include:

- 'computers/robots' are replacing people in industry;
- the only jobs left for people will be routine 'de-humanised' tasks;
- when the 'paperless office' arrives, what will happen to the clerical/administrative worker?;
- skills are becoming irrelevant, as is any desire for autonomy or control;
- we'll never learn to cope with all these new-fangled ways.

Let's look at some of these attitudes.

57. A principle fear is that of *replacement* - ie the substitution of 'intelligent' machines for people at work. (Information technology is in fact often *sold* on this basis - ie it will increase productivity because machines are more efficient than people.) Job opportunities may be lost and redundancies will result, in so far as machines *do* replace people. However, there are certain compensatory mechanisms, in that:

(a) technology generates new products and services (e.g. personal computers, computer games, compact disc players etc.) which encourage investment and expansion, with new employment opportunities;

(b) lower unit costs, arising from higher productivity, can be passed on to the consumer as lower or static prices. There may be increased demand for that - or other - product(s), arising from the extra spending power, again offering new employment opportunities;

(c) there will inevitably be a lapse of time, in any case, between the arrival of a new device or system, and its successful incorporation into existing facilities - which may have to be 'run-down' over a lengthy period; 'natural' labour turnover may sufficiently reduce the workforce during this time to make redundancies unnecessary;

(d) the risks and costs involved in new technologies will make organisations slow to test and initiate changes. They also suggest that an organisation which 'takes the plunge' must be confident of expansion and increased demand - so there is a likelihood of new employment opportunities;

(e) new technology is not all-powerful - nor does it always live up to its advertising. Existing jobs, skills and systems may have to work alongside the new devices, for a while at least.

58. Technical change may even be seen as the way of *preserving* jobs in the face of technologically advanced foreign competitors who innovate faster and produce goods better and more cheaply than British technology-resistant firms. (The economic motive for technological change must not be underestimated: information gathering, storage, display, processing and transmission can be achieved with greater speed, accuracy and consistency through the use of information technology - and this must be desirable from the organisation's point of view.)

59. Another fear is that skills will die out, or become irrelevant and wasted. However, Buchanan and Huczynski suggest that: "as machines do more, people do not necessarily do less. Computer technology may be tools that *complement* human skills and create more interesting and meaningful work.... The outcome depends to a large extent on *management decisions* on how to organise the work around the new devices."

60. Computerised processes - for the 'process supervisor' in a computerised factory, as for the word processor operator in the office - *can* offer satisfaction - eg:

(a) retained discretion to control the process, and responsibility for its correct, safe operation (in the case of a word-processor, responsibility for file management, since errors may cause files to be lost or erased);

(b) new 'user' skills in a high-status field - with opportunities to develop those skills as the technology progresses;

(c) rapid feedback on performance;

(d) satisfaction from more efficient and productive performance;

(e) often, modern and highly 'designed', working environment - the 'modern office' etc;

(f) identification with the 'new revolution', innovation, high-tech etc.

61. In comparisons of the word processor typist's job with the copy typist's, it has been found that the VDU operators:

(a) had more variety (associated with greater output), but fewer breaks in the rhythm of work - ie. more continuous time at the keyboard;

(b) felt they had more control over the quality and appearance of the end product -with text manipulation and corrections etc on screen, and not showing up on the printed version;

(c) had less to do in the way of preparation and other tasks; they did not have to handle or load paper, file finished documents or lay out pages (taking account of line ends, page ends etc) which was done automatically. Corrections were simple and worry-free (compare the copy typist reaching the end of an otherwise perfect page...). However, the VDU operators had other tasks of file management, data protection etc. and needed to acquire skills in the use of codes, menu selection and other operating mechanisms;

(d) found it physically easier to use - lighter touch, flatter keyboard, quieter operation (particularly with the new, silent laser printers) etc. - though more demanding on the concentration.

Introducing new systems

62. Management should be aware of the effect of a new system on the people who will use it. Resistance to a new system can develop, both during the design phase (of a tailor-made system) and the implementation phase of the project, and resistance of this kind will be damaging. For example, to design an efficient system, the analyst needs the co-operation of the user department's staff. They can supply the essential details that the analyst needs, and they can judge whether the system an analyst proposes will 'work' in practice and resolve all the problems it is intended to. Without user department co-operation, participation and enthusiasm for the new system, the analyst will face an uphill struggle.

63. The human problems with systems design can fall into several different categories.

(a) *Job security and status.* Employees might think that the new system will put them out of a job, because the computer will perform routines that are currently done manually, and so reduce the need for human intervention. An office staff of, say, 10 people might be reduced to 8, and the threat of being out of work would unsettle the entire office staff.

Even when there is no threat of losing a job, a new system might make some staff, experienced in the existing system, feel that all their experience will be worthless when the new system goes live, and so they will lose 'status' within the office.

In some cases, the resistance to a new system might stem from a fear that it will result in a loss of status for the *department* concerned. For example, the management of the department might believe that a computer system will give 'control' over information gathering and dissemination to another group in the organisation. Dysfunctional behaviour might therefore find expression in:

(i) interdepartmental squabbling about access to information;

(ii) a tendency to disregard the new sources of information, and to stick to old methods of collecting information instead.

(b) *Career prospects.* In some instances, managers and staff might think that a new system will damage their career prospects by reducing the opportunities for promotion. When the effect of a system is to reduce the requirement for staff in middle management and supervisory grades, this could well be true. On the other hand, today's successful manager should be able to adapt to information technology, and developing a career means being flexible, accepting change rather than resisting it.

(c) *Social change in the office.* New systems might disrupt the established 'social system' in the office. Individuals who are used to working together might be separated into different groups, and individuals used to working on their own might be expected to join a group. Office staff used to moving around and mixing with other people in the course of their work might be faced with the prospect of having to work much more in isolation at a keyboard, unable to move around the office as much. Where possible, new systems should be designed so as to leave the 'social fabric' of the workplace undamaged. Group attitudes to change should then be positive rather than negative.

(d) *Bewilderment.* It is easy for individuals to be confused and bewildered by change. The systems analyst must explain the new system fully, clearing up doubts, inviting and answering questions etc, from a very early stage in systems investigation onwards through the design stages to eventual implementation.

64. Dysfunctional behaviour might manifest itself in the antagonism of operating staff towards data processing specialists who are employed to design and introduce a computer system. It might take the form of:

(a) an unwillingness to explain the details of the current system, or to suggest weaknesses in it that the new system might eradicate. Since DP staff need information from and participation by the operating staff to develop an efficient system, any such antagonism would impair the system design;

(b) a reluctance to be taught the new system;

(c) a reluctance to help with introducing the new system.

65. A new system will reveal weaknesses in the previous system, and so another fear of computerisation is that it will show up exactly how poor and inefficient previous methods of information gathering and use had been. If individuals feel that they are put under pressure by the revelation of any such deficiencies, they might try to find fault with the new system too. When fault-finding is not constructive - ie not aimed at improving the system - it will be dysfunctional in its consequences.

In extreme cases, dysfunctional behaviour might take a more drastic, aggressive form. Individuals might show a marked reluctance to learn how to handle the new equipment, might be deliberately slow keying in data, or might even damage the equipment in minor acts of vandalism.

66. To overcome the human problems with systems design and implementation, management and DP systems analysts must recognise them, and do what they can to resolve them.

(a) Employees should be kept fully informed about plans to install the new system, how events are progressing and how the new system will affect what people do.

(b) Employees should be encouraged to participate fully in the design of the system, when the system is a tailor-made one.
   (i)   Their suggestions about problems with the existing system should be fully discussed.
   (ii) The systems analyst's ideas for a new system should be discussed with them, and their views considered.
   (iii) Their suggestions for features in the new system should be welcomed.

   Participation should be genuine.

(c) Change should be planned. Reductions in jobs should be foreseen, and redundancies can be avoided if plans are made well in advance (eg staff can be moved to other job vacancies in the organisation). Training (and retraining) of staff should be organised.

(d) A member of the staff should be appointed as the office expert or 'guru' in the system, to whom other members of staff can go to ask for help or advice.

Job design

67. We have already discussed job design in relation to the motivatory effect of job enlargement, job enrichment and job rotation: these are alternative approaches to the way in which work is organised and allocated.

   We should mention another approach which ties in with our discussion of fatigue and monotony above.

68. Job enlargement has often been described as an approach to job design which is at the opposite end of a spectrum to the 'micro-division' of labour. The micro-division of labour is based on a production line organisation of work.

(a) A job is divided up into the smallest possible number of sequential tasks. Each task is so simple and straightforward that it can be learned with very little training.

(b) Since skills required are low, the effects of absenteeism are minimised: workers can be shifted from one task to another very easily.

(c) Similarly, high labour turnover is not critical, because replacements can be found and trained without difficulty.

(d) Tasks are closely defined, standardised and timed, so output and quality are more easily predicted and controlled.

69. The arguments against the micro-division of labour run as follows.

(a) The work is monotonous, which leads to boredom, fatigue and (arguably) dissatisfaction. The consequences may include high labour turnover, absenteeism, spoilage and industrial unrest.

(b) Men, unlike machines, actually work more efficiently when their work is varied.

(c) An individual required to do a single, simple task feels like a small cog in a large machine. This prevents him from having any sense of contribution to the job or organisation as a whole.

(d) Extreme specialisation isolates the individual in his work and inhibits social contact with other employees.

70. A 'well-designed' job, according to most accounts, should therefore:

(a) give the individual scope for setting his own work standards and targets;

(b) give the individual control over the pace and methods of working;

(c) provide variety and 'meaning' by allowing related tasks to be done by an individual or team as a whole job, or more complex component of a job;

(d) give the individual a chance to give feedback to management about the product or the job;

(e) provide feedback to the individual about his role and performance.

71. Job enlargement, enrichment and rotation are attempts at offering more satisfying and performance-enhancing jobs - but do they really work as well as prevailing theories promise? There area number of varities that must be taken into account, and no easy formula for success.

Lawler, Hackman and Kaufman reported the results of an early job enrichment programme in 1973. They issued attitude survey questionnaires to all employees, before and after job design changes were made, and conducted interviews. (In fact, only 17 operators actually completed before *and* after questionnaires, due to labour turnover.)

Initial organisation

1   Chief operator
7   Group chief operators
14 Service assistants
39 Operators - 'directory assistance'
         'toll' - ie dealing with, timing and charging long distance calls

Enrichment programme

Conducted by company employees, with *no* consultation with operators or service assistants. The project was entitled 'Initiative and Judgement programme', and the following changes were implemented.

1. Operators were allowed to reply to customer requests in their own words, rather than scripted phrases, and no longer had to give their number at the start of each call.
2. They no longer required supervisor's permission to leave their posts to check records etc, or to visit the toilets.
3. 'Directory assistance' operators could help out 'toll' operators in busy periods, at their own discretion.
4. They were given discretion to handle lengthy enquiries, eg during busy periods, as they thought best.

Management's appraisal

Management felt that the programme was a success.

- Training time (eg for set phrases) was reduced - with cost reductions.
- Less supervision was required.
- Absenteeism and labour turnover fell (during the study).
- Productivity was not adversely affected.

However:

Questionnaire replies did not indicate that jobs had been significantly changed in areas which contributed to job satisfaction or motivation. It did not appear that participants were lacking in the *desire* for discretion, responsibility etc, so it was inferred that the job design was still flawed.

In particular, it was recognised that the programme had failed to anticipate the affect changes would have on the service assistants. They no longer made decisions for the operators, nor were relied on to do so, and lost some of their traditional tasks to operators. The established relationship between the groups was unsettled, and the service assistants' position felt to be under threat.

THE NATURE OF WORK GROUPS

Points to be covered

- Function of groups
- Elton Mayo and the Hawthorne experiments
- The formation of groups
- Group norms
- Group cohesion and competition
- Effective and ineffective work teams
- Communicating in groups

Introduction

1. Handy in *Understanding Organizations* defines a group as 'any collection of people who perceive themselves to be a group'. The point of this definition is the distinction it implies between a random collection of individuals and a 'group' of individuals who share a common sense of identity and belonging.

2. A group has certain attributes that a random 'crowd' does not possess. For example:

   (a) *a sense of identity*. Whether the group is formal or informal, its existence is recognised by its members: there are acknowledged boundaries to the group which define who is 'in' and who is 'out', who is 'us' and who is 'them'. People generally need to feel that they 'belong', that they share something with others and are of value to others. Organisations try to establish a sense of corporate identity or company image among their employees as well as among outsiders through advertising and public relations;

   (b) loyalty to the group, and acceptance within the group. This generally expresses itself as *conformity* or the acceptance of the 'norms' of behaviour and attitude that bind the group together and exclude others from it. This type of 'solidarity' may formalise itself in entrance qualifications, rule books, oaths of allegiance etc. or may be an unspoken acceptance of norms: if you have ever travelled on a commuter train you will know how a group can develop a 'style' of its own, without its existence ever having to be formalised. Again, organisations try to encourage employee loyalty and commitment to the rules and objectives of the organisation, and a sense of solidarity against competition and problems;

   (c) *purpose and leadership*. Most groups have an expressed purpose, aim or set of objectives, whatever field they are in: most will, spontaneously or formally, choose individuals or sub-groups to lead them towards the fulfilment of those goals. Strength of personality, a high level of expertise, seniority of age or status and other factors will determine who 'rises to the top' in any group. This hierarchy will be desirable so that the group can co-ordinate and control its members and their activities: it will of course be highly developed in formal organisations.

3. You should bear in mind that although an organisation as a whole may wish to project itself as a large group, with a single, united identity, loyalty and purpose, any organisation will in fact be composed of many sub-groups, with such attributes of their own. Each individual is likely to be the member of several formal or informal groups: a work organisation, a department, a trade union, a club or society, a committee, a social 'clique' etc.

    People in organisations will be drawn together into groups by:

    (a) a preference for small groups, where closer relationships can develop;
    (b) the need to belong and to make a contribution that will be noticed and appreciated;
    (c) familiarity: ie. a shared office, canteen etc.;
    (d) common rank, specialisms, objectives and interests;
    (e) the attractiveness of a particular group activity (eg. joining an interesting club);
    (f) resources offered to groups (eg. sports facilities);
    (g) 'power' greater than the individuals could muster (eg. trade union, pressure group).

4. Some such groupings will be the result of *formal* directives from the organisation: for example, specialists may be 'thrown together' in a committee set up to investigate a particular issue or problem; a department may be split up into small work teams in order to facilitate supervision.

    Informal groups may spring up as a result of those formal arrangements, (eg. if the members of the committee become friends), and will invariably be present in any organisation.

5. *Formal* groups will have a formal structure; they will be consciously organised for a function allotted to them by the organisation, and for which they are held responsible - ie. they are task oriented.

    Permanent formal groups include standing committees, management teams (eg the board of directors) or specialist services (eg information technology support).

    Temporary formal groups include task forces, designed to work on a particular project, ad hoc committees etc.

6. It is worth looking again at Trist's ideas on the role of the *primary working group*.

    Primary groups are important in an industrial organisation because:

    * they form the smallest units within it;
    * they are the immediate social environment of the individual worker; and
    * the methods and team-spirit which prevail there will determine the efficiency and inter-relationships of the whole company.

7. The optimum size of a primary working group is important; the intimate, face-to-face relationships on which a primary group depends cannot be formed among more than, say, a dozen people. Anthony Jay (*Corporation Man*) identifies a group of ten - a 'ten group' - as the linear descendant of the primaeval hunting-band, balancing the individuality which is necessary for *generating* new ideas with the support and comradeship necessary for *developing* them.

8. In the sense that most industrial work falls naturally into small groups of up to a dozen or so, primary groups are commonly found in industry. In the sense that these groups are provided for in the plan of organisation and given *official* leaders, primary groups are rarely found. Too often, the official organisation of a company comes to an end well above the primary group level.

9. Whenever the formal organisation of a company fails to provide for primary groups, informal primary groups will spring up. These will usually have a self-protective purpose and will offer roles to unofficial leaders whose aims will not necessarily be in harmony with the official aims of the organisation.

10. There are many roles in the organisation (those of setters, overlookers and the like) which are in effect leadership roles. In many cases, however, these are recognised only for their technical content and not for their man management content. If the people in such positions were held responsible for the whole of their leadership role - for relationships and team spirit among the group as well as for its technical working - management organisation would extend to the primary working groups.

The function of groups

11. The function of groups may be looked at from two different standpoints: that of the organisation and that of the individuals who comprise the group.

12. From the organisation's standpoint, groups can be used for:

    - performing tasks which require the collective skills of more than one person;
    - creating a formal organisation by which management can control work, by defining responsibilities and delegating as appropriate;
    - testing and ratifying decisions made outside the group;
    - consulting or negotiating, especially to resolve disputes within the organisation;
    - creating ideas (ie acting as a 'think tank');
    - exchanging ideas, collecting and transmitting information;
    - co-ordinating the work of different individuals or other groups;
    - enquiring into what has happened in the past;
    - motivating individuals to devote more energy and effort into achieving the organisation's goals.

13. From the individual's standpoint groups also perform some important functions.

    (a) They satisfy social needs for friendship and belonging.

    (b) They help individuals to develop images of themselves (eg a person may need to see himself as a member of the corporate planning department or of the works snooker team).

    (c) They enable individuals to help each other in matters which are not necessarily connected with the organisation's purpose (eg people at work may organise a baby-sitting circle).

    (d) They enable individuals to share the burdens of any responsibility they may have in their work.

14. Brayfield and Crockett suggested that an individual will always identify with some group or other.

    (a) If he identifies with a social group, outside work, this will have no effect on his job performance.

    (b) On the other hand, if he identifies with his work-mates and work group:

        (i) a congenial work group, creating high morale, can either raise or lower productivity, depending on the 'norm' adopted by the group. The group norm will probably be based on its collective idea of a fair day's work for a fair day's pay but such an attitude is a subjective one, so what is 'fair' may be a high or low standard of efficiency;

        (ii) Coch and French conducted experiments in 1948 to demonstrate the importance of group psychology in setting performance levels. The most productive member of a work group is likely to be the 'social outcast' and not the one with the greatest ability.

    (c) If he identifies with his trade union, and seeks advancement in the union hierarchy, this 'group attachment' will not motivate him to produce more.

    (d) An employee who identifies with his company may not be the most productive, through caring for quality rather than output level. It has been suggested that the employees who are most likely to win recognition and promotion within the company are those who are critical of its policies, and not those who identify with them.

Elton Mayo and the Hawthorne experiments

15. Mayo was an academic based at Harvard University. His work sheds light on the importance of groups within an organisation. His most interesting findings emerged from the 'Hawthorne experiments', so called because they were conducted at the Hawthorne plant of the Western Electric Company.

16. The experiments arose from an attempt by Western Electric to find out the effects of lighting standards on worker productivity. As a test, it moved a group of girls into a special room with variable lighting, and moved another group of girls into a room where the lighting was kept at normal standards. To the astonishment of the company management, productivity shot up in rooms. When the lighting was then reduced in the first room, as a continuation of the test, not only did productivity continue to rise in the first room, but it also rose still further in the second room. Mayo was called in to investigate further.

17. In Mayo's opinion, earlier researchers had paid insufficient attention to the human factor in productivity. He believed that the economic motive was unimportant compared to emotional and non-logical attitudes and sentiments in improving the efficiency and productivity of employees at work.

18. Mayo brought to his researches a background of psychology. As a professor of industrial research at the Graduate School of Business, Harvard University, from 1927 to 1947, he had a great influence on the development of the social sciences and on other students of management and practising managers as well.

19. His Hawthorne experiments took place in Chicago during the thirties. The researchers were trying to find a relationship between fatigue and output. Five girls were the 'guinea pigs' of the experiment. At every point in the programme, the workers were consulted. Checks were kept in quarterly periods, with records not only of their work conditions, lighting, heating, rest periods etc, but also of their private lives. Nothing of any value came out of the experiments until they returned to the conditions of work that they had started with - a 48 hour week, with no rest breaks and not very good lighting: output in the experiment still kept rising.

20. The improvements in productivity could not be explained by lighting, rest periods, hours of work or any other physical work conditions, but Mayo suspected that the attitudes of the girls in the experiment might explain the results.

21. Following a series of interviews with the guinea pigs in the experiments, the Hawthorne researchers concluded that it was the interest, and attention paid to them, that was the (previously unrecognised) motivator. This, they decided, was of far greater importance than all the improved conditions and other variables that they had been introducing. They said 'Attitudes to people, as people, may be more important than such factors as rest periods, benefits, money etc. People are not merely instruments'.

> 'Management, by consultation with the girl workers, by clear explanation of the proposed experiments and the reasons for them, by accepting the workers' verdict in several instances, unwittingly scored a success in two most important human matters - the girls became a self-governing team, and a team that co-operated wholeheartedly with management'.
>
> *Elton Mayo*

22. A hypothesis was developed that motivation to work, productivity and the quality of output were all related to:

   • the 'psychology of the work group' - resting on social relations among the workers; and
   • the relationship between the workers and their supervisor/boss.

23. The hypothesis was tested further by Roethlisberger and Dickson, who selected a new group of 14 men, wirers and solderers, who were put under observation. The results of the experiments were as follows.

   (a) The group developed a keen sense of its own identity; however, it divided into two separate cliques, one of which felt that it did more difficult, 'higher status' work than the other.

   (b) The group as a whole developed certain 'norms' with regard to both output and supervision.

      (i) With regard to output:

         1. the group appeared to establish a standard amount of production which was 'fair' for the pay they received;

         2. members of the group who produced above this normal level of output, or who shirked work and did less than the norm, were put under 'social pressure' by work-mates to get back into line.

     (ii)   With regard to supervision, the group view was that supervisors should not be officious and take unpleasant advantage of their position of authority. One officious supervisor was put under 'social pressure' by the group, so that he asked for a transfer out of the group.

(c)   The group did not follow company policy on some issues, with regard to work practices. In addition, daily reports of output were 'fiddled'; sometimes workers recorded more output than they actually produced, and on other days they recorded less than they produced. The effect was to report constant volumes of daily production, whereas actual daily volume, according to tiredness or morale on the day, fluctuated considerably.

(d)   Individual production rates varied significantly, but not according to individual ability or intelligence. Members of the 'high status' clique produced more than members of the other clique; but both the highest-producing employees and lowest-producing employees were the 'social outcasts' from either group. The men were paid a productivity incentive, and the high-status group felt that the other group were shirking; this resulted in considerable ill-feeling, and an eventual decline in the productivity of the group as a whole.

24.   The experiments appeared to confirm that human attitudes (both of individuals and work groups) and the relationship between management and whole groups or individual subordinates were of key importance in establishing motivation to work and production efficiency.

The formation of groups

25.   Groups are not static. They mature and develop. Four stages in this development are commonly identified: forming, storming, norming and performing.

26.   During the first stage (*forming*) the group is just coming together, and may still be seen as a collection of individuals. Each individual wishes to impress his personality on the group, while its purpose, composition, and organisation are being established. The individuals will be trying to find out about each other, and about the aims and norms of the group. There will at this stage probably be a wariness about introducing new ideas, and the established line will be the respected and stated one: members will not wish to appear radical or unacceptable to the group, even if their minds are full of ideas which would 'rock the boat'. Individuals will also be 'feeling out' each other's attitudes and abilities: no-one will want to appear less informed or skilled than the others. The objectives being pursued may as yet be unclear and a leader may not yet have emerged.

This settling down period is essential, but may be time wasting: the team as a unit will not be used to being autonomous, and will probably not be an efficient agent in the planning of its activities or the activities of others. It may resort to complex bureaucratic procedures to ensure that what it is doing is at least something which will not get its members into trouble.

27.   The second stage is called '*storming*' because it frequently involves more or less open conflict between group members. There may be changes agreed in the original objectives, procedures and norms established for the group. If the group is developing successfully this may be a fruitful phase as more realistic targets are set and trust between the group members increases. The element of risk enters solutions to problems and options may be proposed which are more far-reaching than would have been possible earlier. Whilst the first stage of group development involved 'toeing the organisational line', the second stage brings out the identification of

team members with causes: this may create disagreement, and there may also be political conflict over leadership.

28. The third stage (*norming*) is a period of settling down. There will be agreements about work sharing, individual requirements and expectations of output. Group procedures and customs will be defined and adherence to them secured. The enthusiasm and brain-storming of the second stage may be less apparent, but norms and procedures may evolve which enable methodical working to be introduced and maintained. This need not mean that initiative, creativity and the expression of ideas are discouraged, but that a reasonable hearing is given to everyone and 'consensus' sought.

29. Once the fourth stage (*performing*) has been reached the group sets to work to execute its task. Even at earlier stages some performance will have been achieved but the fourth stage marks the point where the difficulties of growth and development no longer hinder the group's objectives.

30. It would be misleading to suggest that these four stages always follow in a clearly-defined progression, or that the development of a group must be a slow and complicated process. Particularly where the task to be performed is urgent, or where group members are highly motivated, the fourth stage will be reached very quickly while the earlier stages will be hard to distinguish.

Group norms

31. A work group establishes 'norms' or acceptable levels and methods of behaviour, to which all members of the group are expected to conform. This group attitude will have a negative effect on an organisation if it sets unreasonably low production norms. Groups often apply unfair treatment or discrimination against others who break their 'rules'.

32. 'Norms', as we discussed in an earlier chapter, are partly the product of 'rôles' and rôle expectations of how people in certain positions behave, as conceived by people in related positions. Rôle theory will be important in understanding relationships within groups, and the conflicts and ambiguities that may arise.

> In a classic experiment by Sherif, participants were asked to look at a fixed point of light in a black box in a darkroom. Although the point of light is fixed, it so happens that in the darkness, it *appears* to move. Each participant was asked to say how far the light moved, and their individual estimates were recorded.
>
> They were next put into a small group where each member of the group gave their own estimates to the others. From this interchange of opinions, individuals began to change their minds about how far the light had moved, and a group 'norm' estimate emerged.
>
> When the groups were broken up, each individual was again asked to re-state his estimate; significantly, they retained the group norm estimate and rejected their previous individual estimate.

> The experiment showed the effect of group psychology on establishing norms for the individual himself; even when, as in the case of the experiment, there is no factual basis for the group norm.

33. The general nature of group pressure is to require the individual to share in the group's own identity, and individuals may react to group norms, customs etc with:

- compliance - 'toeing the line' without real commitment;
- internalisation - ie. full acceptance and identification; or
- counter-conformity - ie. rejecting the group and/or its norms.

34. Pressure is strongest on the individual when:

(a) the issue is not clear-cut;
(b) he lacks support for his own attitude or behaviour; and
(c) he is exposed to other members of the group for a length of time.

Intelligent and independent individuals conform less readily. Those who *do* conform easily tend to be more conventional in their social values, less self-confident and lacking in spontaneity.

35. Norms may be reinforced in various ways by the group:

(a) *identification* - the use of 'badges', symbols, perhaps special modes of speech, 'in-jokes' etc - ie. the marks of belonging, prestige and acceptance. There may even be 'initiation rites' which mark the boundaries of membership;

(b) *sanctions* of various kinds. Deviant behaviour may be dealt with by ostracising or ignoring the member concerned ('sending him to Coventry'), by ridicule or reprimand, even by physical hostility. The threat of expulsion is the final sanction.

In other words the group's power to induce conformity depends on the degree to which the individual values his membership of the group and the rewards it may offer, or wishes to avoid the negative sanctions at its disposal.

36. This 'concensus' power is often demonstrated in the ways in which work groups 'manipulate' output.

Roethlisberger and Dickson quote employees who were told by their colleagues that if an operation turned out more than x units in a day "they'll just raise the rate and ask you to do more for the same money". The same discouragement was offered to an individual who had a suggestion to improve work methods.

"There is a widely held belief that if a piece rate setter catches an operator working at top speed he may cut the piece rate, on the assumption that the operator was holding back when his timings were made."

37. The Hawthorne investigations, in their third stage, observed a group of employees in the Bank Wiring Observation Room. It was found that they restricted their output: the group's own norm for output was not exceeded by any of its individual members, as it was considered that:

    (a) too much work would be 'rate-busting'; but
    (b) too little work would be 'chiselling' - ie. not carrying your weight.

    The group was generally indifferent to the company's pay incentive scheme and was firm in its own code of behaviour and against management.

38. From findings that an individual's opinions can be changed or swayed by group consensus, it may be argued that it would be more effective, and probably also easier in practice, to change group norms than to change individual norms. Motivation should therefore involve the work group as a whole, because changes agreed by a group are likely to be more effective and longer-lasting.

Group cohesion and competition

39. In an experiment reported by Deutsch (1949), psychology students were given puzzles and human relation problems to work at in discussion groups. Some groups ('co-operative' ones) were told that the grade each individual got at the end of the course would depend on the performance of his group. Other groups ('competitive' ones) were told that each student would receive a grade according to his own contributions.

40. No significant differences were found between the two kinds of group in the amount of interest and involvement in the tasks, or in the amount of learning. But the co-operative groups, compared with the competitive ones, had greater productivity per unit time, better quality of product and discussion, greater co-ordination of effort and sub-division of activity, more diversity in amount of contribution per member, more attentiveness to fellow members and more friendliness during discussion.

41. Another experiment, conducted in 1949 by Sherif and Sherif, set out to investigate how groups are formed, and how relationships between groups are created. The 'guinea pigs' of the experiment were 24 boys of about 12 years old who were taken to a summer camp. After a few days, 'natural' affinities were discounted by breaking up friendships which had formed, and dividing 'the boys' into two 'formal' groups, the Bulldogs and the Red Devils.

42. It was found that when the groups were formed there was a noticeable switch of friendships. Boys whose previous 'best friends' were moved into the other group began to switch 'best friendships' to someone else who belonged to their group. The group identity thus had a significant effect on the attitudes of individual members.

43. The experimenters also tried to create friction between the groups; these efforts were so successful that by the end of the experiment there was such intense inter-group rivalry that subsequent attempts to re-unite the entire camp were insufficient to restore common goodwill. From this, and other research, it is argued that new members of a group quickly learn the norms and attitudes of the others, no matter whether these are 'positive' or 'negative', friendly or hostile. It is also suggested that inter-group competition may have a positive effect on group cohesion and performance.

44. Within each competing group:

    (a) members close ranks, and submerge their differences; loyalty and conformity are demanded;
    (b) the 'climate' changes from informal and sociable to work and task-oriented; individual needs are subordinated to achievement;
    (c) leadership moves from democratic to autocratic, with the group's acceptance;
    (d) the group tends to become more structured and organised.

45. Between competing groups:

    (a) the opposing group begins to be perceived as 'the enemy';
    (b) perception is distorted, presenting an idealised picture of 'us' and a negative stereotype of 'them';
    (c) inter-group communication decreases - facilitating the perceptual distortion.

46. In a 'win-lose' situation, ie where competition is not perceived to result in benefits for both sides, the winning group will:

    (a) retain its cohesion;
    (b) relax into a complacent, playful state ('fat and happy');
    (c) return to group maintenance, concern for members' needs etc; and
    (d) be confirmed in its group 'self-concept' with little re-evaluation.

47. The losing group will:

    (a) deny defeat if possible, or place the blame on the arbitrator, the system etc;
    (b) lose its cohesion and splinter into conflict, as 'blame' is apportioned;
    (c) be keyed-up, fighting mad ('lean and hungry');
    (d) turn towards work-orientation to regroup - rather than members' needs, group maintenance etc;
    (e) tend to learn by revaluating its perceptions of itself and the other group. It is more likely to become a cohesive and effective unit once the 'defeat' has been accepted.

48. Members of a group will act in unison if the group's existence or patterns of behaviour are threatened from outside. Cohesion is naturally assumed to be the result of positive factors such as communication, agreement and mutual trust - but in the face of a 'common enemy' (competition, crisis or emergency) cohesion and productivity benefit.

49. In an ideal functioning group:

    (a) each individual gets the support of the group, a sense of identity and belonging which encourages loyalty and hard work on the group's behalf;

    (b) skills, information and ideas are 'pooled' or shared, so that the group's capabilities are greater than those of the individuals;

    (c) new ideas can be tested, reactions taken into account, persuasive skills brought into play in group discussion for decision-making and problem-solving;

(d) each individual is encouraged to participate and contribute and thus becomes personally involved in and committed to the group's activities;

(e) goodwill, trust and respect can be built up between individuals, so that communication is encouraged and potential problems more easily overcome.

50. Unfortunately, group working is rarely such an undiluted success. There are certain constraints involved in working with others.

(a) Awareness of 'role' and group norms for behaviour, the desire to be acceptable to the group, may restrict individual personality and flair. This may perhaps create pressure or a sense of 'schizophrenia' for the individual concerned who can't 'be himself' in a group situation.

(b) Conflicting roles and relationships (where an individual is a member of more than one group) can cause difficulties in communicating effectively, especially if sub-groups or cliques are formed in conflict with other groupings.

(c) The effective functioning of the group is dependent upon each of its members, and will suffer if members dislike or distrust each other, or if one member is so dominant that others cannot participate, or so timid that the value of his ideas is lost, or so negative in attitude that constructive communication is rendered impossible etc.

(d) Rigid leadership and procedures may strangle initiative and creativity in individuals. On the other hand, differences of opinion and political conflicts of interest are always likely and if all policies and decisions are to be determined by consultation and agreement within the group, decisions may never be reached and action never taken.

Cohesion and 'group think'

51. It is possible for groups to be *too* cohesive, too all-absorbing. Handy notes that "ultra-cohesive groups can be dangerous because in the organisational context the group must serve the organisation, not itself."

If a group is completely absorbed with its own maintenance, members and priorities, it can become dangerously blinkered to what is going on around it, and may confidently forge ahead in a completely wrong direction. I L Janis describes this as 'group think'.

52. The cosy consensus of the group prevents consideration of alternatives, constructive criticism or conflict. Symptoms of 'group think' include:

(a) sense of invulnerability - blindness to the risk involved in 'pet' strategies;
(b) rationalisations for inconsistent facts;
(c) moral blindness - 'might is right';
(d) tendency to stereotype 'outsiders' and 'enemies';
(e) strong group pressure to quell dissent;
(f) self-censorship by members - ie. not 'rocking the boat';
(g) perception of unanimity - filtering out divergent views;
(h) mutual support and solidarity to 'guard' the decision.

53. Victims of 'group think' - which is rife at the top and centre of organisations - take great risks in their decisions, fail to recognise failure, and are highly resistant to unpalatable information. Such groups must:

- actively encourage self-criticism;
- welcome outside ideas and evaluation; and
- respond positively to conflicting evidence.

Creating an effective work group

54. The management problem is how to create an effective, efficient work group. If managers can motivate groups (and individuals) to work harder and better to achieve organisational goals, the sense of pride in their own competence *(competence motivation)* might create job satisfaction through belonging to the group and performing the group's tasks. Competitive motivation is often strong in successful football teams and highly trained army units.

55. Handy takes a contingency approach to the problem of group effectiveness, which, he argues, depends on:

- the group   }
- the group's task   }   The 'givens'
- the group's environment }

- motivation of the group }
- leadership style   }   The 'intervening factors'
- processes and procedures }

- productivity of the group }   The 'outcomes'
- satisfaction of the group members }

These factors are important, and they are worth learning carefully. They are considered in more detail below.

56. The personalities and characteristics of the individual members of the group, and the personal goals of these members, will help to determine the group's personality and goals. An individual is likely to be influenced more strongly by a small group than by a large group in which he may feel like a small fish in a large pond, and therefore unable to participate effectively in group decisions.

57. It has been suggested that the effectiveness of a work group depends on the blend of the individual skills and abilities of its members. A project team might be most effective if it contains:

(a) a man of originality and ideas;
(b) a 'get-up-and-go' man with considerable energy, enthusiasm and drive;
(c) a quiet, logical thinker, who ponders carefully and criticises the ideas of others;
(d) a plodder, who is happy to do the humdrum routine work; and
(e) a conciliator, who is adept at negotiating compromises or a consensus of thought between other members of the group.

58. Belbin, in a study of business-game teams at Carnegie Institute of Technology in 1981, discovered that a differentiation of influence among team members (ie. agreement that some members were more influential than others) resulted in higher morale and better performance. Belbin's picture (which many managers have found a useful guide to team working) of the most effective character-mix in a team involves eight necessary roles which should ideally be balanced and evenly 'spread' in the team:

   - the *chairman* - presides and co-ordinates; balanced, disciplined, good at working through others;

   - the *shaper* - highly strung, dominant, extravert, passionate about the task itself, a spur to action;

   - the *plant* - introverted, but intellectually dominant and imaginative; source of ideas and proposals but with disadvantages of introversion;

   - the *monitor-evaluator* - analytically (rather than creatively) intelligent; dissects ideas, spots flaws; possibly aloof, tactless - but necessary;

   - the *resource-investigator* - popular, sociable, extravert, relaxed; source of new contacts etc. but not an originator; needs to be made use of;

   - the *company worker* - practical organiser, turning ideas into tasks - scheduling, planning etc. Trustworthy and efficient - but not excited (or exciting, often); not a leader, but an administrator;

   - the *team worker* - most concerned with team maintenance - supportive, understanding, diplomatic; popular but uncompetitive - noticed only in absence;

   - the *finisher* - chivvies the team to meet deadlines, attend to details etc; urgency and follow-through important, though not always popular.

59. The nature of the task must have some bearing on how a group should be managed. If a job must be done urgently, it is often necessary to dictate how things should be done, rather than to encourage a participatory style of working. Jobs which are routine, unimportant and undemanding will be insufficient to motivate either individuals or the group as a whole. If individuals in the group want authoritarian leadership, they are also likely to want clearly defined group targets.

60. The group's environment relates to factors such as the physical surroundings at work and to inter-group relations. An open-plan office, in which the members of the group are closely situated, is more conducive to group cohesion than a situation in which individuals are partitioned into separate offices, or geographically distant from each other. Group attitudes will also be affected, as described previously, by relationships with other groups, which may be friendly, neutral or hostile.

61. Of the 'intervening factors', motivation and leadership are discussed in separate chapters of this text. With regard to processes and procedures, research indicates that a group which tackles its work systematically will be more effective than a group which lives from hand to mouth, and muddles through - but this is often true of individuals as well.

62. High productivity may be achieved if work is so arranged that satisfaction of individuals' needs coincides with high output. Where teams are, for example, allowed to set their own improvement goals and methods and to measure their own progress towards those goals, it has been observed (by Peters and Waterman among others) that they regularly *exceed* their targets.

63. Individuals may bring to the group their own 'hidden agendas' for satisfaction: these are goals which may have nothing to do with the declared aims of the group - eg. protection of a sub-group, impressing the boss, inter-personal rivalry etc.

Peters and Waterman (*In Search of Excellence*) outline the cultural attributes of successful *task force* teams. They should:

- be small - requiring the trust of those who are not involved;
- be of limited duration and working under the 'busy member theorem' - ie. "get off the damned task force and back to work";
- be voluntary - which ensures that the business is 'real';
- have an informal structure and documentation - ie. no bulky paperwork, and open communication;
- have swift follow-up - ie. be *action* oriented.

Case study

64. As an example, suppose that a work group consists of five people, who work closely together in an open-plan office. Their supervisor has his office two floors above in the same building. All the group members are well-educated, but most of them are new to the company.

The task of the group is to prepare market forecasts, which are submitted to marketing managers whose offices are in a different building. The forecasts are mostly routine, although occasionally 'one-off' requests for special information are received. The volume of work is not really sufficient to keep all five group members busy.

The group's leader is more concerned with the special responsibilities which keep him fully occupied, and he is inclined to leave the group alone, ie he displays a 'laissez-faire' approach to leadership.

Many members of the group are frustrated because much of the work is boring, and seemingly unimportant, although they sometimes enjoy doing 'one-off' work. They would like to initiate more of their own projects, and are angry that their supervisor does not show any interest in this idea when they speak to him, which is rarely.

65. You may appreciate that in this situation there is a strong possibility that the work group as a whole will tend to develop negative feelings towards their work and the organisation, to become slack and uncaring about their work, to develop strong interests outside work and to display a hostile attitude to other departments in the organisation. This may result from:

(a) *the nature of the group*. Its size is small, so individuals will more readily identify with it. Individual members may be too well qualified for the work they do, especially the routine report preparation;

(b) *the task*: routine work is unsuited to individuals who seek more challenging work. A shortage of work is likely to lead to boredom;

(c) *the environment*: the group is 'physically intact' in its own office space, but remote from its supervisor and the marketing managers it serves;

(d) *the 'laissez-faire' style of leadership*: unlikely to encourage group motivation, as is the lack of a clear purpose for the group's task, the absence of the right to show initiative and the apparent absence of any kind of reward for doing the job efficiently;

(e) *processes and procedures*: left to its own devices, and without a specific sense of purpose, the organisation of the group is likely to be 'muddled' and lacking a task focus.

66. A management approach to dealing with this particular situation might be:

(a) to further reduce the size of the work group;

(b) to upgrade the work of the group, or to employ less skilled individuals, so that the group is more suited to the task;

(c) to change the supervisor, and to introduce a leader whose style is more suited to the reorganised group;

(d) to re-arrange office space so that the supervisor works close to his group, and maintains effective communication links with the marketing department;

(e) to consider various methods of motivating the group to be more efficient;

(f) to provide the group with an identifiable task, and to organise their work procedures and processes.

As a result the group might be motivated so as to achieve a more clearly thought-out purpose more efficiently.

The characteristics of effective and ineffective work teams

67. If a manager is to try to improve the effectiveness of his work team he must be able to identify the different characteristics of an effective group and an ineffective group. Some pointers to group efficiency are quantifiable measures; others are more qualitative factors and are difficult to measure.

68. A number of different factors should be considered, because a favourable showing in some aspects of work does not necessarily mean that a group is operating effectively. No one factor on its own is significant, but taken collectively the factors will present a picture of how well or badly the group is operating.

Effective work group	Ineffective work group

Quantifiable factors

(1) Low rate of labour turnover	(1) High rate of labour turnover
(2) Low accident rate	(2) High accident rate
(3) Low absenteeism	(3) High absenteeism
(4) High output and productivity	(4) Low output and productivity
(5) Good quality of output	(5) Poor quality of output
(6) Individual targets are achieved	(6) Individual targets are not achieved
(7) There are few stoppages and interruptions to work	(7) Much time is wasted owing to disruption of work flow
	(8) Time is lost owing to disagreements between superior and subordinates

Qualitative factors

(1) There is a high commitment to the achievement of targets and organisational goals	(1) There is no understanding of organisational goals or the role of the group
(2) There is a clear understanding of the group's work	(2) There is a low commitment to targets.
(3) There is a clear understanding of the role of each person within the group	(3) There is confusion and uncertainty about the role of each person within the group
(4) There is a free and open communication between members of the group and trust between members	(4) There is mistrust between group members and suspicion of group's leaders
(5) There is idea sharing	(5) There is little idea sharing
(6) The group is good at generating new ideas	(6) The group does not generate any good new ideas
(7) Group members try to help each other out by offering constructive criticisms and suggestions	(7) Group members make negative and hostile criticisms about each other's work
(8) There is group problem solving which gets to the root causes of the work problem	(8) Work problems are dealt with superficially, with attention paid to the symptoms but not the cause
(9) There is an active interest in work decisions	(9) Decisions about work are accepted passively
(10) Group members seek a united consensus of opinion	(10) Group members hold strongly opposed views
(11) The members of the group want to develop their abilities in their work	(11) Group members find work boring and do it reluctantly
(12) The group is sufficiently motivated to be able to carry on working in the absence of its leader	(12) The group needs its leader there to get work done

69. The importance of a group for social contact among its individual members is worth a bit more thought. You might think that the social nature of groups is obvious. However, some formal groups do not provide strong social links, when their individual members do not work closely together and do not meet often. One example is a committee. Committee members in a large business organisation often do not have strong social links.

70. It will be helpful if you try to make a distinction in your mind between:

(a) what work groups can be organised to do (perform a task, control work, make decisions, ratify decisions, create ideas, exchange ideas and co-ordinate work etc); and

(b) the implication for management of group tendency to develop certain characteristics and norms; it would be advisable to give some attention to the leadership of groups and to making group norms and attitudes work in the organisation's favour (perhaps through participation in decision-making etc).

Communicating in groups

71. In a well-known 'laboratory' test (1951) H J Leavitt examined the effectiveness of four communication networks for *written* communication between members of a small group. The four network patterns were:

(a) the circle:

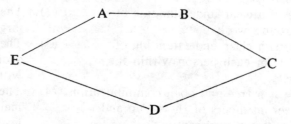

in which each member of the group could communicate with only two others in the group, as shown:

(b) the chain: A - B - C - D - E

Similar to the circle, except that A and E cannot communicate with each other and are therefore at both ends of a communication chain;

(c) the 'Y':

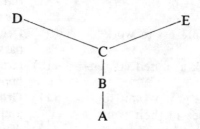

the wheel:

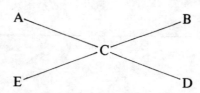

In both the 'Y' and the 'wheel' patterns, C occupies a more central position in the network.

72. In Leavitt's experiment, each member of a group of five people has to solve a problem and each has an essential piece of information. Only written communication, channelled according to one of the four patterns described above, was allowed.

The findings of the experiment were as follows:

(a) *speed of problem-solving*: the wheel was fastest, followed by the Y, the chain and finally the circle;

(b) *leadership*: in the circle, no member was seen as the leader, but in the other three types of groups, C was regarded as a leader (more so in the wheel and the Y);

(c) *job satisfaction*: the enjoyment of the job was greatest among members of a circle, followed by the chain, the Y and lastly the wheel (but see paragraph 75(c) below).

73. The progression (one way or the other) of Circle-Chain-Y-Wheel emerged in all these findings. Leavitt wrote: 'the Circle, one extreme, is active, leaderless, unorganised, erratic and yet is enjoyed by its members. The Wheel at the other extreme is less active, has a distinct leader, is well and stably organised, is less erratic and yet is unsatisfying to most of its members'. He concluded that in organisations where there is minimal 'centrality' and 'peripherality' of individuals in a communication system, the organisation will be active, error-prone, leaderless, slow and enjoyed by its members; whereas in organisations where there is greater 'centrality' of some individuals and 'peripherality' of others, the organisation will be stable and efficient, consisting of leaders and the led (with low enjoyment among the members).

74. One significant communication pattern which was omitted from Leavitt's experiment was the 'all-channel' communication system which might be practically employed in group working:

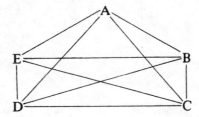

75. In a comparison of the all-channel system, the wheel and the circle, as methods of group communication and operations, the following results emerged.

(a) *Simple problem-solving*: the wheel system solves problems quickest, and the circle is the slowest, with the all-channel system in between.

(b) *Complex problem-solving*: the all-channel system, with its participatory style, and more open communication system, generally provides the best solutions to complex problems. The efficiency of the wheel depends on the ability of the leader, or central figure. In the circle, there is a lack of co-ordination and solutions to problems are poor.

(c) *Job satisfaction*: contrary to Leavitt's findings, it is now argued that job satisfaction in the circle is low, because of poor, or slow performance in decision-making and a lack of co-ordination and although job satisfaction in the wheel system is low for individuals away from the centre, the man at the centre has high satisfaction. The all-channel system provides fairly high job satisfaction to all group members (although the size of the group must not be so large that some individuals feel excluded from participation).

76. It must not be supposed that an all-channel system is best under all circumstances. It solves complex problems well, but slowly, and it tends to disintegrate under pressure (eg time pressure to get results) into a wheel system.

Conclusion

77. It is worth noting, too, that for all its opportunities for exchanged ideas and knowledge, immediate feedback, 'brainstorming' etc, the 'group' as a work unit is not necessarily superior to the individual in terms of performance in all situations.

(a) Decision-making may be a cumbersome process where consensus has to be reached. However, it has been shown (rather surprisingly) that groups take *riskier* decisions than the individuals comprising them - perhaps because of the sense of shared responsibility.

(b) Group norms may work to lower the standard rate of unit production - though, again, individuals need groups psychologically, and isolation can produce stress and hostile behaviour, and can impair performance just as surely as 'rate fixing'.

(c) Group cohesion may provide a position of strength - solidarity - from which to behave in hostile or deviant (from the organisation's point of view) ways.

(d) Groups have been shown to produce less ideas - though better evaluated - than the individuals of the group working separately. A group *will* often produce a better solution to a quiz than its best individual, since 'missing pieces' can be added to his performance.

LEADERSHIP AT WORK

Points to be covered

- Management: Drucker, Handy
- The manager as leader
- Trait and style theories of leadership
- The Ashridge studies
- The views of the scientific management school
- The 'behaviourist' school views - Lewin, Lippit & White - Likert
- Task management: a return to traditional views - Blake's grid
- Reddin's 3-D views on leadership style
- John Adair: action-centred leadership
- A systems approach to leadership
- A contingency approach to leadership: F E Fiedler

Introduction

1. The process of management and the functions of management have been analysed many times in various ways by different writers, who have taken the view that:

    (a) management is an operational process, which can be understood by a close study of management functions;

    (b) the study of management should then lead to the development of certain principles of good management, which will be of value when put into practice.

2. Henri Fayol, a French management theorist working in the early decades of this century, listed the functions of management as follows:

    (a) *Planning*. This involves selecting objectives, and the strategies, policies, programmes and procedures for achieving the objectives either for the organisation as a whole or for a part of it. Planning might be done exclusively by managers who will later be responsible for performance: however, *advice* on planning decisions might also be provided by 'staff management' who do not have 'line' authority for putting the plans into practice. Expert advice is nevertheless a part of the management planning function.

    (b) *Organising*. This involves the establishment of a structure of tasks which need to be performed to achieve the goals of the organisation, grouping these tasks into jobs for an individual, creating groups of jobs within sections and departments, delegating authority to carry out the jobs, and providing systems of information and communication, and for the co-ordination of activities within the organisation.

    (c) *Commanding*. This involves giving instructions to subordinates to carry out tasks over which the manager has authority for decisions and responsibility for performance.

(d) *Co-ordinating*. This is the task of harmonising the activities of individuals and groups within the organisation, which will inevitably have different ideas about what their own goals should be. Management must reconcile differences in approach, effort, interest and timing of these separate individuals and groups. This is best achieved by making the individuals and groups aware of how their work is contributing to the goals of the overall organisation.

(e) *Controlling*. This is the task of measuring and correcting the activities of individuals and groups, to ensure that their performance is in accordance with plans. Plans must be made, but they will not be achieved unless activities are monitored, and deviations from plan identified and corrected as soon as they become apparent.

3. Fayol's analysis of management functions is only one of several similar types of analysis. Other functions which might be identified, for example, are staffing (ie filling positions in the organisation with people), leading (unlike commanding, 'leading' is concerned with the interpersonal nature of management) and acting as the organisation's representative in dealing with other organisations (ie an ambassadorial or public relations role).

Drucker on the management process

4. Peter Drucker worked in the 1940s and 1950s as a business adviser to a number of US corporations. He was also a prolific writer on management. Drucker grouped the operations of management into five categories.

(a) *Setting objectives for the organisation*. Managers decide what the objectives of the organisation should be and quantify the targets of achievement for each objective. They must then communicate these targets to other people in the organisation.

(b) *Organising the work*. The work to be done in the organisation must be divided into manageable activities and manageable jobs. The jobs must be integrated into a formal organisation structure, and people must be selected to do the jobs.

(c) *Motivating* employees and communicating information to them to enable them to do their work.

(d) *The job of measurement*. Management must:

(i) establish objectives or yardsticks of performance for every person in the organisation;

(ii) analyse actual performance, appraise it against the objectives or yardsticks which have been set, and analyse the comparison;

(iii) communicate the findings and explain their significance both to subordinate employees and also to superiors.

(e) *Developing people*. The manager 'brings out what is in them or he stifles them. He strengthens their integrity or he corrupts them'.

6. Drucker has also argued that there is a further basic function of management in business: economic performance. In this respect, the business manager is different from the manager of any other type of organisation. Management of a business can only justify its existence and its authority by the economic results it produces, even though as a consequence of their actions, significant non-economic results occur as well.

6. He then described the jobs of management within this basic function of economic performance as:

   (a) *managing a business*. The purposes of the business are:
      (i)   to create a customer; and
      (ii) innovation;

   (b) *managing managers*. The requirements here are:
      (i)   management by objectives;
      (ii)   proper structure of managers' jobs;
      (iii)   creating the right spirit in the organisation;
      (iv)   making a provision for the managers of tomorrow;
      (v)   arriving at sound principles of organisation structure;

   (c) *managing worker and work*.

7. These three jobs are carried out within a time dimension.

   (a) Management must always consider both the short-term and longer-term consequences of their actions. A business must be kept profitable into the long-term future, but at the same time short-term profitability must be maintained to avoid the danger that the long term will never be reached, and the business liquidated or taken over.

   (b) Decisions taken by management are for the future, and some have a very long 'planning horizon' - ie the time between making the decision and seeing the consequences of that decision can be very long. For example, if a decision is made to build a factory, it might be years before the building is erected, equipped and in operation, and years more before it earns sufficient profits to pay back the investment.

Being a manager: the views of Handy

8. Charles Handy suggested that a definition of a manager or a manager's role is likely to be so broad as to be fairly meaningless. His own analysis of being a manager was divided into three aspects:

   ● the manager as a general practitioner;
   ● the managerial dilemmas;
   ● the manager as a person;

9. *The manager as a general practitioner*. A manager is the first recipient of an organisation's problems and he must:

   (a) identify the symptoms in the situation (eg low productivity, high labour turnover, severe industrial relations problems etc);
   (b) diagnose the disease or cause of the trouble;
   (c) decide how it might be dealt with - ie develop a strategy for better health;
   (d) start the treatment.

10. Typical strategies for health were listed as:

    (a) *people:* ie changing people, either literally or figuratively;
        (i)   hiring and firing;
        (ii) re-assignment;
        (iii) training and education;
        (iv) selective pay increases;
        (v)   counselling or admonition;

    (b) *the work and the structure:*
        (i)   re-organisation of reporting relationships;
        (ii   re-definition of the work task;
        (iii) job enrichment;
        (iv) re-definition of roles;

    (c) *the systems and procedures:* ie to amend or introduce:
        (i)   communication systems;
        (ii) rewards systems (payment methods, salary guides);
        (iii) information and reporting systems;
        (iv) budgets or other decision-making systems (eg stock control, debtor control).

11. *The managerial dilemmas.* Managers are paid more than workers because they face constant dilemmas which they have to resolve. These dilemmas are:

    (a) *the dilemma of the cultures.* The cultures of organisations were described earlier in this text. It is management's task to decide which culture of organisation and management is required for his particular task. As a manager rises in seniority, he will find it necessary to behave in a culturally diverse manner to satisfy the requirements of his job and the expectations of his employees. In other words, managers must be prepared to show flexibility and good judgement in their choice of organisation culture.

    > The manager 'must be flexible but consistent, culturally diverse but recognisably an individual with his own identity. Therein lies the dilemma. Those ....who relapse into a culturally predominant style will find themselves rightly restricted to that part of the organisation where their culture prevails. Middle layers of organisations are often overcrowded with culturally rigid managers who have failed to deal with this cultural dilemma';

    (b) *the dilemma of time horizons.* This is the problem of responsibility for both the present and the future at the same time, described above in paragraph 7(a);

    (c) *the trust-control dilemma.* This is the problem of balance between management's wish to control the work for which they are responsible, and the necessity to delegate work to subordinates, trusting them to do the work properly. The greater trust a manager places in subordinates, the less control he retains himself. Retaining control implies a lack of trust in subordinates. 'The managerial dilemma is always how to balance trust and control';

    (d) *the commando leader's dilemma.* In many organisations, junior managers show a strong preference for working in project teams, with a clear task or objective, and working outside the normal bureaucratic structure of a large formal organisation. Unfortunately, there can be too many project groups (or 'commando groups') for the good of the total organisation, and a manager's dilemma is to decide how many project groups he should create to satisfy the needs of his subordinates, and how much bureaucratic organisation structure should be retained for the benefit of the total organisation despite the wishes of his subordinates.

12. *The manager as a person.* Management is developing into a 'semi-profession' and managers expect to be rewarded for their professional skills. The implications for individual managers are that 'increasingly it will come to be seen as the individual's responsibility to maintain, alter or boost his skills, to find the right market for his skills and to sell them to the appropriate buyer'. In other words, management must continue to develop their own professional skills and sell them to the best bidder.

The 'traditional' view that an organisation should employ 'raw recruits' and nuture them into its management structure might in future no longer be accepted. 'There will then be no obligation to continue to employ the individual when the benefit of his skills begins to be less than their costs'.

The manager as leader

13. Leadership is the process of influencing others to work willingly towards an organisation's goals, and to the best of their capabilities. ' The essence of leadership is *followership*. In other words it is the willingness of people to follow that makes a person a leader' (Koontz, O'Donnell, Weihrich). Leadership would also be listed as *one* of the functions of management.

14. Leadership comes about in a number of different ways.

   (a) A manager is appointed to a position of authority within the organisation. He relies mainly on the (legitimate) authority of that position. Leadership of his subordinates is a function of the position he holds (although a manager will not necessarily be a 'leader', if he lacks leadership qualities).

   (b) Some leaders (eg in politics or in trade unions) might be elected.

   (c) Other leaders might emerge by popular choice and through their personal drive and qualities. Unofficial spokesmen for groups of people are leaders of this style.

15. Leaders are *given* their roles by their putative followers; their 'authority' may technically be removed if their followers cease to acknowledge them. The *personal, physical* or *expert* power of leaders is therefore more important than position power alone.

16. Leaders are the creators and 'sellers' of culture in the organisation. "The [leader] not only creates the rational and tangible aspects of organisations, such as structure and technology, but is also the creator of symbols, ideologies, language, beliefs, rituals and myths." (*Pettigrew*).

17. If a manager had indifferent or poor leadership qualities his subordinates would still do their job, but they would do it ineffectually or perhaps in a confused manner. By providing leadership, a manager should be able to use the capabilities of subordinates to better effect, ie leadership is the 'influential increment over and above mechanical compliance with the

routine directives of the organisation' (Katz and Kahn *The Social Psychology of Organisations*). Managers therefore need – and should seek – to become leaders in situations where they require co-operation ie. not merely compliance by their immediate subordinates.

> "Leadership over human beings is exercised when persons with certain motives and purposes mobilize, in competition or conflict with others, institutional, political, psychological and other resources so as to arouse, engage and satisfy the motives of followers."
>
> *Gregor Burns*

18. Since leadership is concerned with influencing others, it is necessary to have some understanding about what motivates people to work. Motivation is the subject of an earlier chapter of this text, but it may be summarised briefly as the process which determines how much effort, energy and excitement a person is prepared to expend in his work. Koontz, O'Donnell and Weihrich formulate the principle that 'since people tend to follow those whom they see as a means of satisfying their own personal goals, the more managers understand what motivates their subordinates and how these motivations operate, and the more they reflect this understanding in carrying out their managerial actions, the more effective leaders they are likely to be.'

Trait theories of leadership

19. Early theories suggested that there are certain qualities, personality characteristics or 'traits' which make a good leader. These might be aggression, self-assurance, intelligence, initiative, a drive for achievement or power, interpersonal skills, administrative ability, imagination, a certain upbringing and education, the 'helicopter factor' (ie the ability to rise above a situation and analyse it objectively) etc.

20. This list is not exhaustive, and various writers attempted to show that their selected list of traits were the ones that provided the key to leadership. The full list of traits is so long that it appears to call for a man or woman of extraordinary, even superhuman, gifts to be a leader.

21. Jennings (1961) wrote that 'Research has produced such a variegated list of traits presumed to describe leadership, that for all practical purposes it describes nothing. Fifty years of study have failed to produce one personality trait or set of qualities that can be used to distinguish between leaders and non-leaders.'

22. The 'great men' theory (ie that people are born with leadership qualities or traits, and either do or do not 'have what it takes' to be leaders) has been challenged by writers of the human relations school. Stodgill wrote (1948) 'A person does not become a leader by virtue of the possession of some combination of traits, but the pattern of personal characteristics of the leader must bear some relevant relationship to the characteristics, activities and goals of the followers'. As early as 1928, Mary Parker Follett had suggested that different work situations called for different types of leadership.

The conclusion was that if leadership is not an innate gift, a style of leadership appropriate to a given work situation could be learned and adopted.

Other theories of leadership

23. Alternative approaches to leadership theory have been developed over the years, and some of these will be described under the headings of:

- style theories, mainly of the 'behaviouralist' school of thought;

- systems theory and leadership;

- contingency theories of leadership.

Leadership and leadership styles

24. Four different types or styles of leadership were identified by Huneryager and Heckman (1967):

- *dictatorial style:* the manager forces subordinates to work by threatening punishment and penalties. The psychological contract between the subordinates and their organisation would be coercive.

    Dictatorial leadership might be rare in commerce and industry, but it is not uncommon in the style of government in some countries of the world, nor in the style of parenthood in many families;

- *autocratic style:* decision-making is centralised in the hands of the leader himself, who does not encourage participation by subordinates; indeed, subordinates' ideas might be actively discouraged and obedience to orders would be expected from them.

    The autocratic style is common in many organisations, and you will perhaps be able to identify examples from your own experience. Doctors, matrons and sisters in hospitals tend to practise an autocratic style; managers/directors who own their company also tend to expect things to be done their way;

- *democratic style:* decision-making is decentralised, and shared by subordinates in participative group action. To be truly democratic, the subordinate must be willing to participate.

    The democratic style is described more fully later;

- *laissez-faire style:* subordinates are given little or no direction at all, and are allowed to establish their own objectives and make all their own decisions.

    The leader of a research establishment might adopt a laissez-faire style, giving individual research workers freedom of choice to organise and conduct their research as they themselves want (within certain limits, such as budget spending limits).

25. These four divisions or 'compartments' of management style are really a simplification of a 'continuum' or range of styles, from the most dictatorial to the most laissez-faire.

Dictatorial	Autocratic			Democratic			Laissez-faire
Manager makes decisions and enforces them	Manager makes decisions and announces them	Manager 'sells' his decisions to subordinates	Manager suggests own ideas and asks for comments	Manager suggests his sketched ideas, asks for comments and amends his ideas as a result	Manager presents a problem, asks for ideas, makes a decision from the ideas	Manager presents a problem to his group of subordinates and asks them to solve it	Manager allows his subordinates to act as they wish within specified limits

This 'continuum' of leadership styles was first suggested by Tannenbaum and Schmidt (1958).

The Ashridge studies

26. A slightly different analysis of leadership styles, based on this continuum, was made by the Research Unit at Ashridge Management College, based on research in several industries in the UK (reported 1966). This research distinguished four different management styles.

(a) The autocratic or *'tells'* style. This is characterised by one-way communication between the manager and the subordinate, with the manager telling the subordinate what to do. The leader makes all the decisions and issues instructions, expecting them to be obeyed without question.

(b) The persuasive or *'sells'* style. The manager still makes all the decisions, but believes that subordinates need to be motivated to accept them before they will do what he wants them to. He therefore tries to explain his decisions in order to persuade them round to his point of view.

(c) The *consultative* style. This involves discussion between the manager and the subordinates involved in carrying out a decision, but the manager retains the right to make the decision himself. By conferring with his subordinates before making any decision, the manager will take account of their advice and feelings. Consultation is a form of limited participation in decision-making for subordinates, but there might be a tendency for a manager to appear to consult his subordinates when really he has made up his mind beforehand. Consultation will then be false and a facade for a 'sells' style of leadership whereby the manager hopes to win acceptance of his decisions by subordinates by pretending to listen to their advice.

(d) The democratic or *'joins'* style. This is an approach whereby the leader joins his group of subordinates to make a decision on the basis of consensus or agreement. It is the most democratic style of leadership identified by the research study. Subordinates with the greatest knowledge of a problem will have greater influence over the decision. The joins style is therefore most effective where all subordinates in the group have equal knowledge and can therefore contribute in equal measure to decisions.

27. The Ashridge studies made one or two very interesting findings with regard to leadership style and employee motivation. (You should compare these with the views of other writers described in the rest of this chapter.)

    (a) There was a clear preference amongst the subordinates for the *consultative* style of leadership but managers were most commonly thought to be exercising the 'tells' or 'sells' style.

    (b) The attitudes of subordinates towards their work varied according to the style of leadership they thought their boss exercised. The most favourable attitudes were found amongst those subordinates who perceived their boss to be exercising the *consultative* style.

    (c) The least favourable attitudes were found amongst subordinates who were unable to perceive a consistent style of leadership in their boss. In other words, subordinates are unsettled by a boss who chops and changes between autocracy, persuasion, consultation and democracy. The conclusion from this finding is that *consistency* in leadership style is important.

28.

		Strengths		Weaknesses
•	*Tells style*	(1) Quick decisions can be made when speed is required	(1)	It does not encourage the subordinate to give his opinions when these might be useful.
		(2) It is the most efficient type of leadership for highly-programmed routine work.	(2)	Communications between the manager and subordinate will be one-way and the manager will not know until afterwards whether his orders have been properly understood.
			(3)	It does not encourage initiative and commitment from subordinates.
•	*Sells style*	(1) Employees are made aware of the reasons for decisions.	(1)	Communications are still largely one-way. Subordinates might not buy his decisions.
		(2) Selling decisions to staff might make them more willing to co-operate.	(2)	It does not encourage initiative and commitment from subordinates
		(3) Staff will have a better idea of what to do when unforeseen events arise in their work because the manager will have explained his intentions.		

- *Consultative style*

(1) Employees are involved in decisions before they are made. This encourages motivation through greater interest and involvement.

(1) It might take much longer to reach decisions.

(2) An agreed consensus of opinion can be reached and for some decisions consensus can be an advantage rather than a weak compromise.

(2) Subordinates might be too inexperienced to formulate mature opinions and give practical advice.

(3) Employees can contribute their knowledge and experience to help in solving more complex problems.

- *Joins style*

(1) It can provide high motivation and commitment from employees.

(1) The authority of the manager might be undermined.

(2) It shares the other advantages of the consultative style.

(2) Decision-making might become a very long process, and clear decisions might be difficult to reach.

(3) Subordinates might lack enough experience.

29. It is important to get the consultative and 'joins' styles in perspective. A leader cannot try to forget that he is the 'boss' by being friendly and informal with subordinates, or by consulting them before making any decision. Douglas McGregor (*Leadership and Motivation*) wrote about his own experiences as a college president that : 'It took a couple of years, but I finally began to realise that a leader cannot avoid the exercise of authority any more than he can avoid responsibility for what happens in the organisation.' A leader can try to avoid acting dictatorially, and he can try to act like 'one of the boys', but he must accept all the consequences of being a leader. McGregor wrote that 'since no important decision ever pleases everyone in the organisation, he must also absorb the displeasures, and sometimes severe hostility, of those who would have taken a different course'.

Lewin, Lippitt and White (1939)

30. Although Elton Mayo is considered to be the pioneer of the human relations movement, Lewin was another important theorist who did much research on group dynamics and leadership styles. With his colleagues Lippitt and White he reported the results of well-known experiments which were carried out in boys' clubs established for the purposes of their studies.

31. Club leaders were trained to act as autocratic, democratic or laissez-faire leaders, and the purpose of the experiments was to learn how the children reacted to different styles of leadership. The leaders were moved from one club to another every six weeks and by means of rotation each club (consisting of 10-year-old boys) experienced three different styles of leadership, under three different leaders.

    (a) The *autocratic* leader tended to give orders, and to interrupt the activities of the boys by giving commands to do something else. Criticism and praise were given out non-objectively, ie at the whim of the leader.

    (b) The *democratic* leader suggested what the boys should do, showed concern for each boy's individual welfare, participated in the activities of the group, but left the decisions about what to do to the boys themselves.

    (c) The *laissez-faire* leader also made suggestions, but was more 'stand-offish' and did not involve himself with the boy's welfare, nor did he join in the group activities, so that the boys were effectively left to do what they wanted by themselves.

32. Lewin, Lippitt and White were particularly interested in aggressive social behaviour, either within the group or shown to outsiders. Their findings may be summarised as follows.

    (a) In one experiment, aggressive behaviour was very much more common among the autocratic group than the democratic group, but none of the aggression or hostility was directed at the leader himself.

    (b) In a subsequent experiment, boys in four out of five autocratic groups showed 'apathetic' behaviour and lack of aggression. This apathy was attributed by the experimenters to the repressive style of the club leader.

    (c) 95 per cent of boys preferred a democratic to an autocratic leader, and 70 per cent preferred a laissez-faire leader to an autocratic one.

    (d) Aggression is only partly caused by leadership style. Other factors arousing hostile behaviour are tension, restriction of physical space and the cultural background of the boys in the group. Nevertheless, leadership style contributes towards such behaviour.

33. In a subsequent publication many years later (1960) Lippitt and White investigated the effect of leadership on productivity in different groups. They concluded that:

    (a) work-orientated conversation was greatest in a democratic group, less in an autocratic group and, interestingly, least in a laissez-faire group;

    (b) the amount of work actually done was greatest in an autocratic group and least in a laissez-faire group. Motivation was strongest in a democratic group where boys often carried on working even when a leader left the room. Interestingly, however, motivation was not sufficient to increase output above the level of the autocratic group;

    (c) as mentioned above, hostility and discontent were greatest in an autocratic group. Four boys dropped out of the experiment, and all belonged to an autocratic group at the time. Boys in an autocratic group were more dependent on their leader, and submissive; their hostility was towards each other. In contrast, originality, group-mindedness and friendly playfulness were greatest in a democratic group.

Rensis Likert

34. Rensis Likert distinguished four systems of management:

    • exploitive authoritative;

    • benevolent authoritative;

    • consultative authoritative;

    • participative group management.

35. Likert attempted to show that the effective manager is one who uses the participative style of management, although the ideal manager must be able to use the right leadership style for any given situation. Everyone in an organisation is interdependent: authority alone is insufficient to obtain good performance, and can only be effective in certain situations and with certain people. The complete manager is one who uses (normally) a supportive, participative approach but who can use any style effectively in a particular situation.

36. In his books *New Patterns of Management* and *The Human Organisation* Likert attempted through research to answer the question 'what do effective managers have in common?' His research showed that four main elements are normally present in any effective manager.

    (a) *They expect high levels of performance.* Their standards and targets are high and apply overall, not only to their subordinates' performance, but also to other departments and their own personal performance.

    (b) *They are employee-centred.* They spend time getting to know their workers and develop a situation of trust so that their employees feel able to bring problems to them. When necessary, their actions can be hard (though fair), akin to the actions of a responsible parent. Such managers are typified by their ability to face unpleasant facts in a constructive manner and help their staff to grow and develop a similar constructive attitude.

    (c) *They do not practise close supervision.* The truly effective manager is aware of the performance levels that can be expected from each individual and he has helped them to define their own targets. Once this has been achieved, the manager judges results and does not closely supervise the actions of his staff. In this way he not only develops his people, he also frees himself to spend more time on other aspects of his work (for example, planning decisions, communications with other areas and personnel problems).

    (d) *They operate the participative style of management as a natural style.* This means that if a job problem arises they do not simply impose a favoured solution. Instead, they put the problem to the staff member involved. Having agreed a solution, the participative manager would assist in implementing it.

37. Likert emphasises that all four features must be present for a manager to be truly effective. For example, if a manager is employee-centred, if he delegates and is participative, then he will have a happy working environment but he will not produce a high performance unless he also establishes standards of performance. A manager's concern for people must be matched by his concern for achieving results.

This linking of the human relations approach with scientific management targets will provide the recipe for effective performance. It is important to remember that management techniques such as time and motion study, financial controls etc are used by high producing managers 'at least as completely as by the low producing managers, but in quite different ways.' The different application is caused by a better understanding of the motivations of human behaviour.

38. In *New Patterns of Management* Likert examined the results achieved by managers and supervisors who were practising the participative style of management. He analysed these results in terms of output, wastage rates, labour turnover and absenteeism. In summary, his research showed that on the whole, supervisors with the best performance were those who concentrated their main efforts on the human aspects of their staff's problems and attempted to build work groups with high performance standards. On the other hand, supervisors with poor performance are described as spending more time in ensuring that their staff were busily employed in fulfilling specified stages of work.

His research further showed that the participative, supportive supervisor who was transferred to a low-production unit was able to raise the performance at a fast rate.

39. It is necessary to understand how the principle of supportive relationships would affect an organisation structure.

(a) The integration of organisational goals and objectives with those of every individual in the organisation is essential. Each individual must believe that the organisation has desirable, significant objectives, and that he makes an indispensable contribution to the objectives of the organisation. Jobs which do not fulfil this purpose must be re-organised so that they do.

> 'Experiences, relationships etc are considered to be supportive when the individual involved sees the experience (in terms of his values, goals, expectations, and aspirations) as contributing to or maintaining his sense of personal worth and importance.'

(b) An organisation must recognise the importance of the well-motivated work group in setting high-performance goals.

> 'Management should deliberately endeavour to build these effective groups, linking them into an overall organisation by means of people who hold overlapping group membership.'

257

(c) 'Linking pins' perform a key function in the 'overlapping group form of organisation'. A leader of one group is also a subordinate member of a group higher in the hierarchical structure, so that he acts as a link between his subordinates and a higher authority. Diagrammatically this would be shown as follows:

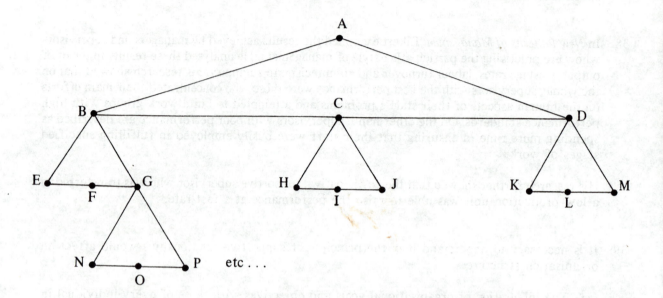

40. In this example, G is a linking pin between the group led by B and his own group of N, O and P. Similarly, B is a linking pin to decisions at the top level - ie A's group of A, B, C and D.

The group leader retains responsibility for what occurs, even though the group practises collective decision-making.

41. Likert's conclusion was that the style of supervision is more important in achieving better results than any more general factors such as job interest, loyalty towards the company etc. (However, it remains true that employees must receive rewards (pay etc) which give them compensation for their efforts. Intrinsic satisfactions cannot *replace* equitable reward systems.)

42. There are clearly difficulties involved in the practical application of Likert's ideas.

(a) For the overlapping group structure to be applied, the entire organisation must adopt the new management style. This 'new style' however, tends to be 'localised' in individual managers and their own work groups.

(b) In a large organisation, a worker at the bottom of the hierarchy will have difficulty in relating his own contributions to the setting of the organisation objectives at the top of the hierarchy.

(c) The ever-present problems of conflict between the self-interest of rival sub-units (eg production, sales, marketing and accountancy departments) will tend to blur a proper appreciation of what company objectives really are.

The Financial Times of 25 June 1986 reported the ideas of Rosabeth Moss Kanter on leadership styles. Moss Kanter is a business consultant whose services are much in demand. She criticises excessively authoritarian and non-participative management on the ground that it stifles innovation and entrepreneurship.

Her list of 'Rules for stifling innovation' is a critique of 'management by terror'.

1.   Regard any new idea from below with suspicion.

2.   Insist that people who need your approval first go through several other levels of management.

3.   Get departments/individuals to challenge each other's proposals.

4.   Express criticism freely, withhold praise, instil job insecurity.

5.   Treat identification of problems as signs of failure.

6.   Control everything carefully. Count everything in sight - frequently.

7.   Make decisions in secret, and spring them on people.

8.   Do not hand out information to managers freely.

9.   Get lower-level managers to implement your threatening decisions.

10. Above all, never forget that you, the higher-ups, already know everything important about the business.

Task management: a return to traditional views – Blake's grid

43. The writings of the human relations school (McGregor etc) tended to obscure the 'task' element of a manager's responsibilities. By emphasising style of leadership and the importance of human relations, it is all too easy to forget that a manager is primarily responsible for ensuring that tasks are done efficiently and effectively.

44. Robert R Blake and Jane S Mouton designed the management grid (1964) based on two aspects of managerial behaviour, namely:

●   concern for production, ie the 'task'; and

●   concern for people.

45. The results of their work were published under the heading of 'Ohio State Leadership Studies', but are now commonly referred to as Blake's grid.

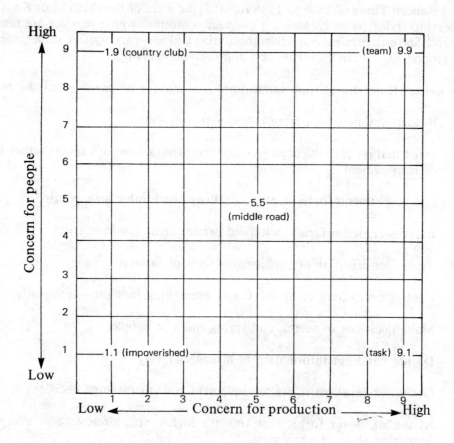

46. The extreme cases shown on the grid are defined by Blake as being:

    (a) 1.1 *impoverished:* manager is lazy, showing little effort or concern for staff or work targets;

    (b) 1.9 *country club:* manager is attentive to staff needs and has developed satisfying relationships. However, there is little attention paid to achieving results;

    (c) 9.1 *task management:* almost total concentration on achieving results. People's needs are virtually ignored and conditions of work are so arranged that people cannot interfere to any significant extent;

    (d) 5.5 *middle of the road or the dampened pendulum:* adequate performance through balancing the necessity to get out work while maintaining morale of people at a satisfactory level;

    (e) 9.9 *team:* high performance manager who achieves high work accomplishment through 'leading' committed people who identify themselves with the organisational aims.

47. The conclusion is that the most efficient managers combine concern for the task with concern for people.

48. It is worth being clear in your own mind about the possible usefulness of Blake's grid. Its primary value is obtained from the appraisal of a manager's performance, either by the manager himself or by his superiors. The ideal manager is a 9.9 man (or woman) with high concern for both production and people. An individual manager can be placed on the grid, and his position on the grid should help him to see how his performance as a leader and a manager can be improved. For example, a manager rated 3.8 has further to go in showing concern for the task itself than for developing the work of his subordinates.

49. You should also be aware that Blake's grid is based on the assumption that concern for production and concern for people are not incompatible with each other - which may or may not be true within the systems and personnel profile of a given organisation.

Reddin's 3-D views on leadership style

50. W J Reddin (1970) argued that a leader's concern for task and concern for people might be high or low (and in this respect he follows Blake and Mouton's ideas); however, a leader might be effective or ineffective in any style of leadership, depending on the circumstances. The following table summarises his analysis.

Concern for task	Concern for human relations	Effectiveness of manager	Description of leadership style
Low	Low	Low	The active deserter.
Low	Low	High	The positive deserter, a rule-follower or bureaucrat.
High	Low	Low	Autocrat
High	Low	High	Benevolent autocrat, a good persuader of staff.
Low	High	Low	Missionary.
Low	High	High	The developer who tries to bring out the best in sub-ordinates.
High	High	Low	The compromiser.
High	High	High	The real executive.*

(*Equivalent to position 9.9 on Blake's grid).

John Adair: action-centred leadership

51. Adair (*Effective Leadership* 1983) identified three aspects of a leadership situation which overlap, but are distinct, ie:

    (a) the requirements of the task;
    (b) the needs of the individual;
    (c) the needs of the group (for self maintenance) etc.

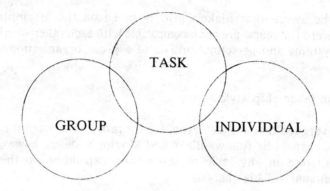

   Adair recognised that there will seldom be complete harmony between the three sets of needs, and the resulting tensions must be diagnosed and managed by the leader of the group.

52. Around this framework, Adair developed a scheme of leadership training based on precept and practice in each of eight leadership activities:

    - defining the task
    - planning
    - briefing
    - controlling
    - evaluating
    - motivating
    - organising
    - setting an example.

53. Adair identified leadership style in this essentially *functional* approach: the common perception of leadership as 'decision-making' was, he argued, inadequate to describe the range of action required by the complex situation in which the manager finds himself.

A systems approach to leadership

54. Systems theory is concerned with the complex inter-relationships between the many different parts of a system (eg the organisation), and the effect of the environment on the system (and vice versa). Katz and Kahn have developed ideas on how leadership can contribute to the functioning of a system.

55. Early research by Katz and Kahn (reported in 1951) into the effect of leadership style on productivity suggested that there were three aspects of leader behaviour which affected productivity:

- assumption of the leadership role;
- closeness of supervision;
- degree of employee-orientation.

56. Comparisons were made between high-production and low-production groups and it was found that:

   (a) in the most efficient groups the supervisor assumed the leadership role and used his supervisory talents to get the best out of his group. The leader has special functions and cannot therefore behave as an ordinary group member (ie be 'one of the boys'). In large organisations the assumption of the supervisory role is often made easier by transferring staff on promotion so that they can make a fresh start among strangers; ✳

   (b) supervision was closer in low-production than in high-production groups. Workers expect to have some control over the means by which they perform a set task, and they resent having means specified in too much detail. Supervisory behaviour was found to reflect management leadership styles, ie the organisational context affects leadership;

   (c) studies of the attitudes held by supervisors towards their subordinates revealed that the men in charge of high-production groups were more employee-oriented (ie intent on promoting their welfare). In the research experiment, the attitudes of a manager were gauged by asking subordinates to rate bosses; results showed that the efficient bosses were seen by their subordinates to be more *considerate*.

57. Katz and Kahn have since developed their ideas and have suggested that the reason why the most effective managers show consideration and understanding towards their subordinates is because they supplement their formal position in the organisation and appreciate that their employees:

   (a) have interests and roles outside their job;
   (b) are subject to pressures and influences from their external environment;
   (c) need information to do their job with greater understanding;
   (d) need to be guided in the dynamic, changing organisation, and to understand the significance of change.

58. Good leaders show a true awareness that organisations are 'open' systems, reacting to and changing with their environment, of which their subordinates are also a part. Leaders influence those aspects of their subordinates' interests, energies and drive which cannot be harnessed by simple organisation structure, job definitions, or more formal management techniques.

A contingency approach to leadership

59. A contingency approach to leadership is one which argues that the ability of a manager to be a leader, and to influence his subordinate work group, depends on the particular situation, and will vary from case to case. Factors which vary in different situations are the personality of the leader, his leadership style, the nature of the group's tasks, the nature and personality of the work group and its individual members, conditions of work and 'external environmental' factors.

F E Fiedler's contingency theory

60. Perhaps the leading advocate of contingency theory is F E Fiedler. In an earlier work (1960) he studied the relationship between style of leadership and the effectiveness of the work group. Two styles of leader were identified:

- *psychologically distant managers* (PDMs) who maintain distance from their subordinates by:

    (i)   formalising the roles and relationships between themselves and their superiors and subordinates;
    (ii) being withdrawn and reserved in their inter-personal relationships within the organisation;
    (iii) preferring formal consultation methods rather than seeking opinions of their staff informally;

- *psychologically close managers* (PCMs) who:

    (i)   do not seek to formalise roles and relationships with superiors and subordinates;
    (ii) are more concerned to maintain good human relationships at work than to ensure that tasks are carried out efficiently;
    (iii) prefer informal contacts to regular formal staff meetings.

61. Fiedler further developed his account of the significant qualities of the psychologically distant manager.

    (a) He judges subordinates on the basis of their performance, expects them to make mistakes and plans accordingly.
    (b) He prefers ambitious subordinates.
    (c) He attempts to obtain considerable freedom of action from his superiors.
    (d) Though reserved in his interpersonal relationships he nevertheless displays good interpersonal skills.
    (e) He is primarily task-orientated, and gains satisfaction from seeing a task performed.

62. Given these qualities of the PDMs, it is perhaps not surprising that in his 1960 study Fiedler concluded that the most effective work groups were led by psychologically distant managers and not by psychologically close managers. The explanation for this appeared to be that a manager cannot properly control and discipline subordinates if he is too close to them emotionally.

63. Fiedler went on to develop his contingency theory in *A Theory of Leadership Effectiveness*. He suggested that the effectiveness of a work group depended basically on two factors:

- the relationship between the leader and his group;
- the nature of the work or tasks done by the group.

64. He concluded that:

    (a) a structured (or psychologically distant) style works best when the *situation* is either very favourable, or very unfavourable to the leader;

    (b) a supportive (or psychologically close) style works best when the *situation* is moderately favourable to the leader.

65. A situation is 'favourable' to the leader when:
    (a) the leader is liked and trusted by the group;
    (b) the tasks of the group are clearly defined;
    (c) the power of the leader to reward and punish with organisation backing is high.

> 'Group performance will be contingent upon the appropriate matching of leadership styles and the degree of favourableness of the group situation for the leader, that is, the degree to which the situation provides the leader with influence over his group members.' (*Fiedler*)

66. Fiedler's analysis can be described by a 3-dimensional cube in which one dimension represents the level of respect and trust for the leader amongst subordinates, a second dimension is the degree to which the tasks of the group are clearly defined, and a third dimension is the degree to which the leader has power and authority to reward or punish subordinates.

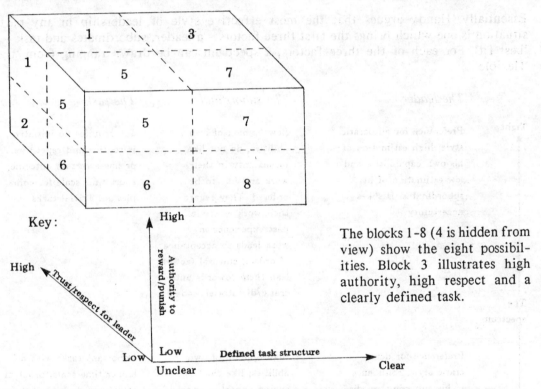

The blocks 1-8 (4 is hidden from view) show the eight possibilities. Block 3 illustrates high authority, high respect and a clearly defined task.

67. (a) When the situation is very favourable for the leader, he can afford to concentrate on the task, and be a task-orientated, psychologically distant manager. The leader of a research group might be in this position.

    (b) When the situation is only moderately favourable for the leader, he will need to show more concern for people - ie be a psychologically close manager.

    (c) When the situation is unfavourable for the leader, he will need to be task-orientated, and a psychologically distant autocrat.

    (d) Concern for task and concern for people should be balanced according to the needs of the situation, and the degree to which it favours the leader.

68. The *situation* is the key to deciding how effective a leadership style can be. 'If we wish to increase organisational and group effectiveness we must learn not only how to train leaders more effectively, but also how to build an organisational environment in which the leader can perform well.'

Handy's 'best fit' approach

69. Handy has also suggested a contingency approach to leadership. The factors in any situation which contribute to a leader's effectiveness are:

- the leader himself - ie his personality, character and preferred style of operating;
- the subordinates - ie their individual and collective personalities, and their preference for a style of leadership;
- the task - ie the objectives of the job, the technology of the job, methods of working etc;
- the environment - which is discussed separately.

70. Essentially, Handy argues that the most effective style of leadership in any particular situation is one which brings the first three factors - a leader, subordinates and task - into a 'best fit'. For each of the three factors, a spectrum can be drawn ranging from 'tight' to 'flexible'.

	The leader	*The subordinates*	*The task*
Tight ↑	Preference for autocratic style; high estimation of his own capabilities and a low estimation of his subordinates. Dislikes uncertainty.	Low opinion of own abilities, do not like uncertainty in their work and like to be ordered. They regard their work as trivial; past experience in work leads to acceptance of orders, cultural factors lean them towards auto-cratic/dictatorial leaders.	Job requires no initiative, is routine and repetitive, or has a certain outcome; short time scale for completion. Trivial tasks.
The spectrum			
↓ **Flexible**	Preference for demo-cratic style, confidence in his subordinates, dis-likes stress, accepts reasonable risk and uncertainty.	High opinion of own abilities; like chall-enging important work; prepared to accept un-certainty and longer time scales for results; cultural factors favour independence.	Important tasks with a longer time scale; problem-solving or decision-making involved, complex work.

71. A best fit occurs when all three factors are on the same level in the spectrum, though this is rare in practice. Confronted with a lack of fit, the leader must decide which factor(s) should be changed to bring all three into line. The factor over which a leader has most influence is himself and his style; hence, Handy argues, the great emphasis on 'leaderships' in management literature. 'However, although the leader's style is theoretically the easiest to alter in the short term, there are often long-term benefits to be achieved from re-defining the task (eg job enlargement) or from developing the work group.'

72. The fourth factor identified by Handy in the situational jig-saw is the environment, ie:

   (a) *the position of 'power' held by the leader in the organisation and the relationship of the leader and his group.* Power might be a position of authority but it might also be the expertise or the charisma of the leader. A person with great power has a bigger capacity to set his own style of leadership, select his own subordinates and re-define the task of his work group;

   (b) *organisational 'norms' and the structure and technology of the organisation.* No manager can flout convention and act in a manner which is contrary to the customs and standards of the organisation. If the organisation has a history of autocratic leadership, it will be difficult to introduce a new style. If the formal organisation is highly centralised, there will be limits to how far a task can be re-structured by an individual manager. In mass-production industries, where routine, repetitive work is in-built in the production technology, challenging tasks will be difficult to create, and leadership will tend to be autocratic;

   (c) *the variety of tasks and the variety of subordinates.* If the tasks of a work group are simple, few in number and repetitive, the best style of leadership will be different from a situation in which tasks are varied and difficult. In many groups, however, tasks vary from routine and simple, to complex 'one-off' problem-solving. Managing such work is complicated by this variety.

   Similarly, the individuals in a work group might be widely different. One member of the group might seek participation and greater responsibility, whereas another might want to be told what to do. Furthermore, where labour turnover is frequent, the individuals who act as leaders or subordinates are constantly changing; such change is unsettling because the leadership style will have to be altered to suit the new situation, each time a personnel change occurs.

74. The 'environment' can be improved for leaders within an organisation if top management act to ensure that:

   (a) leaders are given a clear role and 'power';
   (b) organisational 'norms' can be broken - ie the culture is responsive and adaptive;
   (c) the organisational structure is not rigid and inflexible;
   (d) subordinates in a work group are all of the same quality or type;
   (e) labour turnover is reduced, especially by keeping managers in their job for a reasonably lengthy period of time.

LEADERSHIP AT WORK

Summary

75. The relevance of leadership style to the practice of management may be summarised as follows.

   (a) Leadership involves a concern for the task itself and also a concern for people.

   (b) Concern for people requires an understanding of what will motivate individuals to work harder and more effectively, and also an understanding of what can make a work group as a whole improve its motivation and norms of working.

   (c) Leadership style is a factor influencing the motivation of individual subordinates and the attitudes of work groups.

   (d) Leadership style is susceptible to improvement through training and management development programmes.

   (e) The most appropriate style of management for raising the level of employee efficiency and effectiveness will vary according to circumstances. This means that either:

      (i) a manager might have to change his leadership style as the circumstances of his job change (eg when he is moved to a new job). However, since it is difficult to turn an autocrat into a democrat, or vice versa - ie since a leopard cannot change its spots....

      (ii) ....it might be necessary instead to appoint managers who have a particular style of leadership to jobs where that style will be the most productive in the circumstances.

WORK AND NON WORK

Points to be covered

- Importance of work to the individual
- Work as a central life interest: the work ethic
- Individual orientation to work
- Work and leisure
- Sex differences: occupational and family roles

Introduction

1. Our study of people in organisations has concentrated on those *employed* by work organisations of one type or another. In this chapter we will look at 'work' itself as an activity, and as a social and psychological force in people's lives.

2. The modern definition of work is specifically related to paid employment – not just to activity, effort or achievement. Studying for your exams may be 'hard work'; the full-time housewife may be 'worked off her feet' - but this is not technically 'work' as defined by the sociologist. Work means hiring out one's labour in return for a wage, salary or other payment.

3. Drucker (*Management*) points out that the term 'work' is an ambivalent and emotive one.

"In the pairing 'work and rest', 'rest' is clearly good. But whether 'retirement' is better than 'work' is already questionable. And work is definitely preferable to 'idleness'. Being 'out of work' is far from good - is, indeed, a catastrophe. In 'work and play', 'play' carries a favourable connotation. But 'playing at being a surgeon' is not good at all. Work can be high achievement, as in the phrase 'an artist's life work'. Or it can be sheer drudgery, back breaking, and utter boredom."

Drucker

---

4. Drucker suggests that working, as an activity, has five dimensions:

- *psychological*. Man is not a machine and does not work like one. He lacks strength and stamina for continuous, unvarying tasks - but excels in co-ordination and flexibility. The speed, rhythm and attention spans with which he is capable of working vary widely;

- *psychological*. Work is both a burden and a need, as we discuss further below;

- *social*. In a work-oriented society or community, work provides access to society, and almost comes to define the worker's social position and rôle: "What do you do?" (ie. 'for a living') is often assumed to be the key to a person's identity. Work is also a means to satisfy man's need for affiliation and for meaningful relationships with others;

- *economic*. Work is a living for the worker - and also produces capital for the economy;

- *power*. Working within a group or organisation implies power relationships. Structures, schedules, control systems etc. imply authority - an essential dimension of organisation, and of work.

Importance of work to the individual

5. If we look back at some of the 'need theories' of human motivation, we can see why work may be important to individuals.

6. Starting at the bottom of Maslow's pyramid, for example, it is clear that the economic attractions of work (adequate pay, security etc) are important in satisfying the physiological and safety or 'existence' needs of the individual.

7. Work may also be an important factor in satisfying social, 'relatedness' or 'affiliation' needs and esteem, power or achievement needs. Individuals usually want to feel that they are accepted, and that their work has importance. Ambition plays a part here, both in a negative sense (an individual must accept work or risk rejection by the community around him) and in a positive sense (the harder and more effectively a person works the more he advances in his job, satisfying his needs for esteem and status).

8. Finally, work can be important in enabling an individual to realise what he perceives to be his full potential. This will be so if his abilities are challenged by his work and he feels his powers develop to cope with the challenge. Few individuals will find that all their needs are satisfied (directly or indirectly) by the work they do, but particularly in the case of highly trained craftsmen and professionals it may be an important part of their maturity and self-development.

Work as a central life interest: the work ethic

9. The jobs people do affect many aspects of their lives, since:

(a) they spend their prime waking hours at work;

(b) many of their closest relationships will be formed at work;

(c) the way other people regard them is often perceived to be based on what they do; and

(d) work also defines how they regard themselves - ie. their self-concept, and identity as a 'useful' member of society.

Redundancy, unemployment and retirement can cause acute psychological disturbances undermining not only a person's status (in a society where men, in particular, are expected to work) and financial security but also his self-image, sense of belonging etc.

10. Work has been a concern in human development for thousands of years. The making of tools, the systematic, purposeful approach to necessary tasks, has always been a specifically human activity: man has long admired and identified himself with those creatures that practice social organisation based on work - ants, bees etc.

Since the Industrial Revolution, work has become the focal point of economic and social theory.

11. Parental models, education and the whole socialisation process so conditions the individual to the idea and habit of work that it may become an extension of personality, the sole criterion of achievement, worth and humanity.

The Western (or Protestant) concept of the 'work ethic' attached certain positive values to work. It glorified work *per se* and preached that *all* work is worthwhile and deserving of respect (unlike earlier, more elitist concepts of work which suggested that some forms of work and worker - eg. the artist, or teacher - were intrinsically more valuable than others). 'Service' in itself was considered ennobling - a 'high calling'.

12. The commercial and industrial revolutions of the past two centuries brought a sharp rise in the hours worked by individuals in Britain - not just because of this 'work ethic' but because:

(a) improvements in living conditions and nutrition increased the health of workers and the energy they had available for work; and

(b) there was a shift in values towards economic rewards - partly because economic satisfactions became more available: workers increasingly desired purchasing power because consumer goods were arriving on the market.

13. We are told that this century has seen a significant rejection of the work ethic. This may represent a redressing of the balance between work and leisure, a social reaction against the ethos of self-denial, overwork, child labour etc - not just pleasure-seeking, moral degeneracy or idleness (as is still sometimes suggested to those who are out of work).

14. The crumbling of the work ethic has also been attributed to the comparative affluence that now exists for the majority of people in developed countries (ie. we can sit back and take it easier now). In fact, people are more likely to 'get a taste' for economic rewards than to be satisfied by them and may work more or harder. In that case, work will not lose its importance, but it may be true that work 'for its own sake' will no longer be a central interest.

15. On the other hand, more and more people are demanding more than just a *living* from their work. Workers on subsistence level incomes are not likely to be fussy about 'job satisfaction' or 'self actualisation' but - as the Human Relations school noted - increasing numbers of employees are achieving a measure of economic security, and are demanding that their work be satisfactory *as a way of life* - since so much of their time and energy is invested in it.

16. The centrality of work in an individual's life can become obvious in the psychological effects of redundancy or unemployment. The kind of effects unemployment might have - especially, it has been suggested, in the case of a working-class man of middle age who is highly committed to his job - include:

- financial insecurity;
- loss of variety - fewer activities and places to go;
- less opportunity for development;
- loss of structure and sense of purpose;
- fewer options;
- loss of social contact;
- loss of status and self-esteem;
- more rejection and psychological threats;
- insecurity about the future.

Work orientation and job choice

17. The extent to which work will be the central life interest for any given individual will depend on the relative strengths of his various needs and goals and the choices he makes about how to achieve them - ie. his *orientation*.

18. Many people regard work as the least rewarding aspect of their lives: they derive their personal satisfaction (if not their social definition) from their non-work relationships and pursuits. Work is thought of as a 'necessary evil' - ie. financial goals dictate whatever positive attitude to work there may be (acceptance or resignation), while the fulfilment of social and 'growth' needs is sought elsewhere. Particularly in times of high unemployment, people may feel grateful to *have* a job - even if they hate it, and watch the clock eagerly until they can escape to their non-work world.

19. Other individuals derive a sense of satisfaction from their work. As we have seen, this is highly subjective, and depends on what the individual wants and expects from his work and working conditions. People who are positively oriented towards their job - finding it interesting, challenging, rewarding etc. - may be fulfilling a number of personal goals, and may require less satisfaction of their non-work time and relationships.

20. 'Relatedness' or social needs can be a prime orientation to work. Work is for most individuals in Western society the most important source of relationships, the closest bond outside of the immediate family: for young single people or parents of grown-up children, it may even take the place of the family unit.

    Drucker quotes a retired senior vice-president of a big company: "Don't, please, send me the annual report ....I'm no longer interested in sales. Send me the gossip. I miss even the people I couldn't stand."

21. The greatest strength of the work relationship is that it does not depend purely on like and dislike, but has an objective outward-looking focus: the work itself. It can also - if desired - become a very close bond between individuals which spills over into non work life.

    A sense of unity and mutual support among workers can be the result of poor working conditions, or arduous or dangerous work, and can significantly enhance the acceptability, or even attraction, of that work for the individuals - eg. in coal-mining.

22. The desire to 'serve' is another possible orientation to work. Jobs which involve service, or 'caring responsibility' for others are often referred to as 'vocations' - eg. nursing, teaching, social work. A 'sense of vocation' is rather assumed to be a source of job satisfaction in itself, and the commitment of such workers to their patients/clients etc. may be taken for granted as a stronger orientation than money, working conditions etc.

23. In the 1950s, Nancy Morse and Robert Weiss interviewed 401 American employees, to study the function and significance of work to a random sample of individuals.

    - Asked if they thought they would work - even if they somehow came into enough money to keep them comfortably without working:

        - 80% overall said they would (90% of interviewees in their 20s, with percentages falling slightly towards retirement age, and rising again *after* retirement age);
        - 20% overall said they wouldn't.

    - Asked why:

        - 44% professional/management
        - 10% working class   said: *interest and sense of accomplishment*
        - 18% farmers

        - 37% professional
        - 71% working class   said: *to keep occupied*
        - 64% farmers

    - Asked what they would miss if they didn't work:

        - 31% said the people they knew through work;
        - 25% said the feeling of doing something;
        - 12% said the kind of work they do;
        - 9% said the feeling of doing something important, worthwhile;
        - 6% said the regular routine;
        - 5% said the interest
        - 6% said other
        - 6% said nothing.

24. The way in which people regard work in general, and the reasons they have for working, will be important elements in vocational choice.

    Holland (*Making Vocational Choices*) describes how people with different personal orientations seem to choose certain work environments to suit their needs and abilities.

    (a) *Intellectual* people are at home with ideas and symbols and are suited to work requiring abstract or creative abilities - say, writing, teaching or science.

    (b) *Artistic* people are imaginative, intuitive and creative and are most obviously suited to the arts.

    (c) *Social* people are characterised by their skills in inter-personal relations - management, social work and counselling may be fruitful areas.

(d) *Realistic* people need concrete goals and tasks, and tend to be manipulative; they are suited to engineering, farming and other 'practical' fields.

(e) *Conventional* people like rule books and 'socially acceptable' goals - accounting, office administration etc suit them.

(f) *Enterprising* people are energetic, enthusiastic and explorative - and 'go for' sales, entrepreneurship, politics etc.

25. Goldthorpe, Lockwood *et al* developed a model of the way in which workers choose jobs, through their 'affluent worker' research in the Luton car industry (1968). (The study was intended to be representative only of a certain type of worker - ie unskilled but highly-paid - of which car assembly was a prime example.)

The car assembly workers were found to experience their work as routine and dead-end. However, the researchers concluded that they had made a rational decision to enter employment which offered high monetary reward rather than intrinsic interest, having an instrumental orientation to work: they were getting out of their jobs what they most wanted from them. The researchers inferred a causal link between orientations to work and vocational choice: depending on individual orientation, a person would seek out a job which offered a suitable balance of:

(a) the rewards which were important to him; and
(b) the deprivations he felt able to put up with.

26. The Luton study - although never claiming to be representative of the manual working class as a whole - raises interesting issues about job choice, and the extent to which it exists in practice.

(a) The Luton researchers took for granted the existence of prior orientations to work - ie, in the case of the car assembly workers, instrumental orientations. However, the origins of such predispositions should be questioned. The experience of the workers in the labour market may have conditioned their expectations of what was available to them in work, and therefore what they 'wanted' (ie felt they had to accept) from it.

(b) The affluent worker model implies voluntary acceptance of unskilled, monotonous work, without addressing the issue of the extent to which job choice is limited by opportunity, educational attainment, class models etc. In other words, Goldthorpe *et al* may have assumed a more 'rational' job market than in fact exists. Wedderburn and Crompton point out that the sample chosen for study was situated in the South-East of England and based on a mobile, fairly young group of workers: such a sample maximised the apparent degree of job choice. Their own research - among North-East chemical workers, in an area of higher unemployment - indicated highly restricted freedom of choice.

27. The idea of 'choice' is a key factor in the labour market. In order to distribute and allocate labour rationally and effectively, and in order for workers to obtain advantageous employment, freedom of choice must be encouraged for both employers and workers. However current sociological debate centres on serious doubts raised about this in practice. How much choice constitutes 'real' choice? How many apparently free choices really represent a bowing to 'the inevitable', the lessons of experience, the restrictions imposed by low self-image etc?

Structural forces – race, gender, class, education etc – influence:

(a) the opportunities open to individuals; and
(b) the image individuals develop of the opportunities open to them, and therefore their perceived field of choice.

Work and leisure

"What distinguishes work from play is an old question that has never been answered satisfactorily. Work and play may be the very same activity, down to the smallest detail – wood finishing is work when done by a furniture factory worker and play when done by a weekend hobbyist. Psychologically and socially, the two are quite different. The distinction may well be that work, unlike play, is impersonal and objective. The purpose of play lies in the player; the purpose of work lies with the user of the end product. Where the end product is not determined by the player but by others, we do not speak of play, we speak of work." Drucker (*Management*)

28. As we have suggested, individuals tend to define themselves by the job they do: it is the first item of information that people disclose about themselves. Very few people, when asked: 'what do you do?', will reply: 'I play the piano, and tennis, read novels, breed goldfish' etc. Work is a powerful social symbol, and as such spills over into the 'non-working' life of the individual.

29. This is true in other ways as well. Work may impinge on non work where:

(a) there is a certain amount of role conflict involved e.g. in work and home life. It is not easy for a person to 'switch off' immediately after work, and he or she may bring the work role home – e.g. the manager who tries to be autocratic with the family;

(b) the social contacts and friendships made at work spill over into leisure-time relationships: studies have shown that this is particularly true of workers in dangerous jobs like trawling and mining, which foster a sense of trust and mutual dependence. Work loyalties may even conflict with non work loyalties – going to the pub with 'mates' instead of seeing the girlfriend, staying with a friend who's working late instead of going home to cook the dinner etc.;

(c) the individual's income (ie from the job) determines his lifestyle. Where and how a person lives, and the kind of leisure pursuits he enjoys will depend on spending money (as well as the amount of spare *time* and energy he has left over after working hours);

(d) the physical and/or psychological state of the individual is affected by work. The worker may be so fatigued or numbed by monotony at work that he just 'crashes out' into frankly monotonous leisure time activity; he may be so tense and anxious that he snaps at his family, is unable to sleep, or takes his work frustrations to the nearest pub; he may be so 'switched on' to his work that he can never put it down.

30. The worker's attitude to his/her leisure time may vary widely, and the clarity of the distinction between work and leisure may also differ.

   (a) Some people have jobs that involve their hobbies or leisure interests: leisure time may therefore be an extension of work (or vice versa). Writers, sportsmen and politicians, for example, may not be able to point to 'work hours' with any specificity.

   (b) Workers in routine, boring and low-paid work are more likely to draw a clear line between work and leisure. Leisure time may provide their only opportunity for self-determination, interest, fulfilment, social contact etc. It will be all the more precious if they have had to work overtime or shifts, in order to earn a sufficient wage.

   (c) Leisure time may provide an antidote to monotony at work - and some people in unsatisfying jobs make a real effort to utilise their leisure time to the full, participating in sports, educational courses, amateur artistic pursuits etc. On the other hand, as mentioned above, all too many people return from a tedious job and simply collapse in front of the TV, or 'potter' around the home. The 'leisure industry' seems increasingly geared to maximum 'stimulation' (of a sort) with minimum initiative or effort: TV, hi-fi, video games etc.

   (d) Professional and other skilled workers are more likely to have an active leisure life which offers them further opportunities for self development. Higher income helps, enabling greater variety of pursuits and venues, opportunities for time off, travel abroad etc. Past educational experience also makes a difference to the individual's confidence (e.g. to undertake part-time study, or evening classes, or learning hobbies) as well as to the range of interests which may or may not have been kindled at an earlier age.

31. These factors and attitudes may well come into focus as the working week gets shorter and the ideal of 'full employment' grows more distant. People are likely to have more leisure time in the future. Will they fill it with supplementary jobs? How will the leisure industry respond? Will individuals embrace their new 'freedom' with open arms, or will guilt and insecurity attend the displacement of work as the central life interest?

Sex differences: occupational and family roles

32. There has been a huge increase in the number of women in the workforce in Britain since the Second World War, and in the proportion of married women, in particular, in employment. However, the proportion of women in top professional jobs is low: women are more generally accepted in the less socially powerful professions such as teaching and nursing, but even here women are not promoted to key posts in the hierarchy in proportion to their numbers in the lower grades.

   Most working women in Britain are still in either clerical/secretarial work, domestic/catering work, unskilled factory work and shop work.

"Most employed women in Britain are doing a job that provides a background against which other people can carry out what society believes are the more productive and important kinds of work. The woman employed outside her home is much more likely to be making biscuits than cars, serving coffee than building ships, doing the dry cleaning rather than the dock work." Mackie and Pattullo (*Women at Work*)

276

33. Many women take on part-time rather than full-time work, because they are still expected to run the household and look after the family, while a second income is necessary.

    A 1978 report by the Low Pay Unit explained that female part-time workers' "attachment to work, need for money and potential for workplace militancy is low compared with full-time male workers. It is thought that female part-time workers will accept not only low wages but less favourable conditions of service as well."

34. Leisure time, for working women, is less likely to be 'free' time than it is for male workers, because, although the roles of men and women within the family have adapted somewhat to the higher proportion of women in work outside the home, attitudes still persist. Housework and childcare are still considered (by both sexes) to be women's responsibilities.

    Professional women may have the earning capacity to use domestic help, child-minders etc. to cope with the demands on their time, but the role conflict is likely to be, if anything, *more* acute. Some women are made to feel profoundly guilty at 'neglecting' their traditional role as wife, mother, cook, subordinate etc.

35. Of course, social stereotypes of family and occupational roles can be as stressful to the male as to the female. The pressure placed on men as 'breadwinners' for the family can be crippling – not only because of the continuous weight of responsibility over a long time period, but because of the pressure it puts on educational and career choices at all stages. Getting and keeping 'a good job' becomes the central criterion for all sorts of decisions.

36. We should also bear in mind that family roles vary from culture to culture. The family unit may consist of the nuclear (ie. husband, wife and dependent children) or extended family: polygamy is accepted or encouraged in some societies (ie. a husband may have several wives or, more rarely, a wife several husbands); the permanence of marital relations varies.

    In some societies, child-care is seen as a woman's responsibility; in others, fathers play a role; in others, communal child-rearing by relatives or elders is the norm.

    Some societies are more 'child-centred' than others. In Britain, it is generally considered that children are 'deprived' if they do not have the full-time care and attention of their mother. In many tribal societies, however, it is common for children to be reared by adults other than their parents.

37. Marxist sociology describes family life in capitalist societies as the socialisation of the future labour force. There is division of labour in the family into *wage labour* and *domestic labour*; the major breadwinner (usually the man) is enabled to go out to work by the other partner taking on domestic responsibilities. Children learn these appropriate sex roles in the family – which are reinforced by experience in later life – and the system perpetuates itself.

38. Despite the increasing need for women to work to supplement the family income, women are often discouraged from getting attached to their work roles, which are regarded as secondary or casual. Meagre state support for nurseries and child-care facilities contribute to the attitude problem. Women are often regarded as 'risky' recruits for long-term or responsible positions, because they 'tend to go off and get married/have babies' etc.

39. It is true that in this century, women have been increasingly emancipated from the home, child-bearing and their husbands' incomes. Depending on the viewpoint, this may 'only be the beginning' or 'have gone too far'. Research conducted by sociologists in the last few decades has shown, however, that both attitudes and behaviour have undergone less substantial alteration than might have been expected: rigid division of labour and stereotypical attitudes to family roles have been largely preserved.

Ray and Jan Pahl, in a study of managers and their wives found that: "the majority of the wives saw their role in relation to their husband's work as being essentially a supportive and domestic one... The typical wife saw herself as someone who cares for the house and children while her husband is at work and who helps him to sort out his worries and relax when he comes home to the nest in the evening."

Clearly, it is not only *male* attitudes that the feminist movement is up against!

40. According to a report "Inside the Family: Changing roles of men and women" published by the Family Policy Studies Centre in November 1987, the women's movement and rising unemployment have begun to challenge traditional sex roles, but domestic arrangements remain little changed.

(a) In couples where the wife works *part-time*:

- 83% of wives do most of the cleaning
- 95% do most of the washing and ironing
- 79% have the main responsibility for cooking evening meals
- 64% do most of the routine household shopping

(Though 74% of men do household repairs.)

(b) Even where the wife works *full-time*:

- 61% of women do the cleaning
- 81% do the washing and ironing
- 61% prepare the dinner
- 52% do most of the shopping

(Though 83% of men do the household repairs.)

(c) "While it is true that men - on average - probably take a more active role in the home than in the past, this is typically a helping role, rather than an egalitarian allocation of domestic responsibility."

(d) "While mothers do still take the major responsibility for the care of young children, there is a *sense* of fathers having more involvement than previously."

41. The report also released some interesting statistics on hours worked.

(a) *Free time*.

Wives in full time work: 7 hours on weekend days
                            2.1 hours during the week

Husbands: 10 hours on weekend days
                            2.6 hours during the week

(b) *Full-time employment.*

27% of wives work full-time (7% of mothers of under fives)
33% of wives work part-time (20% of mothers of under fives)
The overwhelming majority of men work full time.

The presence of children is the most important influence on women's decision to work at all, or full- or part-time etc. It has, says the report, virtually no influence on men's decision to work.

(c) *Hours worked in full-time employment.*

Husbands: 45.1 hours per week (often irregular, and involving time away from home)

Wives: 37.4 hours per week

4% of wives work longer hours than their husbands.
11% work the same hours as their husbands.

(d) *Income.*

Most family income is still provided by men. Only about 50% of couples pool their incomes with equal access to resources: about 25% of women are dependent on an allowance from their husbands, with no independent access to money. Most women use their earnings to augment the housekeeping: only 'extra' earnings eg. bonuses or overtime, are considered to be personal spending money.

CONFLICT AND CO-OPERATION AT WORK

Points to be covered

- Theories of conflict in organisations
- Constructive and destructive conflict
- Causes, symptoms and tactics of conflict
- Managerial response to conflict
- Interest groups
- Ideologies of conflict
- Managerial models of the worker
- Theory X and Theory Y; Theory Z
- Class and class-consciousness in Britain
- Alienation
- Counter-organisations and sub-cultures

Introduction

1. 'Conflict' is not as clear a concept as one might think. We have already considered it in the context of stress and frustration (ie. conflict between the individual and his environment) and role theory (ie. intra-personal conflict within the individual). In this chapter we will look at conflict as a social process - ie. between individuals and groups, departments, levels in the hierarchy, or *perceived* groups in the organisation - ie. 'us and them'.

2. You should be clear in your mind, however, that there is no clear-cut definition of, or approach to, 'conflict': there is much controversy in conflict research, as to what should be studied, and how, and how meaningful the results are. Various 'interest groups' in a conflict situation are likely to have different perspectives on the nature of the situation itself, as well as on the particular issues that create it.

   For some parties - eg. management - conflict will be a 'problem' to be 'solved'. From the point of view of the behavioural scientist, however, conflict may seem to be part of the steady state of organisations, so that co-operation, order and stability are more interesting phenomena to study.

3. Since the 1960s, there has been a shift in the management perspective on conflict, from theories which stated:

   - conflict is avoidable, caused by disruptive elements (ie. troublemakers) and detrimental to organisational effectiveness

   to • conflict is inevitable, part of change, caused by structural factors, eg. the class system, and is useful (in small doses) if constructively handled.

4. In other words, existing social/organisational arrangements are still considered to be legitimate, or natural, and the main question which remains is how to control or utilise inevitable conflicts. The goals of the organisation are on the whole shared or accepted by its members: only the means of achieving them are in dispute. That is not the only possible view, however: radical Marxist perspectives do not regard organisational goals as legitimate, and the goals themselves, as well as the means of achieving them, need to be overthrown in the interests of humanity.

We will look at three main approaches.

Theories of conflict in organisations

5. *The 'happy family' view*
This view presents organisations as:

   (a) co-operative structures, designed to achieve agreed common objectives, ie. with no systematic conflict of interest; and

   (b) harmonious environments, where conflicts are exceptional and arise from:

      (i) misunderstandings;
      (ii) personality factors;
      (iii) the expectations of inflexible employees; or
      (iv) factors outside the organisation and its control.

6. Drucker (*The Practice of Management*) writes that "Any business must mould a true team and weld individual efforts into a common effort. Each member of the enterprise contributes something different, but they must all contribute towards a common goal. Their efforts must all pull in the same direction, without friction, without unnecessary duplication of effort".

7. This kind of view is reasonably common in managerial literature, which attempts to come up with training and motivational techniques for dealing with conflicts which arise in what are seen as potentially 'conflict-free' organisations.

Conflict is thus blamed on bad management, lack of leadership, poor communication, or 'bloody-mindedness' on the part of individuals or interest groups that impinge on the organisation. The theory is that a strong culture, good two-way communication, co-operation and motivational leadership will 'eliminate' conflict.

8. The 'happy family' view starts from a belief in 'social order' or 'industrial peace': conflict is a threat to stability, and must be avoided or eradicated.

9. *The conflict view*
In contrast, there is the view of organisations as arenas for conflict on individual and group levels. Members battle for limited resources, status, rewards, professional values etc. Organisational politics involve constant struggles for control, and choices of structure, technology and organisational goals are part of this process. Individual and organisational interests will not always coincide.

10. The extreme form of this perspective is the Marxist view, which is that:

    (a) organisations are one of the 'theatres of war' in which the class struggle is fought. Within an organisation, this war may have different 'fronts' - eg. industrial democracy, wages, equal opportunities, health and safety;

    (b) the organisation is the home of the bourgeoisie - opponents of the working class;

    (c) organisational conflict is part of an inevitable struggle, as long as some own and control the means of production, and others do not.

11. This view still colours many people's perspective on trade unionism, big business, the worker/management divide etc.

    It starts from a belief that 'social order' or 'industrial peace' are themselves the problem: conflict is a way of instituting necessary revolutionary change.

"The history of all hitherto society is the history of class struggles. Freeman and slave, patrician and plebeian, lord and serf, guildmaster and journeyman, in a word, oppressor and oppressed, stood in constant opposition to one another, carried on an uninterrupted, now hidden, now open fight ..."   Marx and Engels. *The Communist Manifesto* (1888)

---

12. *The 'evolutionary' view*
    This view regards conflict as a means of maintaining the status quo, as a useful basis for evolutionary - rather than revolutionary - change. Conflict keeps the organisation sensitive to the need to change, while reinforcing its essential framework of control. The legitimate pursuit of competing interests can balance and preserve social and organisational arrangements.

    A flexible society benefits from conflict because such behaviour, by helping to create and modify norms, assumes its continuance under changed conditions.

13. This 'constructive conflict' view may perhaps be the most useful for managers and administrators of organisations, as it neither:

    (a) attempts to dodge the issues of conflict, which is an observable fact of life in most organisations; nor

    (b) seeks to pull down existing organisational structures altogether.

    Ideology apart, managers have to get on with the job of managing, maintaining society as a going concern, and upholding organisational goals with the co-operation of other members. We will therefore look more closely at the idea of 'managing' conflict.

Constructive and destructive conflict

14. Given that conflict is inevitable, and assuming that organisational goals are broadly desirable, there are two aspects of conflict which are relevant in practice to the manager or administrator.

    (a) Conflict can be highly desirable. It can energise relationships and clarify issues. Hunt suggests that conflict is constructive, when its effect is to:

        (i)   introduce different solutions to problems;
        (ii) define power relationships more clearly;
        (iii) encourage creativity, the testing of ideas;
        (iv) focus attention on individual contributions;
        (v)   bring emotions out into the open;
        (vi) provide opportunity for catharsis - ie. the release of hostile feelings etc that have been, or may be, repressed otherwise.

    (b) Conflict can also be destructive, or negative ie. injurious to social systems, (although the radical perspective regards this as positive and desirable). Hunt suggests that conflict of this kind may act in a group of individuals to:

        (i)   distract attention from the task;
        (ii) polarise views and 'dislocate' the group;
        (iii) subvert objectives in favour of secondary goals;
        (iv) encourage defensive or 'spoiling' behaviour;
        (v)   result in disintegration of the group;
        (vi) stimulate emotional, win-lose conflicts, ie. hostility.

15. Tjosvold and Deerner researched conflict in different contexts. They allocated to 66 student volunteers the roles of foremen and workers at an assembly plant, with a scenario of conflict over job rotation schemes. Foremen were against, workers for.

    One group was told that the organisational norm was to 'avoid controversy'; another was told that the norm was 'co-operative controversy', ie. *trying* to agree; a third was told that groups were out to win any arguments that arose, ie. 'competitive controversy'. The students were offered rewards for complying with their given norms. Their decisions, and attitudes to the discussions, were then monitored.

    • Where controversy was avoided, the foremen's views dominated.

    • Competitive controversy brought no agreement - but brought out feelings of hostility and suspicion.

    • Co-operative controversy brought out differences in an atmosphere of curiosity, trust and openness: the decisions reached seemed to integrate the views of both parties.

    But can *real* managers and workers be motivated to comply with useful organisational 'norms' in this way?

16. Charles Handy redefined the term 'conflict' to offer a useful way of thinking about destructive and constructive conflict and how it might be managed.

(a) Organisations are political systems within which there is competition for scarce resources and unequal influence.

(b) *Differences* between people are natural and inevitable. Differences emerge in three ways:

    (i)   argument;
    (ii) competition; and
    (iii) conflict - which alone is considered wholly harmful.

Argument and competition are potentially beneficial and fruitful; both may degenerate into conflict if badly managed.

17. *Argument* means resolving differences by discussion; this can encourage integration of a number of viewpoints into a better solution. Handy suggests that in order for argument to be effective:

(a) the arguing group must have shared leadership, mutual trust, and a challenging task; and

(b) the logic of the argument must be preserved - ie. the issues under discussion must be classified, the discussion must concentrate on available information, and the values of the individuals must be expressed openly and taken into account.

Otherwise, argument will be frustrated. If this is so, or if the argument itself is merely the symptom of an underlying, unexpressed conflict, then conflict will be the result.

18. *Competition* can:

(a) set standards, by establishing best performance through comparison;
(b) motivate individuals to better efforts; and
(c) sort out the 'men from the boys'.

19. In order to be fruitful, competition must be *open*, rather than *closed*; or, rather, must be *perceived* by the participants to be open, rather than closed.

'Closed' competition is a win-lose (or 'zero-sum') situation, where one party's gain will be another party's loss. One party can only do well at the expense of another, in competition for resources, recognition etc. 'Open' competition exists where all participants can increase their gains - eg. productivity bargaining.

20. If competition is perceived to be open, the 'rules' are seen to be fair, and the determinants of success are within the competitors' control, competition can be extremely fruitful. The observations of Peters and Waterman on the motivational effect of comparative performance information supports this view.

If these preconditions are not met, competition may again degenerate into conflict.

Causes, symptoms and tactics of conflict

21. Conflict may be caused by differences in the *objectives* of different groups or individuals. It is a function of management:

(a) to create a system of planning whereby individual or group objectives are formulated within the framework of a strategic plan. A poor planning structure leaves the door open for conflict to enter where formal objectives, roles, authority relationships etc overlap or are unclear; and also

(b) to provide leadership, and to encourage individuals to accept the goals of the organisation as being compatible with their personal goals. Poor leadership might also lead to conflict, with the goals of individuals or groups diverging and at odds with each other.

22. Conflict may also be caused by disputes about the *boundaries of authority*. For example:

(a) staff managers may attempt to encroach on the roles or 'territory' of line managers and usurp some of their authority;

(b) one department might start 'empire building' and try to take over the work previously done by another department.

23. Personal differences, as regards goals, attitudes and feelings, are also bound to crop up. Ideologies - which we discuss below - may also effect the objectives of individuals and interest groups, and may render 'co-operative controversy' impossible.

24. According to Handy, the observable symptoms of conflict in an organisation will be:

(a) poor communications, in all 'directions';
(b) interpersonal friction;
(c) inter-group rivalry and jealousy;
(d) low morale and frustration;
(d) proliferation of rules, norms and myths; especially widespread use of arbitration, appeals to higher authority, and inflexible attitudes towards change.

25. The tactics of conflict may be as follows:

(a) One manager will withhold information from another. A manager who lacks some important information will be in a weak position for making decisions or urging his own views. Keeping information away from a 'rival' manager is a very effective tactic for increasing influence and extending the boundaries of one's own authority and influence.

(b) Information might be presented in a distorted manner. This will enable the group or manager presenting the information to get their own way more easily. For example, if the engineering department wants to introduce a new item of equipment into service, they might give biased information about likely 'teething troubles' with the equipment's technology or the expected costs of maintenance, or breakdown times.

(c) A group (especially a specialist group such as accounting) which considers its influence to be neglected might seek to impose rules, procedures, restrictions or official requirements on other groups, in order to bolster up their own importance.

(d) A manager might seek to by-pass formal channels of communication and decision-making by establishing informal contacts and friendships with people in a position of importance. A departmental manager might establish informal contacts with the managing director's personal assistant, and so get 'one up' on other departmental managers, by having a friend close to the managing director's ear.

(e) Line managers might refuse to accept the member of a staff department to fill a vacancy in their department. Similarly, line managers might refuse to accept the recommendations of staff department experts. This attitude of conflict by line towards staff management is more likely to occur where staff departments use tactics of their own to obtain more influence over line department operations.

(f) Conflict might also take the form of fault-finding in the work of other departments: eg. Department X might duplicate the work of department Y - hoping to prove department Y 'wrong' - and then report the fact to senior management.

Managerial response to conflict

26. Hunt identifies five different management responses to the handling of conflict - not all of which are effective.

- *Denial/withdrawal*, ie. 'sweeping it under the carpet'. If the conflict is very trivial, it may indeed 'blow over' without an issue being made of it, but if the causes are not identified, the conflict may grow to unmanageable proportions.

- *Suppression* - ie. 'smoothing over', to preserve working relationships despite minor conflicts. As Hunt remarks, however: "Some cracks cannot be papered over".

- *Dominance* - ie. the application of power or influence to settle the conflict. The disadvantage of this is that it creates all the lingering resentment and hostility of 'win-lose' situations.

- *Compromise* - ie. bargaining, negotiating, conciliating. To some extent, this will be inevitable in any organisation made up of different individuals. However, individuals tend to exaggerate their positions to allow for compromise, and compromise itself is seen to weaken the value of the decision, perhaps reducing commitment.

- *Integration/collaboration*. Emphasis must be put on the task, individuals must accept the need to modify their views for its sake, and group effort must be seen to be superior to individual effort. Not easy.

27. Hardy suggests two types of strategy which may be used to turn conflict into competition or argument, or to manage it in some other acceptable way.

(a) *Environmental ('ecological') strategies*. These involve creating conditions in which individuals may be better able to interact co-operatively with each other: they are wide-ranging, time-consuming, and unpredictable, because of the sheer range of human differences. Such strategies involve:

      (i)   agreement of common objectives;

      (ii)   reinforcing the group or 'team' nature of organisational life, via culture;

      (iii) providing feedback information on progress;

      (iv) providing adequate co-ordination and communication mechanisms;

      (v)   sorting out territorial/role conflicts in the organisational structure.

(b) *Regulation strategies.* These are directed to control conflict - though in fact they make it so much a part of the formal structure of the organisation that they tend to legitimise and even perpetuate it. Possible methods include:

      (i)   the provision of arbitration to settle disputes;

      (ii)   the establishment of detailed rules and procedures for conduct by employees;

      (iii) appointing a person to 'manage' the area of conflict - ie. a liaison/co-ordination officer;

      (iv) using confrontation, or inter-group meetings, to hammer out differences, especially where territorial conflicts occur;

      (v)   separating the conflicting individuals; and

      (vi) ignoring the problem, if it is genuinely likely to 'go away', and there is no point in opening fresh wounds.

Interest groups

28. 'Conflicts of interest' may exist throughout the organisation - or even within a single individual. There may be conflicts of interest between local management of a branch or subsidiary and the organisation as a whole; or between sales and production departments in a manufacturing firm (over scheduling, product variation etc); or between trade unions and management. These are three common examples: you can no doubt identify many others.

29. There are also formal *'interest groups'*, ie. groups which are perceived to represent the interests of their members. Such groups tend to wield greater power in conflict situations than their members, and indeed the very existence of the groups may be seen to anticipate and perpetuate conflict, to harden and formalise a set of attitudes and values that their individual members may not themselves have recognised or expressed.

30. Trade Unions are organisations whose purpose it is to promote their members' interests, and, in the view of many trade unionists, to bring about social change for the betterment of society as a whole.

Situations occur where trade union negotiators set targets for achievement of these goals which appear to be at odds with the targets set by management for the organisation (and its employees).

31. Disputes between management and unions may therefore be seen in the context of inter-organisational conflict, and individual members of both organisations may then feel a tug of loyalties in opposing directions. However, the officials of both organisations might succeed in reconciling their apparently conflicting goals.

32. Trade unions have a vested interest in the success of the commercial or government organisation to which their members belong because unless this organisation prospers, the security and rewards of their members will be restricted. For this reason, trade unions might be active in co-operative efforts with management to achieve growth through greater efficiency. They also share with management responsibility for good industrial relations.

33. It is important to be aware that trade unions are organisations in their own right, and we must not assume too hastily or too readily that the goals of a trade union organisation are the same as those of its members or full-time officials. The potential divergence between individual goals and organisational goals exists for a union as well as for a company. This view was given a political edge by the present Conservative government's Industrial Relations Code of Practice, which states that it should be the responsibility of a union to ensure that:

   (a) its members understand the organisation, policy and rules of the union;
   (b) its members understand the powers and duties of the members themselves and those of their union representatives;
   (c) its officials are adequately trained to look after their members' interests in an efficient and responsible way.

34. Like trade unions, occupations and professions are 'interest groups', in that they represent the interests of their members and of their clients. Professional bodies and other occupational associations are concerned:

   (a) to preserve standards of skill and knowledge - by requiring training, experience or some qualification for membership, and by fostering the exchange of knowledge between members - both for the 'honour' or social respect of the members, and in the public interest; and

   (b) to preserve appropriate financial rewards, theoretically commensurate with their skills and knowledge; and

   (c) (particularly in the case of the professions) to create a measure of independence - eg. in the regulation of conduct and ethics, the right to control their own concerns. This may be considered a kind of 'deal' made with society and other organisations, in which self-determination is allowed in return for high standards of service.

35. Labour and financial resources being scarce, and social status being desirable, there is bound to be competition between different occupational groups. One of the principle ways of promoting the interests of one, as opposed to another, is to gain influence over public policy decisions. Popular strategies for occupations which desire to do this include:

   (a) trade union organisations; and
   (b) professionalisation. Professional workers may best be able to serve the interests of their clients if they are part of a strong, independent and highly qualified group - which, of course, may also serve the personal ends of the members.

36. Other interest groups include other organisations (eg. suppliers or customers), shareholders, consumer associations, government, regulatory bodies etc all of whom are in positions to bring a certain amount of pressure to bear on organisations to have their interests preserved.

Ideologies of conflict

37. Ideologies, or 'philosophies', are 'clusters' of specific beliefs that individuals or groups hold. Clashes of ideology will be a primary cause of conflict in organisations, whether related to work and the organisation itself (eg. ideologies of the relationship between manager and worker, about the value of work etc) or to non-work factors (eg. political, religious or cultural ideologies which may bring an individual into conflict with others). Political and social ideologies, in particular, are carried into the workplace: we will discuss class and class-consciousness later.

38. Alan Fox (in "Industrial Relations and a Wider Society: Aspects of Interaction" 1975) identifies three broad ideologies which are involved in industrial relations:

    (a) *unitary ideology*. All members of the organisation, despite their different roles, have common objectives and values which unite their efforts. Workers are loyal, and the prerogative of management is accepted as paternal, and in everyone's best interests. Unions are a useful channel of communication, but are no longer necessary, and can offer unhelpful encouragement to disruptive elements.

    > "The occurence of strikes is a persistent practical contradiction of the ideology of harmony of interests which assigns legitimacy to managerial power."
    >
    > Hyman; *Strikes*

    (b) *pluralist ideology*. (This is the perspective we have discussed in relation to Handy and others). Organisations are political coalitions of individuals and groups which have their own interests. Management has to create a workable structure for collaboration, taking into account the objectives of all the various interest groups or 'stakeholders' in the organisation. A mutual survival strategy, involving the control of conflict through compromise, can be made acceptable in varying degrees to all concerned.

    (c) *radical ideology*. This primarily Marxist ideology argues that there is an inequality of power between the controllers of economic resources (ie. shareholders, managers etc) and those who depend on access to those resources (ie. wage earners). Those in power exploit the others by indoctrinating them to accept the legitimacy of their rights to power, and thus perpetuate the system. Conflict between these strata of society - ie. the proletariat and bourgeoisie - does not aim for mutual survival, but revolutionary change.

Managerial models of the worker

39. As we discussed earlier, a managers approach to motivation, direction and control of workers will depend on the assumptions he makes about them. We have already discussed scientific management and the human relations school of management theory, and the 'picture' of the worker that they put forward. We will here describe two other important descriptions:

    • the work of Edgar Schein (*Organisational Psychology*);
    • Douglas McGregor's Theory X and Theory Y.

40. Edgar Schein developed four models of individuals in general, which have implications for their roles in employing organisations.

41. The *rational-economic man* is primarily motivated by economic incentives. He is mainly passive and can be manipulated by the organisation; he is emotional and unpredictable, and organisations will have to control him. In the context of an employing organisation, such a man would be influenced in his behaviour mainly by salary and fringe benefits. Fortunately, not all men are like this, and the self-motivated, self-controlling individuals must assume responsibility for those that are.

42. The *social man* looks for self-fulfilment in social relationships. In the context of an employing organisation, this would imply that an individual's major motivation would be not so much the job itself as the opportunity to mix with other people.

43. The *self-actualising man* is influenced by a wider range of motivations. At the simplest level, these may include the need for food and security; but they range beyond this to the need felt by self-actualising man to realise his own full potential. He is capable of maturity and autonomy and will (given the chance) voluntarily integrate his goals with the organisation.

44. The *complex man* represents Schein's own view of people. According to his model, individuals are variable and driven by many different motives. The motives influencing a particular individual may change from time to time, and their relative importance may also vary, depending on the situation. The complex man will respond to no single managerial strategy, but will consider its appropriateness to circumstances and his own needs.

45. Douglas McGregor, in his book *The Human Side of Enterprise*, discussed the way in which managers see themselves in relation to others. He identifies two extreme sets of assumptions (Theory X and Theory Y) and explores how management style differs according to which set of assumptions is adopted.

Theory X and Theory Y

46. Theory X is the theory that the average human being has an inherent dislike of work and will avoid it if he can. The human being prefers to be directed, wishing to avoid responsibility. He has relatively little ambition and wants security above all. He is self-centred, with little interest in the organisation's needs. He is resistant to change, gullible and easily led. He must be coerced, controlled, directed, offered reward or threatened with punishment to get him to put forth adequate effort towards the achievement of organisation objectives.

47. According to Theory Y, however, the expenditure of physical and mental effort in work is as natural as play or rest. The ordinary person does not inherently dislike work: according to the conditions it may be a source of satisfaction or punishment. Extensive control is not the only means of obtaining effort. Man will exercise self-direction and self-control in the service of objectives to which he is committed: he is not naturally passive, or resistant, to organisational objectives, but has been made so by experience.

48. The most significant reward that can be offered in order to obtain commitment is the satisfaction of the individual's self-actualising needs. The average human being learns, under proper conditions, not only to accept but to seek responsibility. Many more people are able to contribute creatively to the solution of organisational problems than do so. At present the potentialities of the average person are not being fully used: management's responsibility is to create conditions and methods that will enable individuals to integrate their own and the organisation's goals, by personal development.

49. Theory Y implies the optimum *integration* of organisational requirements with individual goals.

    'Authority is an inappropriate means for obtaining commitment to objectives. Other forms of influence - help in achieving integration for example - are required for this purpose'. Management should adopt policies that promote satisfaction of needs in the job, and individual development and self-expression.

50. You will have your own viewpoints on the validity of Theory X with Theory Y. In fact McGregor intentionally polarised his theories, and recognises that people are in reality too complex to be categorised in this way.

51. McGregor also recognised that the assumptions were self-perpetuating, even where the 'types' did not exist. If people are treated *as though* they are 'Theory X' people, because of management assumptions, 'Theory X' behaviour will in fact be induced - thus confirming management in its beliefs and practices (eg. 'clocking on', timekeeping systems, close supervision and management controls etc), ie: 'Theory X explains the consequences of a particular managerial strategy'.

52. McGregor supported the ideas of Maslow about man's hierarchy of needs, and suggested that a Theory X approach will work well where man is concerned with his physiological and safety needs. 'But the "carrot and stick" theory does not work at all once man has reached an adequate subsistence level and is motivated by higher needs ...'

53. Theory X is often misunderstood, and confused with a 'hard' or 'soft' style of direction. 'Theory X is not a straw man for purposes of demolition, but is in fact a theory which materially influences managerial strategy in a wide sector of American industry today.' What was true in 1960 remains true even now.

    'What sometimes appear to be new strategies - decentralisation, management by objectives, consultative supervision, "democratic" leadership - are usually but old wine in new bottles, because the procedures derived to implement them are derived from the same inadequate assumptions about human nature ... These new approaches are no more than different tactics - programmes, procedures, gadgets - within an unchanged strategy based on Theory X'.

In more general terms, lip service is paid to Theory Y but Theory X is practised.

CONFLICT AND CO-OPERATION AT WORK

54. Theory X stresses domination and dependence in work relationships; Theory Y emphasises independence. But the seeming 'either/or' conflict suggested by these opposing views does not exist; leadership styles can vary in degrees, ranging from extreme Theory X to extreme Theory Y. McGregor was unable to prove that one extreme was objectively better than another (ie more productive) nor could he disprove that a middle of the road leadership style might not be better.

   (a) Theory X supervision, when the 'rules' are properly applied, should be successful in achieving stated objectives. It is unlikely, however, that the stated objectives will be surpassed, ie. the minimum objectives become the maximum objectives as well. Much potential might be unrealised.

   (b) Theory Y supervision has been implemented on occasions. For example, the Lincoln Electric Company in the USA made each employee responsible for his own supplies (both purchasing and control) and for setting the quality and quantity of his own output. Theory Y, however, depends on mature individuals; maturity, given the influence of group psychology etc, does not exist sufficiently on the shop floor to be practicable in its extreme form. *Progress* along the road to Theory Y is all that is realistically possible.

   McGregor concluded that 'Theory Y is an invitation to innovation'.

Theory Z

55. Theory Z was put forward by W G Ouchi as an 'advance' on Theory Y. It attempts to draw on the successful management techniques of large Japanese companies, and suggests how the key elements of successful Japanese management methods can be applied to Western management and organisation.

56. To understand Theory Z, it will be helpful to know something about the characteristics of large Japanese firms.

   (a) In Japan, there are a number of very large firms, such as Sony, Hitachi and Mitsubishi. Each of these has a large number of small firms as 'satellites' around it. The small firms provide goods and services to a large firm, which is in effect a monopoly buyer. The small supplier firm will often be located near to the big firm, and will be expected to provide supplies on demand. The big firm thus minimises its holding of stock, and the small firm must bear the brunt of stockholding costs by holding sufficient stocks of its own finished goods to meet any order which comes from the big firm. The big firms therefore benefit from 'domination' of their small suppliers.

   (b) Large firms are able to provide lifetime employment for their employees who are expected in return to be dedicated 'company men'. Lifetime employment gives employees greater career stability, and tends to contribute to better industrial relations.

   (c) For a large part of their career, employees retain the same job status and pay, and are not promoted. Only employees with sufficient seniority (typically, half way through their career) become eligible for promotion. Since young managers cannot expect to be rewarded for good short-term performances, there is less incentive to work for short-term results at the expense of longer-term benefits. Inter-departmental disputes are less likely to arise and co-operation between managers is more easily achievable in the absence of 'political' in-fighting.

   (d) Large firms spend large amounts of money on the welfare of their employees - housing, sports and social facilities, and medical care as well as training.

57. Broadly speaking, large Japanese firms are characterised by co-operation between management and employees and between managers and departments. Decisions are usually reached by consensus, rather than by a senior manager taking a decision and selling it or imposing it on his subordinates.

58. Theory Z is based on the belief that it is the spirit of co-operation, and the consensus approach to decision-making, that gives Japanese firms the advantages of higher employee motivation, better productivity and higher output quality. Theory Z therefore argues that:

    (a) although individual managers might have to accept responsibility for decisions, there should be a *consensus in decision-making*, reached by agreement with the manager's subordinates and colleagues. In Japan, the concept of *collective responsibility* is sometimes used;

    (b) although there is a formal organisation and management hierarchy, *decisions are nevertheless democratic and based on trust* between managers and subordinates;

    (c) this participative approach to decision-making encourages the free flow of information between departments as well as between managers and subordinates;

    (d) work activities should be 'humanised'. Individual employees are not simply regarded as a functional cog in the wheel.

59. For consensus decision-making to work and for an atmosphere of trust to develop between managers and subordinates, there must be an erosion of status-consciousness. Separate canteens for managers and workers cannot be permitted and managers should really dress in the same way as workers, in standard-type overalls. Employees must also be rewarded for their commitment to the firm, but not in such a way that the desire for rewards affects what they think and do - eg. secure lifetime employment is a more effective reward than early promotion.

60. Theory Z is thus an extension of Theory Y, with the participative approach to decision-making emphasised as a need for consensus, and with an emphasis on personal commitment and the humanisation of work activities.

Class and class-consciousness in Britain

61. 'Working class', 'middle class' and 'upper class' are common terms, but they do not adequately express the complexities of social class in Britain. We all have stereotypes about the typical attributes of a particular class, and the whole topic tends to be very emotive, on the basis of these perceptions.

    In assessing realistically the nature and influence of social class, then, we must consider not only class itself, but class-consciousness.

62. 'Subjective' definitions of class relate to the way in which people consider themselves. A white-collar job, owning a home or indulging in particular leisure pursuits may cause a person to identify himself as 'middle class'; others may consider anyone who 'works' to be 'working class'; others may preserve a sense of being 'working class' because of their family background, though their own social circumstances have changed.

63. Sociologists have more objective criteria for defining social class, based on categories such as occupation, income and wealth (most importantly), and - broadly speaking, following on from these - education, lifestyle (housing, leisure pursuits, dress, schooling for children etc), and behavioural characteristics.

64. In general, seven categories are used to distinguish groups in the class structure:

   - *upper class*: aristocracy and large property owners;
   - *upper middle class*: professionals, eg. lawyers;
   - *middle class*: managerial and technical, eg. retail managers, computer operators;
   - *lower middle class*: non-manual, white-collar and clerical, eg. office workers, supervisors;
   - *upper working class*: skilled manual, eg. mechanics, electricians;
   - *working class*: semi-skilled manual, eg. machine operators;
   - *lower working class*: unskilled manual - eg. cleaners, waitresses.

65. Another method of classification takes only five occupational categories, which are used for census and other statistical purposes: the social classes 1 - 5 on the Registrar General's Scale.

   (a) Social class 1 consists of occupations requiring a university degree or high professional equivalent.

   (b) Social class 2 consists of occupations which also frequently demand a professional qualification, eg. teachers, higher civil servants, and managers (even if 'unqualified').

   (c) Social class 3, the largest group, is usually subdivided into:

       (i)   non-manual, consisting of most of the remaining non-manual jobs, eg. foremen, shop assistants, clerical workers; and
       (ii) manual - regarded as skilled manual.

   (d) Social class 4 consists of semi-skilled manual occupations.

   (e) Social class 5 consists of unskilled manual occupations.

66. The trouble with such five-category classifications in practice is that they describe a two-class society: the working class - producers of goods and services - and middle class - the managers and organisers - are identified, but the 'upper class' seems to have disappeared altogether. The aristocracy - ie. titled landowners - do still exist, and have been joined by the very wealthy (through ownership or investment): it has been reckoned that this 1% of adult population owns one quarter of all the wealth in Britain.

67. You may have noticed that social class is defined:

   (a) *economically*, relying on analysis of the distribution of economic resources in society, in terms of *income* (money earned from paid employment and dividends on investment) and *wealth* (other financial assets eg. land, property, shares); and

   (b) *culturally* - ie. when the general behaviour, lifestyle and attitudes of people are emphasised. It has been argued that you can identify a person's class according to his dress, manner of speech, address, attitude to education, leisure habits etc.

But...

"It is certainly the case that people in the same social class have many things in common - the same monopoly or lack of access to scare resources, for example; the same good or bad standards of housing; the same access to, or restrictions on, educational opportunity; the same shared experiences of comfort, travel, hardship or enjoyment. But all of these cultural characteristics are the *consequences* of social class rather than the *causes* of it. People's lifestyles are a reflection of their economic condition in society, not the reason for their position." Jane Thompson: *Sociology Made Simple*

68. Cultural definitions of class also run into the problem of stereotyping, and overgeneralisation about 'working class attitudes', 'middle class values' etc. - often accompanied by value judgements (depending on one's viewpoint).

69. In the 1950s, attention was directed to the fact that manual workers had increasingly been earning wages directly comparable to those of white-collar and supervisory staff. In other words, the working class characteristics of low economic resources and consumer power no longer applied. It was suggested that cultural differences would gradually be eroded also, and that working class people would take on bourgeois, or middle class, lifestyles. This was called 'embourgeoisement'.

70. It was assumed that the spread of middle class attitudes would radically alter allegiances at work, in particular. Instead of 'us and them' perceptions of their relationships with their employers, the manual workers would forgo hitherto strong class loyalties, and increasingly associate themselves with middle-class conformity.

71. John Goldthorpe and his associates followed up these arguments in 1962 with a study of affluent workers in the car industry: how far had they become middle class in their behaviours and attitudes, with increased spending power?

   Their conclusion was that although surface characteristics had changed, and even values and aspirations were 'converging' to some extent, there was no evidence of radical reshaping of the class structure; the relationship between status groups within it remained significantly unaltered.

   The notion of 'embourgeoisement' was replaced by that of *'class convergence'*.

72. In the Marxist view, 'classes' are groups of people who share the same relationship to the means and organisation of production. Two products of the class situation were:

   • *class conflict:* the bourgeoisie and proletariat have interests which are irreconcilably different; and

   • *class consciousness.* The proletariat represented 'a class *in* itself' while they shared the conditions of labour. They did not act as 'a class *for* itself' until they became aware of their common interests and acted collectively, ie developed 'class consciousness'. As long as members of the proletariat saw their struggles as 'personal problems', or were coerced or conditioned into behaving against their class interests, they were in a state of *'false consciousness'*.

73. Max Weber criticised the Marxist view for being over-generalised. He distinguished between different aspects of social stratification, including dimensions which could overlap class boundaries, e.g.:

(a) *status*. Weber argued that people's social standing, as well as economic position, was significant in their position in society, and that the link between job/income and status is not always direct, e.g. respect for the sense of vocation attributed to nursing, social work etc. which is not reflected in economic reward or social power; and

(b) *party*. Parties for Weber were groups organised to attract and wield power - not just political parties, but trade unions, professional associations and other interest and pressure groups. Weber argued that such groups could overlap class distinctions e.g. the present day Labour Party.

Class and work

74. There are two main class responses to work, ie cultural responses derived from class differences. So far as society is concerned, the middle class culture of work is part of the mainstream social culture; the working class culture of work is subordinate in terms of social power.

(a) The *working class culture of work* (based on the ideal values and assumptions of the class, rather than the actual experiences of work) is:
    (i)   'dead straight' - ie work and non work selves are in harmony: concepts of career, 'job satisfaction', 'vocation' etc. are central to this;
    (ii) rational - ie based on expectations of having choice in and control over career prospects and progress;
    (iii) monopolistic over definitions - ie the way things are, the only sensible way of doing things etc. You can't beat the system - and shouldn't want to, because it represents a co-operative progress towards shared goals.

(b) The working class culture of work is not socially dominant - but relates to the numerical majority of people. The essential characteristics of those who work to create profit in return for wages have remained the same despite surface changes since Marx. Boring, repetitive or even hazardous employment may still be acceptable to capitalist morality: the job is done not out of interest but as a way of earning money, not out of loyalty, but a fear of redundancy.

Two great strengths of shopfloor culture have been identified as:
    (i)   the strength of sheer mental and physical power to survive in a hostile environment. This provides the focus for pride, self-esteem and a certain mystique attached to strength (and particularly masculinity, which, on the debit side, helps to perpetuate sexist attitudes at work and at home); ie 'the lads' culture;
    (ii) confidence expressed in the culture, based on common sense, ability and cheek. Informal resistance against formal organisation gives the illusion of regaining control. A sense of solidarity and comradeship enables workers to enforce their 'own terms' to a certain extent - e.g. practical jokes, subversive humour etc.

75. It is arguable that differences in attitude between workers and management – 'us and them' – are inevitable while there are groups of people who carry those labels: the great divide is too much a fact of organisational life, part of the fabric of 'norms' that each new recruit is taught.

Social class becomes significant when we realise that patterns of recruitment are not distributed randomly from all social strata: managerial and worker classes tend to reproduce themselves. There will obviously be a certain amount of *social mobility* – upwards and downwards – depending on education, motivation, and personality variables, but this is not so significant that social background can be altogether dismissed as a relevant factor in work behaviour.

Alienation

76. We have already referred to 'alienation' in connection with Blauner's studies of various technologies. When an individual or group feels separated from some aspect of their lives (psychologically, but usually in connection with the work situation in particular), they suffer 'alienation' – the symptoms include feelings of powerlessness, meaninglessness, isolation and self-estrangement. Marx argued that the division of labour in capitalist society causes the worker to lose control over the conditions and fruits of his labour, with the result that he becomes estranged both from himself and from his fellow men. Marx argues that the capitalist worker is inevitably alienated – whether he knows it or not.

77. One of the main themes repeatedly emerging in personal accounts of manual work is the experience of alienation suffered by workers in mindless, routine, satisfaction-less jobs.

However, sociological accounts of the meaninglessness of boring work, and the experience of alienated working class labour, commonly fail to recognise that people respond surprisingly well to bad conditions, lack of control and a sense of exploitation; they do seek meaning, enjoyment and structure. This may, as we mentioned in connection with shopfloor culture, occur in spite of work conditions, and often as a form of resistance or opposition to the dominant culture of the workplace.

78. Alienation is in any case a difficult concept. Seeman tried to render it useful by identifying five meanings for it:

- powerlessness – the worker is dominated and controlled by others;
- meaninglessness – he feels isolated from organisational goals;
- normlessness – inability to use socially acceptable means to reach prescribed goals;
- self-estrangement – adherence to the instrumental work orientation; and
- self-evaluative involvement – concerning the self-concept.

Dahrendorf, however, has argued that alienation is irrelevant to empirical social science, 'since no amount of empirical research can either confirm or refute it'.

Counter-organisations and sub-cultures

79. It is worth re-iterating the point that the dominant, mainstream cultures of organisations are broadly acceptable within the framework of the formal organisation structure. The dominant culture may well be one that has been fostered or actively imposed by the Organisation in the person of its managers.

However:

(a) cultures exist in all organisation, including sub-units of the whole employing organisation; and

(b) not all cultures will 'buy in' to the attitudes and values the organisation wishes to promote.

80. If managers wish to integrate divisionalised structures or geographically dispersed branches, for example, by promoting a strong 'central' culture, they may encounter resistance among the sub-units.

81. 'Sub-cultures' are cultures which exist in a context dominated by the decisions, values and attitudes of others. The shopfloor culture referred to earlier is a sub-culture of this kind. A.K. Cohen, among other sociologists, defines sub-cultures as 'cultures which exist *within* cultures', with three major characteristics.

(a) The group shares a distinctive way of life, knowledge, beliefs, codes, tastes and prejudices.

(b) These are learned from others in the group who already exhibit these characteristics.

(c) Their way of life has 'somehow become traditional' among those who inherit and share the social conditions to which the subcultural characteristics are a response.

82. 'Counter cultures' are groups of people within society whose values and norms are different from and go against those held in the wider society.

> "The power to create and manipulate culture as a means of controlling others is well entrenched in the social, economic and political institutions of a society but it is also continually resisted by opposing cultural forms".
>
> Bryn Jones *(The Politics of Popular Culture)*

83. Some sociologists have researched 'counter school' youth cultures, and how they are naturally carried over onto the shopfloor. In collective opposition to the dominant culture of the school, 'the lads' (as Willis calls them) are conventionally regarded as violent, undisciplined 'trouble makers'. In fact, school is an institution which has little meaning for 'the lads': it has merely to be 'got through' as enjoyably as possible - ie by 'having a laff' and rehearsing the loyalties and possibilities for defiance and resistance which will be carried over into work. Wage labour, like school, is essentially meaningless - as is the 'work ethic' designed to perpetuate it.

According to Willis, "when 'the lads' arrive on the shopfloor, they need no telling (from those already there) to 'take it easy', 'take no notice' or that 'they' (the management) always want more; you've had it if you let them get their way." They have no illusions about social mobility and success: they refuse to acknowledge or accomodate the values on which the ultimate security of the main-stream culture depends. Those that are 'seduced' by middle-class culture are despised as traitors.

Co-operation

84. We have discussed 'co-operation' by implication in our study of conflict, but we will summarise its nature briefly here.

- Co-operation is a common cultural belief, and one that is basic to any economic system. In work organisations it is universally believed that co-operation is a Good Thing, and achieve greater productivity than lack of co-operation. For most tasks, this is proven by experience.

- Co-operation is a set of shared values, to the extent of submission of individual needs and differences to the needs of the 'team'.

- Co-operation has a rational appeal. It is demonstrable that a suitable number of people co-operating on a task will achieve a better result than one person doing the same task. Synergy may enable 2+2 to equal 5.

- Co-operation has an emotional appeal. It incorporates values about unity, teamwork, comradeship, insiders (versus outsiders).

- Some cultures encourage this value-cluster more than others. In the UK, individualsism is a major aspect of the national culture - despite stated views on the virtues of co-operation. Hofstede's studies of West German, Japanese and Swedish cultures, however, demonstrate an emphasis on co-operation and inter-dependence, rather than individuality.

- Methods of encouraging co-operation have already been discussed in connection with reinforcing cultures, communication, team cohesiveness and the control of conflict. (Remember that co-operation itself may even involve a certain amount of argument or competition.)

AN OVERVIEW OF THE
BEHAVIOURAL SCIENCES
IN ORGANISATIONS

AN OVERVIEW OF THE BEHAVIOURAL SCIENCES IN ORGANISATIONS

Points to be covered

- Why managers and administrators need to use the behavioural sciences
- Peculiar difficulties of the behavioural sciences
- Experimentation in the behavioural sciences
- Other research methods
- Problems of application for behavioural science research
- The 'rational' model and its limitations
- Politics in organisations

Introduction

1. We have already dealt with some of the matters covered in this section of your syllabus, in more detailed contexts: the value of the behavioural sciences and how they can usefully be applied to work contexts; some of the distinctive perspectives they offer; difficulties of applying research to organisation practice etc.

   In this chapter however, we will draw together the strands of these issues to gain an overview of the behavioural sciences themselves, and their use in organisations.

Why managers and administrators need to use the behavioural sciences

2. The behavioural sciences embrace several different - though closely related - disciplines, including:

   (a) psychology and social psychology - the study of mental processes, personality and behaviour in individuals and groups;

   (b) sociology - the study of group behaviour and social organisation;

   (c) the social sciences - history (study of the past), economics (study of the financial business and trading arrangements made by societies), and political science (study of how societies govern themselves and distribute political power and responsibility); and

   (d) anthropology - the study of human cultures and their origins, of man as an evolving social animal.

303

3. What these disciplines offer the manager or administrator are ways of *understanding* himself and others that impact on his organisational roles and tasks. This understanding may be the basis from which he designs, implements, directs and adapts all the systems and mechanisms which affect, or are affected by, people in organisations. For example, as we have discussed elsewhere, an awareness of the behavioural sciences enables managers to ask questions about:

    (a) selection of personnel and allocation of tasks. Who is right for the job? What job will bring out the best in this person?

    (b) motivation, incentives and morale-building. What are people's needs and wants? Will they want to expend energy, enthusiasm etc. in order to obtain certain rewards? Why is productivity low: are the people frustrated, stressed, hostile? Is there anything the organisation can do about it? Does their satisfaction or happiness *matter*?

    (c) leadership. What 'style' of leadership will the people respond to? Can I become a leader as well as a manager? What type of 'influence' do I have?

    (d) co-ordination and control. Are control systems having an adverse effect on the people? Are our assumptions about their need to be controlled and directed correct? Are there communication problems here, and if so, why?

    (e) the work environment. Are working conditions contributing to the emotional and physical well-being of the people? If not, why not - and is it affecting performance?

    (f) organisation structure and job design. Is the size or 'shape' of the organisation allowing the people to realise their potential for effectiveness? Are they frustrated, challenged, stressed, alienated by the type of job they do? Are there role conflicts, ambiguities or other problems? Can we do anything about it?

    (g) organisational change. How do we plan change so that the people will not actively resist it? Can we 'sell' the new idea so that we will have their active support?

    (h) inter-personal relations. Is there conflict at individual or group level? What is causing it? How can it be controlled? Can we build 'teams' into cohesive and effective units? Does communication need to be improved, and what are the existing barriers? Are inter-personal frictions, arguments or competition impairing, enhancing or irrelevant to organisational effectiveness?

4. Handy suggests that "analysis is an important prerequisite of action. It is no substitute for action, and analysis without action or implementation remains mere analysis and is often seen as irritating sophistry. Or just as the centipede was reduced to lying on its back in a ditch by pondering the question 'How do I use my legs?', so excessive management analysis can lead to management paralysis. But action without analysis becomes mere impulse."

5. We need understanding, or workable theories, of how all the many organisational variables affect each other, of which variables to alter and how that will change the whole situation. Understanding gives better predictive ability and power over the future, though, of course, dilemmas still remain: conflicts of interest, unknown or unpredictable variables etc.

    The most important variable in the organisation is the human individual: he is the bottom line, on which all the other aspects of organisational structure, systems, social interactions and environmental factors depend. They cannot be 'got right' in a vacuum; they have to be perceived and utilised as right by the members of the organisation.

6.   The importance of the human element in organis-
     ations is the prime reason why managers need
     to know about the behavioural implications of
     their plans, systems and actions. As we will
     discuss later, 'rational' views of organis-
     ation often fail to take into account the
     personality variables, persistent habits,
     inconsistencies, barriers and surprises
     that humans tend to bring to the best planned
     structures.

> The concepts expressed by
> behavioural science, properly
> understood and used, may help
> managers to:
> * explain the past
> * understand the present
> * predict the future
> * influence future events
> * reduce disturbance from
>   the unexpected

Peculiar difficulties of the behavioural sciences

7.   There are certain difficulties associated with the behavioural and social sciences that do not
     occur in the study of natural phenomena, and the 'behaviour' of chemicals, metals, fields etc.
     People are not susceptible to the same kind of controlled investigation. Some social scientists
     have themselves denied that they are 'scientists' in the same way that physicists or biologists
     are: the number of forces working on individuals, the intricacies of the interactions between
     them and the complexity of environmental variables all demand insight, intuition and even
     imagination to make sense of them. They are not consistent, not reproducable in tightly
     controlled laboratory conditions.

8.   One problem faced by the behavioural sciences is a lack of credibility. They are sceptically
     regarded in a way that the natural sciences are not: the *practical value* of the latter is not
     called into question, and is clearly visible in the march of 'progress', in medecine,
     technology, transport, communications and other familiar areas of life. The practical value of
     the behavioural sciences is still undervalued.

9.   Moreover, natural science findings, and published material associated with them, tends to be
     prescriptive in nature ie. 'we now know how and why x happens, therefore the way to make it
     happen is to ...'. Student mechanics, doctors, chemists etc. can base their actions on these
     instructions: students of the behavioural sciences are more likely to find new questions than
     answers.

10. Sociologists, psychologists and other behavioural scientists are also human, with their own
     values, attitudes and traditions. It is almost impossible for them to maintain 'scientific
     detachment' or *neutrality* about what is being studied - ie. other people. The results of
     research will depend on the prior assumptions and selective perceptions of the researcher to a
     much larger extent than the rigorously objective controlled experimentation of the natural
     scientist. That is why we have had to describe various 'perspectives' on many of the major
     issues eg. learning, motivation, perception etc.

11. There are also problems with the methodology of the study. The goals of science are, broadly: description, explanation, prediction and control of events.

    To this end, natural science is able to rely on:

    (a) direct observation;
    (b) consistent relationships between variables;
    (c) controlled experimentation to test hypotheses; and
    (d) mathematical logic.

12. The behavioural sciences have few of these advantages. They run into problems associated with:

    (a) *observing and measuring*. If events are to be described, they must be measured. Natural science problems are easy to express, in terms of fixed laws and definitions, while human beings change constantly, and their problems are not easily quantified. Behavioural sciences deal with too many variables, many of which are ambiguous and intangible (ie. you can't 'see' motives or feelings); they rely heavily on the judgement and intuition of the scientist, rather than precision instruments;

    (b) *explanation*. Explaining events implies establishing cause and effect. Behavioural sciences deal in events, the relative timing of which is not always clear. Moreover, the interaction between variables is not consistent: people do not behave consistently, so they cannot be observed in a 'steady state'; they change, so experiments cannot be repeated under identical conditions for confirmation of findings. This means that controlled experiments to test hypotheses are impossible. To complicate matters further, the presence of the researcher himself may be a variable in the subjects' behaviour;

    (c) *prediction*. This implies the generalisation of findings from one setting to other, or all, settings - ie. the formulation of 'laws'. Nature is relatively well-ordered in this way, but human beings are irrational and subject to all sorts of pressures. They are also complex, unique, changeable and not consistently comparable with each other: practical and accurate generalisation is impossible.

13. These problems need not devalue the contribution of the behavioural sciences if we accept that they are fundamentally different from the natural sciences, and not to be judged by the same criteria. Some social scientists *do*, however, argue that human behaviour is governed by universal laws, and that the methods of natural science are applicable to behavioural science, as long as greater attention is given to rigorous definition, measurement, control and neutrality.

Experimentation in the behavioural sciences

14. Behavioural sciences use experimentation to study social and psychological phenomena in much the same way as natural sciences. In some cases, the two overlap - ie. where animal behaviour is observed eg. in experimental psychology, as an indicator of likely human responses to the same conditions.

15. Experiments are used to measure the effects of *variables* on each other. There are:

    (a) *dependent* variables - ie. factors which depend on, or vary according to, the influence or variation of other variables; and

    (b) *independent* variables - ie. those factors which are the object of study, as the cause of change in the dependent variable.

    So, for example, in a study of the effect of financial rewards on productivity, productivity would be the dependent variable; we expect it to be affected by changes made to the independent variable, financial reward.

    The problem for behavioural scientists, remember, is that there may be too many independent variables (personality, education, motivation, the task, organisation structure etc.) affecting each dependent variable (in organisational terms, usually 'productivity' or 'motivation'). The variables are unlikely to be identical in two subjects, or in the same subject over time.

16. There are three main types of experimentation available to the behavioural scientist:

    (a) *laboratory experiments*. The advantage of this is that the researcher has a modicum of control over the relevant variables: the laboratory is an artificial situation, so some of the extraneous variables can be 'filtered out'. You may recall the student role-play exercise set up by Tjosvold and Deerner (see the previous chapter). The 'foremen' and 'workers' were given certain limited information about their situation (which created some consistency as to that particular attitude variable). They worked under the same conditions. Only one variable - ie methods of approaching the controversial discussions - was manipulated to vary between the three different groups. It could then be identified as the source of behavioural differences. The trouble with this - as with all laboratory experiments - is that:

        (i) the situation *is* artificial, and filters out other variables, individual, group and environmental pressures, which occur in real life; and

        (ii) people are self-conscious subjects. Their behaviour may be altered by their awareness that they are part of an experiment, being watched, expected to behave in a certain way etc.

    (b) *field experiments*. These allow researchers to work 'in context' by manipulating events in the real world. Remember the Hawthorne studies, where working conditions of one group in the organisation were changed, while those of another group remained the same; the effects on job satisfaction and performance were then compared. The main advantage of a field experiment is that is it conducted in a real, familiar setting. The disadvantages, however, are that:

        (i) the researcher cannot control the variables so vigorously. In fact, the Hawthorne researchers found that observed behavioural changes were actually mainly caused by factors *other* than those they had set out to change and study, including, again, the *awareness* of being part of the research, which creates a false situation.

        (ii) Organisations rarely want their operations to be disrupted and their members 'experimented on'.

(c) *Naturally occurring experiments*. Researchers may *simulate* the conditions of a field experiment, by being simple observers of situations where one section or group of an organisation has changed while others have not. Since organisations tend to change gradually, this may well be possible. Again, however, there is even less control over the many intervening variables, of a work and non-work nature, that may affect behaviour.

You might like to consider the ethical questions raised by the following experiment, by Stanley Milgram, on human tendencies to obedience.

A naive subject, told that he is participating in an experiment on the effect of punishment on learning, is instructed to administer electric shocks to another subject - who is in fact a confederate of the researcher. The subject is instructed to administer shocks for each error made by the victim, with increasing intensity. A convincing simulated generator is used, with voltage designations 0 - 450, marked from 'slight shock' to 'danger' to 'XXX'. When the subject pulls the switch, the generator buzzes - but (in reality) no shock is actually administered. The supposed victim is unseen in an adjacent room: after the 300 volt level, he has been instructed to pound on the wall, and thereafter cease to respond at all. Of 40 subjects, *all* continued up to 300 volts, and 26 reached the XXX voltage. This is interesting for the experimenter: why do subjects continue to honour a presumed obligation to an unknown scientist (some, merely on the assertion 'the experiment requires that you continue') to accomplish vague goals which are believed to involve serious, gratuitous injury to another person?

But Milgram noted that his subjects were placed under considerable stress: "I observed a mature and initially poised businessman enter the laboratory smiling and confident. Within twenty minutes, he was reduced to a twitching, stuttering wreck who was rapidly approaching a point of nervous collapse."

All in the name of science?

Other research methods

17. Other research methods favoured by behavioural scientist include:

(a) *observation*, ie using the senses. This can be done through:

   (i) un-obtrusive methods, whereby the researcher does not come into direct contact with the objects of his study, but studies related physical evidence - eg. consumption of coffee, tracks worn on carpets etc.;

   (ii) non-participatory observation, whereby the researcher is present, but only as an observer. This may cause self-conscious behaviour in the subject;

   (iii) participatory observation, whereby the researcher is himself involved in the activities under investigation, becoming a member of the group being studied. The researcher is no longer as 'outsider', and subjects' behaviour is likely to be more natural - but ethical considerations may be raised by studying people without their knowledge. Jaques adopted this approach in the last phase of the Glacier Investigations, becoming a part time employee, with the consent of workers' representatives;

(b) *analysing documentation.* Documentary evidence - textual or pictorial - exist in organisations in the form of letters, memoranda and notices, accounts and other records, minutes of meetings, organisation manuals, statistical analyses etc. There may also be published case study material about similar incidents or situations, arising from previous investigations;

(c) *asking questions,* including:
   (i) face-to-face interviews. These may involve predetermined sequences of questions, or may be unstructured; they are useful, if time and cost allows, for gathering complex varied, data;
   (ii) questionnaires. These need not be conducted in person, and are therefore useful for large numbers of respondents. Some people are hostile to impersonal methods like these, especially if there are 'forced choice' questions with no opportunity for self expression. The uniform format may aid analysis, but will inevitably fail to do justice to human uniqueness and complexity.

(d) *surveys* - which may involve any or all of the above. If the coverage is wide enough, over a range or cross-section of people, the researcher will have an insight into the variables operating, when he comes to compare sub-group results.

Description, explanation and prediction

18. The research methods outlined above are ways in which behavioural scientists produce *descriptions* of various phenomena.

    The definitions used for various concepts e.g motivation, perception or learning, may not be clear-cut, or based on 'observable' phenomena, but as long as those who *use* the concepts come to some agreement of a working definition, this need not make the concepts themselves any less useful. It is possible to *infer* that such processes have been in operation, by the observation of behaviour 'before' and 'after'; we are also able to observe inputs and outputs, in the form of abilities, time, energy, resources and changes in behaviour.

19. Observation itself is limited: any given behaviour may be indicative of any number of motives, attitudes etc. That is why the behavioural sciences, unlike the natural sciences, also rely on the subject's own evaluation of what is going on, in order to describe it. The validity of such data, however, is dubious because, as we noted in the case of personality testing:

    (a) the person may deliberately falsify the data, for various reasons;
    (b) the person may give what he thinks are 'acceptable' or 'expected' answers, especially where value judgements are involved; or
    (c) the person may himself be imperfectly aware of the situation, or of his own mental processes. The researcher only gets a description of the situation as the subject perceives it.

20. *Explanation* identifies those events that can be inferred to have caused others. This is not always a precise science, especially if some of the variables are not themselves visible, or if the relative timing of events is not clear (ie so that causes and effects get mixed up). The debate about whether tight management controls are the *result* of observations of 'Theory X' behaviour in workers, or *cause* such behaviour, is one such chicken and egg situation.

21. 'Causality' in human affairs must be considered differently to that in natural phenomena, which are governed by 'laws' in a stricter sense. Events do not *cause* human actions: freedom of choice (for good or bad), irrationality, carelessness etc. enter into considerations of causality in human terms, as do cultural variations in behavioural norms.

    In terms of nature sciences, causality primarily means *how* things happen - ie the sequence of events. In human terms, one must also ask *why:* people attach meanings and reasons to their behaviour, in accordance with their peculiar understanding of their world, which is not systematic or 'scientific'. Reality is blurred and complicated by perception, so in explaining behaviour and events, many more variables are introduced.

22. This is one reason why a knowledge of the behavioural sciences may be useful to the manager: he will have a better understanding of the range of human variables involved when he attempts to infer causality between, say, participative management and higher productivity. (Nevertheless, managers can't afford to be crippled by the complexity of the issue: they have to base their practices on *something* and will have to make certain assumptions, inferences and 'leaps of faith' if they are to function at all.)

23. One of the criteria on which research findings may be evaluated is *internal validity:* ie the degree of confidence with which it can be claimed that a particular independent variable (as opposed to any other factors) really did cause the observed changes in the dependent variable.

24. *Prediction* in the behavioural sciences in generally 'probabalistic'. It points to the likely effects of particular management strategies in a certain type of organisation, or to the rate of employee turnover under particular working conditions: it can rarely indicate whether a given manager will succeed, or a specific employee will leave. Fortunately, organisations are generally more interested in 'people' than in a particular person. Again, as with explanation, there are broad regularities or patterns in human behaviour which are enough to go on with - even if they cannot be relied on as fixed or universal laws.

25. Predictions made by behavioural scientists tend to have certain peculiar effects, because they are communicated to the very people they concern. They may be:

    (a) self-fulfilling. If a reasonably contented, unquestioning worker reads about the need for employees to accept responsibility in order to gain job satisfaction, he may be 'turned on' to the idea. The scientist's findings have *become true* for that individual; or

    (b) self-defeating. Many behavioural predictions imply warnings or evaluated options: eg. if conflict is allowed to develop, co-ordination will suffer. The scientist expects that the prevailing conditions will be changed to choose the better option: his findings will *become* irrelevant or untrue to the new situation.

26. Another criterion on which research findings may be evaluated (related to the process of prediction) is *external validity:* ie. the extent to which the findings from the particular research setting can be generalised and applied to other social settings.

Problems of application for behavioural science research

27. The application of behavioural science research in organisations - even with the employment of a full-time behavioural scientist - does, however, encounter certain obstacles and limitations, eg:

    (a) the suspicion which may attach in managers' minds to 'soft' information of this sort. Sympathy and understanding, consideration of the 'human factor', may be perceived as having no direct relationship with hard results which are the manager's responsibility; they may even be perceived to undermine his authority;

    (b) the pressure it may put on managers. As Drucker says: "Managers should indeed know more about human beings. They should at least know that human beings behave like human beings and what that implies... But most managers find it hard enough to know all they need to know about their own immediate area of expertise.";

    (c) organisational politics. This will be discussed in more detail below, but broadly speaking, efforts to apply the behavioural sciences systematically run into problems with the power/control struggle which is endemic in organisations. Biased perceptions complicate all issues; 'enlightened' management may be seen by suspicious workers as 'psychological manipulation', or by power-orientated managers as an unacceptable relinquishing of legitimate management control etc.;

    (d) other problems associated with the application of research in the 'real world'.

        (i) We have already referred to problems such as the difference research or experimental conditions make to the responses of the participants.
        (ii) Being the focus of management attention, as the Hawthorne researchers found, may be enough to alter behaviour.
        (iii) Simulations using schoolboys (Sherif) or students (Tjosvold and Deerner) may not apply to adult employees with experience of real life in organisations.
        (iv) Findings successfully applied to one group or department will not necessarily work in another, or under different leadership, or with *any* such variable altered.
        (v) The assumptions of the researchers themselves may colour the findings (eg. Peters and Waterman glossing over problems in their 'excellent' companies that might mar their central thesis);

    (e) there are very many variables that may not be within the control of the organisation. Managers may be able to manipulate motivator factors, working conditions etc. to a certain extent, in keeping with research findings, but non-work circumstances, experience, attitudes etc. are still likely to intervene and frustrate the predictability of worker behaviour;

    (f) studies, counselling programmes, the appointment of communication officers, and other methods and results of behavioural science may be unacceptably *costly* to the organisation, for little in the way of measureable benefits.

311

28. Perhaps the most famous instance of the engagement of behavioural scientists by an organisation are the Hawthorne Studies, discussed earlier. You should revise them, bearing in mind that:

    (a) the studies have had practical impact on organisation practice - beyond the Western Electric Company where the research was originally carried out. Organisations like Marks and Spencer have flourished by the application of an approach consciously geared to positive human relations - though also ensuring rigorous selection procedures and tight management control;

    (b) the Hawthorne studies are enduringly popular with managers, not least because they have an apparent simplicity and a straightforward, enthusiastically 'sold' message, without over-attention to academic rigour, cautious qualification etc. The Hawthorne human-relations approach - like Maslow, Herzberg, Theory X and Y and other well-known examples - is simple and memorable, and so seems more 'practical' to managers than more complex, difficult to operate theories like Expectancy Theory;

    (c) Elton Mayo's human relations ideas *were* applied in the Western Electric Company - but didn't work. The company set up a programme of employee counselling which commenced in 1936 with a team of five counsellors for 600 employees, and grew to 55 counsellors for 21,000 employees in 1948. However, the scheme declined and died out in 1956. The programme was time-costly, as well as expensive; enthusiasm waned as the founders left. The conditions which made the initial experiments a success (ie. the sense of status enjoyed by the girls in the Relay Assembly Test Room, because of their participation in the research) were no longer present when the experimental situation ie. the counselling service, was made available organisation-wide.

29. You should look back at some of the other case studies in this text, at least the major ones:

    • Trist/Bamforth: coalmine research
    • Jaques: 'Glacier' investigations
    • Joan Woodward
    • Taylor, Gilbreth and Gantt: Bethlehem Steel Works

    You might also take the Examiner's advice and have a look at some of the more modern research. The Business section of quality daily newspapers are also worth reading for up-to-date research, reports and applications.

30. It is important to get the behavioural sciences in proportion. They are a useful aid to understanding - not a magic wand or panacea for all ills. The manager should use what he thinks will help him to manage in the real world - but shouldn't expect miracles.

    Fortunately for the manager's sanity, most of the variables do remain constant most of the time; most interpretations which held true in the past will do so in the future; most individuals do not override the identifiable influences on their behaviour; and groups tend to be more predictable than individuals.

31. Two further complicating factors remain to be discussed:

    • the essential 'irrationality' of management decision-making and organisations in general; and
    • organisational politics.

AN OVERVIEW OF THE BEHAVIOURAL SCIENCES IN ORGANISATIONS

The 'rational' model and its limitations

32. The rational model of decision-making, and of organisational activity in general, have been central to Western thinking. Complex logical and mathematical methods have been developed for the decision-making process: decision trees, critical path analysis, and other quantitative methods that you may already have covered in Part One of your exams.

Such models may be useful for managers:

(a) to explain and therefore predict how individuals make decisions, how they can be motivated to behave in particular ways; and

(b) to organise their own decision-making processes.

> "We can... identify goals individuals have; on the other hand, we can watch outcomes of overt behaviour. The problem for models of decision-making is that the black box linking goals to behaviours remains just that, a black box. Certainly, there *are* descriptions of how people make decisions, but these descriptions simply reveal something of those people. They reveal very little about how the decision was reached."
> *Hunt (Managing People at Work)*

33. A traditional framework for decision making may be as follows.

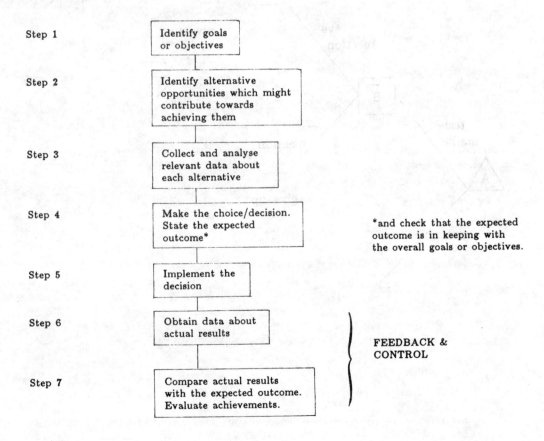

Step 1 — Identify goals or objectives

Step 2 — Identify alternative opportunities which might contribute towards achieving them

Step 3 — Collect and analyse relevant data about each alternative

Step 4 — Make the choice/decision. State the expected outcome*

*and check that the expected outcome is in keeping with the overall goals or objectives.

Step 5 — Implement the decision

Step 6 — Obtain data about actual results

Step 7 — Compare actual results with the expected outcome. Evaluate achievements.

FEEDBACK & CONTROL

34. Other models are based on decision trees eg:

(Decision points = △, possible outcomes = ◯)

Decision Tree

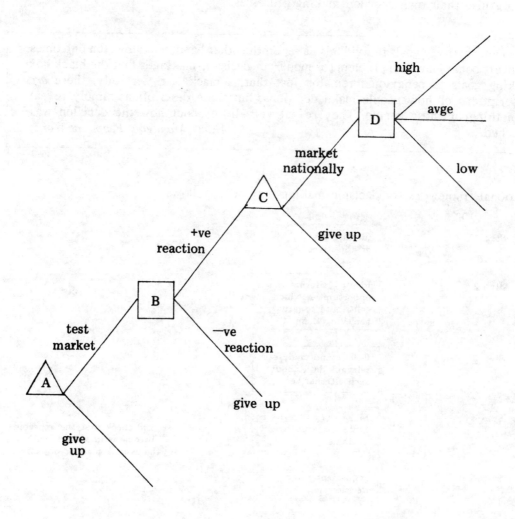

35. Yet, as we have discussed, there are very many variables which impinge on such a process, not all of which can be known to the decision maker, or quantified. The rational model is a constant compromise with the untidiness of reality.

36. Organisations in general are permeated by a belief in rationality: clear structures, authority relationships, objectives and strategies, systems and procedures, logical decisions based on factual information, statistical analyses etc. Undeniably, this is useful in allowing the primary task to be fulfilled within prescribed limits of time and cost, and without wastage of human or other resources.

37. However, behaviour in organisations is also about creativity, emotion, hunches, gut reactions, politics, enthusiasm and other unquantifiable human qualities that do not fit well into the rational model.

> " 'Rational' has come to have a very narrow definition in business analysis. It is the 'right' answer, but it's missing all of that messy human stuff, such as good strategies that do not allow for persistent old habits, implementation barriers and simple human inconsistencies." (*Peters and Waterman*)

38. Drucker argues that the most successful approach to decision-making is the Japanese approach which, according to the Western rational model, shouldn't be able to arrive at any decision, let alone an effective one.

    (a) The Japanese do not focus on giving an answer, but on defining the question - ie. what the decision is really about, not just what the decision should be.
    (b) They bring out dissenting opinions, encourage arguments, and then seek consensus.
    (c) They focus on alternatives, rather than on the 'right' answer.

    While decisions take longer, they do not then have to be 'sold' to the people who have to act on them.

39. Drucker also suggests that, contrary to common models, effective decisions do not flow from a 'consensus on the facts' but from 'the clash and conflict of opinions'.

40. All decision makers work with imperfect information.

    (a) There may be some uncertainty about objectives, or an inclination to settle for an acceptable or 'satisficing' performance rather than maximum achievement.

    (b) There may be incomplete information about alternative opportunities. For example, managers may face a choice between opportunities A and B, not realising that opportunities C, D and E exist as well.

    (c) There is a reluctance to go for radical changes, and so managers have a tendency to reject opportunities that involve big changes or a step into the unknown.

    (d) There is a limit to the quantity of information that managers can digest.

41. Since managers cannot know everything there is to know that might be relevant to a decision, they should try to take rational decisions *within the limitations* of what information is available, digestible and understandable to them. This is referred to as *bounded rationality* in decision-making.

42. Simon, March & Simon, and Cyert & March have all written about the limits to rational decision-making.

'Because individuals in organisations cannot make complex decisions with complete rationality, organisations take action to limit the scope of decisions members can make. They define individual roles and specify sub-goals to guide decision-making. They establish rules, information channels and training programmes to narrow the range of alternatives considered in making decisions.

In the accomplishment of these purposes, there are inadvertent consequences on information flow. As information passes through organisations, successive editing (gatekeeping) takes place and inferences must be drawn from evidence such that the inferences fit the organisation's available classification schemes and are transmitted instead of the evidence.'

March & Simon

This substitution of inferences for evidence is labelled by March and Simon (1958) as *uncertainty absorption*.

43. Peters and Waterman enumerate several shortcomings of the rational model of organisation, including the fact that:

- the numerative analytical component has in-built conservative bias and stifles innovation;
- it does not celebrate informality, internal competition and experimentation;
- it denigrates the importance of values; culture is essentially irrational;
- 'the rationalist approach takes the living element out of situations that should, above all, be alive'.

They suggest that the 'technology of reason' should be supplemented with a 'technology of foolishness': that sometimes, individuals should be free to act before they think. The right side of the brain - artistic and irrational - has its place in human behaviour. The decision making process should be like a 'garbage can': lots of ideas swirling around, mixing etc.

(Note that these comments reflect the researchers' own attitudes as to what is desirable in an organisation to a large extent.)

44. Above all, Peters and Waterman find that the central problem with the rationalist view of organising people is that people are not very rational.

"Logic, reason and analysis are necessary, but not sufficient for success. To ignore this is to confuse a part of the process with the whole. And such a confusion can lead to a state of corporate constipation known as 'analysis paralysis'." *Ray Proctor*

---

45. One of the main spheres in which 'untidy' reality disrupts the rational ideal of organisations is politics.

Politics in organisations

46. The topic of 'political' behaviour is broadly concerned with competition, conflict, rivalry and power relationships in organisations. Organisations are political systems in the sense that they are comprised of individuals and groups who have their own interests, priorities and goals: there is competition for finite resources, power and influence; there are cliques, alliances, pressure groups and blocking groups, centred around values, opinions and objectives which may be opposed by others.

47. Aspects of organisational politics include the following.

   (a) Individuals wish to experience 'victory' and avoid 'defeat'. They have their own objectives which are not always reconcilable with those of the organisation.

   (b) There are inevitable disparities of power and influence in hierarchical organisations - and despite rational organisation designs, events are in reality decided by dominant individuals or coalitions within and/or outside the organisation. Other individuals tend to want to influence, join or overthrow the dominant coalition.

   (c) Organisations are constantly involved in compromise, reconciling or controlling differences, and settling for 'reality' rather than 'ideal'.

   (d) 'Territory' is a useful analogy for the jealousies and rivalries over boundaries of authority, specialisms, spheres of influence etc. Ardrey, in *The Territorial Imperative*, suggests that the animal impulse to possess, acquire and preserve territory and territorial rights also applies to human societies.

48. We have already dealt with the politics of organisations, and managerial involvement in it, in our discussion of conflict, competition and argument in the previous chapter.

   Some of the power games played out in the political arena are, as we saw, not constructive for the organisation as a whole. They may degenerate into conflict, and may divert too much attention and energy away from the task in hand.

49. Mintzberg (*Power In and Around Organisations*) identifies various political games, which can be stimulating for the organisation, but can also degenerate into harmful, all-absorbing conflict:

   - games to resist authority - ie. to sabotage the aims of superiors;
   - games to counter this resistance - ie. the imposition of rules and controls by superiors;
   - games to build power bases - ie. associating with useful superiors, forming alliances among colleagues, gaining the support of subordinates, getting control of information or resources;
   - games to defeat rivals - ie. inter-group or inter-departmental conflict; and
   - games to change the organisation - ie. higher power struggles, or rebellion.

50. Rational models must be set against the hard reality of organisational politics: decisions are not made purely in the interests of the organisation. So must 'enlightened' ideas about the value of human relations policies, improved communication, job enlargement, team work etc.: management will not always be willing, nor workers always grateful and responsive.

The political process should be a welcome invitation to managers to reinterpret their theories, styles and specialisms in the face of the slings and arrows of everyday life in the organisation.

"Since my intention is to say something that will prove of practical use to the inquirer, I have thought it proper to represent things as they are in real truth, rather than as they are imagined. Many have dreamed up republics and principalities which have never in truth been known to exist; the gulf between how one should live and how one does live is so wide that a man who neglects what is actually done for what should be done learns the way to self-destruction rather than self-preservation." Machiavelli: *The Prince*

APPENDIX

ILLUSTRATIVE QUESTIONS

1. Assess the value of Maslow's hierarchy of needs for managers trying to devise effective motivational strategies for their subordinates. (ICSA June 1986)

2. How can a knowledge of motivation help managers? Illustrate and explain your answer with examples.

3. Communication is often said to be the key to effective manager/subordinate relationships. What are the typical causes of communication breakdown between managers and subordinates, and what steps should management take to ensure that such breakdowns are kept to a minimum? (ICSA Pilot Paper, and similar June 1986)

4. "Personality" is simply a term used to describe the way in which an individual is perceived by others." How far would you agree? (ICSA June 1986)

5. "It is a mistake to assume that all change is resisted; some changes, in fact, are positively welcomed." Comment on this statement with particular reference to those features in a situation which may generate resistance to a proposed change, and the ways in which such anticipated resistance may be overcome by a management anxious to introduce innovation with the minimum of disruption. (ICSA June 1987)

6. Assuming you are a manager, what behavioural signs might lead you to believe that a subordinate was experiencing stress of some sort? What would you endeavour to do about it? What are the principal factors that contribute to stress at work and how are these factors likely to change in the foreseeable future? (ICSA June 1987)

7. What are the problems which cause role stress in organisations? How might managers use an understanding of role theory to carry out their job?

8. As a manager, how far would you feel able to rely on the results of Intelligence testing in your staff selection programme?

9. What problems typically arise for management from the existence of low-skilled, repetitive tasks? What options are available to enable management to resolve such problems, where they occur or are likely to do so? (ICSA Pilot Paper)

10. Since the publication of *In Search of Excellence*, the concept of 'culture' has become very fashionable. What exactly is meant by the term 'culture' when applied to an organisation. How can the 'culture' of an organisation be so designed as to promote 'excellence'? (ICSA June 1986)

ILLUSTRATIVE QUESTIONS

11. What are the human problems typically associated with shift work? What practical steps can an employer take to minimise these problems? (ICSA June 1986, similiar in Pilot Paper)

12. What is 'leadership'? How far is it possible and desirable for managers to become leaders? (ICSA June 1986 and similar in Pilot Paper)

13. Discuss the degree to which, in your judgement, the social class system in the United Kingdom is a useful and relevant explanatory variable in the analysis of the behaviour of both shop-floor workers and managers. (ICSA June 1986)

14. What are the benefits to managers from viewing organisations as 'systems'? (ICSA December 1986)

15. "Conflict is not necessarily good or bad, but must be evaluated in terms of its individual and organisational functions and dysfunctions." Comment. (ICSA December 1986)

16. Assess the behavioural implications of the spread of computers and information technology within large organisations. (ICSA December 1986)

17. What do you understand by the term 'a group norm'? What is the importance to management of an understanding of group norms?

18. How would you define bureaucracy? What are its main characteristics, strengths and weaknesses?

19. What, in terms of management theory, is the distinction between a formal and an informal organisation? What are the advantages and disadvantages of informal groups from a managerial point of view? What can managers do to overcome the disadvantages?

20. Describe the 'contingency' approach to organisation and its influence on the design of organisation structures.

21. What are the potential benefits to be derived by managers and administrators from a systematic study of the behavioural sciences? Illustrate your answer with examples showing how organisations have utilised the insights and techniques of the behavioural sciences. (ICSA Pilot Paper)

22. Why does 'political' behaviour occur in organisations? (ICSA June 1986)

23. Discuss the extent to which experimentation is a possible method for acquiring knowledge in the field of organisational behaviour, illustrating your case with examples of both effective and less effective experimental studies. What other research methods are used as alternatives to experimentation? (ICSA June 1987, and similar in Pilot Paper)

SUGGESTED SOLUTIONS

1. *Maslow's hierarchy of needs*

    Maslow's hierarchy of needs is a content theory of motivation - ie. a theory which assumes that human beings have a 'package' of motives which they pursue. Maslow argued that man has seven innate needs:

    (a) physiological needs;
    (b) safety needs;
    (c) love needs;
    (d) esteem needs;
    (e) self-actualisation needs;
    (f) freedom of inquiry and expression needs; and
    (g) knowledge and understanding needs.

    According to Maslow, the last two are the channels through which we find ways of satisfying all the other needs.

    In his motivation theory Maslow put forward certain propositions about the motivating power of these needs.

    (a) Man's needs can be arranged in a 'hierarchy of relative pre-potency'.

    (b) Each 'level' of need is dominant until satisfied; only then does the next level of need become a motivating factor.

    (c) A need which has been satisfied no longer motivates an individual's behaviour. The need for self-actualisation can never be satisfied.

    Logical appeal of the hierarchy

    There is a certain intuitive appeal to Maslow's theory. Humans are unlikely to be concerned with status or recognition while they are hungry or thirsty. Likewise, once your hunger is assuaged, the need for food is unlikely to be a motivating factor.

    Unfortunately, research does not bear out the proposition that needs become less powerful as they are satisfied, except at the very primitive level ie. of 'primary' needs, hunger and thirst etc. Maslow himself said that the various levels of the need hierarchy overlap to some extent, and an individual may still be motivated by needs at a lower level when he acquires needs at a higher level. For example, a manager might want something which fulfils his need for esteem, but he might also be concerned about reducing the threat of redundancy, which would take away the satisfactions afforded by his job with regard to social needs and safety needs.

    It is also worth noting that Maslow did not intend his views to be applied to the specific context of behaviour at work: needs can be satisfied by aspects of a person's life outside work.

SUGGESTED SOLUTIONS

Problems with the hierarchy in practice

There are various problems associated with Maslow's theory.

(a) Empirical verification for the hierarchy is hard to come by. Physiological and safety needs are *not* always uppermost in the determination of human behaviour. It is still not clear, either, whether the higher order needs are innate or learned: it would be pleasant to believe, with Maslow, that they are innate, but, as Buchanan and Huczynski suggest: "Maslow may simply have reflected American middle class values and the pursuit of the good life, and may not have hit on fundamental universal truths about human psychology."

(b) It is difficult to predict behaviour using the hierarchy: the theory is too vague. It is impossible to define how much satisfaction has to be achieved before the individual progresses to the next level in the hierarchy. Different people emphasise different needs. Also, the same need may cause different behaviour in different individuals: one person may seek to satisfy his need for esteem by winning promotion, whereas another individual might seek esteem by leading a challenge against authority.

(c) Application of the theory in work contexts presents various difficulties. The role of money or 'pay' is problematic, since it arguably acts as a representative or 'stand in' for other rewards - status, recognition, independence etc. Moreover, as Drucker notes, a want changes in the act of being satisfied: 'incentives' such as remuneration, once regularly provided, come to be perceived as 'entitlements', and their capacity to create dissatisfaction, to become a deterrent to performance, outstrips their motivatory power. Self actualisation, in particular, is difficult to offer employees in practice: research has even suggested that as time in the same job goes on, an individual becomes less concerned about the intrinsic value or interest of his task, and more concerned about pay, equity, relationships with colleagues etc.

(d) The 'ethnocentricity' of Maslow's hierarchy has also been noted - ie. it does seem broadly applicable to Western English-speaking cultures, but is less relevant elsewhere. In 1963, in a cross-cultural survey of 3,500 managers from 14 countries, Haire, Chiselli and Porter found that 'the theoretical classification of the five types of need according to their priority of prepotency exactly fits the pattern of results for the United States and England, but not for any other group of countries' (although there was substantial agreement between countries about the relative importance of any given 'need').

Possible uses of the hierarchy

Nevertheless, on a common sense level, the manager may be able to use Maslow's hierarchy to offer employees the opportunity to satisfy their needs: physiological and security needs (via financial incentives, job security), love needs (opportunities for social interactions in work groups), esteem needs (promotion, recognition and praise) and self actualisation. This last depends, however, on the employee's own perceptions of it, his self concept, sense of his own potential etc. Herzberg's ideas about job enrichment and job enlargement offer one practical formula for offering self-actualisation - but management should not expect that such methods *in themselves* will create a happy and/or more productive workforce.

Maslow's categorisation of human needs (like those of McClelland or Roethlisberger and Dickson) may perhaps be more useful to the manager as *one* of the variables in *process* theories of motivation, such as expectancy theory, or Charles Handy's motivation calculus. Such theories fit the facts better, although they are harder for managers to make use of in practical ways: they describe the process by which individuals come to particular, subjective decisions about how to behave.

2. (a) One of the functions of management is to manage people in order to get the best out of them, so that they work efficiently and effectively. To this end, managers should try to understand what motivates their subordinates, and to harness their efforts to the advantage of the organisation. Barnard suggested that if employees are not positively motivated by management, they will tend to be negative and hostile towards the aims of the organisation: 'The preponderance of persons in a modern society always lies on the negative side'.

    (b) If the subordinates of a manager are hostile towards him and their work, the problem might be one of inter-personal relationships, but it might also be due to dislike or apathy about the work. Writers such as Handy have suggested that there is a psychological contract between an individual and his organisation. Negative attitudes arise when this contract is 'coercive' and the employee feels that too many demands are being made of him for the low level of rewards he gets in return. A knowledge of motivation should help a manager to consider whether 'coercive' contracts and hostile attitudes can be removed - either by reducing demands on the employee, or by increasing the rewards.

    (c) It is important to put the importance of motivation into perspective, and a manager should be aware that by trying to improve the motivation of his staff, he will not necessarily achieve the improvements in performance that he is hoping for. This is because several factors affect performance. Suppose, for example, that an office manager is faced with an ever-increasing mountain of unfinished work in his section, and he needs to find some way of increasing the work rate in the section in order to keep up with the work flow. The solution to the problem might be obtaining extra staff, or introducing new equipment into the office to help out (eg office computers). The problem might also be resolved by a better organisation of work procedures carried out by existing staff with existing equipment.

    (d) A manager needs to understand that the link between motivation and better performance is not a clear one, and that it might take time and patience before any benefits materialise. An individual might put more energy and enthusiasm into his work, but unless it is properly channelled by his superior, the extra energy might not be applied usefully. For example, an employee who is motivated to work better might spend a long time trying to raise the quality of his work to a level of 'perfection', with the result that his work rate might slow down. If his manager wants greater productivity, the employee would not be responding in the required way.

    (e) Managers need to understand that motivation will only work if:

        (i)   an individual's greater efforts will have a significant effect on performance. It might be a waste of time, for example, trying to motivate an individual on a production line where the pace of working is dictated by the speed of machinery (although some efforts should be made to avoid hostile and negative attitudes amongst employees);

        (ii) better performance is rewarded - eg by more pay, by promotion, by some sort of official recognition or by an elevated status within the work group;

        (iii) the individual values those rewards, and gets sufficient satisfaction out of them to continue his extra efforts in his work.

        A system of rewards should therefore be designed so as to give the employee a sense of achievement from his efforts and real satisfaction from those achievements.

    (f) A knowledge of the theories of Herzberg might help managers to understand the effects of different policies for trying to provide employee satisfaction. If the theories of Herzberg are accepted, management must continually pay attention to improvements in 'hygiene' factors, such as pay, quality of supervision, job security, working conditions, and interpersonal relations, in order to prevent dissatisfaction at work. However, if employees are to be motivated to put more energy into their work managers must offer them something extra and different - ie 'motivator' factors such as challenging work, responsibility, and advancement and recognition. These are not easily offered and managers need to be aware of the size of the task they are undertaking if they try to motivate their subordinates.

(g) A knowledge of motivation is necessary for managers to plan the way they try to manage people and motivate them. Paying lip service to motivation without offering real incentives to employees will only result in failure. For example, if a manager says that he wants to encourage participation by subordinates in his decision-making responsibilities, or will delegate more of his authority to them, or will reward them for effort, he will only stand a chance of succeeding if his intentions are genuine. He must create a decision-making procedure which provides for participation, he should delegate authority freely without trying to keep looking over his subordinate's shoulder to see what he is doing, and he must be able to provide the rewards he has promised. In this respect, since rewards through pay and promotion can only be provided if the company has such a reward system, the encouragement of employee motivation must stem in the first instance largely from top management.

3. *Causes of communication breakdown*

Potential barriers to any interpersonal communication include:

(a) distortion or omission of information by the sender;

(b) misunderstanding due to lack of clarity or technical jargon;

(c) non-verbal signs contradicting the verbal message, so that its meaning is in doubt;

(d) 'overload' ie. a person being given too much information to digest in the time available;

(e) differences in social, racial or educational background, compounded by age and personality differences creating barriers to understanding and co-operation;

(f) perceptual bias or selectivity - ie. people hearing only what they want to hear in a message.

Additional problems may be caused in communication between managers and subordinates because of:

(a) a subordinate mistrusting his superior and looking for 'hidden meanings' in a message. This mistrust may arise because of class-related attitudes to the role of manager and worker ('us' and 'them'), the manager's style of man-management, the political climate of an organisation where everyone is 'after something' etc.;

(b) hostility or resentment of subordinates towards management, resulting in deliberate attempts to 'sabotage' communication;

(c) subordinates otherwise giving superiors incorrect or incomplete information (eg. to protect a colleague, or to avoid 'bothering' the superior);

(d) the relative status in the hierarchy of the sender and receiver of information. A senior manager's words are listened to more closely and, if there is a conflict of interests, the immediate superior's perhaps discounted or ignored;

(e) people from different job or specialist backgrounds (eg. accountants, marketing managers, engineers) having difficulty in talking on the same wavelength. Managers, especially from specialist areas may, unintentionally or to assert their superiority, talk 'over the heads' of their subordinates. On the other hand, shopfloor experts may be frustrated by general management's lack of understanding of their operations and needs;

(f) managers who are prepared to make decisions on a 'hunch' without proper regard to the communications they may or may not have received. This may cause frustration for those subordinates who offer management information;

(g) lack of opportunity, formal or informal, for a subordinate to say what he thinks or feels.

Steps to prevent breakdown

It may be apparent that communication problems fall into three broad categories. Firstly, there may be a bad formal communication system; secondly there may be misunderstanding about the actual content of a message; and thirdly, there may be inter-personal difficulties causing a break-down even though the formal communications organisation may be adequate under normal circumstances.

Bad organisation must be improved. The ways in which this may be achieved will depend on the individual circumstances of each problem, but the aim should be to set up more or better communication links in all 'directions'. Standing instructions should be recorded in easily accessible manuals which are kept fully up-to-date; management decisions should be sent to all people affected by them, preferably in writing.

To improve upward and downward communication, regular staff meetings, or formal consultation with trade union representatives should be held, and a house journal should be issued regularly. For the same reason, there should be formal 'appraisal' interviews between a manager and his subordinates, to discuss the job performance and career prospects of the subordinates. The informal organisation should supplement this increased freedom of communication: if status consciousness can be reduced in management (as in Japanese companies) there will be more opportunity for exchange of views, motivatory 'good news swapping', and general 'keeping in touch', in the open plan office, the canteen, the corridor etc.

Misunderstandings about the actual content of a message could be improved by using the principle of redundancy - ie issuing a message in more than one form (eg by word of mouth at a meeting, confirmed later in minutes, discussed and re-confirmed on the telephone and subsequently in a written memo or letter) - so that if the message fails to get through the first time, it may do so on one of the subsequent occasions. Reporting by exception should operate to prevent information overload on managers. Managers who do not express themselves clearly and concisely could be sent on courses to improve their fluency and style. The use of jargon should be discouraged, but also taught in some degree to people new to the organisation or unfamiliar with the terminology of the specialists. (Again, this may happen informally as part of the process of socialisation, but formal training will be more dependable.)

Inter-personal communication difficulties cannot really be improved by teaching personnel skills on formal courses, and the best solutions might be for top management to set an example by expressing their intentions openly to subordinate managers, to choose staff for vacant jobs very carefully so that 'personableness' becomes an important criterion in selection for the job, and to set up facilities within the organisation (eg a comfortable canteen and coffee lounge, or a sports and social club) to improve the likelihood of a good atmosphere at work and better informal communications. These are what Handy refers to as 'ecological' methods of controlling conflict and improving communication: they are aimed at providing an environment conducive to co-operation.

Research has also suggested that communication between superiors and subordinates will be improved when an interpersonal trust exists. Exactly how this is achieved will depend on the management style of the manager, the attitudes and personality of the individuals involved, and other environmental variables. Peters and Waterman have suggested that a strong central 'culture' is the key to uniting employees to their manager's objectives, and removing the resentment inherent in some methods of managerial control. They advocate 'management by walking around' (MBWA), and informality in superior/subordinate relationships as a means of establishing closer links, and suggest that comparative performance information and cultural peer pressure are 'non aversive' ways of excercising control.

There are no easy solutions, however. Attitudes are difficult to change, and as long as there are 'managers' and 'subordinates', there is likely to be a perceived gulf between them, which may create mistrust or hostility - even where intentions are good. Moreover, organisations are political systems, and the acquisition and control of information is one of the political 'games' identified by Mintzberg: managers may try to keep subordinates in a weak position by withholding information; subordinates may deliberately distort information to preserve the illusion of power; both parties are likely to suspect what is going on, and perceptions of the other's motives will be even more distorted. Obvious measures like the introduction of journals, negotiating machinery, counselling interviews or standing rules for communication procedures may have a short-term affect, and may change behaviour - but compliance is not the same as internalisation, and the radical cultural changes required for *that* are unlikely to be wholly within the control of management (let alone a single manager).

4. The term 'personality' may be defined as the pattern of characteristic ways of thinking, feeling and behaving that comprise an individual's distinctive method of relating to his environment.

It is true that 'personality' depends to some extent on the perception of others for its usefulness as a concept in everyday social interactions. We use our informal assessments of personality to explain and predict the behaviour of others, and to regulate the way in which we ourselves behave towards them.

To the extent that emotions and thought-processes may be *inferred* from behaviour, other individuals may be able to form some idea of one's personality, but:

(a) any given behaviour may be caused or influenced by any number of motives, trains of thought etc. - which are not readily 'observable', and not necessarily those inferred by the observer, on the basis of his *own* experience;

(b) 'personality' focuses on consistent or stable properties, which an observer may not be in a position to assess. His perception of occasional or random behaviours will not form a useful basis for an understanding of the other's personality;

(c) perceptual selectivity or distortion may be operating. The 'halo effect', 'stereotyping' etc. may give a false impression of personality, not doing justice to the uniqueness and complexity of the individual. The attitudes of the observer may colour his assessment.

One must make a distinction between *popular* use of the term 'personality' and psychologists' use of it. Everyday usage is based on perception alone, and is faulty in that:

(a) it tends to be defined by a single, key characteristic eg. 'an outgoing personality';

(b) it tends to be confused with a perception of social success, which leads to notions of 'quantity' eg. 'lots of personality'.

According to the nomothetic approach to personality, the term is not related to the perception of others. Individuals possess certain traits or types – and the job of the psychologist is to identify them. Unfortunately, this begs the question of how far the psychologist, questionnaire designer or researcher impose their *own* perceptions and assumptions on the results of their scientific study.

The idiographic approach raises another question: how far is personality used to describe the way in which an individual is perceived *by himself?* Personality is the product of the processes through which an individual learns to be what and who he is. Again, the reseacher's perceptions of the individual's self-awareness, or what he is trying to say about himself will influence the 'portrait' emerging.

Individuals are only imperfectly self-aware, so their perception of their 'personality' is likely to be at best incomplete and at worst wildly inaccurate. Other individuals have even less to 'go on', to base their perceptions on: some aspects of personality eg. complex motivations, obsessions etc. may be hidden, while others are displayed eg. extraversion. The psychologist, however, may be in a better position: projective testing (eg. Thematic Apperception Test, Rorschach Inkblot Test) and psychoanalysis (embodied in the work of Freud) have shed light on hidden aspects of personality. If the term is used in such a context to describe 'perceived' aspects of a person, it may at least be a fairer reflection of human complexity and uniqueness.

5. *Features which may generate resistance to change*

It is true that people in organisations often welcome the concept of 'progress', long for change, and, if asked, have their own ideas about how things in their own area of work could be improved. However, change in general, when it is proposed, tends to encounter resistance, not all of which can be attributed to the way in which it is announced and implemented. It may be true that 'some changes are positively welcome', and that an intended programme of change merely has to be 'sold' to employees on those terms ie. appealing to their sense of adventure (if the organisation has a particularly innovative culture), to new opportunities for acquiring skills, to increased status, better lifestyle resulting from a relocation etc. However, some aspects of a change programme may cause real inconveniences, and will also almost inevitably attract irrational fears and insecurities.

We may list the reasons for resistance to change as:

(a) *Insecurity*
    With the removal of vital components of Maslow's pyramid not only actual job security is threatened, but also status, and potential promotion prospects at all levels. People do not know where they stand any longer.

(b) *Disruption of known relationships*
    Existing relationships with members of the work group are threatened and this is feared. Good groups can work well together and members fear the loss of good comradeship and cooperation. A production director may fear the loss of his highly supportive cost accountant.

(c) *Relative position*
    Changes may be proposed which affect the relationship of groups in terms of remuneration, status and so on. A merger may downgrade a former finance director to the level of a divisional accountant, resulting in loss of status and, perhaps, of perks such as a company car.

(d) *Disruption of social life*
Changes of shiftworking, or relocation of the work will cause social life to be disordered. The closure of the Lewis Merthyr coalmine did not destroy jobs, but it forced miners to commute and had serious effects on the local community.

(e) *Immobility*
Employees usually resist a change which obliges a move to another (unknown) district. Again, despite the ostensible aesthetic unpleasantness of pit community life, and the prospect of moving to a new home with better facilities, the breakup of a mining community is a swap of the unknown for the known and is usually resisted no matter how pleasant the change.

Townsend proves that this is a factor of confidence. Those who are confident in their future with the firm, will move anywhere. Those who are not, will be reluctant. However, recent events in the UK have tended to remove that sense of security for many people.

(f) *Reduction of the value of previous training/experience*
The computer controlled photo-typesetter made the special skill of compositors unnecessary and, without industrial action, reduced their bargaining strength.

(g) *Determination to survive*
Even when offered alternative employment, workers tend to resist the removal of their specific work.

Reducing resistance to change

There is certainly no set method of reducing resistance of this kind. However, these ideas may contribute.

(a) Full information in advance (thus minimising unnecessary concern about the future) except that if badly handled or communicated it will cause more concern.

(b) Explain why and how employees will not lose out. Offer compensation, jobs guaranteed, remuneration assurances, no additional travel cost, assistance with removal.

(c) Implement change through participation in the identification of the need for the change concerned, so that, once this is understood, the need is evidenced and willingness to make some sacrifices more likely.

(d) Agreement on the basis of change. For example, can miners be persuaded that coalfaces are damaged beyond repair?

(e) Trust and good relations between management and operatives.

6. *Symptoms of stress*

It is worth mentioning that stress (ie. demands made on an individual's physical and mental energies) can be stimulating. Excessive stress, however, can be damaging, and the behavioural signs which might point to it include:

(a) signs of nervous tension. This may manifest itself in various ways: irritability, increased sensitivity to pressure, pre-occupation with details, polarised perspectives on issues, sleeplessness etc. Various physical symptoms - eg. skin and digestive disorders - are also believed to be stress-related;

(b) withdrawal. This is a method of coping with stress, usually manifested in unusual quietness, reluctance to communicate, or physical withdrawal ie. absenteeism, poor time-keeping or even leaving the organisation;

(c) low morale: lack of self confidence, dissatisfaction, expressions of frustration or hopelessness;

(d) signs that the individual is repressing the problem, trying to deny it. Forced cheerfulness, boisterous playfulness, excessive drinking etc, may indicate this. Irritability *outside* work (if noticed by the manager) may point to transference of the problem to the non-work environment.

Managerial action

Managerial action in the face of stress symptoms will depend on the perceived causes of the stress, which will require discussion with the individual concerned.

If the problem is simply one of over-work, the manager may be able to re-allocate some of the individual's tasks to others, or may advise him to take some time off to replenish his energy reserves, and to 'get things in proportion'.

If the problem is related to the individual's role(s) in the organisation, (ie. stress arising from role ambiguity, incompatibility, conflict etc), there may have to be some redrafting of his job description, redrawing of boundaries of authority, or rethinking of schedules (to make room for conflicting demands). This will require a co-operative effort on the part of other members of the individual's role set who will be affected: it may involve counselling, then staff or departmental meetings.

If the problem is caused by insecurity - eg. because the individual is involved in risk-taking or innovation, or because he is worried about his career - the manager should ensure that he is being supportive, positively reinforcing the employee's self-concept, establishing trust. In a 1987 American study "Working Well: Managing for Health and High Performance", management style was found to be held responsible for causing stress and stress-related health problems.

Causes of stress

As suggested above, prime causes of stress are:

(a) role problems;

(b) insecurity;

(c) management style; and also

(d) personality factors. Friedman and Rosenheim identified Type A and Type B people: Type A (competitive, dynamic, sensitive to pressure) were found to be prone to ill health through stress. People who are emotionally sensitive, incompetent in interpersonal relations and weighed down by a sense of responsibility suffer stress more acutely; and

(e) the nature of the job (related to role overload and underload). In a study of Swedish and American workers, Robert Karasek found that stress was high in jobs with *work overload* and *low discretion:* low workload/low discretion jobs made few demands on the physical *or* mental energies, while high discretion jobs - of whatever workload - provided stimulation and satisfaction.

It would be nice to think that these factors would soon change, and eliminate stress. However, personality variables are unlikely to do so; insecurity is, if anything, likely to increase as the pace of technological change increases, and unemployment remains high. Role problems and management style are gradually coming into focus, with the popular work of Handy, Peters and Waterman etc. and the emphasis on 'productivity through people': greater *awareness* on the part of management is likely to help in the 'ecological' control of stress ie. creating conditions in which it is less likely to become a serious problem. High workload/low discretion jobs, too, will not disappear overnight, but the increasing automation eg. of production processes may help both to ease the workload of human operators and to offer opportunities of development of high-status skills with a measure of apparent discretion or control. Again, *awareness* of the problem and movement away from the scientific management school of thought, is helping: the introduction of autonomous work groups (eg. at Volvo), job enrichment programs, and the emergence of 'culture' as a way of adding 'meaning' to people's jobs all contribute at least to *compensate* for stressful elements, if not to eliminate them.

The philosophy of 'productivity through people' (observed by Peters and Waterman in excellent American companies such as IBM, 3M and MacDonalds) may also encourage the provision of leisure facilities, flexible working hours and non-work social activities as areas of stability, so that individuals can come to terms with stress, and keep it to useful proportions.

7. Role theory is one way of explaining the attitude and behaviour of individuals within an organisation. An individual sees his job in terms of a role, which is defined by the expectations of people who come into contact with him in performance of that role.

There are several problems which may arise which may put an individual under role stress. These are:

(a) role ambiguity, which occurs when there is some uncertainty about what the role should be. It may occur, for example, when an individual's authority and job description are not clear, or when a manager is not sure whether he is expected to be a man of constructive ideas, or whether his boss wants him to be a 'yes man';

(b) role incompatibility, which occurs when an individual's idea of himself clashes with the expectations of other people about what he should be doing in his job; for example, an individual might not want to be a ruthless executive;

(c) role conflict, which occurs when an individual has to perform two incompatible roles, perhaps as a manager of the organisation and as a trade union official;

(d) role overload, which occurs when an individual is expected to perform too many roles; for example, a manager may be expected to act as commander, conciliator, counsellor and advisor, expert, fire-fighter, innovator, administrator, planner, decision-maker, controller, committee man etc, all in the same job;

(e) role underload, which occurs when an individual believes that he can carry out more roles than he is currently expected to.

These problems, according to role theory, create role stress. Some individuals may thrive on stress, and react positively to their challenge, seeking a clarification of their role and attempting to expand into the role demands of any new job they take on. Other individuals react badly to stress, become tense, lose morale and tend to become withdrawn and difficult to communicate with.

Role stress will occur in any organisation and will be felt particularly by management. Clearly, anything which can be done to promote beneficial stress and remove harmful stress is desirable. The selection of managers to new jobs, for example, should be made with some consideration for their ability to cope with the role demands of their job. Jobs should be clearly defined to reduce role ambiguity and conflict, ideally in consultation with those in related positions whose roles will be affected by an individual's attempt to enlarge, abdicate or redefine his own role. Education of members of the organisation into the significance of roles may help to reduce some of the problems, for example:

(a) it is wrong to categorise or stereotype people according to the job they do, and individuals should avoid falling into the trap of behaving according to their stereotype in the role, by a kind of self-fulfilling prophecy;

(b) role perceptions influence inter-personal and inter-group relationships in much the same way. In addition, an individual in a group may be influenced by a wish to conform (or not to conform) within his group, by adopting the common role of members of the group.

Unfortunately, the problems of role stress are easier to recognise than to do anything about. They are unavoidable. Apart from structuring an organisation efficiently, selecting staff carefully and showing an awareness of role problems, management can do little except recognise the symptoms of harmful role stress when they occur and attempt to deal with a problem through an understanding of its causes.

8.   *Value of IQ testing to the manager*

One major criticism of IQ testing is the narrow and unproblematic use of the concepts 'intelligence' and 'ability', which almost come to be defined solely by the individuals' response to such tests. 'High IQ' should perhaps not be synonymous with 'intelligent': education, experience, wisdom, judgement and even emotional stability might also be taken into consideration. If certain personality traits are required in a job - eg. emotional stability, willingness to shoulder responsibility, high tolerance for monotony, extraversion, etc - intelligence (as 'IQ') may not be what the manager most wants to assess in a potential employee. Likewise, while numerical, verbal and visuo-spatial abilities are commonly tested, athletic, manual and musical ability, practical intelligence, 'inter-personal' intelligence and other observed facets of human intelligence are not. Nor is *learning* ability and potential taken into account.

The equation of intelligence with IQ test success is not a good basis for the assessment of 'ability' in all contexts. Mintzberg, Peters and Waterman and others have stressed the importance of 'vision' and 'flair' to successful management.

John W Hunt notes that while most top managers do possess above average intelligence, and most middle managers average or above average intelligence, no study has been able to show a positive correlation between intelligence per se and 'better' management. On the contrary, some 'super intelligent' individuals have been shown to be 'distinctly untalented' managers.

Validity of IQ testing

Research has been performed into the assumptions behind, and effectiveness of, IQ testing. The tests are supposedly scientifically rigorous and neutral, but there is considerable debate centred on:

(a) the reliability and sufficiency of results. Although the tests appear to rely on sound principles, social and emotional factors affecting performance are not taken into account.

Moreover, research has demonstrated that experience of completing IQ tests improves performance - ie. 'practice makes perfect': where does 'intelligence' end and memory or habit take over?;

(b) the cultural neutrality of the tests. Research by sociologists has suggested that the basis of the questions is the experience of white, Anglo-Saxon, middle-class individuals, and that results which show other groups to have 'low ability' are therefore subject to this bias.

H J Eysenck, author of bestselling IQ testing books, admits that 'intelligence tests are subject to practice and coaching effects', but argues that this disadvantage can be overcome by giving *everyone* a familiarity with test methods: meaningful *comparisons* between individuals can then still be made.

On the cultural bias of tests, Eysenck again admits that the measurement of intelligence requires 'certain fundamental elements of knowledge, motivation, habit and experience in common among testees', which present problems in comparing people from different social, national or ethnic groups. However, given a fairly homogeneous group - such as is arguably the case in some areas of staff selection eg. at management level - IQ testing is a reasonable indication of intelligence (in its rather limited, 'analytical' sense).

There is much that IQ tests do not tell a manager, that he or she would wish to know about a prospective employee.

9. *Problems for management*

The existence of low-skilled, repetitive tasks poses the following typical problems for management.

(a) Monotony, and the experience of boredom, is part of what may be called 'industrial *fatigue*', an element which interferes with the 'steady state' in which workers work best. Tasks which provide little mental stimulation for the worker may result in inattention, daydreaming or preoccupation with social interactions and diversions. Errors and even accidents may result from this. If the worker has *no* social outlet, however, the strain of monotony is even worse.

(b) According to a study of Swedish and American workers by Robert Karasek, *stress* is related to high workload, low discretion jobs. Its symptoms - including nervous tension, withdrawal and low moral - will invariably affect production, and may increase absent-eeism, labour turnover etc. Frustration and aggression (including hostile or destructive behaviour) may emerge: Handy reports an incident where an assembly line worker literally 'threw a spanner in the works' one day, to the cheers of his fellow workers.

(c) Motivation will suffer, unless particular efforts are made to compensate the workers for lack of satisfaction in the work itself. According to various theories of 'needs' in workers, personal 'growth', 'achievement', 'self-esteem', 'self-actualisation' etc are the highest forms of job satisfaction. Low-skilled, repetitive tasks, however, offer little opportunity for mental stimulation, personal development or indeed self esteem. With little control over, or interest in, their work, workers may experience what Blauner called 'alienation': a sense of powerlessness, meaninglessness and isolation. Although a positive relationship between satisfaction and high productivity has not been conclusively proved, the 'symptoms' of alienation and low morale - absenteeism or genuine ill-health, withdrawal to the point of leaving the organisation, hostility etc - are a likely to be a problem for management. The informal organisation may also start to absorb the time, energy and loyalty that the workers do not feel able to give to the job itself.

(d) If such tasks, and the alienation that may accompany them, are perceived to be the lot of the worker/proletariat (or simply 'us'), under the control of management/bourgeoisie (or 'them'), hostile attitudes may be hardened. Interpersonal relations between manager and workers will be hampered, trade union militancy will strengthen and a subversive counter-culture may flourish on the shop floor.

The extent to which workers suffer boredom and stress from 'role underload' in low-skilled repetitive tasks will depend on the mental capacity and self concept of the individual. Handy reports a scheme to replace human inspectors at the conveyor belt of a pill factory with pigeons: the pigeons worked longer hours - and made fewer errors!

Options available

The general conclusions of studies of monotony have been that it is less likely to arise if:

(a) the activity is changed from time to time, and rest pauses allowed; workers might be trained to alternate jobs, or might simply be allowed to move around a bit - e.g. by fetching their own materials or tools. The Health and Safety Executive suggest that short, frequent breaks seem to prevent fatigue and that natural pauses are preferable to fixed rest break schedules, giving workers some control;

(b) work is grouped into whole, self-contained tasks - rather than the repetition of a single part of a job by each individual. Eric Trist and his colleagues designed the 'composite longwall' method of working in mines, whereby a whole task was completed by the work team, which therefore had autonomy, self-regulation, multi-skilled roles and a sense of 'seeing the task through';

(c) workers are permitted the outlet of social interaction, ie are allowed to form groups, rather than being isolated by the way the work place is designed; 'chatting' is usually permitted within reason; Volvo, in the 1970s, decided 'to bring people together by replacing the mechanical line with the human work group. In this pattern, employees can act in co-operation, discussing more, deciding more among themselves how to organise the work - and, as a result, doing much more'.

(d) payment by results is used - depending on the significance of pay as a motivation to the individual.

Herzberg suggested that job enrichment, enlargement and rotation are three options available to managers.

(a) Job enrichment is the 'planned process of up-grading the responsibility, challenge and content of the work'. Typically this would involve increasing the delegation and the provision of feedback on performance, to involve workers in their jobs. This may not of itself make workers more productive, however: they would expect to be rewarded fairly for their 'new' position.

(b) Job enlargement is the process of increasing the number of operations in which a worker is engaged. Herzberg regarded this as more limited in value since a man who is required to complete several tedious tasks is unlikely to be much more highly motivated than a man performing one continuous tedious task. However, by lengthening the 'time cycle' of repeated operations, the number of repetitions will be decreased, and some of the effects of monotony may therefore be alleviated.

(c) Participation is a form of job enlargement and enrichment. It is not easy to implement without an element of mistrust on all sides, but it can be effective in the right context. At IBM, final details of the design of the first electronic computers were worked out on the factory floor in consultation with the workforce. Management found that worker satisfaction increased, speed of production increased and the product design was improved.

(d) Job rotation is the planned operation of a system whereby staff exchange positions, breaking monotony in the work and providing opportunity for training in new skills. It is generally accepted, however, that the value of job rotation as a motivation is limited, partly because of the sense of 'traineeship' that accompanies it.

It is worth noting, in conclusion, a study by Katz of the motivation of managers who stay in the same job for a long period. Katz found that concern for the 'value', 'meaning' and skill requirements of a job become progressively less important: even 'self actualisation' seems to become monotonous and routine!

10. *Culture*

Culture may be defined as the complex body of shared values and beliefs of an organisation.

Peters and Waterman, in their study (In Search of Excellence) found that the 'dominance and coherence of culture' was an essential feature of the 'excellent' companies they observed. A 'handful of guiding values' was more powerful than manuals, rule books, norms and controls formally imposed (and resisted). They commented: 'If companies do not have strong notions of themselves, as reflected in their values, stories, myths and legends, people's only security comes from where they live on the organisation chart.'

Handy sums up 'culture' as 'that's the way we do things round here'. For Schein, it is 'the pattern of basic assumptions that a given group has invented, discovered, or developed, in learning to cope with its problems of external adaption and internal integration, and that have worked well enough to be considered valid and, therefore, to be taught to new members as the correct way to perceive, think and feel in relation to these problems.'

All organisations will generate their own cultures, whether spontaneously, or under the guidance of positive managerial strategy. The culture will consist of:

(a) the basic, underlying assumptions which guide the behaviour of the individuals and groups in the organisation, e.g. customer orientation, or belief in quality, trust in the organisation to provide rewards, freedom to make decisions, freedom to make mistakes, the value of innovation and initiative at all levels etc;

(b) overt beliefs expressed by the organisation and its members, which can be used to condition (a) above. These beliefs and values may emerge as sayings, slogans, mottos etc. such as 'we're getting there', 'the customer is always right', or 'the winning team'. They may emerge in a richer mythology - in jokes and stories about past successes , heroic failures or breakthroughs, legends about the 'early days', or about 'the time the boss...'. Organisations with strong cultures often centre themselves around almost legendary figures in their history. Management can encourage this by 'selling' a sense of the corporate 'mission', or by promoting the company's 'image'; it can reward the 'right' attitudes and punish (or simply not employ) those who aren't prepared to commit themselves to the culture;

(c) visible artifacts - the style of the offices or other premises, dress 'rules', display of 'trophies', the degree of informality between superiors and subordinates etc.

Promoting excellence

Peters and Waterman define 'excellent' as 'continuously innovative' - ie. the whole culture is prepared to adapt to the needs of customers, the skills of competitors etc. Excellent companies "experiment more, encourage more tries, and permit small failures".

They identify various attributes of 'excellent' companies including:

1. *A bias for action* - ie. experiment, try, *do* rather than overanalyse, focus on problems etc. The 'results first' approach means not asking "What's standing in the way?" but "What can we do *now?*"

2. *Closeness to the customer*. Customer-orientation and concern for quality at all levels can be an intense motivator, as well as a spur to innovation, because the workers' actions have measurable, even tangible, effects - a better product.

3. *Autonomy and entrepreneurship:* giving teams and individuals control over their improvement goals and methods, and encouraging stimulating competition and adventurism.

4. *Productivity through people* - ie. 'turning people on' to their work and to organisational objectives, by positive reinforcement, 'reaffirming the heroic element' of the job, treating people decently; 'demanding extraordinary performance from the average man'.

5. Simultaneous loose-tight properties - ie. autonomy, but control through central faith, guiding values, replacing manuals and rules.

The creation or reinforcement of all of these will depend on the culture of the organisation, and the extent to which it can be 'sold' to all the employees. Indeed, Peters and Waterman noted the success of companies with such 'strong' cultures that employees had to 'buy in or get out'. They argue that 'dominance and coherence of culture proved to be an essential quality of excellent companies.' Although they present a rather 'rosy' and unqualifiedly approving picture of their excellent companies, in pursuit of their central thesis, culture is becoming a real force in management thinking.

11. *Human problems of shiftwork*

The effects of shiftwork have been well researched. They include:

(a) *physiological or medical effects* - a disruption of body-temperature, disturbance of digestion, inability to sleep during the day etc. resulting from the disorientation of the body's 'clock', its regular cycle of meals, sleep, energy expenditure etc. Shiftwork tends to conflict with the body's 'circadian rhythms', or 24-hour body cycles. Stress-related ill-health may also be caused. Some people suffer more from the physical disruption than others: in particular, diabetics, epileptics and those prone to digestive disorders;

(b) *psychological effects*. The experience of variety can be stimulating. On the other hand, the fatigue and sense of physical disorientation can be stressful. Those with strong security or structure needs may feel threatened by a lack of 'rhythm' in working life. A sense of isolation and lack of variety arising from the social problems of shiftwork may also be threatening - particularly if strain is being put on non-work relationships and roles;

(c) *social effects*. Some forms of shiftwork involve high social costs, though others - in particular double-day working, very little. In some systems, the normal hours of socialising - ie afternoon and evening - are taken up at work, which may isolate the individual from his non-work social circle. Family problems may be acute - especially where weekends are lost: not only is the worker absent, leaving a role gap in the family, but the routine of the whole family will be disrupted by his sleeping and eating patterns;

(d) *economic effects*. Overtime is not necessarily eliminated by shiftwork: premiums for double-shift and Sundays are common in practice. Shiftworking itself is inherently unpopular, and its appeal will largely depend on financial incentives.

Practical steps to minimise problems

Employers may be able to minimise problems by the choice of shift pattern used. A recent study by Folkard and Monk suggests that the best way of adapting to the physiological problems of conflict with the body's circadian rhythms is by working permanently on one shift (ie. allowing the body to develop a revised 'schedule'). This is in practice unlikely to be implemented because of social problems with evening and night work. The best compromise solution may be to alternate frequently between shifts, with longer rest periods.

Three shift-patterns in common use are:

(a) *the double-day system* - ie two standard working day shifts, say from 6am - 2pm, and 2pm - 10pm. The physical and social problems of such a system are much less acute than where night-work is required - although the hours may seem somewhat 'anti-social' and hard on the evening social life;

(b) *the three-shift system* - ie three eight-hour shifts covering the whole 'day' (say 6am - 2pm, 2pm - 10pm, 10pm - 6am). The main problem here is the 'unnaturalness' of night-time work, on the third shift. Most complaints are directed at the so-called 'dead fortnight', when the pattern of afternoon and night shifts interfere most with normal social life;

(c) *the Continental or 3-2-2 system*. This entails more frequent changes than the traditional system, enabling employees to have 'normal' leisure time at least two or three time per week! Over a four-week cycle, shifts rotate so that workers do 3 mornings, 2 afternoons, 2 nights, 3 rest days. This gets away from the 'dead fortnight', but it may cause confusion initially, and also means that there are no entirely free weekends - which may be important to families.

The 3-2-2 system is becoming increasingly popular - and is already established in the chemical and iron and steel industries. ICI operate it in two factories, and surveys show 80% of the workforce in favour because:

(a) shorter, though more frequent, spells on each shift were found to be less fatiguing than longer periods on, say, the night shift;
(b) the variety was more enjoyable;
(c) employees felt that they had more time off for social and family life; and
(d) senior staff found it easier to keep in touch with the shiftworkers.

In addition to selecting a congenial shift pattern, management should operate a screening process to exclude people who are prone to stress or certain physical disabilities from shiftwork, for health reasons.

The EEC Commission Report on 'The Problems of Shiftworking', in 1977, proposed to reduce the extent of shiftworking, and to improve conditions by:

(a) giving older shiftworkers, or those with a certain length of shift service, the right to return to day work - to counter negative physical and psychological effects; and

(b) reducing the length of the working week, lengthening rest periods and offering earlier retirement to shiftworkers.

12. *Leadership*

Leadership is the process of influencing others to work willingly towards an organisation's goals, and to the best of their capabilities. 'The essence of leadership is *followership*. In other words it is the willingness of people to follow that makes a person a leader' (Koontz, O'Donnell, Weihrich).

A manager is appointed to a position of authority within the organisation. He relies mainly on the (legitimate) authority of that position. Leadership of his subordinates is a function of the position he holds - but a manager will not necessarily be a 'leader'. Some leaders (eg in politics or in trade unions) might be elected; others might emerge by popular choice and through their personal drive and qualities. Unofficial spokesmen for groups of people are leaders of this style.

Leaders are *given* their roles by their putative followers; their 'authority' may technically be removed if their followers cease to acknowledge them. The *personal, physical* or *expert* power of leaders is therefore more important than than position power alone.

Leaders are the creators and 'sellers' of culture in the organisation. "The [leader] not only creates the rational and tangible aspects of organisations, such as structure and technology, but is also the creator of symbols, ideologies, language, beliefs, rituals and myths." (Pettigrew).

Making managers into leaders

Early writers like Taylor believed the capacity to 'make others do what you want them to do' was an inherent characteristic. Early studies on leadership concentrated on personal *traits* of existing and past leaders. One study by Ghiselli did show a significant correlation between leadership effectiveness and the personal traits of intelligence, initiative, self assurance and individuality. It is obvious that these personal characteristics are important since it is unlikely that a person who lacks self assurance and initiative would command much respect from others. The 'helicopter ability' (ie. 'seeing the big picture') has also been identified (Hunt and others) as the only ability positively correlated with management success.

Jennings (1961), however, wrote that 'Research has produced such a variegated list of traits presumably to describe leadership, that for all practical purposes it describes nothing. Fifty years of study have failed to produce one personality trait or set of qualities that can be used to distinguish between leaders and non-leaders.' Trait theory, although superficially attractive, is now largely discredited.

There have since been many classifications of leadership 'styles'. The Hawthorne studies directed by Mayo demonstrated that the productivity shown by the girls in the Relay Assembly Room was a function of democratic (ie participative, people-oriented) leadership. Later studies by Lippitt and Whyte (Boys Clubs) and Likert in his Michigan studies confirmed that democratic rather than autocratic leadership appeared to encourage productivity. Most businesses (under the general influence of the Human Relations Approach) then set about training and making these new styles of leaders. This was done by intensive training in supervisory techniques and in particular human behaviour. The assumption was that if the supervisors and managers could understand the sociological theory explaining the success in the Hawthorne studies, they would automatically adopt this approach to 'good' leadership. This approach assumed leaders could be *made* through the right type of training and understanding.

Blake and Mouton (1964) suggested that an exclusive concentration on 'people' was unlikely to prove effective in productivity leadership and what was necessary was a balanced approach between 'concern for people' and 'concern for production'. Their Managerial Grid approach was a very particular approach to training and making such 'good' leaders.

It consisted of using 'peer group pressure' to correct supervisors who showed one particular orientation (eg over concern for production or over concern for people) into this new balanced concern for both people and task. The underlying assumption is that people can adopt such leadership patterns through training and development and therefore be *made* into good leaders by the adoption of a particular style of leadership.

The current approach to making a good leader takes more account of the factors involved in any leadership situation. This contingency approach commenced with Fiedler's study which demonstrated the importance of:

(a) the relationship between the leader and his group (eg liked, trusted);
(b) the structure of the task (eg task clearly laid down);
(c) the power of the leader in relation to the group (eg the value of rewards and punishments).

This has been followed by a further development of contingency approaches. The 'best fit' approach (C Handy) suggests that the leader to be effective must take four sets of influencing factors into consideration.

(i)   The leader: his preferred style and personal characteristics;
(ii) The subordinates: their preferred style in the light of the situation;
(iii) The task: the job, its objectives and its technology;
(iv) The environment: the organisational setting of the leader and his group.

This 'best fit' approach maintains there is no such thing as the right style of leadership but that leadership will be most effective when the requirements of the leader, group and task fit together. This latest flexible style approach still begs the question as to whether those in authority be made (by training, influence, development) to adopt such approaches or does it still require some *inborn* characteristics of the person?

Desirability of becoming a leader

Research has shown the apparent effect on motivation, efficiency and productivity of the chosen leadership style of managers. But does it really matter whether a manager is a leader or not?

The belief is that if a manager had indifferent or poor leadership qualities his subordinates would still do their job, but they would do it ineffectually or perhaps in a confused manner. By providing leadership, a manager should be able to use the capabilities of subordinates to better effect, ie leadership is by definition the 'influential increment over and above mechanical compliance with the routine directives of the organisation' (Katz and Kahn *The Social Psychology of Organisations*).

Handy suggests that position power (or legitimate authority) is insufficient in itself to bring about lasting attitude change in employees, though it may be sufficient to change behaviour in a desirable direction. Personal or expert power are perceived as more 'meaningful' to the worker, and the psychological dissonance involved in opposing them more acute. The most influential managers, then, are those who wield these sorts of power - ie. the leaders.

Managers therefore need - and should seek - to become leaders in situations where they require co-operation ie. not merely compliance by their immediate subordinates.

13. It may seem most valuable to consider social class in the context of *conflict* in organisations, as it emerges in the behaviour of shop-floor workers and managers. The 'us and them' attitudes which continue to impair industrial relations in the UK may be traced to 'social class' as, in the Marxist view, it relates to the relationship of groups of people to the means and organisation of production. Class will be a relevant variable in behaviour if we accept Marx's view that class conflict is inevitable: the bourgeoisie and proletariat have interests which are irreconcilably different.

Max Weber, however, argued that class boundaries (ie. socio-economic stratifications) could be overlapped by other aspects, such as 'status' and 'party'. Weber argued that social standing is significant in a person's position in society - and not always directly linked to job/income - and that groups (parties) organised to attract and wield power (eg. trade unions, political parties and other interest groups) could also give power to members from all classes. 'Class' in its job/income related sense, therefore, is not always a useful concept for the explanation and prediction of behaviour.

'Cultural' definitions of class might be considered relevant, ie. by considering the general behaviour, lifestyle and attitudes (particularly attitudes to work) of different classes. For example, the 'middle class culture of work' has been described as a cluster of ideal attitudes which are:

(a)   'dead straight'. Work and non-work selves are in harmony. Work is an important source of satisfaction, even self-identity. Concepts of 'career', 'job satisfaction' and 'vocation' are meaningful;

(b)   rational - ie. based on expectations of having the power of choice, and control over career prospects, skill acquisition, progress etc; and

(c)   culturally dominant - ie. this is the way things are, the sensible way; the status quo is for the good of everybody, etc.

The 'working class culture of work', however, has none of these attributes. The job is done not out of interest, loyalty or ambition, but as a way of earning money and staying in work. A certain amount of resilience - and resistance - is manifested in the sense of comradeship, commonsense, subversive humour at the expense of 'them', and a mystique attached to strength and masculinity.

These attitudes may be relevant in behavioural analysis, but the problem with cultural definitions of class is that they involve a large measure of stereotyping and generalisation. It is arguable that as long as there are people who are labelled 'manager' and 'worker', hostile attitudes will be perpetuated - even where socio-economic stratification does not enter into the picture.

It is worth emphasising, too, that cultural characteristics are the *consequences* of social class (eg. spending power) rather than the *causes* of it. This raises the question of social mobility, and whether it makes 'class' irrelevant as an aid to behavioural analysis. There is, clearly, a measure of upward (and downward) mobility - both in socio-economic and cultural terms. An individual *may* be elevated by intelligence or learned skill into a higher 'bracket', based on job/income - but this presupposes such variables as self confidence, ambition, educational opportunities, etc. which may not be present precisely because of the individual's economic and cultural background. Managerial and labour classes do tend to reproduce themselves, because of the continuing monopoly over, or lack of access to, scarce resources, access to, or restrictions on, educational opportunity, parental career models, etc. (Goldthorpe's investigation of affluent workers in the Luton car industry served to discredit the notion of 'embourgeoisement': despite changes in surface characteristics, associated with increased income, there was no evidence of radical reshaping of the class structure.) In terms of patterns of recruitment, therefore, the concept of social class is highly relevant, despite the possibility of social mobility as applied to career choice and success.

14. *The systems approach*

There is no universally accepted definition of a 'system', although Ludvig von Bertalanffy, a pioneer of general system theory in the 1930s, said it is 'an organised or complex whole' and 'organised complexity'. Alternatively, it is 'an entity which consists of interdependent parts', so that system theory is concerned with the attributes and relationships of these inter-acting parts.

An *open system* is a system connected to an interacting with its environment. It takes in influences (or 'energy') from its environment, ie. inputs (and outputs from other systems) and through a series of activities, converts these inputs into outputs (or inputs into other systems). In other words it influences its environment by its behaviour. An open system is a stable system which is nevertheless continually changing or evolving. All social systems are open systems.

Inputs to the organisation include labour, finance, raw materials, components, equipment and information. Outputs include information, services provided, goods produced etc.

The organisation 'open system' must remain sensitive to its external environment, with which it is in constant interaction: it must respond to threats and opportunities, restrictions and challenges posed by markets, consumer trends, competitors, the government etc. Changes in input will influence output.

An organisation is not simply a structure: the organisation chart reflects only one sub-system of the overall organisation. Trist and his associates at the Tavistock Institute have suggested that an organisation is a 'structured sociotechnical system', ie. it consists of at least 3 sub systems:

(a)   a structure;

(b)   a technological system (concerning the work to be done, and the machines, tools and other facilities available to do it);

(c)   a social system (concerning the people within the organisation, the ways they think and the ways they interact with each other.)

The systems model therefore emphasises the interdependence of the component parts comprising the system: one facet can rarely be changed without impacting on another.

The contribution of the systems approach

General systems theory can contribute to the principles and practice of management in several ways, not least by enabling managers to learn from the experience of experts and researchers in other disciplines.

(a)   It draws attention to the *dynamic* aspects of organisation, and the factors influencing the growth and development of all its sub-systems.

(b)   It creates an awareness of sub-systems, each with potentially conflicting goals which must be integrated. *Sub-optimisation* (ie. where sub-systems pursue their own goals to the detriment of the system as a whole) is a feature of organisational behaviour.

(c)   It focuses attention on interrelationships between aspects of the organisation, and between it and its environment, ie. the needs of the system as a whole: management should not get so bogged down in detail and small political arenas that they lose sight of the overall objectives and processes.

(d)   It teaches managers to reject the deterministic idea that A will always cause B to happen. 'Linear causality' may occur, but only rarely, because of the unpredictability and uncontrollability of many inputs.

(e)   The importance of the *environment* on a system is acknowledged. One product of this may be customer orientation, which Peters and Waterman note is an important cultural element of successful, adaptive companies.

Like any other approach, managers should take what they find useful in practice in the systems view, without making a 'religion' of it.

15.   Conflict may appear in organisations in various contexts eg. within the individual himself (eg. over two alternative objectives, or roles), between the individual and his environment (a form of stress), between individuals, departments, groups, levels in the hierarchy etc.

There is no clear-cut definition of, or approach to, 'conflict': there is much controversy in conflict research, as to what should be studied, and how, and how meaningful the results are. Various 'interest groups' in a conflict situation are likely to have different perspectives on the nature of the situation itself, as well as on the particular issues that create it.

Theories of conflict include the following.

(a)   The 'happy family' view starts from a belief in 'social order' or 'industrial peace': conflict is a threat to stability, and must be avoided or eradicated.

Conflicts are exceptional and arise from:
(i)   misunderstandings;
(ii)   personality factors;
(iii) the expectations of inflexible employees; or
(iv)   factors outside the organisation and its control.

(b) The 'conflict view' regards organisations as arenas for inevitable conflict over limited resources, status, rewards, values, etc. Individual and organisational interests will not always coincide. According to Marx, organisational conflict is part of the necessary class struggle: 'social order'and 'industrial peace' are themselves the problem.

(c) The 'constructive conflict view' suggests that conflict is inevitable, but can be used as a way of maintaining society (or the organisation) as a going concern, by creating and modifying norms and stimulating evolutionary change.

Given that conflict is inevitable, and assuming that organisational goals are broadly desirable, there are two aspects of conflict which are relevant in practice to the manager or administrator.

(a) Conflict can be highly desirable. It can energise relationships and clarify issues. Hunt suggests that conflict is constructive, when its effect is to:
  (i)   introduce different solutions to problems;
  (ii)   define power relationships more clearly;
  (iii) encourage creativity, the testing of ideas;
  (iv)   focus attention on individual contributions;
  (v)   bring emotions out into the open;
  (vi)   provide opportunity for catharsis - ie. the release of hostile feelings etc that have been, or may be, repressed otherwise.

(b) Conflict can also be destructive, or negative (ie. injurious to social systems, which the radical perspective regards as desirable). Hunt suggests that conflict of this kind may act in a group of individuals to:
  (i)   distract attention from the task;
  (ii)   polarise views and 'dislocate' the group;
  (iii) subvert objectives in favour of secondary goals;
  (iv)   encourage defensive or 'spoiling' behaviour;
  (v)   result in disintegration of the group;
  (vi)   stimulate emotional, win-lose conflicts, ie. hostility.

Charles Handy redefined the term 'conflict' to offer a useful way of thinking about destructive and constructive conflict and how it might be managed.

(a) Organisations are political systems within which there is competition for scarce resources and unequal influence.

(b) *Differences* between people are natural and inevitable. Differences emerge in three ways:
  (i)   argument;
  (ii)   competition; and
  (iii) conflict - which alone is considered wholly harmful.

Argument and competition are potentially beneficial and fruitful; both may degenerate into conflict if badly managed.

If one looks at the complexity of the politics in organisations, one might note that in the final analysis, 'conflict' is good or bad according to whether you are the winner or loser. Conflict over control of budgeting between a departmental manager and Finance manager, for example, will be perceived as 'good' by whichever individual gains control: ie. it has borne fruit for him. On an ideological level, conflict is bad if you are the manager whose plans are disrupted - but good if you are instigating the shop floor revolution!

16. *Impact of information technology*

Seven areas can be identified where changes in technology will have an impact.

(a) Jobs. Technological innovations allow organisations to reduce the headcount by replacing several workers with one machine without a consequent loss in productivity. Inevitably such moves create in employees feelings of insecurity, fears of redundancy, changed attitudes to other workers, the new technology itself and the organisation. This can have dramatic effects on the psychological contract which exists between employer and employee.

(b) The nature of work. Frequently the new systems may tend to make obsolete or replace whole layers of skilled and semi-skilled traditional activities in the organisation. Recent events in the newspaper industry illustrate this point. Not only has new technology swept away traditional highly skilled tasks such as those of the compositor, but the switch to electronic based automatic equipment has meant that work traditionally within the closely guarded domain of the highly skilled print craftsman, has been transferred to the electricians, traditionally regarded as the under-dog of the newspaper industry. In less dramatic environments what remains might be challenging and demanding jobs for the highly skilled, and a number of menial jobs cannot economically be automated. This can have serious consequences for the level of job satisfaction and motivation of the employees who remain, and may create a wider schism between white and blue collar workers or confrontation between unions or groups of craft workers (as the newspaper industry again demonstrates).

(c) Opportunities for interaction. Almost inevitably the new technology will bring changes in the way in which people relate to one another at work. The new technology might disrupt relationships and reduce the opportunities for social interaction with colleagues. This will hinder the development of often essential informal groups which cross organisational boundaries and which help the organisation to achieve its goals (the Trist and Bamforth research in the coal industry). Conversely, if an individual's social needs are not met at work, or obstructed by work procedures, alienation will develop and he will try to find ways of 'beating the system' to ensure that these needs are met. Absenteeism could also increase in such conditions.

(d) Group relations. The new technology may lead to greater external control and monitoring of work performance. This will give fewer opportunities for informal group 'norms of production' to be set which may limit the volume of production. The employees have much less personal control over the output, the way in which work is done and their own working lives, which might increase feelings of powerlessness at work and again possibly foster alienation. Alternatively employees may show even greater creativity in devising new ways to beat the new sophisticated systems. Additionally 'buck passing' or a loss of accountability may develop as the coal industry studies illustrate.

(e) Leadership. It is inevitable that styles of leadership will be required to change. The supervisor's power is likely to become based much more on skill and expertise than on formal authority. With highly skilled technicians working on interdependent systems, a team management approach will probably be more effective than over-reliance on the scalar relationship.

(f) Structural changes. There are likely to be structural changes in the organisation. Departments will develop to accommodate the new skills required. Older departments which house people with redundant skills will decline in size and influence. This will create problems in inter-departmental relations as the new replace the old and the status and power of each department changes.

(g) Industrial relations. In industrial relations there could well be a substantial switch in the basis of power both between unions and management and between unions representing different workers. However, the risk of 'strategic' strike of one or two key workers will escalate.

A final aspect of the implications of technology change is that many control systems work on the basis of division of duties between clerical grades to maintain control and avoid collusion, which could conceal fraud. Such systems depend upon many clerks being employed in jobs such as wages preparation, bonus calculations and production statistics. With advanced technology automating many of these tasks, fewer people are required, and therefore the risk of collusion returns, unless rigid controls are built into the new systems. For example, the bonus calculations must be keyed in such a way, that they can be readily related to the levels of output and eligibility for bonus, to avoid bonuses being paid to operatives or staff that are not entitled to them. This may require, therefore, more detailed classification of the workers' records in the computer system as well as possible changes in access to initial data, and responsibility for input.

17. *Group norms*

'A group norm' refers to an acceptable level or method of behaviour, to which all members of a group are expected to conform. In a work situation, norms will be developed by informal work groups, which will probably be employees in the same section or department (although informal groups can extend beyond section boundaries). Not all people in a formal work group will belong to the informal group, so that these 'exceptions' do not accept the group norms, but they are regarded as 'outcasts' by the rest of the group. Group norms are therefore the consequence of group psychology, and they are expressed in terms of dress and, more importantly, attitudes. The experiments of Sherif, who asked a group of individuals to say how much a fixed point of light in a black box moved as they looked at it, showed that individuals were prepared to abandon their own opinions in favour of a group norm or consensus in discussion – even though the norm was 'wrong'. The experiments showed how individual perceptions and opinions could be changed by an individual's identification with a group.

Roethlisberger and Dickson, who conducted some of the Hawthorne experiments, identified two important group norms from the point of view of productivity. The first was that a work group appears to set an 'unspoken' standard of output which reflects its view of a fair day's work for a fair day's pay. Secondly, a norm develops for the group's attitude to its supervisor or manager, and 'social pressure' can be placed on someone who is too officious and takes advantage of his authority. If the output norm is low and the attitude to supervisors is hostile, a work group will be unproductive and inefficient.

Implications for management

There are several important implications of group norms for management.

(a) One fundamental problem which a manager must overcome is the antagonism of his subordinates. If a manager remains remote in his office, and avoids contact with his subordinates, he will be encouraging a group attitude which is out of sympathy with himself as a person and in consequence, with the job he is trying to do. Direct contact with members of the group must be maintained in order to become known and accepted. At the same time, it is likely that there will be a group view about the type or style of leadership they expect from their manager, and a manager must be prepared to adapt his style to the requirements of the group. He should avoid officious or bullying behaviour, but he may need to be democratic, authoritarian etc according to the needs of the work group.

(b) If a manager wishes to raise the efficiency of working, he must focus his attention on the group norm. An attempt to persuade individuals to do better may only succeed in the case of the 'social outcasts', if the group attitude is hostile to greater productivity. The manager's task would therefore be to improve group motivation in order to raise the group norm. There is no clear solution to the problem of raising group productivity, and the approach may need to vary according to circumstances. For example, in the economic recession of the early 1980s the fear of redundancy and actual cut-backs in the work force of many companies led to greater industrial activity in Britain, and it appears that group attitudes if 'times are hard' may have contributed to a raising of efficiency levels. Managers might also consider whether consultations with their subordinates and employees and group participation in some decision-making process would improve group motivation, which in turn would raise group norms.

(c) Management must be wary of inter-departmental conflicts and friction. An organisation may consist of many work groups which should co-operate with each other, but an attitude of petty rivalry might develop, preventing constructive co-operation.

(d) Managers need to be aware that new members of a formal work group will need time to become accepted as a member of the informal group. It would therefore be inadvisable to expect that personal changes can occur without initial 'teething troubles', and a manager should not encourage individual new members to do better than their colleagues and thus antagonise them.

In conclusion, it might be said that group psychology can be so important that it overshadows independent individual attitudes and formal work structures and programmes. Management must understand it, although the task of influencing it is much more difficult.

18. *Bureaucracy*

The bureaucratic form of organisation uses the strict application of rules and procedures, the definition of duties and responsibilities to ensure conformity of behaviour of its members. The studies of D Pugh and J Child have shown that this form of organisation is closely related to the size of an organisation where increasing size usually results in increasing use of bureaucratic procedures.

The main characteristics of bureaucracy were described by Max Weber as follows:

(a) The organisation is seen as coming before the people who work in it.

(b) There is a fixed hierarchy of positions and authority.

(c) Positions are obtained by ability, as evidenced by passing specialist examinations.

(d) Work is routine and covered by rules and procedures which are known and carefully applied by everyone.

(e) Jobs are carefully defined and the job is more important than the person. (C Handy refers to this as 'role culture').

(f) Logic: rationality and the impersonal application of the rules are highly practised. Therefore people (eg staff; clients; public) simply become 'cases' within the rules rather than individuals.

(g) Non-routine work is done by specialists.

SUGGESTED SOLUTIONS

(h) There is a clear division between line (operational) and staff (functional) management.

(i) Stability. Employees who do well are rewarded with good pay, job security etc.

(j) A clear distinction is made between ownership and control.

Strengths

Weber argued this was the most efficient form of organisation because:

(a) it is free from the personal bias of the individual managers;

(b) its authority system is based on merit;

(c) it is based on the rational achievements of its objectives;

(d) it is free from human friction and relationships in pursuing the organisation's objectives, that is, the personal element (which can be destructive) is taken out;

(e) it makes full use of technical knowledge;

(f) it encourages close control and co-ordination of activities;

(g) employees find the working environment stable and secure;

(h) it is very useful for businesses where operations are routine.

Weaknesses

In spite of Weber's claims bureaucracies have been criticised by a number of empirical studies by Gouldner, Merton and Burns and Stalker. These criticisms are referred to below:

(a) Bureaucracies respond very slowly in conditions of rapid change.

(b) They are not suited for encouraging innovation.

(c) Rules become more important than the objectives they are supposed to achieve.

(d) The impersonal nature of relationships alienates the staff who cannot identify with the organisation. Individuals are treated as cogs in the machine.

(e) Decision making is 'routinised' (by following the rules) therefore it cannot cope with situations outside the rules. This creates an upward dependency. Also the process of decision making is slowed down by the need to follow procedures.

(f) The work is usually routine and boring.

(g) The organisational structure may not be able to deal with 'one off' situations because it has been developed to take account of only a limited number of eventualities.

(h) Not all factors affecting an organisation's efficiency can be analysed rationally eg some aspects of human behaviour.

(i) There is a tendency for 'red tape' to develop eg excessive attention to laid down procedures rather than the exercising of good managerial sense.

(j)   There may be a tendency to pass the buck and to blame the rules when things go wrong.

(k)   The system can very quickly get out of date but not change because of its inertia.

In spite of these criticisms, the bureaucratic form of organisation is still widely practised. The possible reasons for this are:

(a)   *Size*. Many of the modern organisations are very large (eg the big four banks and bureaucratic procedures ensure a large number of people all react in the same way to the same situation).

(b)   *Nature of the business*. Where conformity of behaviour is an essential part of the business (eg the security and confidentiality expected by customers in banking) their bureaucratic rules ensure strict procedures are followed.

(c)   *Increasing use of specialists in modern organisations*. Bureaucracy makes a clear distinction between line and staff relationships and different functional departments. Bureaucratic procedures provide an approach to ensure that the different activities are co-ordinated and related together in a rational and formal way.

(d)   *Management culture*. Many managers still have a 'deep set of beliefs' (C Handy) that this is the best way to exercise authority and how work should be organised. Bureaucracy often fits the values on the best way to discharge their accountability in achieving objectives since it ensures:

   (i)   a high degree of central control;
   (ii)   close supervision and attention to the 'job';
   (iii) justification of their status and position on the basis of 'merit'.

Other forms of organisation are appearing (eg matrix organisation used by Citibank) but the bureaucratic form still fits the philosophy and values of many managers and (as referred to earlier) by their very nature bureaucracies are slow to change.

19.   *Formal and informal organisations*

Formal organisation refers to the way an organisation is structured to carry out its tasks and achieve its objectives. The primary task and decisions on how to achieve these objectives will directly affect the form of the organisation and impose constraints on the place, time and nature of the work done and the resources used to perform it. Formal organisation reflects the needs of the organisation itself and views on how these might be efficiently achieved. This will include:

(a)   definition of the tasks to be performed;
(b)   chains of command;
(d)   levels of authority and responsibility;
(e)   channels of communication.

In summary, formal organisation defines the way an organisation is designed to work. Earlier writers such as F W Taylor and H Fayol considered this to be the most important aspect of organisational effectiveness.

The studies by E Mayo demonstrated the existence and importance of the informal organisation.

The informal group develops spontaneously as a complex system of its own with a pattern of personal and group relationships, with its own communication channels (grapevine) which differs from the normal organisation from which it was derived. The Hawthorne Studies showed how such groups had a powerful effect on their members which was often quite the opposite to the 'economic man' assumptions of the earlier writers, which were that 'social needs' for 'belonging' will regulate the individual's economic behaviour in relation to output and attitudes to management. The studies also showed the existence of informal leaders who often act as opinion leaders in relation to how the group reacts to particular situations.

In summary, informal organisation rises out of the social relationships necessary in any formal organisation. Such informal grouping or cliques will affect substantially the performance and behaviour of their members quite independently of any formal organisation.

Advantages of informal groups

The advantages of informal groups are that:

(a) individuals satisfy their need for social relationships. It is argued that this will make them work more efficiently, as they will not experience stress, isolation etc.;

(b) individuals gain through the group a sense of identity and status which they find difficult to gain on their own in a large organisation. This again may have a motivating effect;

(c) they may develop their own performance targets, which may be better for motivation, and more consistently adhered to, than goals imposed from above;

(d) communications may be improved because of the existence of the 'grapevine';

(e) the activities of different individuals and departments will be better co-ordinated;

(f) problems will be shared and ideas generated through the interaction of different opinions and backgrounds.

Disadvantages of informal groups

The disadvantages are that:

(a) group norms for performance may be below the required level, but the members of the group may feel bound by them;

(b) loyalty to the group may be more absorbing than, or even conflict with, loyalty to the organisation;

(c) creativity and innovation may be sacrificed because of the need to conform;

(d) groups may indulge in counter-productive competition with each other, rather than co-operating;

(e) the 'grapevine' invariably carries inaccurate and often subversive information;

(f) the group may be resistant to necessary change because it is happy with the way things are;

(g) the informal organisation may not fit into the formal structure eg. where formal authority is undermined by a manager's being 'one of the lads';

(h) 'counter-' or 'sub-cultures' may emerge in opposition to the mainstream system of values that management wishes to promote.

Managerial control of the informal organisation

It is important that managers understand that the organisation is unlikely to work in precisely the way it was designed to work. The existence of such informal groupings is inevitable even within a small branch. Such cliques are likely to regulate the work patterns and work output.

The manager must attempt to understand the 'value system' of such cliques or groupings since they may determine the reaction to his orders or instructions. The 'group attitude' can either help or hinder his task in managing. It will undoubtedly create the 'environment', 'atmosphere' or 'climate' of the organisation. Whilst he may not be able to directly alter the nature of the group or its values he can help by ensuring that adequate 'official' communications exist, instead of allowing rumour and the 'grapevine' to fill the gaps. He can also help by using democratic and participative leadership styles and generally creating an 'openness' between the formal and informal organisations.

Further ways of overcoming these problems are:

(a) ensuring that the formal organisation is flexible enough to accommodate the change and to incorporate the various informal groupings;

(b) making clear what is expected of individuals and groups before collective norms develop;

(c) encouraging individuals to suggest new ideas and procedures;

(d) displaying positive leadership qualities so that the informal group does not become a law unto itself.

20. Contingency theory of organisations has developed out of the results of a whole variety of empirical studies. Each study has shown the importance of different factors on the *structure* and *performance* of an organisation. Contingency theory rejects the assumption there is one right way to design an organisation and argues the appropriate design will depend on a variety of factors. Each factor will have to be considered separately in determining the 'best fit' between the organisation needs and the influence of these 'contingencies'. Some of the important contingencies are:

SIZE — J Child has shown that the larger the organisation the more bureaucratic it will become, because of the benefits of formalisation.

ENVIRONMENT — Burns and Stalker demonstrated that mechanistic structures are more suitable to stable environments and organic structures suitable to unstable environments.

TECHNOLOGY — Trist and Bamforth showed that the organisation of work must be related to the type of technological system being used, that organisation of the social system and the technological system were interdependent.

DIVERSITY — Organisations with a varied range of activities and work practices are more likely to have a decentralised structure.

TYPE OF PERSONNEL — Because of background, education etc employees will differ in their preference for an authoritarian or participative style of leadership.

CULTURE	The structure of an organisation reflects different varieties of organisation culture eg freedom given to subordinates, formalisation of clothing and office layout.
MANAGEMENT PHILOSOPHY	C Handy demonstrated that the type of organisation adopted will be strongly influenced by management philosophy, that is their beliefs on how to work should be organised and authority exercised (eg Theory X views or Theory Y views will give rise to different types of organisation).

These and many more studies have shown that a wide range of factors must be taken into account. It follows that in choosing an organisation structure, the degree of fit depends on analysing the importance of each factor and using the findings of each study to determine the appropriate design. It is possible that the final structure selected is likely to be a compromise between pressures pointing in opposite directions.

Many writers have argued that this is simply a more sophisticated approach to determining the one best way. Similarly, some well-established organisations may be able to ignore 'contingency factors' and adopt any structure they wish (eg Civil Service). Finally, it has never been satisfactorily shown that by taking account of contingency factors in the design of an organisation structure necessarily helps performance.

21. Handy suggests that 'analysis is an important prerequisite of action. It is no substitute for action ... but action without analysis becomes mere impulse.'

    We need understanding, or workable theories, of how all the many organisational variables affect each other, of which variables to alter and how that will change the whole situation. Understanding gives better predictive ability and power over the future, though, of course, dilemmas still remain: conflicts of interest, unknown or unpredictable variables etc.

    The most important variable in the organisation is the human individual: he is the bottom line, on which all the other aspects of organisational structure, systems, social interactions and environmental factors depend. They cannot be 'got right' in a vacuum; they have to be perceived and utilised as right by the members of the organisation.

    What the behavioural sciences offer the manager or administrator are ways of *understanding* himself and others that impact on his organisational roles and tasks. This understanding may be the basis from which he designs, implements, directs and adapts all the systems and mechanisms which affect, or are affected by, people in organisations.

    For example:

    (a) motivation, incentives and morale-building are areas in which the behavioural sciences may contribute to management policy. Herzberg carried out research via surveys into the factors that contribute to job satisfaction and dissatisfaction, to produce a practical and enduringly popular framework for motivation: the 'two factor theory' of 'environmental' (or hygiene) factors, and motivator factors, related to the job itself. Peters and Waterman observed how positive reinforcement, 'good news swapping' and enhancing workers' self esteem contributes to the success of companies like Mars Inc. in America, where every opportunity is taken to reward performance, good attendance etc.;

    (b) the management of change is an important area in which the insights of behavioural science may be used. Understanding, anticipating and overcoming fears and resistance to change in the organisation will require sensitivity to common misconceptions, insecurities etc. Eric

Trist's work for the Coal Board, reducing resistance to new working methods brought about by new technology, is one example: Trist and his team were able to devise a work structure which minimised employee unrest;

(c) group behaviour will also be of interest to the organisation. The Hawthorne research programme at the Western Electric Company developed the hypothesis that productivity and quality of output were related to the psychology of the work group and the relationship between the workers and their supervisor. In the Bank Wiring Room, it was found that 'group norms' significantly influenced work rates and standards. The motivatory effect of team structures was also observed by Peters and Waterman. The insights of researchers like Sherif, Janis and Belbin, into the behaviour of groups in competition, 'group think', and the roles of individuals in successful groups may also be a useful tool for management;

(d) leadership. The Ashridge studies, the work of Lippitt and White and others, into various 'styles' of leadership showed that worker attitudes are most favourable under consultative or democratic leadership, but that the level of output was actually higher, in the short term, under autocratic leadership. Other research findings (eg. the Ohio State leadership Studies - 'Blake's grid') emphasise the need for management concern with the task, as well as the people. Jaques (the Glacier investigations) found that problems in personal relations and employee dissatisfaction occurred where leaders tried to abdicate their expected role.

These are only a few areas. Others include work structuring (eg. Trist and the composite longwall method, Taylor and the Bethlehem Steel Works), design of control systems, design of the work environment, management of interpersonal relations and conflict etc. Job enrichment programmes, the establishment of autonomous work groups, employee counselling and other products of behavioural science have been implemented (though not always with long-term success) by companies consciously geared to human relations: MacDonalds, Marks and Spencer, etc. However, it is dangerous to assume that 'people programmes' will have a predictable or lasting impact, and that knowledge about 'people' will enable accurate prediction and control of events.

22. The topic of 'political' behaviour is broadly concerned with competition, conflict, rivalry and power relationships in organisations. Organisations are political systems in the sense that they are comprised of individuals and groups who have their own interests, priorities and goals: there is competition for finite resources, power and influence; there are cliques, alliances, pressure groups and blocking groups, centred around values, opinions and objectives which may be opposed by others.

Some reasons for political behaviour include the following.

(a) Individuals wish to experience 'victory' and avoid 'defeat'. They have their own objectives which are not always reconcilable with those of the organisation.

(b) There are finite human, material and financial resources available to individuals and groups in organisations, and 'success' is perceived as the maximisation of those resources. There is bound to be competition for influence, information, skilled staff, money and materials.

(c) There are inevitable disparities of power and influence in hierarchical organisations - and despite rational organisation designs, events are in reality decided by dominant individuals or coalitions within and/or outside the organisation. Other individuals tend to want to influence, join or overthrow the dominant coalition.

(d) Organisations are constantly involved in compromise, reconciling or controlling differences, and settling for 'reality' rather than 'ideal'. Trade-offs over quality/cost, quality/quantity, trust/control in leadership style, loyalty to the goals of the group/subsidiary/department/team (ie. problems of 'goal congruence') etc. are bound to occur.

(e) 'Territory' is a useful analogy for the jealousies and rivalries over boundaries of authority, specialisms, spheres of influence etc. Ardrey, in *The Territorial Imperative*, suggests that the animal impulse to possess, acquire and preserve territory and territorial rights also applies to human societies.

(f) Interest groups or 'stakeholders' in the organisation - employees, trade unions, professional associations, shareholders, customers, consumer associations, regulatory bodies etc, - may be bringing pressure to bear, possibly with conflicting interests. Eg. a pay settlement demanded by unions may have to be balanced against shareholder demands for a dividend on their shares.

Political behaviour itself may take different forms. Mintzberg (*Power In and Around Organisations*) identifies various political games, which can be stimulating for the organisation, but can also degenerate into harmful, all-absorbing conflict:

(a) games to resist authority - ie. to sabotage the aims of superiors;

(b) games to counter this resistance - ie. the imposition of rules and controls by superiors;

(c) games to build power bases - ie. associating with useful superiors, forming alliances among colleagues, gaining the support of subordinates, getting control of information or resources;

(d) games to defeat rivals - ie. inter-group or inter-departmental conflict; and

(e) games to change the organisation - ie. higher power struggles, or rebellion.

23. There are certain difficulties associated with the behavioural and social sciences that do not occur in the study of natural phenomena, and the 'behaviour' of chemicals, metals, fields etc. People are not susceptible to the same kind of controlled investigation. Some social scientists have themselves denied that they are 'scientists' in the same way that physicists or biologists are: the number of forces working on individuals, the intricacies of the interactions between them and the complexity of environmental variables all demand insight, intuition and even imagination to make sense of them. They are not consistent, not reproducable in tightly controlled laboratory conditions.

However, the behavioural sciences use experimentation to study social and psychological phenomena in much the same way as natural sciences. In some cases, the two overlap - ie. where animal behaviour is observed eg. in experimental psychology, as an indicator of likely human responses to the same conditions.

The problem for behavioural scientists is that there may be too many independent variables (personality, education, motivation, the task, organisation structure etc.) affecting each dependent variable (in organisational terms, usually 'productivity' or 'motivation'). The variables are unlikely to be identical in two subjects, or in the same subject over time.

There are three main types of experimentation available to the behavioural scientist:

(a) *laboratory experiments*. The advantage of this is that the researcher has a modicum of control over the relevant variables: the laboratory is an artificial situation, so some of the extraneous variables can be 'filtered out'. Eg. the student role-play exercise set up by Tjosvold and Deerner. The 'foremen' and 'workers' were given certain limited information about their situation (which created some consistency as to that particular attitude variable). They worked under the same conditions. Only one variable - ie methods of approaching the controversial discussions - was manipulated to vary between the three different groups. It could then be identified as the source of behavioural differences. The trouble with this - as with all laboratory experiments - is that:

   (i)   the situation *is* artificial, and filters out other variables, individual, group and environmental pressures, which occur in real life; and

   (ii) people are self-conscious subjects. Their behaviour may be altered by their awareness that they are part of an experiment, being watched, expected to behave in a certain way etc.

(b) *field experiments*. These allow researchers to work 'in context' by manipulating events in the real world. A famous example is the Hawthorne studies, where working conditions of one group in the organisation were changed, while those of another group remained the same; the effects on job satisfaction and performance were then compared. The main advantage of a field experiment is that is it conducted in a real, familiar setting. The disadvantages, however, are that:

   (i)   the researcher cannot control the variables so vigorously. In fact, the Hawthorne researchers found that observed behavioural changes were actually mainly caused by factors *other* than those they had set out to change and study, including, again, the *awareness* of being part of the research, which creates a false situation. This was an experimental study that, despite its enduring popularity with managers, was ineffective even in its own setting. The counselling programme set up on the basis of the study declined and died out once the artificial experimental conditions (and the motivating effect of association with them) were dissolved.

   (ii) Organisations rarely want their operations to be disrupted and their members 'experimented on'.

(c) *Naturally occurring experiments*. Researchers may *simulate* the conditions of a field experiment, by being simple observers of situations where one section or group of an organisation has changed while others have not. Since organisations tend to change gradually, this may well be possible. Again, however, there is even less control over the many intervening variables, of a work and non-work nature, that may affect behaviour.

Other research methods

Other research methods favoured by behavioural scientist include:

(a) *observation*, ie using the senses. This can be done through:

   (i)   un-obtrusive methods, whereby the researcher does not come into direct contact with the objects of his study, but studies related physical evidence - eg. consumption of coffee, tracks worn on carpets etc.;

(ii) non-participatory observation, whereby the researcher is present, but only as an observer. This may cause self-conscious behaviour in the subject;

(iii) participatory observation, whereby the researcher is himself involved in the activities under investigation, becoming a member of the group being studied. The researcher is no longer as 'outsider', and subjects' behaviour is likely to be more natural - but ethical considerations may be raised by studying people without their knowledge. Jaques adopted this approach in the last phase of the Glacier Investigations, becoming a part time employee, with the consent of workers' representatives;

(b) *analysing documentation.* Documentary evidence - textual or pictorial - exist in organisations in the form of letters, memoranda and notices, accounts and other records, minutes of meetings, organisation manuals, statistical analyses etc. There may also be published case study material about similar incidents or situations, arising from previous investigations;

(c) *asking questions,* including:

(i) face-to-face interviews. These may involve predetermined sequences of questions, or may be unstructured; they are useful, if time and cost allows, for gathering complex varied, data;

(ii) questionnaires. These need not be conducted in person, and are therefore useful for large numbers of respondents. Some people are hostile to impersonal methods like these, especially if there are 'forced choice' questions with no opportunity for self expression. The uniform format may aid analysis, but will inevitably fail to do justice to human uniqueness and complexity.

(d) *surveys* - which may involve any or all of the above. If the coverage is wide enough, over a range or cross-section of people, the researcher will have an insight into the variables operating, when he comes to compare sub-group results.